6th Workshop on Argument Mining (ArgMining 2019)

Florence, Italy
1 August 2019

ISBN: 978-1-5108-9115-9

ACL 2019

The 6th Workshop on Argument Mining
(ArgMining 2019)

Proceedings of the Workshop

August 1, 2019
Florence, Italy

Introduction

Welcome to the 6th Workshop on Argument Mining (ArgMining 2019), collocated with ACL 2019 in Florence, Italy. The ArgMining workshop series is the premier research forum devoted to the mining, the assessment, and the generation of natural language arguments. Previous editions have been held annually at ACL (2014, 2016), NAACL (2015), and EMNLP (2017, 2018).

Argument mining, also known as argumentation mining, is an emerging research area of computational linguistics. At its heart, it involves the automatic identification of argumentative structures in free text, such as the premises, conclusions, and inference schemes of arguments as well as their interrelations and counter-considerations. To date, researchers have investigated argument mining on various registers including legal texts, scientific papers, product reviews, news editorials, Wikipedia articles, persuasive essays, tweets, and online discussions. Argument mining is tied to stance and sentiment analysis, since every argument carries a stance towards its topic, often expressed with sentiment. Recently, the quality assessment of arguments came into focus; it is considered as an important step to bring computational argumentation to practical impact.

While solutions to basic steps such as component segmentation and classification slowly become mature, many tasks remain largely unsolved, particularly when facing more open genres and topics. Success in computational argumentation requires joint efforts integrating NLP technology, theories of semantics and pragmatics, knowledge of discourse in application domains, artificial intelligence, information retrieval, argumentation theory, and computational models of argumentation.

Computational argumentation gives rise to various applications of great importance. It provides methods that can find and visualize the main pro and con arguments on a topic of interest in a corpus — or even in documents, blogs, and discussions on the web. In instructional and educational contexts, written and diagrammed arguments can be mined to convey and assess students' command of course material, while the retrieval of mined arguments is expected to play a salient role in the emerging field of conversational search. With IBM's Project Debater, technology based on computational argumentation recently received a lot of media attention.

The community around ArgMining is constantly growing. This year's edition of the workshop had 41 valid submissions (after 27 in 2017 and 32 in 2018), among these 22 full papers, 17 short papers, and two demo papers. The submissions came from institutions on five continents, 44% of the first authors being female. Five submissions were withdrawn due to acceptance at other venues, indicating the quality of submissions. Out of the remaining 36 papers, seven have been selected for oral presentation (19%) and 13 for poster presentation, resulting in an overall acceptance rate of 56%. Thanks to the hard work of 46 program committee members and four additional reviewers, all authors got three reviews on time.

14 full papers, five short papers, and one demo paper are included in the proceedings at hand. We were delighted to gain Professor Giovanni Sartor and Professor Marco Lippi as keynote speakers, experts on legal reasoning and its relation to Artificial Intelligence. The ArgMining 2019 workshop program also featured a best paper award, thankfully sponsored by IBM and selected by an independent committee, as well as a special event. Both the award and the event are announced on the official workshop website chaired by Roxanne El Baff: `https://argmining19.webis.de`.

Benno Stein and Henning Wachsmuth
(ArgMining 2019 co-chairs)

Organizers:

Benno Stein, Bauhaus-Universität, Weimar (chair)
Henning Wachsmuth, Paderborn University (chair)

Kevin Ashley, University of Pittsburgh
Claire Cardie, Cornell University
Nancy Green, University of North Carolina Greensboro
Iryna Gurevych, Technische Universität Darmstadt
Ivan Habernal, BIX
Diane Litman, University of Pittsburgh
Georgios Petasis, NCSR Demokritos
Chris Reed, University of Dundee
Noam Slonim, IBM Research AI
Vern R. Walker, Maurice A. Deane School of Law at Hofstra University

Program Committee:

Rahit Aharonov, IBM Research AI
Yamen Ajjour, Bauhaus-Universität Weimar
Ahmet Aker, University of Duisburg-Essen
Khalid Al-Khatib, Bauhaus-Universität Weimar
Milad Alshomary, Paderborn University
Carlos Alzate, IBM Research AI
Kevin Ashley, University of Pittsburgh
Roy Bar-Haim, IBM Research AI
Chris Biemann, University of Hamburg
Yonatan Bilu, IBM Research AI
Andre Blessing, University of Stuttgart
Miriam Butt, University of Konstanz
Elena Cabrio, Université Côte d'Azur, CNRS, Inria, I3S
Claire Cardie, Cornell University
Johannes Daxenberger, Technische Universität Darmstadt
Roxanne El Baff, Bauhaus-Universität Weimar
Annette Frank, University of Heidelberg
Michael Granitzer, University of Passau
Nancy Green, University of North Carolina Greensboro
Ivan Habernal, BIX *
Graeme Hirst, University of Toronto *
Yufang Hou, Yufang Hou IBM Research AI
Jonas Kuhn, University of Stuttgart
Gabriella Lapesa, University of Stuttgart
John Lawrence, University of Dundee
Beishui Liao, Zhejiang University
Diane Litman, University of Pittsburgh
Marie-Francine Moens, KU Leuven
Smaranda Muresan, Columbia University
Elena Musi, University of Liverpool
Joonsuk Park, Williams College
Georgios Petasis, NCSR Demokritos

Peter Potash, Microsoft Research
Olesya Razuvayevskaya, University of Cambridge
Chris Reed, University of Dundee
Ariel Rosenfeld, Bar-Ilan University
Patrick Saint-Dizier, IRIT-CNRS
Jodi Schneider, University of Illinois at Urbana-Champaign *
Noam Slonim, IBM Research AI
Manfred Stede, University of Potsdam
Nicolas Turenne, Université Paris-Est Marne-la-Vallée
Serena Villata, CNRS
Vern R. Walker, Maurice A. Deane School of Law at Hofstra University
Zhongyu Wei, Fudan University
Magdalena Wolska, Bauhaus-Universität Weimar
Adam Wyner, Swansea University

The marked PC members form the Best Paper Committee.

Additional Reviewers:

Wei-Fan Chen, Bauhaus-Universität Weimar
Özge Sevgili Erguven, University of Hamburg
Tobias Mayer, Université Côte d'Azur, CNRS, Inria, I3S
Gregor Wiedemann, University of Hamburg

Invited Speakers:

Marco Lippi, University of Modena and Reggio Emilia
Giovanni Sartor, University of Bologna & European University Institute of Florence

Workshop Program

Thursday, August 1, 2019

08:40–08:50   *Opening Remarks*

Session 1

08:50–09:50   *Keynote: Schemes for Legal Argumentation*
Giovanni Sartor and Marco Lippi

09:50–10:10   *Segmentation of Argumentative Texts with Contextualised Word Representations*
Georgios Petasis

10:10–10:30   *A Cascade Model for Proposition Extraction in Argumentation*
Yohan Jo, Jacky Visser, Chris Reed and Eduard Hovy

10:30–11:00   *Coffee Break*

Session 2

11:00–11:20   *Dissecting Content and Context in Argumentative Relation Analysis*
Juri Opitz and Anette Frank

11:20–11:40   *Aligning Discourse and Argumentation Structures using Subtrees and Redescription Mining*
Laurine Huber, Yannick Toussaint, Charlotte Roze, Mathilde Dargnat and Chloé Braud

11:40–12:00   *Transferring Knowledge from Discourse to Arguments: A Case Study with Scientific Abstracts*
Pablo Accuosto and Horacio Saggion

12:00–12:30   *Poster Lightning Talks*
All poster presenters

12:30–14:00   *Lunch Break*

14:00–15:30   Session 3: Demo and Posters

Demo   *The Swedish PoliGraph: A Semantic Graph for Argument Mining of Swedish Parliamentary Data*
Stian Rødven Eide

Towards Effective Rebuttal: Listening Comprehension Using Corpus-Wide Claim Mining
Tamar Lavee, Matan Orbach, Lili Kotlerman, Yoav Kantor, Shai Gretz, Lena Dankin, Michal Jacovi, Yonatan Bilu, Ranit Aharonov and Noam Slonim

Lexicon Guided Attentive Neural Network Model for Argument Mining
Jian-Fu Lin, Kuo Yu Huang, Hen-Hsen Huang and Hsin-Hsi Chen

Is It Worth the Attention? A Comparative Evaluation of Attention Layers for Argument Unit Segmentation
Maximilian Spliethöver, Jonas Klaff and Hendrik Heuer

Argument Component Classification by Relation Identification by Neural Network and TextRank
Mamoru Deguchi and Kazunori Yamaguchi

Argumentative Evidences Classification and Argument Scheme Detection Using Tree Kernels
Davide Liga

The Utility of Discourse Parsing Features for Predicting Argumentation Structure
Freya Hewett, Roshan Prakash Rane, Nina Harlacher and Manfred Stede

Detecting Argumentative Discourse Acts with Linguistic Alignment
Timothy Niven and Hung-Yu Kao

Annotation of Rhetorical Moves in Biochemistry Articles
Mohammed Alliheedi, Robert E. Mercer and Robin Cohen

Evaluation of Scientific Elements for Text Similarity in Biomedical Publications
Mariana Neves, Daniel Butzke and Barbara Grune

Categorizing Comparative Sentences
Alexander Panchenko, Alexander Bondarenko, Mirco Franzek, Matthias Hagen and Chris Biemann

Ranking Passages for Argument Convincingness
Peter Potash, Adam Ferguson and Timothy J. Hazen

Gradual Argumentation Evaluation for Stance Aggregation in Automated Fake News Detection
Neema Kotonya and Francesca Toni

15:30–16:00 **Coffee Break**

Session 4

16:00–16:20 *Persuasion of the Undecided: Language vs. the Listener*
Liane Longpre, Esin Durmus and Claire Cardie

16:20–16:40 *Towards Assessing Argumentation Annotation - A First Step*
Anna Lindahl, Lars Borin and Jacobo Rouces

16:40–17:25 *Special Event*
Moderated by workshop chairs

17:25–17:30 *Best Paper Announcement*
Workshop chairs

17:30 **Closing Remarks**

Segmentation of Argumentative Texts with Contextualised Word Representations

Georgios Petasis
Software and Knowledge Engineering Laboratory
Institute of Informatics & Telecommunications
National Center for Scientific Research (N.C.S.R.) "Demokritos"
Athens, Greece.
petasis@iit.demokritos.gr

Abstract

The segmentation of argumentative units is an important subtask of argument mining, which is frequently addressed at a coarse granularity, usually assuming argumentative units to be no smaller than sentences. Approaches focusing at the clause-level granularity, typically address the task as sequence labeling at the token level, aiming to classify whether a token begins, is inside, or is outside of an argumentative unit. Most approaches exploit highly engineered, manually constructed features, and algorithms typically used in sequential tagging – such as Conditional Random Fields, while more recent approaches try to exploit manually constructed features in the context of deep neural networks. In this context, we examined to what extend recent advances in sequential labelling allow to reduce the need for highly sophisticated, manually constructed features, and whether limiting features to embeddings, pre-trained on large corpora is a promising approach. Evaluation results suggest the examined models and approaches can exhibit comparable performance, minimising the need for feature engineering.

1 Introduction

Argument mining involves the automatic discovery of *argument components* (such as claims, premises, etc.) and the *argumentative relations* (i.e. support, attack, etc.) among these components in texts. Primarily aiming to extract arguments from texts in order to provide structured data for computational models of argument and reasoning engines (Lippi and Torroni, 2015a), argument mining has additionally the potential to support applications in various research fields, such as opinion mining (Goudas et al., 2015), stance detection (Hasan and Ng, 2014), policy modelling (Florou et al., 2013; Goudas et al., 2014), legal information systems (Palau and

Moens, 2009), fact checking (Naderi and Hirst, 2018), etc.

The identification of argumentative discourse structures typically consists of two main tasks: 1) the identification of the locations in text and the type of the argument components, and 2) the identification of how these argument components related to each other (Persing and Ng, 2016). As a result, argument mining is usually addressed as a pipeline of several sub-tasks. Typically the first sub-task is the separation between argumentative and non-argumentative text units, which can be performed at various granularity levels, from clauses to several sentences, usually depending on corpora characteristics. Detection of argumentative units (AU)[1], as discussed in Section 2, is typically modeled as a fully-supervised classification task, either a binary one, where units are separated in argumentative and non-argumentative ones with argumentative ones to be subsequently classified in major claims, claims, premises, etc. as a second step, or as a multi-class one, where identification of argumentative units and their classification into claims and premises are performed as a single step. Typically the granularity of this task is coarse, with most approaches considering sentences as the smallest argumentative unit (Florou et al., 2013; Moens et al., 2007; Song et al., 2014; Swanson et al., 2015), although some works focused on the most difficult task of detecting units at the *clause level* (Park and Cardie, 2014; Goudas et al., 2014, 2015; Sardianos et al., 2015; Stab, 2017; Ajjour et al., 2017; Eger et al., 2017). According to a recent survey (Lippi and Torroni, 2015a), the performance of proposed approaches depends on highly engineered and sophisticated, manually constructed, features.

Approaches focusing at the clause-level granu-

---

[1] Also known as "Argumentative Discourse Units – ADUs" (Peldszus and Stede, 2013).

1

Proceedings of the 6th Workshop on Argument Mining, pages 1–10
Florence, Italy, August 1, 2019. ©2019 Association for Computational Linguistics

larity, typically address the task as sequence labeling at the token level, aiming to classify whether a token begins, is inside, or is outside of an argumentative unit through the IOB format (Ramshaw and Marcus, 1995). Most of the approaches employ Conditional Random Fields (CRFs) (Lafferty et al., 2001) with hand-crafted features (Goudas et al., 2014), as CRFs are the prominent and most reliable algorithm for many sequential labelling tasks (Zeng et al., 2017), and have been applied to a wide range of segmenting tasks, from named-entity recognition (McCallum and Li, 2003) and shallow parsing (Sha and Pereira, 2003), to aspect-based sentiment analysis (Patra et al., 2014). Sequence labeling algorithms take as input a set of features for each token in a sequence (such as a sentence) and learn to predict an optimal sequence of labels for all tokens in the input sequence, while performance depends on the provided (typically manually engineered features) and how well these features can help the model predicting the likelihood of every label in the sequence. However, as deep learning is slowly replacing CRFs for sequence labelling (i.e. (Ajjour et al., 2017)), it is interesting to examine whether these hand-crafted features are still important, or comparative levels of performance can be achieved without them.

In this paper we examine whether a "CRF-inspired" neural model without the hand-crafted features, can be applied to the task of argumentative unit segmentation at the clause level, and whether its performance is comparable to approaches exploiting such features. In addition, we study whether contextualised word representations can help in this task, and provide an alternative to hand-crafted features. These can be reflected in the following two questions:

1. Can approaches that do not use manually engineered features achieve performances comparable to approaches that exploit such features?

2. Can contextualised word representations (pre-trained in large corpora) replace manually engineered features in argument mining?

The motivation behind the work presented in this paper originates from the advances performed in the state of art of named-entity recognition by Bidirectional LSTM-CRF Models for Sequence Tagging (Huang et al., 2015; Ma and Hovy, 2016), a variation of Long Short-Term Memory (LSTM)

based models with a decoding layer that considers relations between neighbouring labels and jointly decodes the optimal sequence of labels for a given input sequence (Ma and Hovy, 2016), using a Conditionally Random Field. Recognising a similar evolution pattern also in the area of argument mining segmentation – starting with CRF's and manually constructed features (Park and Cardie, 2014; Goudas et al., 2014, 2015; Stab, 2017), then employing word embeddings as features in CRFs (Sardianos et al., 2015) and subsequently applying bi-directional LSTMs (Ajjour et al., 2017) on manually engineered features – poses the question if a similar advancement can be achieved by introducing the currently missing pieces (LSTM-CRF models or contextualised word representations such as (Peters et al., 2018)), in an attempt to eliminate – or reduce the need for – manually engineered features.

In order to approach our research questions we have used the second version of the Argument Annotated Essay Corpus (Stab, 2017), a collection of 402 essays, which has been manually annotated with major claims (one per essay), claims and premises at the clause level. In addition, the corpus contains manual annotations of argumentative relations, where the claims and premises are linked, while claims are linked to the major claim either with a support or an attack relation. We have applied LSTM-CRF models (using the implementation reported in (Akbik et al., 2018)) employing various word embeddings (including contextualised word representations like "ELMo" (Peters et al., 2018), "Flair" (Akbik et al., 2018) and "BERT" (Devlin et al., 2018)). Evaluation results suggest that all studied approaches are comparable or slightly better to the current state of art.

2   Related work

Almost all argument mining frameworks proposed so far employ a pipeline of stages, each of which is addressing a sub-task of the argument mining problem (Lippi and Torroni, 2015a). The segmentation of text into argumentative units is typically the first sub-task encountered in such an argument mining pipeline, aiming to segment texts into argumentative and non-argumentative text units (i.e. segments that do contain or do not contain argument components, such as claims or premises). The granularity of argument components is text-dependant. For example, in Wikipedia articles studied in (Rinott et al., 2015), argument components spanned from less than a sentence to more than a paragraph, although 90% of the cases was up to 3 sentences, with 95% of components being comprised of whole sentences.

Several approaches address the identification of argumentative units at the sentence level, a sub-task known as "argumentative sentence detection", which typically models the task as a binary classification problem. Employing machine learning and a set of features representing sentences, the goal is to discard sentences that are not part (or do not contain a component) of an argument. As reported also by Lippi and Torroni (2015a), the vast majority of existing approaches employ "classic, off-the-self" classifiers, while most of the effort is devoted to highly engineered features. A plethora of learning algorithms have been applied on the task, including Naive Bayes (Moens et al., 2007; Park and Cardie, 2014), Support Vector Machines (SVM) (Mochales and Moens, 2011; Rooney et al., 2012; Park and Cardie, 2014; Stab and Gurevych, 2014; Lippi and Torroni, 2015b), Maximum Entropy (Mochales and Moens, 2011), Logistic Regression (Goudas et al., 2014, 2015; Levy et al., 2014), Decision Trees and Random Forests (Goudas et al., 2014, 2015; Stab and Gurevych, 2014). There is also a limited number of approaches addressing the task in a semi-supervised or unsupervised manner, such as (Ferrara et al., 2017).

The identification of argumentative units at the clause level has been less studied than its more coarse counterpart. (Park and Cardie, 2014) has exploited n-grams and a large number of additional, manually crafted, binary (denoting the presence of features) and numeric (containing counts) features in a supervised manner with Support Vector Machine as classifier, achieving a macro-averaged $F_1 = 68.99\%$ on a corpus manually annotated by the authors. In (Goudas et al., 2014, 2015) the authors have examined segmentation both at sentence and clause level, for the Greek language, using a corpus manually annotated by the authors. They have exploited both features from previous approaches and features proposed by the authors, achieving $F_1 = 42.37\%$, as measured by "conlleval.pl" (taking into account correct sequences and not only labels at the token level). The same Greek corpus has been used in (Sardianos et al., 2015), where word2vec em-

beddings (Mikolov et al., 2013) have been used as features in a supervised setting using CRFs, combined with part-of-speech tags and a small lexicon with cue phrases, to report a small increase in performance ($F_1 = 32.12\%$) over the baseline ($F_1 = 27.04\%$).

CRFs have been also used in (Stab, 2017), along with an extensive set of highly engineered features, including structural, syntactic, lexico-syntactic and probabilistic features. The approach has been evaluated on the second version of the Argument Annotated Essay Corpus (the same corpus has been used for evaluation in this work), created by the authors, achieving macro-averaged $F_1 = 86.70\%$. Similar features (with the addition of pragmatic features) have been exploited in (Ajjour et al., 2017) using a bidirectional LSTM model as classifier in a supervised setting, achieving macro-averaged $F_1 = 88.54\%$ on the second version of the Argument Annotated Essay Corpus, with lower scores on two other corpora. In interesting aspect of this work is the out-of-domain evaluation, performing evaluations on different corpora from the ones used for training. Deep neural networks have been also employed by (Eger et al., 2017), using bidirectional LSTM-CRF models in a supervised setting, as an end-to-end system. Framing argument mining as a sequence tagging at the token level, they learn simultaneously four different sets of labels, encoding both segmentation of argumentative units, their types and their relations. The approach has been evaluated on the second version of the Argument Annotated Essay Corpus (the same corpus has been used for evaluation in this work) achieving $F_1 = 69.49\%$.

In (Persing and Ng, 2016) the authors propose a rule-based approach, with manually constructed rules applied on top of syntactic trees, achieving a performance of 92.1% on the first version of the Argument Annotated Essay Corpus (Stab and Gurevych, 2014). In (Lawrence et al., 2014) the authors propose a two-stage approach: During the first stage text is segmented into propositions using two Naive Bayes classifiers (Nir Friedman and Goldszmidt, 1997) with simple features (words, lengths and a sliding window of three tokens) in a supervised setting. Then, as a second step, propositions are scored based on their similarities to document topic retrieved through Latent Dirichlet Allocation (LDA) and their distances, to decide whether they constitute an argumentative unit or not.

3   Data

For our experiments, we have used the second version of the Argument Annotated Essay Corpus (Stab, 2017; Eger et al., 2017; Stab and Gurevych, 2017), which contains 402 student essays written in response to controversial topics. The corpus has been manually annotated with major claims (one per essay), claims and premises at the clause level. In addition, the corpus contains manual annotations of argumentative relations, where the claims and premises are linked, while claims are linked to the major claim either with a support or an attack relation. Essays are on average 370 tokens long, while most of the tokens ($\sim$ 70%) are part of an argumentative unit. The corpus is split into train and test sets at the essay level, provided by the authors. We have converted the corpus into the CoNLL token-based sequence tagging format (using the tools provided by the "BRAT" annotation toolkit) and we extracted a small development set ($< 10\%$) from the training set randomly, with the help of "scikit-learn" toolkit.

4   Models

Following the typical setting in argumentative unit segmentation at the clause level, we are going to also frame the task as a sequence labelling classification problem. In sequential labelling the label of an instance does not depend only on the instance itself, but also depends on the instances previously seen. A natural choice for sequence labelling are recurrent neural networks (RNNs), which consider "hidden" states computed from previous points in time (instances already classified) during classification. For our experiments we have chosen LSTMs (Hochreiter and Schmidhuber, 1997), a type of RNNs able to learn long-term dependences, as their structure allows them to control how much information is shared across points in time.

However, a single LSTM is able to have access to a single context (typically to the left context of a token) when assigning a label. Bidirectional LSTMs employ two separate LSTM layers, looking at the input from opposite directions, while their output is concatenated into a single vector. Finally, in order to reflect all CRF capabilities, and especially its ability to assign labels taking into account contextual dependencies from all tags

in a sequence, a CRF network can be combined with an LSTM or a bidirectional LSTM to form an LSTM-CRF (or bi-LSTM-CRF model) (Huang et al., 2015), which can use features from all instances in a sequence (past and future) for assigning a label to an instance (Fig 1).

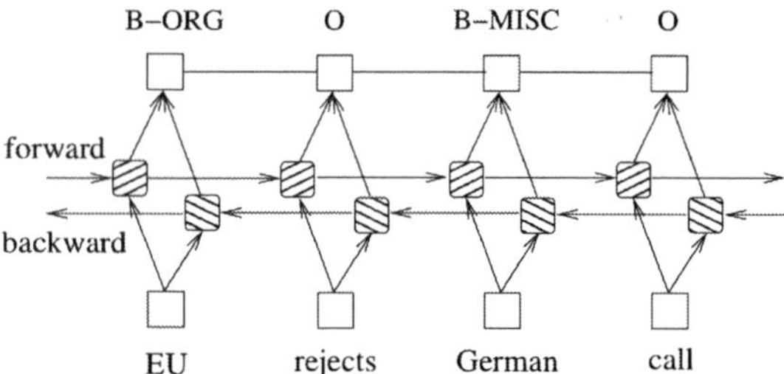

Figure 1: A BI-LSTM-CRF model. (Huang et al., 2015)

4.1   Argument Mining as Sentence Labelling

In a simple scenario, argumentative unit identification can be performed at the sentence level, where labeling consists in distinguishing between sentences that are argumentative units ($y = au$) and sentences that are not argumentative units ($y = \overline{au}$).

4.2   Argument Mining as Sequence Labelling

In a more articulated scenario, argumentative unit identification must decide not only whether a sentence contains an argumentative unit, but in addition to identify the exact words that represent each argumentative unit within each sentence. Framing this task as a sequence labelling task, each token is assigned a label from y, where $y = \{(b, t) \mid b \in \{B, I, O\}, t \in \{au\}\}$.

4.3   Embeddings

As input to the aforementioned model, we are going to use dense representations, and more specifically pre-trained word embeddings, such as GloVe (Pennington et al., 2014). Depending on the way word embeddings were generated and the information they represent, word embeddings can be seen as a form of transfer learning, providing a model additional information, typically acquired from a larger corpus than a training dataset for a task. In addition to these embeddings, we are going to examine more recent *deep contextualised* word representations, such as "ELMo" (Peters et al., 2018), "Flair" (Akbik et al., 2018) and

		Number of tokens				
Part	**# Documents**	B-Arg	I-Arg	O-Arg	Total	Average
Train + Development	322	4,823	75,657	38,195	118,675	368.56
Test	80	1,266	18,837	9,442	29,545	369.31

Table 1: Number of documents, tokens per class, and average number of tokens per document.

"BERT" (Devlin et al., 2018). These representations are able to model "both characteristics of word usage (e.g. syntax and semantics) and how these uses vary across linguistic contexts (i.e. to model polysemy)" (Peters et al., 2018). These representations assign a different vector to each word based on its context, in contrast to embeddings like GloVe that assign the same vector to a word, irrespectively of context.

5 Experiments

5.1 Argument Mining as Sentence Labelling

Using the corpus described in Section 3, we have applied four classifiers to the task of classifying a sentence as argumentative or not. Using as only features the GloVe[2] vectors for each token in a sentence, we have applied Convolutional Neural Networks (CNNs) the following implementation, BI-LSTM-CRF, and bidirectional Sentence-State LSTMs (S-LSTMs) (Zhang et al., 2018)[3]. All approaches involve the usage of non-contextualised embeddings (GloVe), keeping the most frequent 15,000 words in the corpus, following the training details as described in (Zhang et al., 2018). All models are trained using SGD with no momentum (with a mini-batch size of 32), clipping gradients at 5, for a maximum 40 epochs. A simple learning rate annealing method is employed in which we halve the learning rate if training loss does not fall for 5 consecutive epochs, initialising learning rate to 10^{-3}. The hidden states per-layer was set to 300, and variational dropout was used. The number of hidden layers was fine-tuned in the range $1 - 8$, and model selection was performed by choosing the model with the best accuracy on the development set. The split provided by the authors of the corpus regarding the training and test sets was used, while a small development set was extracted from the training set, containing 21 es-

says[4]. Regarding stability and reproducibility of results, we have used 2019[5] as the seed value. The aforementioned approaches were compared to the "BERT" (Devlin et al., 2018) contextual embeddings[6], using a single feed-forward layer on top of the embeddings, with a hidden layer equal to the size of the embeddings (768)[7]. Minimal fine-tuning has been performed, allowing only a single epoch with mini-batch size of 32 and a learning rate equal to $2e^{-5}$.

Embedding	**Architecture**	**Accuracy**
GloVe	CNN	0.8391
GloVe	LSTM	0.8488
GloVe	S-LSTM	0.8619
BERT	Feed Forward	**0.8874**

Table 2: Argument Mining as Sentence Labelling: Evaluation Results.

Our experiment results are summarised in Table 2. While BERT embeddings (even with minimal fine-tuning of a single hidden layer) have outperformed all other approaches, traditional word embeddings ("GloVe" + S-LSTM) may still be useful as their performance is still very close to BERT, while employing 6 Bi-S-LSTM-CRF layers, with a window of 5 tokens, and after 15 epochs of fine-tuning to the task.

5.2 Argument Mining as Sequence Labelling

For our second experiment, which combines the identification of argumentative units with their localisation as textual segments, we have employed

---

[2]Wikipedia 2014 + Gigaword 5, 6B tokens, 400K vocabulary, uncased, 300 dimensions.

[3]We have used the following implementation for CNNs, LSTMs and S-SLTMs: `https://github.com/leuchine/S-LSTM`

[4]The essays randomly selected for the development set are: 13, 38, 41, 115, 140, 152, 156, 159, 162, 164, 201, 257, 291, 324, 343, 361, 369, 371, 387, 389, 400.

[5]The same seed value, 2019, has been used for all experiments performed in this paper.

[6]We have adapted the implementation that can be found here: `https://colab.research.google.com/github/google-research/bert/blob/master/predicting_movie_reviews_with_bert_on_tf_hub.ipynb`

[7]The used embeddings can be found at: `https://tfhub.dev/google/bert_uncased_L-12_H-768_A-12/1`

an end-to-end system that utilises a BI-LSTM-CRF architecture with 2 layers, with each layer employing 256 hidden nodes. This model has been trained and evaluated with a series of traditional "(GloVe", character embeddings) and contextual embeddings ("ELMo", "Flair", and "BERT"). All experiments we have used the "Flair"[8] framework. Fine-tunning was performed for a maximum of 150 epochs, using SGD with a mini-batch size of 32,and simulated annealing, with a starting learning rate of 0.1. The same random seed (2019) was used for all experiments.

We report the macro F-score as an evaluation measure, since this allows for a comparison to related work. The macro F_1-score considers all the classes to be equally important, without taking into consideration the number of instances each class has. (The distribution of classes in the corpus is shown in Table 1.)

5.2.1 Comparison with previous work

Features	Model	Macro F_1
All (Semantic+Syntactic	SVM	61.40
+Structural+Pragmatic)	CRF	79.16
(Ajjour et al., 2017)	BI-LSTM	**88.54**
All (Stab, 2017)	CRF	**86.70**
GloVe + Character	BI-LSTM-CRF	85.92
GloVe + Character + Flair	BI-LSTM-CRF	88.17
ELMo	BI-LSTM-CRF	88.62
BERT	BI-LSTM-CRF	89.31
GloVe + Flair + BERT	BI-LSTM-CRF	**90.13**
GloVe + Flair + ELMo + BERT	BI-LSTM-CRF	87.42

Table 3: Argument Mining as Sequence Labelling: Evaluation Results.

In order to enable comparison with existing approaches, we have tried to imitate the experimental settings found in (Stab, 2017) and (Ajjour et al., 2017). Table 3 shows the results of the approaches presented in (Ajjour et al., 2017) in the upper part of the table, followed by the best overall result presented in (Stab, 2017), including all features (semantic, syntactic and structural) and the CRF classifier. Both approaches employ a large number of highly engineered and sophisticated, manually constructed, features. Finally, in the lower part of the table, we report our results of the BI-LSTM-CRF model with the various tested embeddings.

From Table 3 it can be seen that almost all embeddings (especially the contextual ones) outperform the approaches with manually engineered features (Ajjour et al., 2017; Stab, 2017), with the combination of contextual embeddings achieving new state-of-art ($MacroF_1 = 90.13$) on the Essays v2.0 corpus, especially when considering the absence of manually constructed features.

5.3 Error Analysis

We analysed the results obtained with the GloVe+Flair+BERT experiment. The test dataset contains 1448 annotated sentences, where 1,178 sentences were correctly annotated, while 270 sentences were erroneously annotated by our model. According to the confusion matrix, the two major sources of errors are 1767 "O" tokens erroneously classified as "I-Arg", and 829 "I-Arg" erroneously classified as "O". The majority of the errors (104 sentences) were sentences that the model erroneously annotated as containing argumentative components, while these sentences did not contain any argumentative component according to the gold annotation. Some examples of such sentences are displayed in the following list (annotated segments by the model are highlighted):

1. In spite of this, the disadvantages of the promotion of a universal language cannot be denied.

2. It is obvious that the benefits of the Internet undoubtedly outweigh its disadvantages.

3. It would be highly unpractical to ask people to adopt a simpler way of life.

4. Some people claim that without this punishment our lives would be less secure and crimes of violence would increase.

5. It is evident that technology promotes economy.

The second most important source of errors, are sentences containing argumentative units that were not annotated as such by our model. 43 sentences belong in this category, while some examples are shown as follows:

1. However, it is not sufficient in itself.

---

[8]https://github.com/zalandoresearch/flair

2. Some people claim that the prevalent of English brings a great number of benefits for people.

3. In the modern world, computers are used everywhere.

4. There is no end to the evolution of computers.

5. Many people hold the opinion that past behaviour determines the future actions, which could be the main reason to support the idea of revealing the record to the jury.

The rest of the errors (123 sentences in total) are various errors, like two argumentative units merged in one (errors by our model in red):

1. For instance , some Asians are seeking individualism, previously denied by many Asian countries, due to the fact that they have gradually identified with such values expressed in American movies, which are imported by the governments as a result of the proliferation of English.

2. First and foremost, sports events are good chances for excellent athletes to meet and learn valuable experiences from one another. so that they can improve their results, break records and bring victories to their own countries.

Finally, in some cases, our model missed the beginning of an argumentative unit (in red the part not annotated by our model):

1. From personal level, it fosters a sense of unfairness between the older and younger generations.

2. From social perspective, massively forcing the early retirement would be one of financial burden to the local government.

5.4 Discussion

Evaluation results suggest that omitting highly engineered, manually crafted features, and replacing them with embeddings (pre-trained on large corpora and possibly exploiting multiple sources of information), is a promising approach and a viable alternative.

Research Question 1: Can approaches that do not use manually engineered features achieve performances comparable to approaches that exploit such features?

Evaluation results suggest that a large part of the information provided by the plethora of manually constructed features can be substituted with a fairly standard architecture and word embeddings, especially contextualised embeddings that can be tuned to the task at hand, like the contextualised word representations ELMo (Peters et al., 2018) and BERT (Devlin et al., 2018). Further optimisation is of course possible (especially with respect to the architectures on top of embeddings, the number of layers, and the fine-tune of the many hyper-parameters associated with the employed neural models). However, there are some limiting factors, mainly the absence of a development set in the corpus used for evaluation, and the computational requirements of the models, especially in the case of contextualised word embeddings.

Research Question 2: Can contextualised word representations replace manually engineered features?

Evaluation results are promising, especially since the examined approaches have achieved a small increase over the current state-of-art. However, the examined approaches have not exceeded significantly the current state-of-art, suggesting that manually engineered features are still relevant and significant at least for this task, the segmentation of argumentative units at the clause level. One of the findings in (Ajjour et al., 2017) is that the semantic features appear to be the most significant features, achieving the highest F-scores, an observation that seems to hold also in our experiments, as reverting to embeddings that enhance semantic modelling (through implicit word sense disambiguation performed based on contextual information) seems to provide a significant increase in performance. At the same time, the performance difference with the CRF exploiting the manually constructed features (Stab, 2017) is small, suggesting that removing the highly engineered features may have a small penalty in performance, at least for the approach of (Stab, 2017).

6 Conclusion

The segmentation of argumentative units is an important subtask of argument mining, which is frequently addressed at a coarse granularity, usually assuming argumentative units to be no smaller than sentences. Approaches focusing at the clause-level granularity, typically address the task as sequence labeling at the token level, aiming to classify whether a token begins, is inside, or is outside of an argumentative unit through the IOB format (Ramshaw and Marcus, 1995). Most approaches exploit highly engineered, manually constructed features, and algorithms typically used in sequential tagging – such as CRFs (Park and Cardie, 2014; Goudas et al., 2014, 2015; Stab, 2017), while more recent approaches try to exploit manually constructed features in the context of deep neural networks (Ajjour et al., 2017; Eger et al., 2017). In this context, we examined to what extend recent advances in sequential labelling and contextualised word embeddings allow to reduce the need for manually constructed features, and whether limiting features to embeddings, pre-trained on large corpora is a promising approach. Evaluation results suggest the examined models and approaches can exhibit comparable performance, minimising the need for feature engineering.

Regarding directions for further research, there are several axes that can be explored. Evaluation on more corpora will provide enhanced insights about the performance of the examined approaches on different document types. At the same time, there is a significant optimisation potential, especially in hyper-parameter tuning of the employed algorithms, provided that a suitable development set is available, and the computational requirements of some models (especially the ones employing contextualised word representation) are significantly reduced in order to constitute experimentation more tractable and practical.

Acknowledgments

We acknowledge support of this work by the project "APOLLONIS: Greek Infrastructure for Digital Arts, Humanities and Language Research and Innovation" (MIS 5002738) which is implemented under the Action "Reinforcement of the Research and Innovation Infrastructure", funded by the Operational Programme "Competitiveness, Entrepreneurship and Innovation" (NSRF 2014-2020) and co-financed by Greece and the European Union (European Regional Development Fund).

References

Yamen Ajjour, Wei-Fan Chen, Johannes Kiesel, Henning Wachsmuth, and Benno Stein. 2017. Unit segmentation of argumentative texts. In *Proceedings of the 4th Workshop on Argument Mining*, pages 118–128, Copenhagen, Denmark. Association for Computational Linguistics.

Alan Akbik, Duncan Blythe, and Roland Vollgraf. 2018. Contextual string embeddings for sequence labeling. In *COLING 2018, 27th International Conference on Computational Linguistics*, pages 1638–1649.

Jacob Devlin, Ming-Wei Chang, Kenton Lee, and Kristina Toutanova. 2018. BERT: pre-training of deep bidirectional transformers for language understanding. *CoRR*, abs/1810.04805.

Steffen Eger, Johannes Daxenberger, and Iryna Gurevych. 2017. Neural end-to-end learning for computational argumentation mining. In *Proceedings of the 55th Annual Meeting of the Association for Computational Linguistics (Volume 1: Long Papers)*, pages 11–22, Vancouver, Canada. Association for Computational Linguistics.

Alfio Ferrara, Stefano Montanelli, and Georgios Petasis. 2017. Unsupervised detection of argumentative units though topic modeling techniques. In *Proceedings of the 4th Workshop on Argument Mining*, pages 97–107, Copenhagen, Denmark. Association for Computational Linguistics.

Eirini Florou, Stasinos Konstantopoulos, Antonis Koukourikos, and Pythagoras Karampiperis. 2013. Argument extraction for supporting public policy formulation. In *Proceedings of the 7th Workshop on Language Technology for Cultural Heritage, Social Sciences, and Humanities, LaTeCH@ACL 2013, August 8, 2013, Sofia, Bulgaria*, pages 49–54. The Association for Computer Linguistics.

Theodosis Goudas, Christos Louizos, Georgios Petasis, and Vangelis Karkaletsis. 2014. Argument extraction from news, blogs, and social media. In Aristidis Likas, Konstantinos Blekas, and Dimitris Kalles, editors, *Artificial Intelligence: Methods and Applications: 8th Hellenic Conference on AI, SETN 2014, Ioannina, Greece, May 15-17, 2014. Proceedings*, pages 287–299. Springer International Publishing, Cham.

Theodosis Goudas, Christos Louizos, Georgios Petasis, and Vangelis Karkaletsis. 2015. Argument extraction from news, blogs, and the social web. *International Journal on Artificial Intelligence Tools*, 24(05):1540024.

Kazi Saidul Hasan and Vincent Ng. 2014. Why are you taking this stance? identifying and classifying reasons in ideological debates. In *Proceedings of the 2014 Conference on Empirical Methods in Natural Language Processing (EMNLP)*, pages 751–762, Doha, Qatar. Association for Computational Linguistics.

Sepp Hochreiter and Jürgen Schmidhuber. 1997. Long short-term memory. *Neural Comput.*, 9(8):1735–1780.

Zhiheng Huang, Wei Xu, and Kai Yu. 2015. Bidirectional LSTM-CRF models for sequence tagging. *CoRR*, abs/1508.01991.

John D. Lafferty, Andrew McCallum, and Fernando C. N. Pereira. 2001. Conditional random fields: Probabilistic models for segmenting and labeling sequence data. In *Proceedings of the Eighteenth International Conference on Machine Learning*, ICML '01, pages 282–289, San Francisco, CA, USA. Morgan Kaufmann Publishers Inc.

John Lawrence, Chris Reed, Colin Allen, Simon McAlister, and Andrew Ravenscroft. 2014. Mining arguments from 19th century philosophical texts using topic based modelling. In *Proceedings of the First Workshop on Argumentation Mining*, pages 79–87, Baltimore, Maryland. Association for Computational Linguistics.

Ran Levy, Yonatan Bilu, Daniel Hershcovich, Ehud Aharoni, and Noam Slonim. 2014. Context dependent claim detection. In *COLING 2014, 25th International Conference on Computational Linguistics, Proceedings of the Conference: Technical Papers, August 23-29, 2014, Dublin, Ireland*, pages 1489–1500. ACL.

Marco Lippi and Paolo Torroni. 2015a. Argument mining: A machine learning perspective. In *Theory and Applications of Formal Argumentation: Third International Workshop, TAFA 2015, Buenos Aires, Argentina, July 25-26, 2015, Revised Selected Papers*, pages 163–176, Cham. Springer International Publishing.

Marco Lippi and Paolo Torroni. 2015b. Context-independent claim detection for argument mining. In *Proceedings of the 24th International Conference on Artificial Intelligence*, IJCAI'15, pages 185–191. AAAI Press.

Xuezhe Ma and Eduard Hovy. 2016. End-to-end sequence labeling via bi-directional lstm-cnns-crf. In *Proceedings of the 54th Annual Meeting of the Association for Computational Linguistics (Volume 1: Long Papers)*, pages 1064–1074. Association for Computational Linguistics.

Andrew McCallum and Wei Li. 2003. Early results for named entity recognition with conditional random fields, feature induction and web-enhanced lexicons. In *Proceedings of the Seventh Conference on Natural Language Learning at HLT-NAACL 2003 - Volume 4*, CONLL '03, pages 188–191, Stroudsburg, PA, USA. Association for Computational Linguistics.

Tomas Mikolov, Kai Chen, Greg Corrado, and Jeffrey Dean. 2013. Efficient estimation of word representations in vector space. In *1st International Conference on Learning Representations, ICLR 2013, Scottsdale, Arizona, USA, May 2-4, 2013, Workshop Track Proceedings*.

Raquel Mochales and Marie-Francine Moens. 2011. Argumentation mining. *Artificial Intelligence and Law*, 19(1):1–22.

Marie-Francine Moens, Erik Boiy, Raquel Mochales Palau, and Chris Reed. 2007. Automatic detection of arguments in legal texts. In *Proceedings of the 11th International Conference on Artificial Intelligence and Law*, ICAIL '07, pages 225–230, New York, NY, USA. ACM.

Nona Naderi and Graeme Hirst. 2018. Automated fact-checking of claims in argumentative parliamentary debates. In *Proceedings of the First Workshop on Fact Extraction and VERification (FEVER)*, pages 60–65, Brussels, Belgium. Association for Computational Linguistics.

Dan Geiger Nir Friedman and Moises Goldszmidt. 1997. Bayesian network classifiers. *Machine Learning*, 29:131–163.

Raquel Mochales Palau and Marie-Francine Moens. 2009. Argumentation mining: The detection, classification and structure of arguments in text. In *Proceedings of the 12th International Conference on Artificial Intelligence and Law*, ICAIL '09, pages 98–107, New York, NY, USA. ACM.

Joonsuk Park and Claire Cardie. 2014. Identifying appropriate support for propositions in online user comments. In *Proceedings of the First Workshop on Argumentation Mining*, pages 29–38, Baltimore, Maryland. Association for Computational Linguistics.

Braja Gopal Patra, Soumik Mandal, Dipankar Das, and Sivaji Bandyopadhyay. 2014. Ju_cse: A conditional random field (crf) based approach to aspect based sentiment analysis. In *Proceedings of the 8th International Workshop on Semantic Evaluation (SemEval 2014)*, pages 370–374, Dublin, Ireland. Association for Computational Linguistics and Dublin City University.

Andreas Peldszus and Manfred Stede. 2013. From argument diagrams to argumentation mining in texts: A survey. *Int. J. Cogn. Inform. Nat. Intell.*, 7(1):1–31.

Jeffrey Pennington, Richard Socher, and Christopher D. Manning. 2014. Glove: Global vectors for word representation. In *Empirical Methods in Natural Language Processing (EMNLP)*, pages 1532–1543.

Isaac Persing and Vincent Ng. 2016. End-to-end argumentation mining in student essays. In *Proceedings of the 2016 Conference of the North American Chapter of the Association for Computational Linguistics: Human Language Technologies*, pages 1384–1394, San Diego, California. Association for Computational Linguistics.

Matthew Peters, Mark Neumann, Mohit Iyyer, Matt Gardner, Christopher Clark, Kenton Lee, and Luke Zettlemoyer. 2018. Deep contextualized word representations. In *Proceedings of the 2018 Conference of the North American Chapter of the Association for Computational Linguistics: Human Language Technologies, Volume 1 (Long Papers)*, pages 2227–2237. Association for Computational Linguistics.

Lance Ramshaw and Mitch Marcus. 1995. Text chunking using transformation-based learning. In *Third Workshop on Very Large Corpora*.

Ruty Rinott, Lena Dankin, Carlos Alzate Perez, Mitesh M. Khapra, Ehud Aharoni, and Noam Slonim. 2015. Show me your evidence - an automatic method for context dependent evidence detection. In *Proceedings of the 2015 Conference on Empirical Methods in Natural Language Processing*, pages 440–450, Lisbon, Portugal. Association for Computational Linguistics.

Niall Rooney, Hui Wang, and Fiona Browne. 2012. Applying kernel methods to argumentation mining. In *Proceedings of the Twenty-Fifth International Florida Artificial Intelligence Research Society Conference, Marco Island, Florida. May 23-25, 2012*. AAAI Press.

Christos Sardianos, Ioannis Manousos Katakis, Georgios Petasis, and Vangelis Karkaletsis. 2015. Argument extraction from news. In *Proceedings of the 2nd Workshop on Argumentation Mining*, pages 56–66, Denver, CO. Association for Computational Linguistics.

Fei Sha and Fernando Pereira. 2003. Shallow parsing with conditional random fields. In *Proceedings of the 2003 Conference of the North American Chapter of the Association for Computational Linguistics on Human Language Technology - Volume 1*, NAACL '03, pages 134–141, Stroudsburg, PA, USA. Association for Computational Linguistics.

Yi Song, Michael Heilman, Beata Beigman Klebanov, and Paul Deane. 2014. Applying argumentation schemes for essay scoring. In *Proceedings of the First Workshop on Argumentation Mining*, pages 69–78, Baltimore, Maryland. Association for Computational Linguistics.

Christian Stab and Iryna Gurevych. 2014. Identifying argumentative discourse structures in persuasive essays. In *Proceedings of the 2014 Conference on Empirical Methods in Natural Language Processing (EMNLP)*, pages 46–56, Doha, Qatar. Association for Computational Linguistics.

Christian Stab and Iryna Gurevych. 2017. Parsing argumentation structures in persuasive essays. *Comput. Linguist.*, 43(3):619–659.

Christian Matthias Edwin Stab. 2017. *Argumentative Writing Support by means of Natural Language Processing*. Ph.D. thesis, Technische Universität Darmstadt, Darmstadt.

Reid Swanson, Brian Ecker, and Marilyn Walker. 2015. Argument mining: Extracting arguments from online dialogue. In *Proceedings of the 16th Annual Meeting of the Special Interest Group on Discourse and Dialogue*, pages 217–226, Prague, Czech Republic. Association for Computational Linguistics.

Donghuo Zeng, Chengjie Sun, Lei Lin, and Bingquan Liu. 2017. Lstm-crf for drug-named entity recognition. *Entropy*, 19(6).

Yue Zhang, Qi Liu, and Linfeng Song. 2018. Sentence-state LSTM for text representation. In *Proceedings of the 56th Annual Meeting of the Association for Computational Linguistics (Volume 1: Long Papers)*, pages 317–327, Melbourne, Australia. Association for Computational Linguistics.

A Cascade Model for Proposition Extraction in Argumentation

Yohan Jo[1]**, Jacky Visser**[2]**, Chris Reed**[2]**, Eduard Hovy**[1]
[1]Language Technologies Institute, Carnegie Mellon University
[2]Centre for Argument Technology, University of Dundee
`yohanj@cs.cmu.edu, j.visser@dundee.ac.uk,`
`c.a.reed@dundee.ac.uk, hovy@cmu.edu`

Abstract

We present a model to tackle a fundamental but understudied problem in computational argumentation: proposition extraction. Propositions are the basic units of an argument and the primary building blocks of most argument mining systems. However, they are usually substituted by argumentative discourse units obtained via surface-level text segmentation, which may yield text segments that lack semantic information necessary for subsequent argument mining processes. In contrast, our cascade model aims to extract complete propositions by handling anaphora resolution, text segmentation, reported speech, questions, imperatives, missing subjects, and revision. We formulate each task as a computational problem and test various models using a corpus of the 2016 U.S. presidential debates. We show promising performance for some tasks and discuss main challenges in proposition extraction.

1 Introduction

Most argument mining models for identifying the argumentative structure of a text build upon elementary text spans that serve argumentative functions, such as premise and conclusion. In argumentation theory, it is commonly accepted that these building blocks are propositions (Blackburn, 2016), i.e., statements that are either true or false. Despite the foundational role of propositions, however, proposition extraction from text has been little studied in computational argumentation. Instead, most models rely on argumentative discourse units (ADUs) obtained by surface-level text segmentation (Stede et al., 2016; Al Khatib et al., 2016). In what follows, we discuss limitations of ADUs that potentially impinge upon subsequent argument mining processes, and then describe our approach.

One limitation of ADUs is that they may lack important semantic information, such as the **ref-erents of anaphors** and the **subject of an incomplete sentence**, necessary for subsequent argument mining steps. For example, for two consecutive text segments *Alice complained to Bob* and *He is upset*, if we do not know *he* refers to Bob, it would be confusing whether the first segment supports the second or vice versa. In another example, suppose *Alice was faithful to Bob, keeping the secret* is split into two propositions, each associated with the main clause and the adverbial participle, respectively. While mere text segmentation leaves the subject of the participle (Alice) missing, tracing and reconstructing the subject makes it clear that the participle supports the main clause. As illustrated in these examples, anaphora resolution and subject reconstruction recover semantic information that has potential benefits for argument mining systems.

Moreover, ADUs may completely miss implicit propositions. For instance, **questions** and **imperatives** do not convey explicit propositions, but they are important argumentative components that often imply propositional content in dialogical argumentation. Suppose an arguer asks, *why would you waste your money on tax?*, and someone responds, *tax is a waste of money*. It is not straightforward for an argument mining system to tell whether the response agrees or disagrees with the arguer, without knowing what is implied by the question. Implicit propositions occur in **reported speech** as well. Suppose an arguer says, *the doctor said we need more magnesium*. The arguer is not only claiming the report event having happened, but also bringing the content of the doctor's speech as a proposition into the argumentation structure or even may be asserting it using authority. These examples show the significance of recovering implicit propositions for argument mining systems.

To overcome these limitations, we present a cascade model that aims to extract propositions

Proceedings of the 6th Workshop on Argument Mining, pages 11–24
Florence, Italy, August 1, 2019. ©2019 Association for Computational Linguistics

from argumentative dialogues, with important semantic information and implicit propositional content recovered. Our model consists of 7 modules, namely, anaphora resolution, locution extraction, reported speech, question, imperative, subject reconstruction, and revision (Figure 2). For each module, we formulate the task as a computational problem and test various models to solve it, except for the question and imperative modules, for which we present experimental sketches. Our analyses and evaluation are based on the transcripts of the 2016 U.S. presidential debates and reaction on social media that are manually annotated with propositions (Visser et al., 2019). Our contributions are three-fold.

1. We introduce the problem of proposition extraction as seven tasks.
2. We present various models to tackle each task and evaluate performance.
3. We analyze challenges facing our computational methods and suggest future directions.

For the remainder of the paper, we first review prior work on ADU segmentation and a theoretical framework for obtaining propositions from ADUs (§2). We then explain the annotated data of propositions (§3). Next, we describe our cascade model (§4) and formulation of each task, along with experiments (§5). We conclude the paper by discussing the challenges and future directions (§6).

2   Background

In computational argumentation, the basic unit of an argument is often called an argumentative discourse unit (ADU). In this section, we first review how existing studies define and obtain ADUs from text, and then some theoretical framework to obtain propositions from ADUs.

2.1   From Text to ADUs

In most studies, ADUs are obtained via text segmentation. While some studies leave the choice of the boundary of an ADU to the annotator's judgment (Stab and Gurevych, 2014), many studies employ a set of syntactic rules as a basis. For instance, an ADU can be as fine-grained as a phrase that plays a discrete argumentative function (Stede et al., 2016). In other cases, an ADU may be a clause (Peldszus and Stede, 2015) or a series of clauses that must include a subject, a verb, and an object if necessary (Al Khatib et al., 2016).

Based on annotated ADUs, some studies have

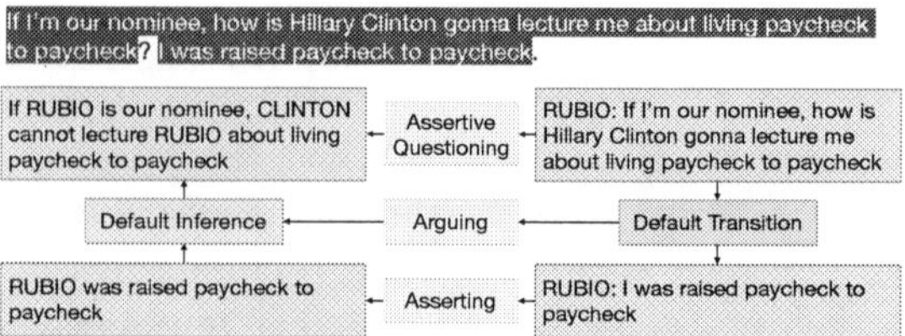

Figure 1: A snippet of the US2016 corpus. The top text is the original utterance. The blue boxes on the right are locutions, which are also highlighted with green on the utterance. The blue boxes on the left are propositions anchored in the locutions, via illocutionary acts (yellow boxes).

proposed methods for automatically segmenting ADUs using machine learning. This task is commonly formulated as tagging each word in the text as either the beginning, inside, or outside of an ADU (BIO tagging). The tagging has been incorporated into an end-to-end argument mining (Eger et al., 2017) or conducted separately on various domains (Ajjour et al., 2017). Instead of tagging, a retrieval approach has also been used, where candidate ADUs are generated and the best is retrieved (Persing and Ng, 2016).

All these approaches to ADU segmentation share most of the concerns mentioned in Section 1. For better-informed argument mining, we need to go further to obtain propositions from ADUs, and thus a relevant framework will be discussed in the following section.

2.2   From ADUs to Propositions

Following Speech Act Theory (Austin, 1962; Searle, 1969), the connection between text segments and propositions can be modeled as illocutionary acts: the application of particular communicative intentions to propositional contents – e.g., *asserting* that a proposition is true, or *questioning* whether it is true. Focusing on argumentatively relevant speech acts (van Eemeren and Grootendorst, 1984), Inference Anchoring Theory (IAT) (Reed and Budzynska, 2011) explains how propositional contents and the argumentative relations between them are anchored in the expressed locutions by means of illocutionary connections.

IAT has been applied to annotate argumentative dialogues of various kinds, including the corpus used in this paper (Section 3). IAT annotation comprises, amongst other things, segmenting the original text into locutions[1], identifying the illo-

---

[1] Analogous to ADUs. We use the terms interchangeably.

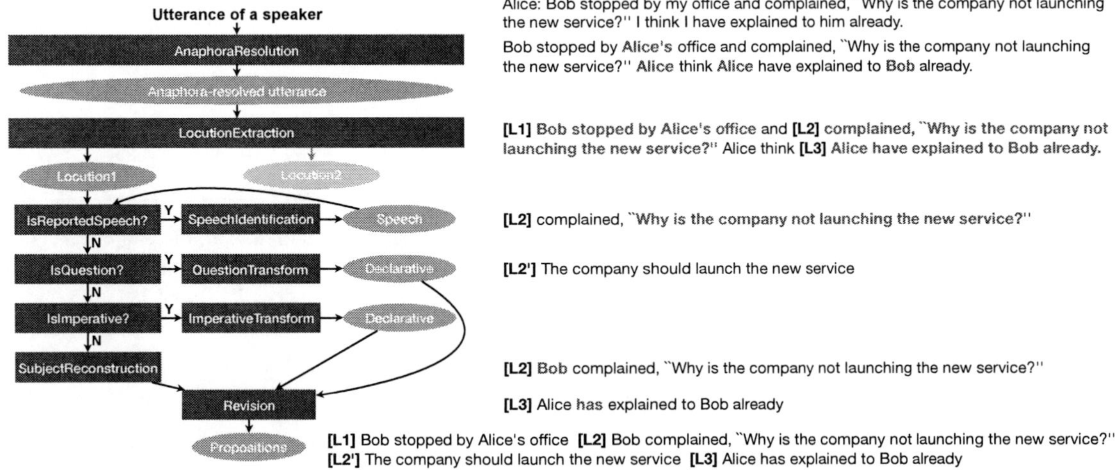

Figure 2: Cascade model of proposition extraction. The input is each utterance, blue boxes are individual (sub)modules and orange circles are the outputs of the modules. We made up the utterance used in the figure in order to cover the functions of most modules.

cutionary force instantiated by the locution, and reconstructing its propositional content (an example snippet shown in Figure 1). Each locution generally conveys a propositional content. Conjuncts conjoined by a conjunction and conditional clauses may be separated if they each fulfill a discrete argumentative function. In addition, punctuation, discourse indicators, and epistemic modalities (e.g., *I think*) should be excluded. For propositions, anaphoric references are typically reconstructed, resulting in full grammatical sentences understandable without context.

3 Data

We use the US2016 corpus (Visser et al., 2019), which contains transcripts of televized debates for the 2016 U.S. presidential election and reaction to the debates on Reddit. All dialogues have been manually segmented and annotated with locutions, illocutionary connections, and propositions based on IAT (Reed et al., 2016) (Figure 1). The corpus was annotated by 4 annotators, yielding an overall Cohen's κ of 0.610 (considered substantial agreement). We downloaded the annotations from the corpus webpage and separately scraped the original dialogues.

For data preparation, we aligned each locution with the original dialogue; e.g., in Figure 1, the locutions (in the right blue boxes) are aligned with the original utterance (at the top) using text matching. This allows us to build a model to extract locutions from utterances, and propositions from

locutions. As our model handles reported speech and questions, we need additional processing to identify those locutions. In the corpus, a locution of reported speech (e.g., *S said P*) is annotated with an intermediate locution, along with the speaker (S) and the content of speech (P). The content of speech, in turn, becomes the proposition of this locution. Locutions of questions are connected with their propositions via four illocutionary acts: pure/assertive/challenge/directive questioning. The processed data includes 2,672 utterances and 8,008 locutions (278 reported speech and 565 questions).

4 Model

Our cascade model takes a speaker's utterance as input, runs seven modules, and outputs a set of propositions extracted from the utterance. Figure 2 shows the model structure and an example utterance processed throughout. The functions of individual modules are as follows:

1. **Anaphora resolution:** Replace pronoun anaphors with their referents.
2. **Locution extraction:** Extract locutions (ADUs) from the utterance.
3. **Reported speech:** Determine if the locution is reported speech; if so, identify the text segment representing the content of speech.
4. **Question:** Determine if the locution or speech content is a question; if so, extract its propositional content.
5. **Imperative:** Determine if the locution or

speech content is an imperative; if so, extract its propositional content.

6. **Subject reconstruction:** Reconstruct the missing subject, if any, of the locution or speech content.

7. **Revision:** Make additional adjustments necessary for final propositions.

5 Method

In this section, we describe how to formulate the task of each module as a computational problem, and present various approaches with their performance. Each module is evaluated separately on the ground truth data, instead of using the result of the previous module. This setting prevents error propagation and helps to evaluate the performance of each module more accurately. Some methods we use are based on machine learning and thus requires a split of training and test sets. Hence, we randomly split the entire corpus into five folds and conduct cross validation with the same folds throughout the paper.

Extensive experiments are focused on anaphora resolution, locution extraction, subject reconstruction, and revision. For the other modules, we present baseline models or experimental sketches, leaving room for improvement for future work.

5.1 Module: **AnaphoraResolution**

Anaphora resolution is based on Stanford CoreNLP 3.8.0. Yet, blindly applying it induces several challenges, such as incorrect resolution of speakers/hearers (this information may be often missing in the text), resolution of non-pronouns, and errors inherent in the tool. To rectify these challenges, we decompose the task into the following subtasks.

- **1st-person singular:** Replace *I, my, me, mine* with the speaker's name.
- **2nd-person singular:** Replace *you, your, yours* with the previous turn's speaker name.
- **3rd-person singular gender:** Resolve *he, his, him, she, her, hers* using CoreNLP.
- **3rd-person singular gender-neutral:** Resolve *it, that* using CoreNLP.
- **3rd-person plural:** Resolve *they, their, them, theirs* using CoreNLP.

Inaccurate anaphora resolution can rather distort the original meaning of text. Hence, the goal here is to find the best combination of the subtasks. The first two subtasks are applied only to TV debates,

	BLEU	Dep	Dep-SO	Noun
Locution (no resol)	69.3	.651	.558	.714
CoreNLP	62.8	.617	.538	.704
1S	**70.1**	**.657**	.589	.748
1S+2S	69.7	.655	.583	.746
1S+3SG	69.3	.654	**.601**	**.757**
1S+3SG+3SN	68.5	.649	.592	.756

Table 1: Performance of anaphora resolution. (**1S:** 1st-person singular, **2S:** 2nd-person singular, **3SG:** 3rd-person singular gender, **3SN:** 3rd-person singular gender-neutral, **Dep:** Dependency, **Dep-SO:** Dependency for subjects and objects.)

as Reddit user names have not been resolved in the corpus. All possessive pronouns are replaced with references suffixed with *'s* (e.g., *his* → *Trump's*).

For evaluation, we assume that effective anaphora resolution would make a locution more "similar" to the annotated proposition. Hence, we compare the similarities between a locution and the annotated proposition before and after anaphora resolution, using the following metrics:

- **BLEU:** Generic string similarity based on n-grams ($n = 1, 2, 3, 4$).
- **F1-score of dependency tuples:** String similarity based on dependencies. Less sensitive than BLEU to the exact locations of words.
- **F1-score of nsubj/dobj dependency tuples:** Rough semantic information pieces representing who did what to whom/what.
- **F1-score of nouns:** How accurately anaphora resolution retrieves nouns (as our anaphora resolution replaces only nouns).

Result

As shown in Table 1, blindly applying CoreNLP (row 2) significantly hurts all similarity measures (compared to row 1). In contrast, speaker resolution (row 3) plays a key role in improving all measures over original locutions, especially semantic information (subject/object) and nouns. Additional resolution of hearers (row 4) does not help, as *you* is used in a more general way than referring specifically to the hearer.

Resolving 3rd-person gender pronouns (row 5) further improves performance for semantic information and noun retrieval over speaker resolution, at the expense of slightly lower BLEU and dependency similarites. Additional resolution of *it, its, and that* turns out to rather hurt performance.

For argument mining, it may be desired to resolve as many anaphors as possible unless the original meaning is significantly hurt, because pronouns provide little information for identifying propositional relations. Hence, we conclude that resolution of speakers and 3rd-person gender pronouns is ideal for this module, and the subsequent modules use the result of this configuration. However, we find that resolution of 3rd-person gender-neutral pronouns is critical, as will be discussed in Section 5.8, and eventually they should be resolved depending on the availability of proper anaphora resolution tools.

5.2 Module: LocutionExtraction

For each utterance with anaphors resolved, the LocutionExtraction module identifies locutions, from which proposition(s) will be extracted. This task is almost identical to ADU segmentation, and several methods have already been proposed (Section 2.1). Beating prior models for this task is beyond the scope of this paper; rather, we focus on understanding what causes confusion for locution boundaries. Following the convention for this task (Eger et al., 2017; Ajjour et al., 2017), the task is formulated as tagging each word with B/I/O (beginning/inside/outside of a locution).

We explore the state-of-the-art BiLSTM model (Ajjour) (Ajjour et al., 2017), as well as a regular CRF (R-CRF) and BiLSTM-CRF (Huang et al., 2015). A CRF showed strong performance for cross-domain segmentation, and BiLSTM-CRF is an extension of CRFs, where emission scores are calculated through BiLSTM. For all models, we use the following features, adopted from or informed by the prior work (Ajjour et al., 2017):

- **word:** Current word (i.e., word index for R-CRF and pre-trained GloVe.840B.300d word embeddings for BiLSTM-CRF and Ajjour).
- **pos:** Part-of-speech tag of the current word.
- **ne:** Named entity type of the current word.
- **prev_1gram:** Previous word of the current word, as conjunctions and discourse markers are good indicators of location boundaries. (R-CRF only, as BiLSTM considers context.)
- **bos/eos:** Indicator of whether the current word marks the beginning/end of a sentence, as locution boundaries are often restricted by sentence boundaries.
- **boc/eoc:** Indicator of whether the current word marks the beginning/end of a clause, as locution boundaries are closely related to clause boundaries. We obtain clauses from the constituency parse of the sentence, taking

R-CRF	BiLSTM-CRF	Ajjour
.788	.789	**.794**

Table 2: F1-score of locution extraction.

	1st locution1	2nd locution
Subordinate clauses	7%	6%
Adverb phrases	4%	8%
Particle phrases	1%	4%
Yes/no	2%	-
Relative clauses	-	5%

Table 3: Breakdown of locution types that are separated by a comma or that are back-to-back (total 293 pairs).

phrases tagged with S. For nested clauses, we take the deepest clauses to avoid overlap.

The model settings are explained in Appendix A.

We evaluate the models using the macro F1-score across the BIO tags with 5-fold CV.

Result

Ajjour et al. (2017)'s model outperforms the CRF-based models (Table 2). The model tends to underproduce locutions (7,767 compared to 8,008 annotated), i.e., produce coarse locutions, missing signals for splitting them further into smaller locutions. To examine those signals, we gathered extracted locutions that overlap with two consecutive annotated locutions, and counted the words between the two locutions (Table 9 in Appendix).

Frequently, the model failed to make a split at a comma (31%) or between locutions that are back-to-back without any separator in between (10%). In the majority of these cases, the locutions are two independent clauses, indicating that the model needs a more robust mechanism to make use of clause boundaries. Although not very common, a locution also serves as a subordinate clause, adverb phrase, particle phrase, yes/no answer, or relative clause (Table 3). Deciding whether to separate a subordinate clause from the main clause is not trivial. For instance, if- and when-clauses, the most common subordinate clauses in the analysis, are separated off or attached to the main clause depending on the strength of their dependency, which is often vague. If we are to build a system to make this decision automatically, we may consider the truth value of the subordinate clause and whether it is idiomatic.

Other frequent separators include conjunctions *and* (21%) and *but* (6%). As in the case above, the

Regex	Prec	Recl	F1
say + said	.404	.363	.383
Reporting marks	.576	.259	.357
Other reporting verbs	.579	.040	.074
All above	.442	.590	.505

Table 4: Accuracy of reported speech detection.

Tregex	F1	Coverage
Reporting verbs	.234	5%
Reporting marks	.371	20%
All above	.395	23%

Table 5: Accuracy of speech identification.

model sometimes has difficulty deciding whether to split conjoined phrases and clauses.

5.3 Module: **ReportedSpeech**

A locution extracted above is examined by the Is-ReportedSpeech submodule to decide if it is reported speech. If so, the content of speech is identified by the SpeechIdentification submodule.

5.3.1 Submodule: **IsReportedSpeech**

To detect if a locution is reported speech, we use 11 regular expressions that capture the existence of reporting verbs (*said, say, called, blamed, argued, insisted*) and reporting marks (*", :*). A matched locution is classified as reported speech.

Result

As shown in Table 4, the method achieves an F1-score of 0.505, which reveals the difficulty of detecting reported speech (the full list of patterns and their accuracy are in Table 10 in Appendix). High-performing patterns capture *say/said* and reporting marks; other reporting verbs have too low recall. Interestingly, regular expressions achieve not only low recall but also low precision. To see why, we examined false-positives made by *said* and opening quotation marks, and found this task quite challenging indeed. Two big challenges are detecting whether the report actually happened and if the content of speech is mentioned, as in the following examples (underlined text increases complexity):

1. **Event factuality:** *I thought reddit said that Paul was supposed to be the rational one here*; *He never even said that he didn't do it*
2. **Mention of speech content:** *He said that the second time anyway*; *I mean, "track the terrorists and not the citizens" is full of so many holes*

These challenges suggest that we need more sophisticated features to identify event factuality and the mention of speech content.

5.3.2 Submodule: **SpeechIdentification**

Speech content is important to identify, as it often contributes to the argumentation structure (e.g., as part of an authority claim). We formulate this task as BIO tagging, as in locution extraction. Individual words in each locution are tagged with B/I/O based on the best alignment between the locution and its content proposition (Section 3).

To identify speech content, we use regular expressions matched to constituency parse trees. A speech is assumed to be a clause, preceded by a reporting verb (*said, say, says, claim.*, argue.*, insist.**) or reporting mark (*", :*). Matching is conducted using Tregex in Stanford CoreNLP.

For evaluation, a matched clause is tagged with B and I, and the other words with O. We compute the macro F1-score of BIO tags and the percentage of locutions matched by patterns (coverage).

Result

As shown in Table 5, the Tregex method has a low F1-score, mostly due to a poor coverage (the full list of patterns and their accuracy are in Table 11 in Appendix). The low coverage stems from several causes, including:

- Speech content may not be a complete clause (e.g., *you say charge the banks more*), or the parser fails to recognize it as a clause.
- Speech content is signaled by various verbs (e.g., *talking about, I'm hearing*).
- A reporting verb may be missing. This usually happens when speech content and main clause are segmented into separate locutions.

We believe that various signals of speech content may be captured better by machine learning models, increasing overall performance.

5.4 Module: **Question**

A locution or speech content is examined by the IsQuestion submodule to decide if it is a question. If so, it is transformed to its propositional content by the QuestionTransformation submodule.

Regex	Prec	Recl	F1
Question mark	.751	.938	.834
Initiating words	.514	.499	.506
All above	.588	.972	.733

Table 6: Accuracy of question detection.

5.4.1 Submodule: **IsQuestion**

To detect if an input text is a question, we use regular expressions that capture if the enclosing sentence has a question mark or begins with words that often initiate a question (e.g., *how*, *do*) (the full list of patterns is in Table 12 in Appendix). The reason for matching the patterns to the entire sentence is that a question mark is often excluded from a locution.

Result

As shown in Table 6, a question mark by itself is strongly indicative of a question and has high recall. While it has fair precision, there exist some confusing false-positives, including:

1. A question merely for emphasis. (e.g., *It also could be somebody sitting on their bed that weighs 400 pounds, ok?*)
2. Reported question. (e.g., *You say to yourself, why didn't they make the right deal?*)
3. A question for expressing confusion. (e.g., *Bernie?... Come again?*)

For questions without a question mark, the regular expressions for question-initiating words increase recall but significantly hurts precision. Some of these words are used as a subordinate conjunction (*when*) or as a relative pronoun (*which*). The low precision of some words is due to incomplete sentences with missing subject *I* (e.g., *Could barely understand*). The error cases show that highly accurate detection of a question requires a combination of several factors.

5.5 Submodule: **QuestionTransformation**

We found no prior work that addresses transforming questions into propositions, although some work identifies different types of questions (Zhang et al., 2017). For this submodule, we only describe the task with examples in the corpus, without models. In the corpus, questions are associated with four illocutionary acts: pure, assertive, challenge, and directive. Pure questions assume no assertion and thus may be transformed to a statement underspecified in the semantic dimension questioned, optionally containing a placeholder *xxx*:

- *Who is Chafee? → Chafee is xxx*
- *Do all lives matter? → All lives do / do not matter*

In contrast, assertive and challenge questions have an assertive force. The difference between them is whether or not a question is to challenge another argument.

- *What does that say about your ability to handle challenging crises as president? → Clinton does not have the ability to handle challenging crises as president.* (assertive)
- *What has he not answered? → He has answered questions* (challenge)

Lastly, directive questions have imperative mood:

- *Any specific examples? → Provide any specific examples*

We may explore various approaches, such as hand-crafted rules and seq2seq models, in future work.

5.6 Module: **Imperative**

There is neither consensus nor common practice on how to extract propositional content from imperatives. Accordingly, the corpus had no guidelines for imperatives, and most imperatives have not been modified. Yet, some imperatives have been modified according to the annotators' own judgment, with examples including:

- *Raise the minimum wage → The minimum wage should be raised*
- *Let me address college affordability → Clinton would like to address college affordability*
- *Look at the mess we're in → We're in a mess*

We argue that more analysis would be useful to understand when and how an imperative can be systematically transformed to a proposition.

5.7 Module: **SubjectReconstruction**

A locution or speech content may miss its subject due to segmentation. Hence, the SubjectReconstruction module aims to reconstruct the subject if it exists within the same sentence. We first trace the subject of each verb in every sentence, and then reconstruct the subject (along with auxiliary verbs) of a segmented text that begins with a verb whose subject is outside the text.

We trace the subject of a verb using the basic dependency relations (from CoreNLP) as follows. When a verb has no subject relation with any words, we move to the word that is connected with the current verb through a dependency relation of the types: conjunct (conj), auxil-

Prec	BLEU-Reconst	BLEU-Locution
.714	62.6	59.1

(a) Performance of subject reconstruction.

Reason	%
Ill-formed sentence	25%
No subject in the sentence	25%
Trace mistake	20%
Complex sentence	10%
Phrasal/clausal subject	10%
Wrong antecedents of relative pronouns	10%

(b) Reasons for subject identification errors.

Table 7: Results of subject identification.

iary (aux/auxpass), copula (cop), and open clausal complement (xcomp). The intuition is that this new word and the current word are likely to have the same subject. We repeat this process until we find a subject or no more move is available. The following dependency parse illustrates the intuition, i.e., why *wanted* and *send* connected with xcomp have the same subject. Examples of the other relations are in Appendix B.

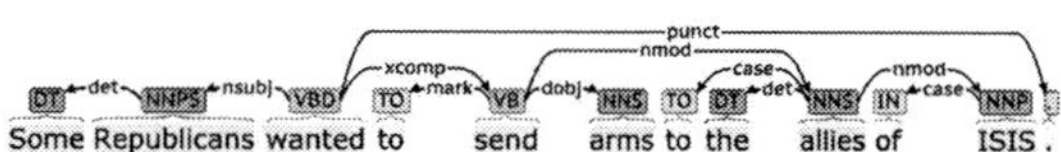

Sometimes a verb's direct subject is a relative pronoun, in which case we move to the word modified by the verb via the acl:relcl relation. However, *which* may often refer to a phrase or a clause, and this method may not be able to capture that.

Result

We identified 96 locutions (1.2% of locutions) beginning with a verb whose subject is identified to be in the sentence yet outside the locution. We focus on 73% of them whose subjects are recovered in annotated propositions. Note that annotated subjects can be lexically different from the ones that are correctly identified by our method, due to imperfect anaphora resolution. Hence, our evaluation is based on manual comparison, checking if identified subjects and annotated subjects refer to the same thing/person.

As shown in Table 7a, the method identified subjects correctly for 71% of the locutions. Accordingly, the BLEU score improved by 3.5, compared to mere locutions. Table 7b breaks down the reasons for errors. Sometimes the tracing method made a mistake (20%) or failed to capture a phrasal/clausal subject (10%). However, more

commonly, CoreNLP could not properly handle sentences that are ill-formed (25%), missing a subject (25%), or too long/complex (10%). In some cases, it incorrectly identified the antecedents of relative pronouns (10%).

There exists other work that addresses recovering elided materials in sentences using dependencies (Schuster et al., 2018). Following some of the work, it would be an interesting direction to explore a richer set of dependency relations, such as the enhanced dependencies (Schuster and Manning, 2016).

5.8 Module: Revision

While the previous modules handle major tasks, a processed locution may still need additional adjustments, including grammar correction. Hence, the Revision module makes adjustments to a processed locution and outputs proposition(s). This task is formulated as a seq2seq problem, i.e., a model automatically learns and decides how to change the input, based on the data.

We explore two models: standard attention (Luong et al., 2015) and copy mechanism. Both encode an input text using BiLSTM and decode proposition(s) using LSTM. The attention model computes the probability of a word being generated, using attention over the encoder's hidden states. It requires a lot of training data, whereas we already know that most input words remain unchanged. The copy model, on the other hand, decides internally whether to copy an input word or generate a new word. Informed by existing copy mechanisms (Gu et al., 2016; Allamanis et al., 2016), we developed a slight variant that worked better on this task. The model and parameters are explained in detail in Appendix C.

We use two evaluation metrics: BLEU and exact match (percentage of outputs identical to the annotated propositions). We exclude locutions of reported speech and questions, to better focus on this module's performance. The baseline is to treat each locution as a proposition without modification. Accuracy is based on 5-fold CV.

Result

As shown in Table 8, the baseline (row 1) already achieves high performance, because locutions are often very similar to the propositions extracted from them unless they are reported speech or questions. For this reason, the attention model (row 2) performs poorly, as it tends to make many

	BLEU	Exact
Locution	75.5	.473
Attention	47.2	.124
Copy	76.2	.493
Copy (short)	**76.6**	**.501**

Table 8: Performance of revision.

unnecessary adjustments to input locutions. The copy model (row 3) performs significantly better than the attention model, but sometimes it could not handle long input texts and generated irrelevant content toward the end of an output. Leaving long input texts (25+ words) unmodified (row 4) slightly improved performance. Overall, the improvement over the baseline is rather modest.

The most notable and useful role of the copy model is correcting a verb case that was left incorrect due to anaphora resolution (e.g., *cooper want to → cooper wants to, webb have had → webb has had*). This behavior is quite desirable. The model also sometimes removed non-propositional content and changed a person's first name to the full name as reflected in annotations. In general, the roles of the model remain lexical conversion rather than semantic conversion.

We found that the differences between generated and annotated propositions are derived mainly from unresolved non-personal anaphors (e.g., *it, this, that*). Furthermore, annotators sometimes insert omitted verb phrases (e.g., *You should. → You should clinge to capitalism.*; *not hard to do → not hard to dominate*). Such semantic information is not recovered by the current copy model.

6 Conclusion

Our decomposition of the proposition extraction task has yielded that: (i) anaphora resolution is crucial for recovering the semantic information of propositions, and the main bottleneck is to resolve 2nd-person singular and 3rd-person gender-neutral pronouns; (ii) locution boundaries are often confused around clause boundaries; (iii) detecting reported speech and speech content suffers poor accuracy with pattern matching. These tasks, along with question detection, reveal the need for sophisticated feature combinations for satisfactory results, and we may need additional training data; (iv) for subject reconstruction, the tracing method is fairly effective, and the accuracy is bounded mainly by the robustness of dependency parsing to ill-formed and complex sentences; (v) the final re-

vision with a seq2seq model remains mostly grammar error correction, and substantial semantic revision may require significantly different models.

Though we are starting to explore the challenges facing complete reconstruction of propositions from natural argumentative discourse, our cascade model already demonstrates improvement over locutions (ADUs) in several modules for this understudied yet crucial task in argument mining.

We are currently working on systematic extraction of propositional content from questions and imperatives, and evaluation of the entire cascade model as a whole. Our future direction is to use extracted propositions to develop argument mining models that identify nuanced types of propositional relations informed by argumentation theory.

Acknowledgements

This research was funded by the Kwanjeong Educational Foundation and grant EP/N014871/1 by the Engineering and Physical Sciences Research Council (EPSRC).

References

Yamen Ajjour, Wei-Fan Chen, Johannes Kiesel, Henning Wachsmuth, and Benno Stein. 2017. Unit Segmentation of Argumentative Texts. In *Proceedings of the 4th Workshop on Argument Mining*, pages 118–128, Copenhagen, Denmark. Association for Computational Linguistics.

Khalid Al Khatib, Henning Wachsmuth, Johannes Kiesel, Matthias Hagen, and Benno Stein. 2016. A News Editorial Corpus for Mining Argumentation Strategies. In *Proceedings of COLING 2016, the 26th International Conference on Computational Linguistics: Technical Papers*, pages 3433–3443. The COLING 2016 Organizing Committee.

Miltiadis Allamanis, Hao Peng, and Charles Sutton. 2016. A Convolutional Attention Network for Extreme Summarization of Source Code. In *International Conference on Machine Learning (ICML)*.

John L. Austin. 1962. *How to Do Things with Words*. Clarendon Press.

Simon Blackburn. 2016. *The Oxford Dictionary of Philosophy*. Oxford University Press.

F. H. van Eemeren and R. Grootendorst. 1984. *Speech acts in argumentative discussions: A theoretical model for the analysis of discussions directed towards solving conflicts of opinion*. Foris.

Steffen Eger, Johannes Daxenberger, and Iryna Gurevych. 2017. Neural End-to-End Learning for

Computational Argumentation Mining. In *Proceedings of the 55th Annual Meeting of the Association for Computational Linguistics (Volume 1: Long Papers)*, pages 11–22, Stroudsburg, PA, USA. Association for Computational Linguistics.

Jiatao Gu, Zhengdong Lu, Hang Li, and Victor O K Li. 2016. Incorporating Copying Mechanism in Sequence-to-Sequence Learning. In *Proceedings of the 54th Annual Meeting of the Association for Computational Linguistics (Volume 1: Long Papers)*, pages 1631–1640. Association for Computational Linguistics.

Zhiheng Huang, Wei Xu, and Kai Yu. 2015. Bidirectional LSTM-CRF Models for Sequence Tagging. *arXiv*.

Thang Luong, Hieu Pham, and Christopher D Manning. 2015. Effective Approaches to Attention-based Neural Machine Translation. In *Proceedings of the 2015 Conference on Empirical Methods in Natural Language Processing*, pages 1412–1421, Lisbon, Portugal. Association for Computational Linguistics.

Andreas Peldszus and Manfred Stede. 2015. Towards Detecting Counter-considerations in Text. In *Proceedings of the 2nd Workshop on Argumentation Mining*, pages 104–109. Association for Computational Linguistics.

Isaac Persing and Vincent Ng. 2016. End-to-End Argumentation Mining in Student Essays. In *Proceedings of the 2016 Conference of the North American Chapter of the Association for Computational Linguistics: Human Language Technologies*, pages 1384–1394, Stroudsburg, PA, USA. Association for Computational Linguistics.

Chris Reed and Katarzyna Budzynska. 2011. How dialogues create arguments. In *Proceedings of the 7th Conference of the International Society for the Study of Argumentation (ISSA)*. SicSat.

Chris Reed, Katarzyna Budzynska, and Jacky Visser. 2016. IAT annotation guidelines for US2016. http://arg.tech/US2016-guidelines.

Sebastian Schuster and Christopher D. Manning. 2016. Enhanced English universal dependencies: An improved representation for natural language understanding tasks. In *Proceedings of the Tenth International Conference on Language Resources and Evaluation (LREC 2016)*, pages 2371–2378, Portorož, Slovenia. European Language Resources Association (ELRA).

Sebastian Schuster, Joakim Nivre, and Christopher D Manning. 2018. Sentences with Gapping: Parsing and Reconstructing Elided Predicates. In *Proceedings of the 2018 Conference of the North American Chapter of the Association for Computational Linguistics: Human Language Technologies, Volume 1 (Long Papers)*, pages 1156–1168, New Orleans, Louisiana. Association for Computational Linguistics.

J. R. Searle. 1969. *Speech acts: An essay in the philosophy of language.* Cambridge University Press.

Christian Stab and Iryna Gurevych. 2014. Annotating Argument Components and Relations in Persuasive Essays. In *Proceedings of COLING 2014, the 25th International Conference on Computational Linguistics: Technical Papers*, pages 1501–1510. Dublin City University and Association for Computational Linguistics.

Manfred Stede, Stergos Afantenos, Andreas Peldszus, Nicholas Asher, and Jérémy Perret. 2016. Parallel Discourse Annotations on a Corpus of Short Texts. In *Proceedings of the Tenth International Conference on Language Resources and Evaluation (LREC 2016)*, Paris, France. European Language Resources Association (ELRA).

Jacky Visser, Barbara Konat, Rory Duthie, Marcin Koszowy, Katarzyna Budzynska, and Chris Reed. 2019. Argumentation in the 2016 US presidential elections: annotated corpora of television debates and social media reaction. *Language Resources and Evaluation*.

Justine Zhang, Arthur Spirling, and Cristian Danescu-Niculescu-Mizil. 2017. Asking too much? The rhetorical role of questions in political discourse. In *Proceedings of the 2017 Conference on Empirical Methods in Natural Language Processing*, pages 1558–1572, Copenhagen, Denmark. Association for Computational Linguistics.

Top 1-8	Top 9-16	Top 17-24
, (31%)	– (2%)	or (1%)
and (12%)	, because (1%)	? (1%)
NONE (10%)	-lrb- (1%)	. and (1%)
, and (9%)	, which (1%)	to (1%)
, but (4%)	; (1%)	as (1%)
. (3%)	... (1%)	, so (1%)
because (2%)	- (1%)	that (1%)
but (2%)	when (1%)	if (0%)

Table 9: Words that separate two annotated locutions that overlap with one predicted locution. NONE indicates that the locutions are back-to-back without any separator.

Regex	Prec	Recl	F1
`(?<!i )said (\S + ){3,}`	.387	.295	.335
`^ ```	.559	.119	.196
`, ```	.552	.115	.190
`you say`	.500	.068	.120
`said that (\S + ){3,}`	.394	.047	.084
`: ```	.875	.025	.049
`said ```	.714	.018	.035
`called (\S +)+```	.556	.018	.035
`blamed`	.500	.014	.028
`argued that (\S + ){3,}`	1.000	.004	.007
`insisted that (\S + ){3,}`	1.000	.004	.007
All above	.442	.590	.505

Table 10: Accuracy of reported speech detection.

Tregex	F1	Coverage
`S $ (VBD < said)`	.234	5%
`S $ (VBD < /says?/)`	.184	0%
`S $ (VBD < /claim.*/)`	.184	0%
`S $ (VBD < /argue.*/)`	.184	0%
`S $ (VBD < /insist.*/)`	.184	0%
`S < ```	.352	15%
`S $- /:/`	.220	5%
All above	.395	23%

Table 11: Regular expressions (Tregex syntax) for speech identification and their accuracy. The first five patterns represent a clause that is a sibling of *said*, *say* or *says*, *claim.**, *argue.**, and *insist.**, respectively. The last two patterns represent a clause that includes an opening quotation mark and follows a colon, respectively.

Regex	Prec	Recl	F1	Regex	Prec	Recl	F1
\?	.751	.938	.834	^should	.800	.014	.028
^do	.485	.087	.147	^would	.538	.012	.024
^how	.759	.078	.141	^will	1.000	.011	.021
^what	.462	.064	.112	^was	.667	.011	.021
^is	.775	.055	.102	^where	.714	.009	.017
^why	.423	.039	.071	^when	.071	.009	.016
^did	.842	.028	.055	^which	.286	.007	.014
^are	.800	.021	.041	^have	.500	.005	.011
^who	.706	.021	.041	^were	1.000	.004	.007
^can	.611	.019	.038	^could	.182	.004	.007
^does	.588	.018	.034	^has	.333	.002	.004
All	.588	.972	.733				

Table 12: Accuracy of question detection.

A   Module: **LocutionExtraction**

For R-CRF, we used sklearn-crfsuite 0.3.6. We conducted grid search, exploring all combinations of the bias feature ($\{1, 0\}$) and the following optimization parameters:

- Gradient descent using the L-BFGS method
  - L1 regularization: 0, 0.05, 0.1
  - L2 regularization: 0, 0.05, 0.1
- Passive Aggressive (PA)
  - Aggressiveness parameter: 0.5, 1, 2

For BiLSTM-CRF, we used the following parameter values:

- BiLSTM hidden dim: 128
- Optimizer: Adam
- Learning rate: 0.001

For Ajjour, we used the following parameter values:

- Encoder BiLSTMs hidden dim: 128
- Output BiLSTM hidden dim: 5, 10, 20
- Optimizer: Adam
- Learning rate: 0.001

B   Module: **SubjectReconstruction**

Conjunct (conj): Two verbs that are conjoined by a conjunction are likely to have the same subject. In the following example, *preserving* has the same subject as *protecting* does.

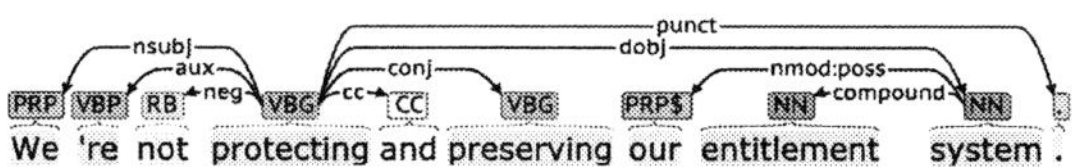

Auxiliary, passive auxiliary (aux, auxpass): An auxiliary verb that modifies a (passive) verb is likely to have the same subject as the modified verb does. In the following example, *got* has the same subject as *carried* does.

Copula (cop): A copula that joins a verb with its subject is likely to have the same subject as the verb. In the following example, *'ve* has the same subject as *wrong* does.

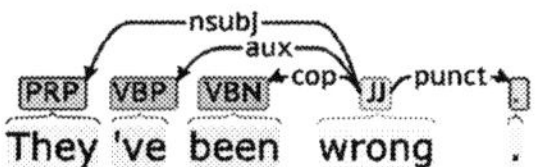

Open clausal complement (xcomp): An open clausal complement of a verb is likely to have the same subject as the verb does. In the following example, *send* has the same subject as *wanted* does.

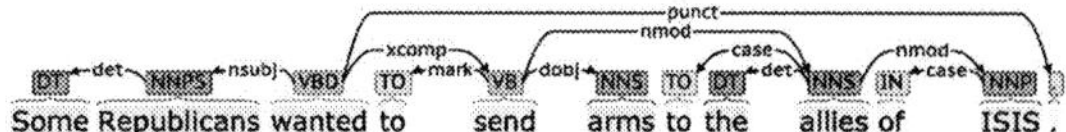

Adverbial clause modifier (advcl): An adverbial clause modifier of a verb may or may not have the same subject as the verb does. In the following examples, the two sentences have the same structure of verb + object + marked adverbial clause modifier. However, in the first sentence, *keeping* has the same subject as *do* does, whereas in the second sentence, *leaving* has a different subject than *stop* does. For reliability, we do not include adverbial clause modifiers for tracing a subject.

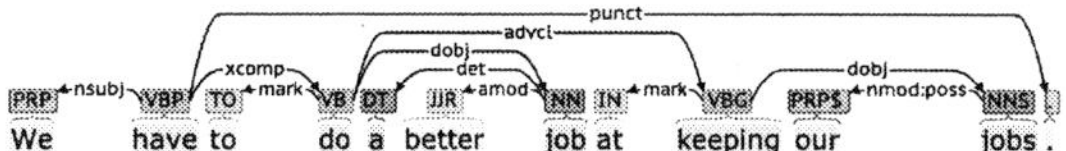

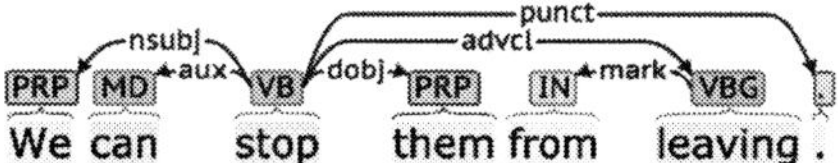

Relative clause modifier (acl:relcl): Sometimes a verb's direct subject is a relative pronoun, in which case we move to the word that is modified the current verb. In the following example, *ran* modifies *campaign*, which is the proper subject.

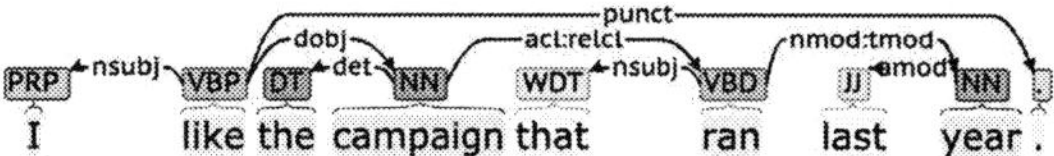

However, *which* may often refer to a phrase or a clause, and this method may not be able to capture that.

C   Module: **Revision**

C.1   Copy Model

Suppose an input text is a sequence of words $w_1^E, \cdots, w_N^E$, and denote the word vector (e.g., word embedding) of w_i^E as $\boldsymbol{w}_i^E$. The BiLSTM encoder encodes each word $\boldsymbol{w}_i^E$ and outputs forward/backward hidden states $\overrightarrow{\boldsymbol{h}}_i^E$ and $\overleftarrow{\boldsymbol{h}}_i^E$ as

$$\overrightarrow{\boldsymbol{h}}_i^E, \overleftarrow{\boldsymbol{h}}_i^E = \overline{\text{BiLSTM}}(\boldsymbol{w}_i^E, \overrightarrow{\boldsymbol{h}}_{i-1}^E, \overleftarrow{\boldsymbol{h}}_{i+1}^E)$$
$$\overrightarrow{\boldsymbol{h}}_0^E = \overleftarrow{\boldsymbol{h}}_{N+1}^E = \boldsymbol{0}.$$

For the jth word to be generated, the LSTM decoder first encodes the concatenation of the previously generated word $\boldsymbol{w}^D_{j-1}$ and context vector $\bar{\boldsymbol{h}}^E_{j-1}$ (explained below), along with the previous hidden state as

$$\boldsymbol{h}^D_j = \text{LSTM}([\boldsymbol{w}^D_{j-1}; \bar{\boldsymbol{h}}^E_{j-1}], \boldsymbol{h}^D_{j-1})$$
$$\boldsymbol{h}^D_0 = [\overleftarrow{\boldsymbol{h}}^E_1; \overrightarrow{\boldsymbol{h}}^E_N].$$

Next, the decoder attends to the encoder's hidden states using an attention mechanism. The attention weight of the ith hidden state is calculated as the dot product of the hidden states from the encoder and decoder:

$$a_{ji} = \boldsymbol{h}^D_j \cdot [\overleftarrow{\boldsymbol{h}}^E_i; \overrightarrow{\boldsymbol{h}}^E_i], \hat{a}_{ji} = \frac{\exp(a_{ji})}{\sum_{i'} \exp(a_{ji'})}$$
$$\bar{\boldsymbol{h}}^E_j = \sum_i a_{ji}[\overrightarrow{\boldsymbol{h}}^E_i; \overleftarrow{\boldsymbol{h}}^E_i].$$

The probability of the ith input word being copied is proportional to the attention weight of the ith hidden state. On the other hand, calculation of the probability of newly generating the vth word in the vocabulary follows the standard attention decoder mechanism. Denoting these probabilities as $P_C(w_v)$ and $P_G(w_v)$, respectively, they are calculated as

$$P_C(w_v) = \sum_{i=1}^{N} \hat{a}_{ji} I(w^E_i = w_v)$$
$$P_G(w_v) = \text{softmax}(W_G[\boldsymbol{h}^D_j; \bar{\boldsymbol{h}}^E_j] + b_G)_v,$$

where W_G and b_G are corresponding weight matrix and bias vector. The final probability of w_v being generated is a weighted sum of $P_C(w_v)$ and $P_G(w_v)$, where the weight δ is automatically calculated as

$$\delta_j = \sigma(W_\delta \boldsymbol{h}^D_j + b_\delta)$$
$$P(w_v) = \delta P_C(w_v) + (1 - \delta) P_G(w_v),$$

where W_δ and b_δ are corresponding weight matrix and bias vector. The original method for calculating the weight (Gu et al., 2016) and a constant weight did not perform well on our task.

Beam search is used to choose the best output. Gradient clipping is used to avoid the exploding gradient problem.

C.2 Model Parameters

We explore the combinations of the following parameter values:

- Encoder hidden dim: 96, 128, 160, 192 (attention model) / 128, 192 (copy model)
- Beam size: 4
- Optimizer: Adam
- Learning rate: 0.001
- Gradient clipping: 1

Dissecting *Content* and *Context* in Argumentative Relation Analysis

Juri Opitz and **Anette Frank**
Research Training Group AIPHES,
Leibniz ScienceCampus "Empirical Linguistics and Computational Language Modeling"
Department for Computational Linguistics
69120 Heidelberg
{opitz,frank}@cl.uni-heidelberg.de

Abstract

When assessing relations between argumentative units (e.g., *support* or *attack*), computational systems often exploit disclosing indicators or markers that are not part of elementary argumentative units (EAUs) themselves, but are gained from their context (position in paragraph, preceding tokens, etc.). We show that this dependency is much stronger than previously assumed. In fact, we show that by completely masking the EAU text spans and only feeding information from their context, a competitive system may function even *better*. We argue that an argument analysis system that relies more on discourse context than the argument's content is unsafe, since it can easily be tricked. To alleviate this issue, we separate argumentative units from their *context* such that the system is forced to model and rely on an EAU's *content*. We show that the resulting classification system is more robust, and argue that such models are better suited for predicting argumentative relations across documents.

1 Introduction

In recent years we have witnessed a great surge in activity in the area of computational argument analysis (e.g. Peldszus and Stede (2013); Stab and Gurevych (2014b); Rasooli and Tetreault (2015); Stab et al. (2018)), and the emergence of dedicated venues such as the ACL Argument Mining workshop series starting in 2014 (Green et al., 2014).

Argumentative relation classification is a subtask of argument analysis that aims to determine relations between argumentative units A and B, for example, A *supports* B; A *attacks* B. Consider the following argumentative units **(1)** and **(2)**, given the topic **(0)** *"Marijuana should be legalized"*:

(1) *Legalizing marijuana can increase use by teens, with harmful results.*

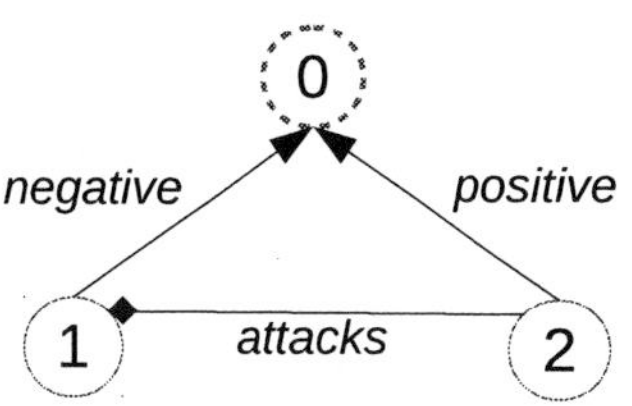

Figure 1: A graph representation of a topic (node w/ dashed line), two argumentative premise units (nodes w/ solid line), premise-topic relations (positive or negative) and premise-premise relations (here: *attacks*).

(2) *Legalization allows the government to set age restrictions on buyers.*

This example is modeled in Figure 1. It is clear that **(1)** has a negative stance towards the topic and **(2)** has a positive stance towards the topic. Moreover, we can say that **(2)** *attacks* **(1)**. In discourse, such a relation is often made explicit through discourse markers: *(1). However, (2); On the one hand (1), on the other (2); (1), although (2); Admittedly, (2)*; etc. In the absence of such markers we must determine this relation by assessing the semantics of the individual argumentative units, including (often implicit) world knowledge about how they are related to each other.[1]

In this work, we show that argumentative relation classifiers – when provided with textual *context* surrounding an argumentative unit's span – are very prone to neglect the actual textual *content* of the EAU span. Instead they heavily rely on *contextual markers*, such as conjunctions or adverbials, as a basis for prediction. We argue that a system's capacity of predicting the correct relation based on the argumentative units' *content* is important in many circumstances, e.g., when an argumentative debate crosses document boundaries.

---

[1] In case of **(1)** and **(2)**: By setting age restrictions on legalization of Marijuana, increased use by teens can be (expected to be) prevented, thus we can infer that **(2)** attacks **(1)**.

Proceedings of the 6th Workshop on Argument Mining, pages 25–34
Florence, Italy, August 1, 2019. ©2019 Association for Computational Linguistics

For example, the *prohibition of marijuana* debate extends across populations and countries – argumentative units for this debate can be recovered from thousands of documents scattered across the world wide web. As a consequence, argumentative relation classification systems should not be (immensely) dependent on contextual clues – in the discussed cross-document setting these clues may even be misleading for such a system, since source and target arguments can be embedded in different textual contexts (e.g., when **(1)** and **(2)** stem from different documents it is easy to imagine a textual context where **(2)** is not introduced by *however* but instead by an 'inverse' form such as e.g. *moreover*).

Contributions   In Section §3 we describe argumentative relation classification systems and their features. Then, to assess the systems' dependency on context, we propose a three-way feature grouping: (i) features which access only the EAU span; (ii) features which access only the context of an EAU; (iii) features which access both EAU span and its context. Our experimental results (§4) indicate that systems, when given the option, tend to focus on the *context* of an EAU, while neglecting its *content*. On the one hand, this leads to strong performance when EAUs appear sequentially in a rhetorically well structured argumentative monologue. Yet, on the other hand, we show that such systems can easily be fooled, e.g., when EAUs are extracted from different documents.

2   Related Work

It is well-known that the rhetorical and argumentative structure of texts bear great similarities. For example, Azar (1999); Green (2010); Peldszus and Stede (2013) observe that elementary discourse units (EDUs) in RST (Mann and Thompson, 1987) share great similarity with elementary argumentative units (EAUs) in argumentation analysis.[2] Wachsmuth et al. (2018) experiment with a modified version of the Microtext corpus (Peldszus and Stede, 2016), which is an extensively annotated albeit small corpus. Similar to us, they separate argumentative units from discursive contextual markers. While Wachsmuth et al. (2018) conduct a *human* evaluation to investigate the separation of *Logos* and *Pathos* aspects of arguments,

our work investigates how (de-)contextualization of argumentative units affects *automatic* argumentative relation classification models.

Notions of context   Various notions of *context* are being used in the area of argumentation mining. For example, Lippi and Torroni (2016) develop a *context-independent* claim detection system, where by *context-independent* they refer to a system which is not tailored to a specific topic (analogously, Levy et al. (2014) aim at *context-dependency*). Another notion of *context* concerns the graph context in which relations and EAUs are embedded (Kuribayashi et al., 2018). On the other hand, we adopt a more *textual* notion of context, that is we take a given EAU span as content and text which is not in the EAU span as context. This goes in the same direction as Stab and Gurevych (2014b, 2017); Persing and Ng (2016) and Aker et al. (2017) who incorporate features derived from EAU-surrounding text in their classification systems. However, they do not clearly separate between a word indicator feature extracted from within (or outside) the EAU span. For example, when computing features for an EAU, they also take into account EAU-preceding tokens. The preceding tokens, often contain shallow discourse markers which highlight the relationship between two EAUs (e.g., *because*, *however*, etc.).

To the best of our knowledge, prior work has not yet thoroughly investigated the impact of features extracted from the EAU vs. features extracted from the EAU-embedding context. Our work fills this gap and shows that the impact of contextual clues from the EAU *context* on classifier performance can be much greater than the impact of features extracted from the EAU *content*.

Context matters   Nguyen and Litman (2016); Nguyen (2018) extract additional features from the text between source and target EAUs (on the StudentEssay-v01 data (Stab and Gurevych, 2014a)) which results in enhanced predictive performance. However, having seen the clear advantages of incorporating context (performance-wise), we find that the downsides of incorporating context remain untold. In this work, we demonstrate that systems which are offered EAU *context* may be prone to neglect the EAU *content*, an issue that can have undesired effects.

Argumentative relation classification   Argumentative relation classification (Mochales and

---

[2]Throughout this work we often drop "elementary" and use the phrases *EAU and (elementary) argumentative unit* and *argumentative component* interchangeably.

Moens, 2011) is the task for which we aim to examine the context-content relationship. It is concerned with predicting and analyzing relations between argumentative units such as, for example, *support* or *attack*. Besides works discussed above (Nguyen and Litman, 2016; Stab and Gurevych, 2014b, 2017), this task has also been addressed by Cocarascu and Toni (2017) who develop a neural model to label the edge between two EAUs with $\{attack, support, \varnothing\}$. The task has also been approached by taking global graph context into account. E.g., Hou and Jochim (2017) jointly model argument relation classification and stance classification in the DebatePedia[3] corpus using Markov logic networks (Richardson and Domingos, 2006). Peldszus and Stede (2015) experiment with Microtexts and show that it can be beneficial to model argumentative relations jointly in a network with a minimum spanning tree decoding algorithm. Our work focuses on local relation prediction and labeling using the well-established StudentEssay-v02 data (Stab and Gurevych, 2017)[4] with 402 argumentative essays and thousands of annotated relations between EAUs.

3 Argumentative Relation Prediction: Models and Features

In this section, we describe different formulations of the argumentative relation classification task and describe features used by our replicated model. In order to test our hypotheses, we propose to group all features into three distinct types.

Three feature types: content-based; content-ignorant; full access We categorize features of Stab and Gurevych (2017) into three types: (i) features derived from the *context* of the argumentative unit (e.g., leading and trailing tokens surrounding the EAU span), (ii) features derived from the argumentative unit's *content* (i.e., the EAU span), and (iii) a joint feature set consisting of the union of features from (i) and (ii). However, in (iii) we additionally include features that capture discourse structures that overlap the boundaries between an EAU and its surroundings.

Notations Henceforth we denote models that only make use of features of type (i), ignoring anything inside the EAU, as **content-ignorant** ($\mathcal{CI}$), and models that are given only features covering the EAU span as **content-based** ($\mathcal{CB}$). A model that combines both is denoted by **full-access** ($\mathcal{FA}$). We distinguish these different model types with a type-variable $\mathcal{T} \in \{\mathcal{CI}, \mathcal{CB}, \mathcal{FA}\}$.

3.1 Models

Now, we introduce a classification of three different prediction models used in the argumentative relation prediction literature. We will inspect all of them and show that all can suffer from severe issues when focusing (too much) on the context.

The model h adopts a discourse parsing view on argumentative relation prediction and predicts one outgoing edge for an argumentative unit (**one-outgoing edge**). Model f assumes a connected graph with argumentative units and is tasked with predicting edge labels for unit tuples (**labeling relations in a graph**). Finally, a model g is given two (possibly) unrelated argumentative units and is tasked with predicting connections as well as edge labels (**joint edge prediction and labeling**).

One-outgoing edge Stab and Gurevych (2017) divide the task into relation prediction l and relation class assignment h:

$$l^{\mathcal{T}} : A \times A \to \{linked, \varnothing\} \tag{1}$$

$$h^{\mathcal{T}} : A \to \{attack, support\}, \tag{2}$$

which the authors describe as *argumentative relation identification* (l) and *stance detection* (h). In their experiments, $\mathcal{T} = FA$, i.e., no distinction is made between features that access only the argument content (EAU span) or only the EAU's embedding context, and some features also consider both (e.g., discourse features). This model adopts a parsing view on argumentative relation classification: every unit is allowed to have only one type of outgoing relation (this follows trivially from the fact that h has only one input). Applying such a model to argumentative attack and support relations might impose unrealistic constraints on the resulting argumentation graph: A given premise might in fact attack or support several other premises.[5] The approach may suffice for the case of student argumentative essays, where EAUs are well-framed in a discourse structure, but seems overly restrictive for many other scenarios.

---

[3] http://debatepedia.idebate.org/
[4] https://tinyurl.com/y269fq3k

[5] E.g., *this decision will improve the living situation for children. It may also support elderly people with low income.*

Labeling relations in a graph Another way of framing the task, is to learn a function

$$f^{\mathcal{T}} : A \times A \to \{support, attack\}, \qquad (3)$$

Here, an argumentative unit is allowed to be in a attack or support relation to multiple other EAUs. Yet, both h and f assume that inputs are already linked and only the class of the link is unknown.

Joint edge prediction and labeling Thus, we might also model the task in a three-class classification setting to learn a more general function that performs relation prediction and classification jointly (see also, e.g., Lippi and Torroni (2016)):

$$g^{\mathcal{T}} : A \times A \to \{support, attack, \varnothing\}. \qquad (4)$$

The model described by Eq. 4 is the most general one: not only does it assume a graph view on argumentative units and their relations (as does Eq. 3); in model formulation (Eq. 4), an argumentative unit can have no or multiple support or attack relations. It naturally allows for cases where an argumentative unit a (supports b | attacks c | *is-unrelated-to* d). Given a set of EAUs mined from different documents, this model enables us to construct a full-fledged argumentation graph.

3.2 Feature implementation

Our feature implementation follows the feature descriptions for *Stance recognition* and *link identification* in Stab and Gurevych (2017). These features and variations of them have been used successfully in several successive works (cf. Stab and Gurevych (2014b); Nguyen and Litman (2016); Aker et al. (2017)).

For any model the features are indexed by $I = \{1, ..., N\}$. We create a function $\Phi : I \to \mathcal{T}$ which maps from feature indices to feature types. In other words, Φ tells us, for any given feature, whether it is content-based ($\mathcal{CB}$), content-ignorant ($\mathcal{CI}$) or full access ($\mathcal{FA}$). The features for, e.g., the joint prediction model g of type $\mathcal{CI}$ ($g^{\mathcal{CI}}$) can then simply be described as $\{i \in I | \Phi(i) = \mathcal{CI}\}$. Recall that features computed on the basis of the EAU span are *content-based* ($\mathcal{CB}$), features from the EAU-surrounding text are *content-ignorant* ($\mathcal{CI}$) and features computed from both are denoted by *full-access* ($\mathcal{FA}$). Details on the extraction of features are provided below.

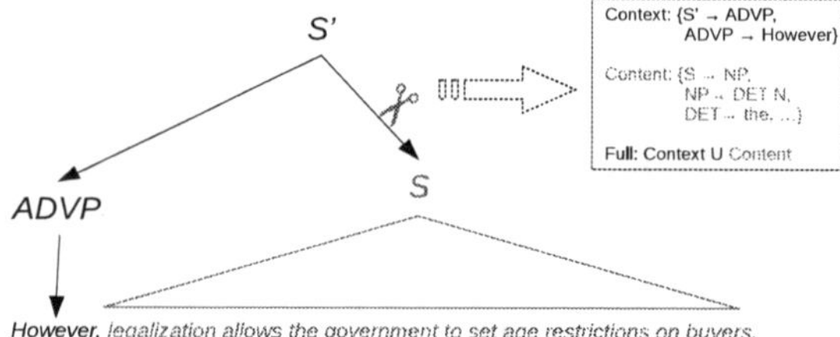

Figure 2: Production rule extraction from constituency parse for two different argumentative units.

Lexical features These consist of boolean values indicating whether a certain word appears in the argumentative source or target EAU or both (and separately, their contexts). More precisely, for any classification instance we extract uni-grams from within the span of the EAU (if $\mathcal{T} = \mathcal{CB}$) or solely from the sentence-context surrounding the EAUs (if $\mathcal{T} = \mathcal{CI}$). Words which occur in both bags are only visible in the full-access setup $\mathcal{T} = \mathcal{FA}$ and are modeled as binary indicators.

Syntactic features Such features consist of syntactic production rules extracted from constituency trees – they are modelled analogously to the lexical features as a bag of production rules. To make a clear division between features derived from the EAU embedding context and features derived from within the EAU span, we divide the constituency tree in two parts, as is illustrated in Figure 2. If the EAU is embedded in a covering sentence, we cut the syntax tree at the corresponding edge (✂ in Figure 2). In this example, the content-ignorant ($\mathcal{CI}$) bag-of-word production rule representation includes the rules $S \to ADVP$ and $ADVP \to however$. Analogously to the lexical features, the production rules are modeled as binary indicator features.[6]

Structural These features describe shallow statistics such as the ratio of argumentative unit tokens compared to sentence tokens or the position of the argumentative unit in the paragraph. We set these features to zero for the content representation of the argumentative unit and replicate those features that allow us to treat the argumen-

---

[6]A notable insight from our experiments is that the production rule features have a considerable intersection with lexical features. This is due to the terminal production rules, which correspond to the leaves of the constituency tree. This explains the surprisingly high scores for production rule features in the production-rule-only ablation experiments in e.g., Stab and Gurevych (2014b, 2017).

tative unit as a black-box. For example, in the content-based ($\mathcal{CB}$) system that has access only to the EAU, we can compute the #tokens in the EAU, but not the #tokens in EAU divided by #tokens in the sentence. The latter feature is only accessible in the full access system variants. Hence, in the content-based ($\mathcal{CB}$) system most of these statistics are set to zero since they cannot be computed by considering only the EAU span.

Discourse   For the content-based representation we retrieve only discourse relations that are confined within the span of the argumentative unit. In the very frequent case that discourse features cross the boundaries of embedding context and EAU span, we only take them into account for $\mathcal{FA}$.

Embeddings   We use the element-wise sum of 300-dimensional pre-trained GloVe vectors (Pennington et al., 2014) corresponding to the words within the EAU span ($\mathcal{CB}$) and the words of the EAU-surrounding context ($\mathcal{CI}$). Additionally, we compute the element-wise subtraction of the source EAU vector from the target EAU vector, with the aim of modelling directions in distributional space, similarly to Mikolov et al. (2013). Words with no corresponding pre-trained word vector and empty sequences (e.g., no preceding context available) are treated as a zero-vector.

Sentiment   Tree-based sentiment annotations are sentiment scores assigned to nodes in constituency parse trees (Socher et al., 2013). We represent these scores by a one-hot vector of dimension 5 (5 is very positive, 1 is very negative). We determine the *contextual* ($\mathcal{CI}$) sentiment by looking at the highest possible node of the context which does not contain the EAU (ADVP in Figure 2). The sentiment for an EAU span ($\mathcal{CB}$) is assigned to the highest possible node covering the EAU span which does not contain the context subtree (S in Figure 2). The full-access ($\mathcal{FA}$) score is assigned to the lowest possible node which covers both the EAU span and its surrounding context (S' in Figure 2). Next to the sentiment scores for the selected tree nodes and analogously to the word embeddings, we also calculate the element-wise subtraction of the one-hot sentiment source vectors from the one-hot sentiment target vectors. This results in three additional vectors corresponding to $\mathcal{CB}$, $\mathcal{CI}$ and $\mathcal{FA}$ difference vectors.

model	#train		#test	
	$h\ \&\ f$	g	$h\ \&\ f$	g
documents	322	322	80	80
support	3820	3820	1021	1021
attack	405	405	92	92
$\varnothing$	-	5474	-	1622

Table 1: Data set statistics.

4   Experiments

Data and pre-processing   We use the corpus of 402 persuasive essays which were annotated with argumentative units, their stances towards the topic and argumentative relations (Stab and Gurevych, 2017). The data is suited for our experiments because the annotators were explicitly asked to provide annotations on a clausal level. This entails that contextual clues tend not to be contained in the annotated span (e.g., only *people should not smoke* is annotated as EAU in the sentence *Therefore, people should not smoke.*). In this work, we are concerned with classifying relations between argumentative units into *support* or *attack* and thus do not consider other annotations. For feature extraction, we process all documents with Stanford CoreNLP (Manning et al., 2014) with the following annotation layers: *sentence tokenize, word tokenize, constituency parse* and *constituency-sentiment*. For extraction of the discourse-features, we proceed by parsing all documents with the PDTB-parser[7] developed by Lin et al. (2014). For the joint task of predicting three link classes (including a non-linked class), we extract as non-linked EAU pairs all EAU pairs which are not linked on a document level. Data set statistics are displayed in Table 1.

Setup   As explained in §3, we are interested in three distinct configurations of the argumentative relation classifier: **content-based ($\mathcal{CB}$)**, **content-ignorant ($\mathcal{CI}$)** and **full-access ($\mathcal{FA}$)**. Naturally, we would expect the latter to perform best and perhaps we would also expect $\mathcal{CB}$ to outperform $\mathcal{CI}$ – a system which has no access to the argumentative unit internals whatsoever should not be able to confidently determine relations between them. Note that some features are only available to $\mathcal{FA}$, which is the case when features cross con-

---

[7]`https://github.com/WING-NUS/pdtb-parser`

system	$F1_{sup}$	$F1_{att}$	macro F1
S&G16	94.7	41.3	68.0
replicated ($h^{\mathcal{FA}}$)	94.7	44.0	69.3

Table 2: Baseline system replication results.

model	$\mathcal{T}$	$F1_{sup}$	$F1_{att}$	$F1_{\varnothing}$	macro F1
h	mfs	95.7	0	-	47.8
	$\mathcal{CB}$	92.9	21.7	-	57.3[†]
	$\mathcal{CI}$	95.0	38.6	-	67.0[†‡]
	$\mathcal{FA}$	94.7	44.0	-	69.3[†‡]
f	mfs	95.7	0	-	47.8
	$\mathcal{CB}$	92.3	20.3	-	56.3[†]
	$\mathcal{CI}$	96.1	41.7	-	70.8[†‡]
	$\mathcal{FA}$	94.4	42.4	-	68.5[†‡]
g	mfs	0	0	74.5	8.3
	$\mathcal{CB}$	54.3	9.9	65.0	43.4[†]
	$\mathcal{CI}$	63.0	34.8	76.5	59.3[†‡]
	$\mathcal{FA}$	46.6	32.3	73.1	56.1[†‡]

Table 3: Argumentative relation classification models h, f, g with different access to content and context; models of type $\mathcal{CI}$ (content-ignorant) have no access to the EAU span. †: significantly better than mfs baseline ($p < 0.005$); ‡ significantly better than content-based ($p < 0.005$).

text and argumentative unit spans (e.g., some of the discourse features), thereby resisting a clear categorization into $\mathcal{CB}$ or $\mathcal{CI}$. Same as most prior work, we use an SVM to learn the feature weights.

4.1 Results

Replication experiments Our first step towards our main experiments is to replicate the competitive argumentative relation classifier of Stab and Gurevych (2017, 2014b). Hence, for comparison purposes, we first formulate the task exactly as it was done in this prior work, using the model formulation in Eq. 2, which determines the type of outgoing edge from a source (i.e., tree-like view).

The results in Table 2 confirm the results of Stab and Gurevych (2017) and suggest that we successfully replicated a large proportion of their features.

Main results The results for all three prediction settings (one outgoing edge: h, support/attack: f and support/attack/neither: g) across all type variables ($\mathcal{CB}$, $\mathcal{CI}$ and $\mathcal{FA}$) are displayed in Table 3. All models significantly outperform the majority baseline with respect to macro F1. Intriguingly,

the content-ignorant models ($\mathcal{CI}$) *always* perform significantly better than the models which only have access to the EAUs' content ($\mathcal{CB}$, $p < 0.005$). In the most general task formulation (g), we observe that $\mathcal{CI}$ even significantly outperforms the model which has maximum access (seeing both EAU spans and surrounding contexts: $\mathcal{FA}$).

At first glance, the results of the purely EAU focused systems ($\mathcal{CB}$) are disappointing, since they fall far behind their competitors. On the other hand, their F1 scores are not devastatingly bad. The strong most-frequent-class baseline is significantly outperformed by the content-based ($\mathcal{CB}$) system, across all three prediction settings.

In summary our findings are as follows: (i) models which see the EAU span (content-based, $\mathcal{CB}$) are significantly outperformed by models that have no access to the span itself (content-ignorant, $\mathcal{CI}$) across all settings; (ii) in two of three prediction settings (f and g), the model which only has access to the context even outperforms the model that has access to all information in the input. The fact that using features derived exclusively from the EAU embedding context ($\mathcal{CI}$) can lead to better results than using a full feature-system ($\mathcal{FA}$) suggests that some information from the EAU can even be harmful. Why this is the case, we cannot answer exactly. A plausible cause might be related to the smaller dimension of the feature space, which makes the SVM less likely to overfit. Still, this finding comes as a surprise and calls for further investigation in future work.

Robustness tests A system for argumentative relation classification can be applied in one of two settings: *single-document* or *cross-document*, as illustrated in Figure 3: in the first case (top), a system is tasked to classify EAUs that appear linearly in one document – here contextual clues can often highlight the relationship between two units. This is the setting we have been considering up to now. However, in the second scenario (bottom), we have moved away from the closed single-document setting and ask the system to classify two EAUs extracted from different document contexts. This setting applies, for instance, when we are mining arguments from multiple sources.

In *both* cases, however, a system that relies more on contextual clues than on the content expressed in the EAUs is problematic: in the single-document setting, such a system will rely on discourse indicators – whether or not they are justi-

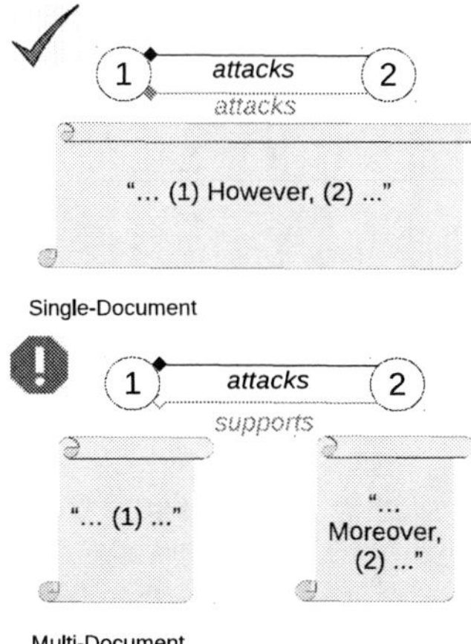

Figure 3: Single-document (top) vs. cross-document (bottom) argumentative relation classification. Black edge: gold label; purple edge: predicted label.

fied by content – and can thus easily be fooled.

In the cross-document setting, discourse-based indicators – being inherently defined with respect to their internal document context – do not have a defined rhetorical function with respect to EAUs in a separate document and thus a system that has learned to rely on such markers within a single-document setting can be seriously misled. We believe that the cross-document setting should be an important goal in argumentation analysis, since it generalizes better to many debates of interest, where EAUs can be found scattered across thousands of documents. For example, for the topic of *legalizing marijuana*, EAUs may be mined from millions of documents and thus their relations may naturally extend across document boundaries. If a system learns to over-proportionally attend to the EAUs' surrounding contexts it is prone to making many errors.[8]

In what follows we are simulating the effects that an overly context-sensitive classifier could have in a cross-document setting, by modifying our experimental setting, and study the effects on the different model types: In one setup – we call it *randomized-context* – we systematically distort the context of our testing instances by exchanging the context in a randomized manner; in the other setting – called *no-context*, we are deleting the context around the ADUs to be classified.

Randomized-context simulates an open world debate where argumentative units may occur in different contexts, sometimes with discourse markers indicating an opposite class. In other words, in this setting we want to examine effects when porting a context-sensitive system to a multi-document setting.[9] For example, as seen in Figure 3, the context of an argumentative unit may change from "However" to "Moreover" – which can happen naturally in open debates. The results are displayed in Figure 4. In the standard setting (Figure 4a), the models that have access to the context besides the content ($\mathcal{FA}$) and the models that are only allowed to access the context ($\mathcal{CI}$), always perform better than the content-based models ($\mathcal{CB}$) (bars above zero). However, when we randomly flip contexts of the test instances (Figure 4b), or suppress them entirely (Figure 4c), the opposite picture emerges: the content-based models always outperform the other models. For some classes (*support*, $\varnothing$) the difference can exceed 50 F1 percentage points. These two studies, where testing examples are varied regarding their context (*randomized-context* or *no-context*) simulates what can be expected if we apply our systems for relation class assignment to EAUs stemming from heterogeneous sources. While the performances of a purely content-based model naturally stays stable, the performance of the other systems decrease notably – they perform worse than the content-based model.

Feature investigation We calculate the ANOVA classification F scores of the features with respect to our three task formulations h, g and f. The F percentiles of features extracted from the EAU surrounding text ($\mathcal{CI}$) and features extracted from the EAU span ($\mathcal{CB}$), are displayed in Figure 5.

It clearly stands out that features obtained from the EAU surrounding context ($\mathcal{CI}$) are assigned much higher scores compared to features stemming from the EAU span ($\mathcal{CB}$). This holds true for all three task formulations and provides further evidence that models – when given the option – put a strong focus on contextual clues while neglecting the information provided by the EAU span itself.

5 Discussion

While competitive systems for argumentative relation classification are considered to be robust, our

---

[8] In fact, similar considerations also apply when moving from argumentative monologue to dialogue, i.e., in interactive debates. Again, systems need to be able to detect relations between EAUs uttered by different speakers and independently from the speaker-specific utterance context.

[9] We concede that this is an artificial setup, but defer more realistic cross-document experiments to future work.

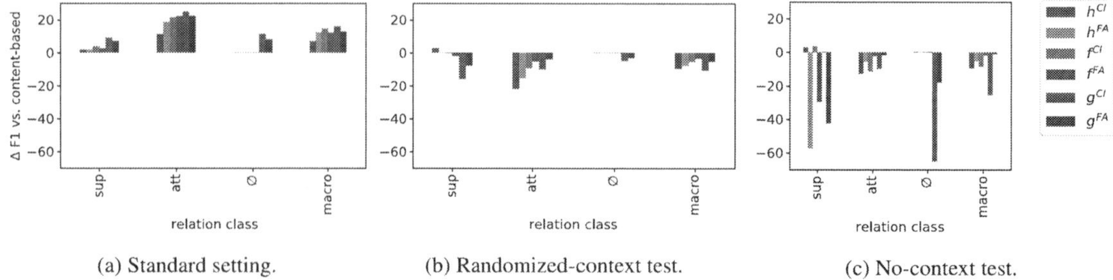

<table>
<tr><td>(a) Standard setting.</td><td>(b) Randomized-context test.</td><td>(c) No-context test.</td></tr>
</table>

Figure 4: *Randomized-context* test set: models are applied to testing instances with randomly flipped contexts. *No-context test set*: models can only access the EAU span of a testing instance. A bar below/above zero means that a system that can access context (content-ignorant $\mathcal{CI}$ or full-access $\mathcal{FA}$) is worse/better than the content-based baseline $\mathcal{CB}$ that only has access to the EAU span (its performance is not affected by modified context, cf. Tab. 3).

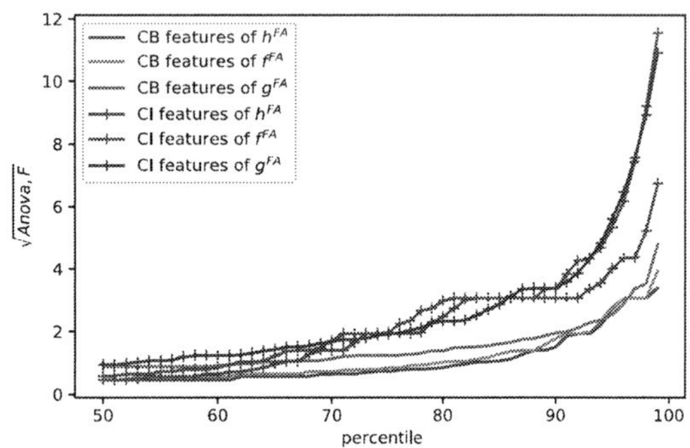

Figure 5: ANOVA F score percentiles for content-based vs. content-ignorant features in the training data. A higher feature score suggests greater predictive capacity.

experiments have shown that despite confidence-inspiring scores on unseen testing data, such systems can easily be fooled – they can deliver strong performance scores although the classifier does not have access to the content of the EAUs. In this respect, we have provided evidence that there is a danger in case models focus too much on rhetorical indicators, in detriment of the context. Thus, the following question arises: *How can we prevent argumentation models from modeling arguments or argumentative units and their relations in overly naïve ways?* A simple and intuitive way is to dissect EAUs from their surrounding document context. Models trained on data that is restricted to the EAUs' content will be forced to focus on the content of EAUs. We believe that this will enhance the robustness of such models and allows them to generalize to cross-document argument relation classification. The corpus of student essays makes such transformations straightforward: only the

EAUs were annotated (e.g., "However, $[_{arg}A]$"). If annotations extend over the EAUs (e.g., only full sentences are annotated, "$[_{arg}$However, A]"), such transformations could be performed automatically after a discourse parsing step. When inspecting the student essays corpus, we further observed that an EAU mining step should involve coreference resolution to better capture relations between EAUs that involve anaphors (e.g., *"Exercising makes you feel better"* and *"It$_{[Exercising]}$ increases endorphine levels"*).

Thus, in order to conduct real-world end-to-end argumentation relation mining for a given topic, we envision a system that addresses three steps: (i) mining of EAUs and (ii) replacement of pronouns in EAUs with referenced entities (e.g., *It is healthy $\rightarrow$ Excercise is healthy*). Finally (iii), given the cross product of mined EAUs we can apply a model of type g to construct a full-fledged argumentation graph, possibly spanning multiple documents.[10] We have shown that in order to properly perform step (iii), we need stronger models that are able to better model EAU contents. Hence, we encourage the argumentation community to test their systems on a decontextualized version of the student essays, including the proposed – and possibly further extended – testing setups, to challenge the semantic representation and reasoning capacities of argument analysis models. This will lead to more realistic performance estimates and increased robustness of systems when addressing desirable multi-document tasks.

---

[10]cf. Peldszus and Stede (2015) for graph prediction within single documents.

6 Conclusion

We have shown that systems which put too much focus on discourse information may be easily fooled – an issue which has severe implications when systems are applied to cross-document argumentative relation classification tasks. The strong reliance on contextual clues is also problematic in single-document contexts, where systems can run a risk of assigning relation labels relying on contextual and rhetorical effects – instead of focusing on content. Hence, we propose that researchers test their argumentative relation classification systems on two alternative versions of the StudentEssay data that reflect different access levels. (i) *EAU-span only*, where systems only see the EAU spans and (ii) *context-only*, where systems can only see the EAU-surrounding context. These complementary settings will (i) challenge the semantic capacities of a system, and (ii) unveil the extent to which a system is focusing on the discourse context when making decisions. We will offer our testing environments to the research community through a platform that provides datasets and scripts and a table to trace the results of content-based systems.[11]

Acknowledgments

This work has been supported by the German Research Foundation as part of the Research Training Group Adaptive Preparation of Information from Heterogeneous Sources (AIPHES) under grant no. GRK 1994/1 and by the Leibniz ScienceCampus "Empirical Linguistics and Computational Language Modeling", supported by the Leibniz Association under grant no. SAS-2015-IDS-LWC and by the Ministry of Science, Research, and Art of Baden-Württemberg.

References

Ahmet Aker, Alfred Sliwa, Yuan Ma, Ruishen Lui, Niravkumar Borad, Seyedeh Ziyaei, and Mina Ghobadi. 2017. What works and what does not: Classifier and feature analysis for argument mining. In *Proceedings of the 4th Workshop on Argument Mining*, pages 91–96, Copenhagen, Denmark.

M. Azar. 1999. Argumentative text as rhetorical structure: An application of rhetorical structure theory. *Argumentation*, 13(1):97–114.

Oana Cocarascu and Francesca Toni. 2017. Identifying attack and support argumentative relations using deep learning. In *Proceedings of the 2017 Conference on Empirical Methods in Natural Language Processing*, pages 1374–1379.

Nancy Green, Kevin Ashley, Diane Litman, Chris Reed, and Vern Walker, editors. 2014. *Proceedings of the First Workshop on Argumentation Mining*. Association for Computational Linguistics, Baltimore, Maryland.

Nancy L Green. 2010. Representation of argumentation in text with rhetorical structure theory. *Argumentation*, 24(2):181–196.

Yufang Hou and Charles Jochim. 2017. Argument relation classification using a joint inference model. In *Proceedings of the 4th Workshop on Argument Mining*, pages 60–66.

Tatsuki Kuribayashi, Paul Reisert, Naoya Inoue, and Kentaro Inui. 2018. Towards exploiting argumentative context for argumentative relation identification. In *Proceedings of the Annual Meeting of the Association for Natural Language Processing NLP*, pages 284–287.

Ran Levy, Yonatan Bilu, Daniel Hershcovich, Ehud Aharoni, and Noam Slonim. 2014. Context dependent claim detection. In *Proceedings of COLING 2014, the 25th International Conference on Computational Linguistics: Technical Papers*, pages 1489–1500, Dublin, Ireland. Dublin City University and Association for Computational Linguistics.

Ziheng Lin, Hwee Tou Ng, and Min-Yen Kan. 2014. A pdtb-styled end-to-end discourse parser. *Natural Language Engineering*, 20(2):151–184.

Marco Lippi and Paolo Torroni. 2016. Argumentation mining: State of the art and emerging trends. *ACM Transactions on Internet Technology (TOIT)*, 16(2):10.

William C Mann and Sandra A Thompson. 1987. Rhetorical structure theory: Description and construction of text structures. In *Natural language generation*, pages 85–95. Springer.

Christopher Manning, Mihai Surdeanu, John Bauer, Jenny Finkel, Steven Bethard, and David McClosky. 2014. The Stanford CoreNLP natural language processing toolkit. In *Proceedings of 52nd Annual Meeting of the Association for Computational Linguistics: System Demonstrations*, pages 55–60, Baltimore, Maryland.

Tomas Mikolov, Ilya Sutskever, Kai Chen, Greg S Corrado, and Jeff Dean. 2013. Distributed representations of words and phrases and their compositionality. In *Advances in neural information processing systems*, pages 3111–3119.

Raquel Mochales and Marie-Francine Moens. 2011. Argumentation mining. *Artificial Intelligence and Law*, 19(1):1–22.

---

[11]http://explain.cl.uni-heidelberg.de/

Huy Nguyen. 2018. *Context-aware Argument Mining and Its Applications in Education*. Ph.D. thesis, University of Pittsburgh.

Huy Nguyen and Diane Litman. 2016. Context-aware argumentative relation mining. In *Proceedings of the 54th Annual Meeting of the Association for Computational Linguistics (Volume 1: Long Papers)*, volume 1, pages 1127–1137.

Andreas Peldszus and Manfred Stede. 2013. From argument diagrams to argumentation mining in texts: A survey. *International Journal of Cognitive Informatics and Natural Intelligence (IJCINI)*, 7(1):1–31.

Andreas Peldszus and Manfred Stede. 2015. Joint prediction in mst-style discourse parsing for argumentation mining. In *Proceedings of the 2015 Conference on Empirical Methods in Natural Language Processing*, pages 938–948.

Andreas Peldszus and Manfred Stede. 2016. An annotated corpus of argumentative microtexts. In D. Mohammed and M. Lewinski, editors, *Argumentation and Reasoned Action - Proc. of the 1st European Conference on Argumentation, Lisbon, 2015*. College Publications, London.

Jeffrey Pennington, Richard Socher, and Christopher Manning. 2014. Glove: Global vectors for word representation. In *Proceedings of the 2014 conference on Empirical Methods in Natural Language Processing (EMNLP)*, pages 1532–1543.

Isaac Persing and Vincent Ng. 2016. End-to-end argumentation mining in student essays. In *Proceedings of the 2016 Conference of the North American Chapter of the Association for Computational Linguistics: Human Language Technologies*, pages 1384–1394, San Diego, California. Association for Computational Linguistics.

Mohammad Sadegh Rasooli and Joel R. Tetreault. 2015. Yara parser: A fast and accurate dependency parser. *Computing Research Repository*, arXiv:1503.06733. Version 2.

Matthew Richardson and Pedro Domingos. 2006. Markov logic networks. *Machine learning*, 62(1-2):107–136.

Richard Socher, Alex Perelygin, Jean Wu, Jason Chuang, Christopher D. Manning, Andrew Ng, and Christopher Potts. 2013. Recursive deep models for semantic compositionality over a sentiment treebank. In *Proceedings of the 2013 Conference on Empirical Methods in Natural Language Processing*, pages 1631–1642, Seattle, Washington, USA.

Christian Stab and Iryna Gurevych. 2014a. Annotating argument components and relations in persuasive essays. In *Proceedings of COLING 2014, the 25th International Conference on Computational Linguistics: Technical Papers*, pages 1501–1510, Dublin, Ireland. Dublin City University and Association for Computational Linguistics.

Christian Stab and Iryna Gurevych. 2014b. Identifying argumentative discourse structures in persuasive essays. In *Proceedings of the 2014 Conference on Empirical Methods in Natural Language Processing (EMNLP)*, pages 46–56.

Christian Stab and Iryna Gurevych. 2017. Parsing argumentation structures in persuasive essays. *Computational Linguistics*, 43(3):619–659.

Christian Stab, Tristan Miller, Benjamin Schiller, Pranav Rai, and Iryna Gurevych. 2018. Cross-topic argument mining from heterogeneous sources. In *Proceedings of the 2018 Conference on Empirical Methods in Natural Language Processing*, pages 3664–3674.

Henning Wachsmuth, Manfred Stede, Roxanne El Baff, Khalid Al Khatib, Maria Skeppstedt, and Benno Stein. 2018. Argumentation synthesis following rhetorical strategies. In *Proceedings of the 27th International Conference on Computational Linguistics*, pages 3753–3765.

Aligning Discourse and Argumentation Structures using Subtrees and Redescription Mining

Laurine Huber[1], Yannick Toussaint[1],
Charlotte Roze[1], Mathilde Dargnat[2] and Chloé Braud[1]

[1] Université de Lorraine, CNRS, Inria, LORIA (UMR 7503), F-54000 Nancy, France
`firstname.lastname@loria.fr,`
[2] ATILF, Université de Lorraine, CNRS (UMR 7118), Nancy, France
et Institut des Sciences Cognitives Marc Jannerod, CNRS (UMR 5304), Bron, France
`mathilde.dargnat@univ-lorraine.fr`

Abstract

In this paper, we investigate similarities between discourse and argumentation structures by aligning subtrees in a corpus containing both annotations. Contrary to previous works, we focus on comparing sub-structures and not only relation matches. Using data mining techniques, we show that discourse and argumentation most often align well, and the double annotation allows to derive a mapping between structures. Moreover, this approach enables the study of similarities between discourse structures and differences in their expressive power.

1 Introduction

This paper presents preliminary results in aligning different text structure representations. Using graph and redescription mining, we compare argumentative and discourse trees. The former represents the way arguments are organized through support or attack relations, the latter accounts for the coherence of texts by linking segments with semantico-pragmatic relations.

Aligning structures such as argumentation and discourse trees could help to understand the links between these representations, to build some bridges between theories, or to allow a better understanding of the expressive power of the different formalisms.

The arg-microtexts-multilayer corpus[1] (Stede et al., 2016) provides three representations of short texts: RST trees (Mann and Thompson, 1988),[2] SDRT graphs (Lascarides and Asher, 2007), and argumentation (ARG) structures as described in (Peldszus and Stede, 2013), based on Freeman's theory (Freeman, 1991).

In this preliminary study, we focus on RST and ARG annotations. We propose to describe each text by two views, one corresponding to the set of subtrees extracted from the RST tree, and the other to the subtrees extracted from the ARG tree. The best alignment between subtrees is computed thanks to a redescription mining approach.

2 Related Work

A manual analysis of the correspondences between RST and argumentation relations (Peldszus and Stede, 2016) has already shown that a 1-to-1 mapping leads to some mismatches. For example, 39% of the `supports`, 72% of the `rebuts`, and 33% of the `undercuts` do not have a corresponding RST edge. These mismatches have been explained by granularity differences in annotations. Thus, we propose here to consider alignment at the level of subtrees allowing more complex combinations of relations.

Cabrio et al. (2013) showed that 5 Argumentation Schemes (AS) from (Walton et al., 2008) can be mapped to Penn Discourse TreeBank (PDTB) relations (Prasad et al., 2008). They built an hypothetical mapping of AS to PDTB relations, and extracted 10 examples from the PDTB. Two annotators had to say whether the AS definition was relevant to the example, and the measured Cohen's kappa showed a significant agreement ($\kappa = 0.71$). Though their goal was to study the link between argumentation and discourse, their approach was based on both human hypothesis and human annotation. Unlike them, we propose an automatic approach based on data mining. To our knowledge, it is the first generic and systematic approach for mapping discourse and argumentation.

3 Methodology

The three-step process aims at finding an exhaustive and systematic alignment over the corpus between "parts" of the RST and "parts" of the ARG representations. First, for each text, its RST and ARG representations are respectively transformed

---

[1] `https://github.com/peldszus/arg-microtexts`
[2] `https://www.sfu.ca/rst/`

35

Proceedings of the 6th Workshop on Argument Mining, pages 35–40
Florence, Italy, August 1, 2019. ©2019 Association for Computational Linguistics

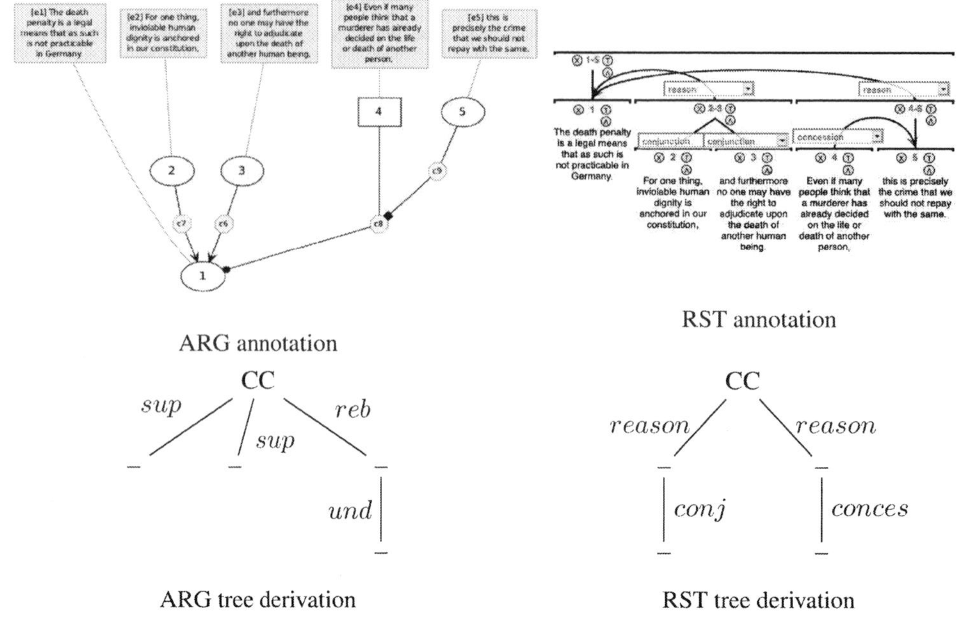

ARG tree derivation

RST tree derivation

Figure 1: Text *micro_b006* annotated in ARG and RST
and trees derived from annotations

into two labeled trees. Then, RST and ARG trees being considered separately, subgraph mining extracts all subtrees common to at least 2 texts. Each subtree becomes a feature used for describing one of the two views (i.e. RST and ARG) of each text. In the last step, redescription mining searches for alignments between features of the RST view and features of the ARG view.

3.1 Encoding RST and ARG representations into trees

RST and ARG representations are encoded into two distinct trees, refered as initial RST or ARG trees in the following. In both ARG and RST trees, we label CC the root node, to represent the central claim and the main nucleus respectively.[3]

As we do not consider the text but only the structure, and because we do not consider the sequentiality of the units in the texts proposed by (Wachsmuth et al., 2017), other nodes are left unlabeled (–). These unlabeled nodes represent the Argumentative Units (AUs) in ARG trees and the Discourse Units (DUs) in RST trees.[4] Labels on the edges correspond to the argumentative or discursive relations between AUs and DUs, respectively. Trees are built in a straightforward

way, except in ARG representations when some relations are not directed to an AU but to a relation (`undercut` for example). Inspired from Wachsmuth et al. (2017), we make them target the premise of the undercutted relation (see ARG tree example in Figure 1).

3.2 Creating two views

In this step, we extract subtrees from the whole set of RST initial trees on the one hand, and subtrees from ARG initial trees on the other hand. Each subtree is given a unique identifier and becomes a boolean feature to be associated with texts: a text has a feature if the subtree is in its initial tree.

Extracting subtrees gSpan (*Graph-Based Substructure Pattern Mining*) (Yan and Han, 2002) is an algorithm to extract frequent subtrees from a graphset $\mathbb{GS}$. Informally, a graph h is a *subtree* of a graph g if h is contained in g, and h is *frequent* if, given a support threshold σ_s, at least s graphs of $\mathbb{GS}$ contain h. We applied gSpan,[5] on the ARG treeset and the RST treeset with $\sigma_s = 2$.

Building the data-tables From the gSpan runs, we represent the boolean features in two binary

---

[3]The "most nuclear" unit or central unit (Stede, 2008).

[4]An AU can comprise multiple DUs, to express that multiple DUs form an argument only when combined.

[5]We use the following python implementation: `https://github.com/betterenvi/gSpan` as we are interested in subtrees that include the central claim, we used the algorithm on undirected graphs.

data-tables, called views, where the rows correspond to the texts and the columns to the features.

3.3 Redescription Mining

In data analysis, redescription mining (Galbrun and Miettinen, 2017) is the task of finding two distinct characterizations of the same set of objects (i.e. texts in this experiment). Inputs of redescription mining are the views of the texts. The goal is to find two boolean expressions, called queries, $q1$ and $q2$, where $q1$ and $q2$ are formulae over the features of the ARG view and the RST view respectively, and where the support of $q1$ and $q2$ are sufficiently similar, so that they explain (approximately) the same set of texts. This similarity is measured by the Jaccard index:

$$J(q1, q2) = \frac{supp(q1 \wedge q2)}{supp(q1 \vee q2)} \qquad (1)$$

where $supp(q)$ is the number of texts where q occurs. In other words, Jaccard quantifies how big the overlapping between the objects that evaluate true in q1 and those that evaluate true in q2 is.

The exploration strategy of ReRemi is based on atomic updates. First, the algorithm computes the Jaccard for all possible pairs of atomic queries, in other words all redescriptions that can be built from one feature for each view. These pairs are ranked following their Jaccard in a decreasing order and the n best pairs are kept. Starting with the best pair, the algorithm applies operations (addition, deletion, edition) on either query to improve the candidate redescription until no further improvement of the Jaccard can be done. The first redescription has been built. The algorithm then iterates on the remaining best pairs. We use the ReReMi Algorithm (Galbrun and Miettinen, 2012) implemented in Siren with the predefined parameters of the tool. Conjunctions and disjunctions are allowed in the queries but the length of a query is restricted to 4. This length restriction has an impact on the redescriptions that are found. The algorithm must maximize the Jaccard with maximum 4 features in each query. Thus some patterns that we may want to observe do not appear in the queries, because if they where used instead of another, they will make the Jaccard lower.

4 Data

The corpus contains 112 micro-texts, each of them answering a controversial issue (e.g., *"Should Germany introduce the death penalty?"*). We use 2 of the 3 types of annotations provided: the RST and argumentation representations (Peldszus and Stede, 2015). RST trees are annotated with 28 relations, with 2 to 12 relations per tree, the most frequent relations are: `reason` (180), `concession` (65), `list` (63), `conjunction` (44), `antithesis` (32), `elaboration` (37), and `cause` (20). ARG trees have 2 to 9 relations, 5 distinct relations are annotated, the most frequent being `support` (263), `rebut` (108) and `undercut` (63).

gSpan produces 311 RST and 98 ARG features, both sharing at least 2 objects.[6] The most frequent RST feature occurs in 105 texts while the most frequent ARG feature occurs in 94 texts. Only 22 RST features are shared by more than 10 texts, and 18 ARG features are shared by more than 13 texts.

5 Results

	q1	q2	J(q1,q2)	# texts
$Rd1$	a57	r40 ∨ r65 ∨ r123	0.691	54
$Rd2$	a58	r61 ∨ r119 ∨ r125	0.351	13
$Rd3$	a23 ∨ a59	r125	0.3	8

Table 1: Examples 3 redescriptions. `aX` and `rX` correspond resp. to ARG and RST subtrees.

Table 1 gives three redescription examples over the 31 obtained. For reason of space, we mainly comment and discuss these three redescriptions. $Rd1$ has the highest Jaccard value (0.691). The support value is 54, meaning that 54 texts share both the left and the right part of the redescription. $Rd2$ is a specialisation of $Rd1$, and, finally, $Rd3$ is a redescription where the conjunction is on the argumentation side. Subtrees corresponding to the query features are drawn in Figure 2, 3 and 4.

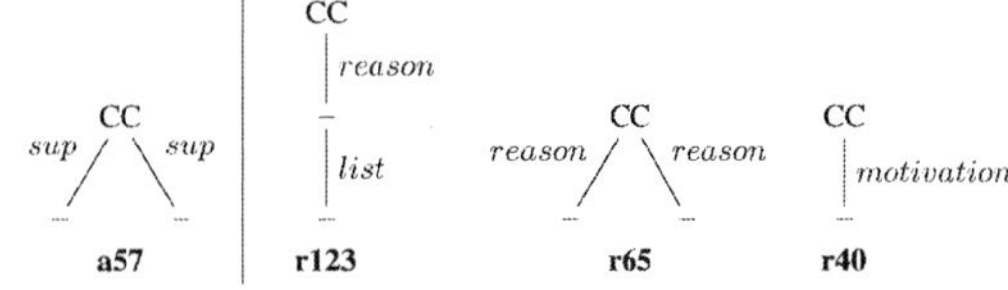

Figure 2: Subtrees corresponding to features of $Rd1$.

The 54 texts described by $Rd1$ all contain feature `a57` in their ARG tree, but the disjunction on the RST query emphasizes a difference in the granularity of ARG and RST formalisms. More precisely from the 54 texts, 30 contain `r123`, 22

---

[6]Because the parameter $\sigma_s = 2$ is given to gSpan.

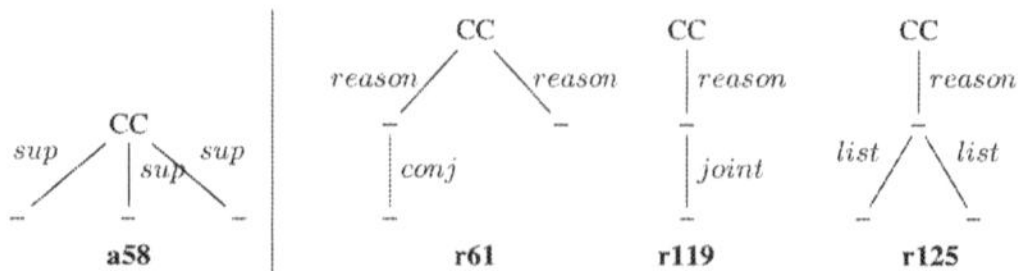

Figure 3: Subtrees corresponding to features of *Rd2*.

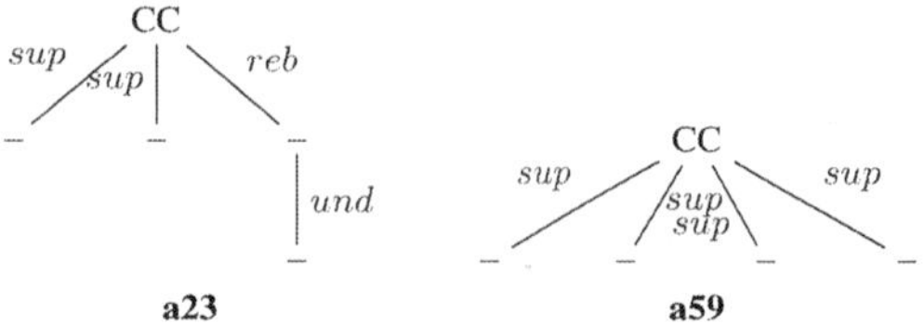

Figure 4: Subtrees corresponding to ARG features of *Rd3*, for `r125` feature see Figure 4

contain `r65`, 2 contain `r40`. In other words, in half of the data, when the ARG structure contains two `support` pointing to the CC, the RST tree includes either a `reason` relation followed by two `list`, or two `reason` relations, or one `motivation` directed to the CC. The objects described by *Rd2* and *Rd3* are also described by *Rd1* so *Rd2* and *Rd3* can be seen as specialisations of *Rd1*. *Rd2* can be read in the same way as *Rd1*, namely from 23 texts containing `a58`, 13 are aligned with either `r61` (3), or `r119` (3) or `r125` (7). Contrary to *Rd1* and *Rd2*, the disjunction on the ARG side in *Rd3* suggests that the feature `r125` (appearing 8 texts) can be mapped into two different ARG structures: `a59` which concerns 2 texts, and `a23` which concerns 5 texts.

6 Discussion

A 1(ARG)-to-many(RST) mapping: One interesting question that arises, when looking at *Rd1*, concerns the disjunction on the discourse side, i.e. different discourse structures that represent the same argumentative structure. Thus, this redescription could be an illustration of granularity difference between the two representations, RST being more fine-grained than ARG. However, by looking more precisely at the texts, we distinguish two different issues related to granularity as described below.

Granularity in labeling relations: We observe that an edge labeled by a given ARG relation can be aligned with RST edges with different labels. The explanation could be that a limited set of 5 relations is used to annotate argumentation while the annotators were given a larger set of 28 relations to annotate discourse.

As shown in (Peldszus and Stede, 2016), a `support` relation can correspond in fact to several distinct RST relations, most often `reason` and `justification` (found in another redescription), but also `motivation`, as also found via our extraction procedure. The lower frequency of `motivation` compared to `reason` could come from the fact that the latter is more generic, the former being used only to motivate actions (Carlson and Marcu, 2001).

Granularity in structure: *Rd1* seems to imply a similarity between RST structures described by `r123` and `r65`, that is a `list` embedded under a `reason`, and two `reason` directed to the CC. The `list` relation links comparable items, which is not mandatory for two `reasons` annotated independently. This fine level of granularity is not expressed in ARG trees.

Moreover, for the two cases with a `motivation` relation, we notice that the embedded node is in fact annotated either with a `list` or with a `conjunction`, the latter being very similar to the former and thus corresponding to another compatible structure. Note here that we do not extract a subtree parallel to `r123` but involving a `motivation` by applying our method: while this structure exists, it only appears once in the data, and thus does not meet our minimum support criterion. Lowering the support treshold is an option, it could be compared to the use of a relation grouping to allow an automatic recognition a priori of similar RST labels.

If we assume that discourse structures are more fine grained than argumentation structures, we could parametrised ReReMi to extract only atomic ARG queries to obtain a redescription of each single ARG structure. However, the following study of *Rd3* comes to contradict this hypothesis.

Depth and width of the subtrees: Some redescriptions with lower support and Jaccard concern deeper or larger subtrees than in *Rd1*. For example in *Rd2*, the `a58` subtree includes `a57`, `r125` includes `r123`, and `r61` includes `r65`.

It thus seems meaningful to consider that a deeper/larger structure in one view is aligned with a deeper/larger structure in the other view. Thus, we would have liked to consider *Rd2* as a specialisation of *Rd1*, emphasizing the following: when embedded within a relation matching a `support`, the multinuclear RST relations `conjunction` and `list` express an additional `support` in ARG.

However, we observe that a new subtree, namely `r119`, occurs in the RST part of *Rd2*. This non parallel new subtree being mapped to `a58` still needs further investigation.

A many(ARG)-to-1(RST) mapping: As RST structures are more fine grained than argumentation structures, we could expect ARG structures to be aligned with a disjunction of RST structures. However, the other way around is also true. *Rd3* emphasizes that some RST (`r125`) structures are aligned with a disjunction of ARG structures.

The `r125` RST tree contains 3 `lists` in a `reason` related to CC. On the ARG side, `a23` contains two `supports` and a sequence of `rebut` and `undercut` directed to the CC. The third expected `support` for `a23` to partially map `r125` comes from the following assertion: if an X `undercuts` a Y, which in turn `rebuts` the CC, then X is in a `support` relation to CC.

The pattern $a59$ is founded in 5 texts, but only 2 of them contain `r125` in their RST representation. Here, 4 `support` nodes in ARG are mapped to 3 `lists` in RST. For these 2 texts, the fourth expected `support` relation comes from deeper elements in the trees. In one of the texts, a segment that is in a `e-elaboration` in one of the `list` element is used as a `support` in the ARG tree. In the second text, a `restatement` plays the same role. Thus, nodes involved in these substructures are split into two `supports` in the ARG annotation. Despite a small Jaccard, this many-to-1 mapping is very informative.

Weakness due to tree representation: One weakness of our tree representation is that we omit the position of the segments in the text. Doing this for ARG and RST subtrees extraction allows to consider the subtrees regardless of their place in the text. However, features aligned by a redescription do not necessarily refer to the same part of the text.

In Figure 1, while text $b006$ illustrates *Rd1*, the segments contained in `a57` and `r123` do not correspond: a correct mapping would align both `support` in ARG with the `conjunction` embedded in the `reason` in RST (segments 2 and 3). In the same way, the ARG `undercut` and `rebut` in sequence would have been mapped to

the RST `concession` and `reason` in sequence (segments 4 and 5).

7 Conclusion

The alignment of text structures can be done with redescription mining applied on subtrees. The automatic process, compared to manual methods, enables a systematic comparison of different formalisms. Applied to a small corpus of argumentative texts, this preliminary experiment demonstrates the effectiveness of our approach to compare structures in different frameworks, but also to get insights on the encoding used within a specific formalism.

Several improvements are currently under study. First, as we only used the predefined parameters of ReRemi, we can reparametrize it. We can restrict the ARG side of the redescription to an atomic query in order to associate a conjunction of RST subtrees to each ARG subtree. We may also reparametrize ReReMi to get a higher number of redescriptions and possibly longer queries. Indeed, the 4-features limitation in a query blocks the emergence of more interesting features (deeper subtrees) in the redescriptions.

Second, tree representations should include links to text segments in order to enable a fairer alignement between ARG and RST structures.

Finally, the methodology could also be extended to other formalisms (e.g. SDRT), or used to provide a grouping of substructures from one theory to another.

8 Acknowledgement

This work was supported partly by the french PIA project "Lorraine Université d'Excellence", reference ANR-15-IDEX-04-LUE, and the PEPS blanc from CNRS (INS2I).

References

Elena Cabrio, Sara Tonelli, and Serena Villata. 2013. From Discourse Analysis to Argumentation Schemes and Back: Relations and Differences. In David Hutchison, Takeo Kanade, Josef Kittler, Jon M. Kleinberg, Friedemann Mattern, John C. Mitchell, Moni Naor, Oscar Nierstrasz, C. Pandu Rangan, Bernhard Steffen, Madhu Sudan, Demetri Terzopoulos, Doug Tygar, Moshe Y. Vardi, Gerhard Weikum, João Leite, Tran Cao Son, Paolo Torroni, Leon van der Torre, and Stefan Woltran, editors, *Computational Logic in Multi-Agent Systems*, volume 8143, pages 1–17. Springer, Berlin, Heidelberg.

Lynn Carlson and Daniel Marcu. 2001. Discourse tagging reference manual. Technical report, University of Southern California Information Sciences Institute.

James B Freeman. 1991. *Dialectics and the macrostructure of arguments: a theory of argument structure*. Foris Publications, Berlin.

Esther Galbrun and Pauli Miettinen. 2012. From black and white to full color: extending redescription mining outside the Boolean world. *Statistical Analysis and Data Mining: The ASA Data Science Journal*, 5(4):284–303.

Esther Galbrun and Pauli Miettinen. 2017. *Redescription Mining*. SpringerBriefs in Computer Science. Springer International Publishing.

Alex Lascarides and Nicholas Asher. 2007. Segmented Discourse Representation Theory: Dynamic Semantics With Discourse Structure. In Harry Bunt and Reinhard Muskens, editors, *Computing Meaning*, volume 3. Springer Netherlands, Dordrecht.

William Mann and Sandra Thompson. 1988. Rhetorical structure theory: Towards a functional theory of text organization. *TEXT*, 8:243–281.

Andreas Peldszus and Manfred Stede. 2013. From Argument Diagrams to Argumentation Mining in Texts: A Survey. *International Journal of Cognitive Informatics and Natural Intelligence (IJCINI)*, 7(1):1–31.

Andreas Peldszus and Manfred Stede. 2015. An annotated corpus of argumentative microtexts. In *Proceedings of the First European Conference on Argumentation: Argumentation and Reasoned Action*, volume 2, pages 801–816.

Andreas Peldszus and Manfred Stede. 2016. Rhetorical structure and argumentation structure in monologue text. In *Proceedings of the Third Workshop on Argument Mining (ArgMining2016)*, pages 103–112, Berlin, Germany. Association for Computational Linguistics.

Rashmi Prasad, Nikhil Dinesh, Alan Lee, Eleni Miltsakaki, Livio Robaldo, Aravind Joshi, and Bonnie Webber. 2008. The Penn discourse treebank 2.0. In *Proceedings of the Sixth International Language Resources and Evaluation (LREC 2008)*, Marrakech, Morocco. European Language Resources Association (ELRA).

Manfred Stede. 2008. Rst revisited: Disentangling nuclearity. *Subordination 'versus' Coordination' in Sentence and Text*, pages 33–59.

Manfred Stede, Stergos Afantenos, Andreas Peldszus, Nicholas Asher, and Jérémy Perret. 2016. Parallel discourse annotations on a corpus of short texts. In *Proceedings of the Tenth International Conference on Language Resources and Evaluation (LREC 2016)*, Paris, France. European Language Resources Association (ELRA).

Henning Wachsmuth, Giovanni Da San Martino, Dora Kiesel, and Benno Stein. 2017. The impact of modeling overall argumentation with tree kernels. In *Proceedings of the 2017 Conference on Empirical Methods in Natural Language Processing*, pages 2379–2389, Copenhagen, Denmark. Association for Computational Linguistics.

Douglas Walton, Christopher Reed, and Fabrizio Macagno. 2008. *Argumentation Schemes*. Cambridge University Press, Cambridge.

Xifeng Yan and Jiawei Han. 2002. gSpan: graph-based substructure pattern mining. In *2002 IEEE International Conference on Data Mining, 2002. Proceedings.*, pages 721–724, Maebashi City, Japan. IEEE.

Transferring knowledge from discourse to arguments:
A case study with scientific abstracts

Pablo Accuosto and Horacio Saggion

Large-Scale Text Understanding Systems Lab (LaSTUS) / TALN Group
Department of Information and Communication Technologies
Universitat Pompeu Fabra
C/Tànger 122-140, 08018 Barcelona, Spain
{name.surname}@upf.edu

Abstract

In this work we propose to leverage resources available with discourse-level annotations to facilitate the identification of argumentative components and relations in scientific texts, which has been recognized as a particularly challenging task. In particular, we implement and evaluate a transfer learning approach in which contextualized representations learned from discourse parsing tasks are used as input of argument mining models. As a pilot application, we explore the feasibility of using automatically identified argumentative components and relations to predict the acceptance of papers in computer science venues. In order to conduct our experiments, we propose an annotation scheme for argumentative units and relations and use it to enrich an existing corpus with an argumentation layer.[1]

1 Introduction

The growing number of scientific publications and the shortening of the research-publication cycles (Bornmann and Mutz, 2015) pose a challenge to authors, reviewers and editors. The development of automatic systems to support the quality assessment of scientific texts can facilitate the work of editors and referees of scientific publications and, at the same time, be of value for researchers to obtain feedback that can lead to improve the communication of their results.

The quality assessment of scientific texts has many dimensions, and each one involves different levels of difficulties. While the relevance of the problem at stake and the novelty of the solutions proposed by the authors are of great significance in terms of weighting the ultimate contributions of the work, aspects such as the argumentative structure of the text are key when analyzing its effectiveness with respect to its communication objectives (Walton and Walton, 1989). A fine-grained

---

[1]Available at `http://scientmin.taln.upf.edu/argmin/scidtb_argmin_annotations.tgz`.

assessment of the contributions made in research articles requires to identify the main claims made by the authors and to determine if the evidence provided to support them is *strong* enough. Or, in other terms, if both the structure and the contents of the arguments proposed by the authors can persuade a potential reader of the validity of their contributions.

In addition to being useful for facilitating the assessment of some quality aspects of a text, the automatic identification of argumentative units and their relations–a set of related tasks known as *argument mining*–is a relevant problem in itself in the context of knowledge mining (Mochales and Moens, 2011). Being able to extract not only what is being stated by the authors of a text but also the reasons they provide to support it can be useful in multiple applications, ranging from a fine-grained analysis of opinions to the generation of abstractive summaries of texts. As an example of a potential application for argument mining, (Lippi and Torroni, 2016) suggest the possibility of developing an argumentative ranking component in a search engine so that it retrieves documents based on claims and evidence on a given topic extracted automatically from texts.

The tasks involved in the extraction of arguments from text–including the identification of argumentative sentences, the detection of argument component boundaries and the prediction of argument structures–are related to other text mining tasks–including sequence labeling, text segmentation, entity recognition and relation extraction–which are in general tackled by means of supervised learning methods (Lippi and Torroni, 2016). The lack of annotated data with argumentative information, however, presents a challenge when trying to apply these well-known approaches to argument mining (Stab and Gurevych, 2017). This is so, in part, due to the inherent difficulty of unambiguously identifying argumentative elements

Proceedings of the 6th Workshop on Argument Mining, pages 41–51
Florence, Italy, August 1, 2019. ©2019 Association for Computational Linguistics

in texts, which is reflected in the low levels of inter-annotator agreement reached in general for this task (Habernal et al., 2014). If this is true in several knowledge domains, it poses a more difficult problem in the case of scientific texts due to their inherent argumentative complexity (Kirschner et al., 2015; Green, 2015). We propose to address this challenge by leveraging data annotated with discourse relations, as previous works suggest potential benefits in linking discourse analysis and argument mining tasks (Peldszus and Stede, 2016; Stab et al., 2014; Cabrio et al., 2013; Biran and Rambow, 2011; Green, 2015).

1.1 Contributions

- We propose to tackle the limitations posed by the lack of annotated data for argument mining in the scientific domain by leveraging existing Rhetorical Structure Theory (RST) (Mann et al., 1992) annotations in a corpus of computational linguistics abstracts (SciDTB) (Yang and Li, 2018). In order to do so:

  1. We propose and test an annotation scheme that we use to conduct a pilot annotation experiment in which we enrich a subset of the SciDTB corpus with an additional layer of argumentative structures.
  2. We explore the potential of a transfer learning approach to improve the performance of an argument mining model trained with a small volume of data annotated with the proposed scheme.

- We report preliminary results on the prediction of acceptance or rejection of scientific papers in computer science conferences based on the automatic identification of argumentative components and relations in their abstracts.

In this work we adopt a pragmatic perspective in relation to exploring the predictive potential of the argumentative structure of an abstract for the acceptance or rejection of the corresponding manuscript in a peer review process. We do not intend to imply that the ultimate quality of the papers–or even the abstracts–could be determined solely by considering this limited information.

The rest of the paper is organized as follows: in Section 2 we describe previous work, focusing, in particular, on works aimed at identifying

arguments in scientific texts. In Section 3 we describe the dataset used in our experiments and our proposed annotation scheme for fine-grained scientific argument mining. In Section 4 we describe our transfer learning experiments, their experimental settings and results and, in Section 5, we do the same with the experiments aimed at predicting the acceptance or rejection of papers in conferences. Finally, in Section 6, we summarize our main contributions and propose additional research avenues as follow-up to the current work.

2 Related work

This work is informed by previous research in the areas of argument mining, argumentation quality assessment and the relationship between discourse and argumentative structures and, from the methodological perspective, to transfer learning approaches. Due to space restrictions, we cannot cover in detail all the relevant background work. We refer the reader to (Lippi and Torroni, 2016) for a thorough summary of argument mining initiatives in various domains and with different approaches. (Wachsmuth et al., 2017) provide a comprehensive survey of quality assessment approaches in the context of computational argumentation and categorize them in relation to how they address logical, rhetorical and dialectical dimensions of argumentation. (Pan and Yang, 2010) provide an in-depth review of current trends in transfer learning, including inductive, transductive and unsupervised approaches. Furthermore, they classify the different approaches based on *what is transferred*: instances, feature representations, parameters or relational knowledge. A more direct antecedent to our work is the research conducted by Peldszus and Stede (Peldszus and Stede, 2016, 2015a; Stede et al., 2016), who annotated 112 argumentatively rich texts using RST and argumentation schemes in order to study the relationship between discourse and argumentation structures. The texts were generated in an experiment in which several participants wrote short texts of controlled linguistic and rhetoric complexity discussing a controversial issue from a pre-defined list. Based on this corpus, the authors conducted experiments in order to derive argumentative components and relations from RST trees, comparing three approaches: a transformation model, an aligner based on sub-graph matching and an evidence graph model (Peldszus and Stede, 2015b).

Our work is one of few that deal with argument mining in scientific texts which, as mentioned in Section 1, is considered as a particularly challenging domain (Kirschner et al., 2015; Green, 2015). (Stab et al., 2014) and (Kirschner et al., 2015) carried out annotation studies with scientific articles in educational research with binary argumentative and discourse relations (*support*, *attack*, *detail*, and *sequence*). In order to calculate the agreement between the annotators that participated in the process they developed a novel graph-based agreement measure, which can identify different annotations with similar meaning, thus obtaining higher agreement than with standard measures. The evaluation of argument annotations is still an open issue. (Stab et al., 2014) suggest that it might be interesting to explore, for this task, evaluation schemes that are able to deal with multiple correct annotations such as those used in text summarization. (Lauscher et al., 2018b) analyze the information shared by rhetorical and argumentative structure of scientific documents. In order to do this, they add an argumentation layer to the DrInventor Scientific Corpus (Fisas et al., 2016), which includes 40 computer graphics papers annotated with four layers including citation contexts, rhetorical role of sentences, subjective information and summarization relevance. The enriched corpus is used to trained new models for the automatic identification of claims and evidence, which are made available as a web service (Lauscher et al., 2018a). Some of the first initiatives aimed at the automatic identification of rhetorical and argumentative components in scientific texts include the Argumentative Zoning (AZ) model (Teufel et al., 1999, 2009) and the CoreSC scheme (Liakata et al., 2012). While AZ considers annotations for knowledge claims made by the authors of scientific articles, CoreSC associates research components to the parts of the texts describing them, thus obtaining a readable representation of the research process described by the paper. Both of them are sentence-based schema that are focused on the identification of the components and do not consider the relations between them. (Feltrim et al., 2006) adapted the AZ model for the automatic annotation of scientific abstracts in Portuguese (AZPort). The AZPort model was integrated as a module of SciPo,[2] a web-based tool aimed at supporting novice writers of academic

texts: given an abstract, the system classifies its sentences by means of AZPort and, based on a set of rules for well-formed rhetorical structures, it provides feedback for potential improvements (e.g., re-ordering the elements of the text or adding missing content). More recently, (Vargas-Campos and Alva-Manchego, 2016) adapted the AZPort model to Spanish (AZEsp), which was also integrated into a computer-assisted writing tool for computer science dissertations in Spanish (Sci-Esp).

3 Annotated data

In order to explore the possibility of leveraging discourse information for the identification of argumentative components and relations we add a new annotation layer to the Discourse Dependency TreeBank for Scientific Abstracts (SciDTB) (Yang and Li, 2018). SciDTB contains 798 abstracts from the ACL Anthology (Radev et al., 2013) annotated with elementary discourse units (EDUs) and relations from the RST Framework. Polynary discourse relations in RST are binarized in SciDTB following a criteria similar to the "right-heavy" transformation used in other works that represent discourse structures as dependency trees (Morey et al., 2017; Stede et al., 2016; Li et al., 2014).

We consider a subset of the SciDTB corpus consisting of 60 abstracts from the Proceedings of the 2014 Conference on Empirical Methods in Natural Language Processing (EMNLP) and transformed them into a format suitable for the GraPAT graph annotation tool (Sonntag and Stede, 2014)[3], which had been previously tailored to the specificities of our proposed annotation scheme, described in Section 3.1.

The corpus enriched with the argumentation[4] level contains a total of 327 sentences, 8012 tokens, 862 discourse units and 352 argumentative units linked by 292 argumentative relations.

3.1 Annotation scheme

Several argumentation mining works (Lippi and Torroni, 2016) use *claims* and *premises* as basic argumentative units. In the case of scientific discourse, however, it is frequent to find that claims

---

[3]http://angcl.ling.uni-potsdam.de/
resources/grapat.html

[4]The annotations are made available to download at
http://scientmin.taln.upf.edu/argmin/
scidtb_argmin_annotations.tgz

are not explicitly stated in an argumentative writing style but are instead left implicit (Hyland, 1998). The description of the problem addressed in the paper, for instance, usually conveys implicit claims in relation to the relevance of the problem at stake and/or the adequacy of the proposed approach. We introduce a fine-grained annotation scheme aimed at capturing information that accounts for the specificities of the scientific discourse, including the type of evidence that is offered to support a statement (e.g., background information, experimental data or interpretation of results). This can provide relevant information, for instance, to assess the *argumentative strength* of a text. The types of proposed units in our scheme were considered so they can be mapped–even if with a different level of granularity–to concepts in CoreSC (Liakata et al., 2010) and AZ categories, which would enable additional research on the potential of using existing annotated corpora for argument mining tasks. Like (Peldszus and Stede, 2016)–and in contrast with CoreSC and AZ–we consider EDUs as the minimal spans that can be annotated. Argumentative units can, in turn, cover multiple sentences.

The proposed units include:

- *proposal* (problem or approach)
- *assertion* (conclusion or known fact)
- *result* (interpretation of data)
- *observation* (data)
- *means* (implementation)
- *description* (definitions/other information)

In line with (Kirschner et al., 2015), we adopt in our annotation scheme the classic ***support*** and ***attack*** argumentative relations and the two discourse relations ***detail*** and ***sequence***.

Figure 1 shows a subset of the argumentative components and relations annotated in an abstract from (Zhang and Wang, 2014),[5] including a *proposal* and two supporting units: an *assertion* and a *result*. Figure 2 shows the original discourse units and relations as annotated in SciDTB.

In the subset of SciDTB annotated for our experiments, the types of argumentative units are distributed as follows: 31% of the units are of type *proposal*, 25% *assertion*, 21% *result*, 18% *means*, 3% *observation*, and 2% *description*. In turn, the relations are distributed: 45% of type *detail*, 42%

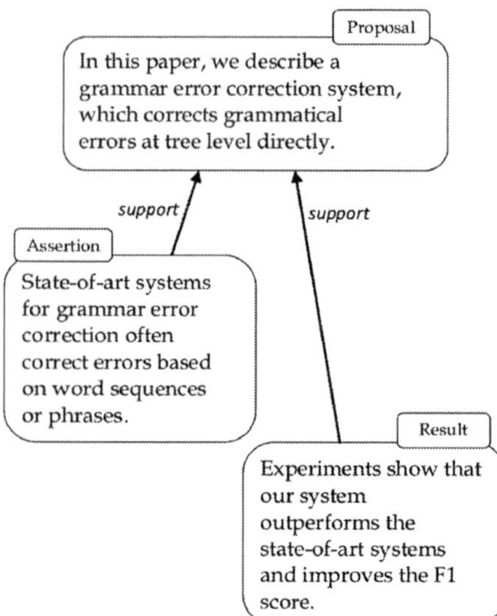

Figure 1: Partial argumentative structure

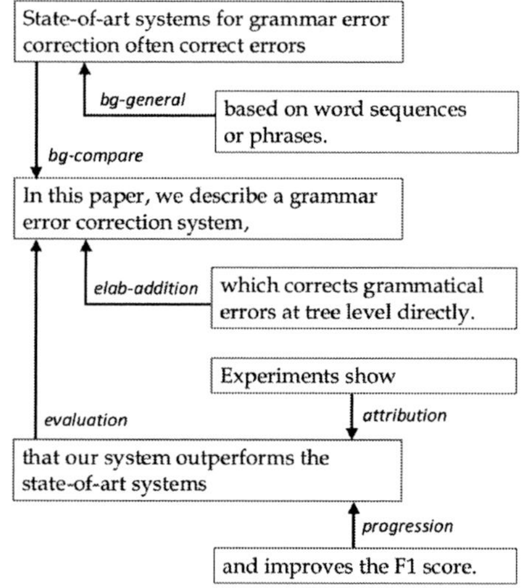

Figure 2: Partial discourse structure

support, 9% *additional*, and 4% *sequence*. No *attack* relations were identified in the set of currently annotated texts. When considering the distance[6] of the units to their parent unit in the argumentation tree, we observe that the majority (57%) are linked to a unit that occurs right before or after it in the text, while 19% are linked to a unit with a distance of 1 unit in-between, 12% to a unit with a distance of 2 units, 6% to a unit with a distance of 3, and 6% to a unit with a distance of 4 or more.[7]

---

[5] http://aclweb.org/anthology/D14-1033

[6] By *distance* we refer to the number of argumentative units that occur between two units in the text.

[7] According to the position of the parent unit, there are 200 relations pointing forward and 92 in which the parent occurs

4 Transfer learning experiment

The first set of experiments, described in this section, are aimed at exploring the potential of applying a transfer learning method to improve the performance of argument mining tasks trained with a small corpus of 60 abstracts by leveraging the discourse annotations available in the full SciDTB corpus.

4.1 Tasks

We define the following set of argument mining tasks:

- **AFu (argumentative function)**: Identify the boundaries and argumentative functions of the components. In the example in Fig. 1, it would imply to identify the boundaries of the three nodes and the two *support* relations that link them.
- **ATy (argumentative unit)**: Identify the boundaries and types of the components. In the example, the *proposal, assertion* and a *results* units.
- **APa (argumentative attachment)**: Identify the boundaries of the components and the relative position of the parent argumentative unit. For instance, the *assertion* unit in Fig. 1 is attached to the *proposal* unit with a relative distance of one unit in the forward direction (as the assertion occurs right before the proposal in the text). The *result* unit, in turn, is attached to the *proposal* with a distance of four units in the background direction (the units that occur between these two nodes are omitted in the figure).

4.2 Experimental setups

We train each of the tasks described in 4.1 separately and compare the results obtained with those obtained by an inductive transfer learning method in which we use encoders trained with the RST annotations available in the SciDTB corpus. These encoders are then used to produce contextualized representations of the input tokens that are fed to the argument mining learning processes.

The discourse parsing tasks considered to train the specialized encoders are:

- **DFu (discourse function)**: Identify the boundaries and discourse roles of the EDUs

before in the text.

(*attribution, evaluation, progression,* etc.).[8]

- **DPa (discourse attachment)**: Identify the boundaries of the EDUs and the relative position of the parent units in the RST tree.

The discourse tasks (DFu and DPa) are trained with the 738 abstracts left in the SciDTB corpus when excluding the 60 abstracts annotated with arguments. This is done in order to avoid introducing a bias that would not reflect the results obtained when no discourse annotations are available.

All the argument mining models (AFu, ATy, APa) are trained and evaluated in a 10-fold cross-validation setting.

In all cases the models are generated by means of bi-directional long short-term memory (BiLSTM) networks, as this type of architecture has proven to perform reasonably well in argument mining tasks across different classification scenarios (Eger et al., 2017). In order to simplify the experiments and the interpretation of their results we use the same architecture for all tasks: two layers of 100 recurrent units, Adam optimizer, naive dropout probability of 0.25 and a conditional random fields (CRF) classifier as the last layer of the network. We use, for the BiLSTMs, the implementation made available by the Ubiquitous Knowledge Processing Lab of the Technische Universität Darmstadt (Reimers and Gurevych, 2017).[9] As our intention is to compare the different approaches and not necessarily obtain the best possible models for these tasks, no hyperparameter optimization is done in these experiments and, in all of the cases, the networks are trained for 100 epochs.

All of the tasks are modeled as sequence labeling problems in which the tokens are tagged using the beginning-inside-outside (BIO) tagging scheme. The tokens are encoded as the concatenation of 300-dimensional dependency-based word embeddings (DEmb)[10] ($\vec{k}$) (Komninos and Manandhar, 2016) and 1024-dimensional contextualized word embeddings (ELMo) ($\vec{e}$) (Peters et al., 2018). In these experiments we use the 5.5 billion-token version of ELMo trained with Wikipedia and monolingual news from the WMT 2008-2012

---

[8]Please refer to (Yang and Li, 2018) for a description of the discourse roles used in SciDTB.

[9]`https://github.com/UKPLab/elmo-bilstm-cnn-crf`

[10]`https://www.cs.york.ac.uk/nlp/extvec/`

corpora.[11] For the experiments with the RST encoders we include the 200-dimensional embeddings obtained from the concatenation of the backward and forward hidden states of the top layers of the DFu or DPa models (RSTEnc) ($\vec{f}$ and $\vec{p}$, respectively). Table 1 summarizes the sets of embeddings used in these experiments and their dimensions.

Each argument mining task is paired with one discourse parsing task for the transfer learning experiments. While AFu and ATy are paired with DFu, APa is paired with DPa. This means that the input for the AFu and ATy tasks is obtained as the concatenation of the vectors $[\vec{k}, \vec{e}, \vec{f}]$, while in the case of APa the input is $[\vec{k}, \vec{e}, \vec{p}]$.

Abbreviation	Notation	Dimensions
DEmb	$\vec{k}$	300
ELMo	$\vec{e}$	1024
GloVe	$\vec{g}$	200
RSTEnc (DFu/DPa)	$\vec{f}$ / $\vec{p}$	200

Table 1: Word embeddings used in the experiments

4.3 Results

We adopt the ConNLL criteria for named-entity recognition[12] to evaluate the performances obtained in the identification of argumentative components and relations. Table 2 shows the average F1-measures obtained for each of the settings considering the epochs 10 to 100.[13] The argument mining models trained with the representations produced by the RST encoders (*DEmb+ELMo+RSTEnc*) yield better performances, with gains of 0.03, 0.04 and 0.02 F1 points for AFu, ATy and APa, respectively, over the models trained solely with the dependency-based and ELMo embeddings (*DEmb+ELMo*).

Setting	AFu	ATy	APa
DEmb+ELMo	0.66	0.63	0.38
DEmb+ELMo+GloVe	0.65	0.65	0.38
DEmb+ELMo+RSTEnc	**0.69**	**0.67**	**0.40**

Table 2: Average F1-measures in epochs 10-100

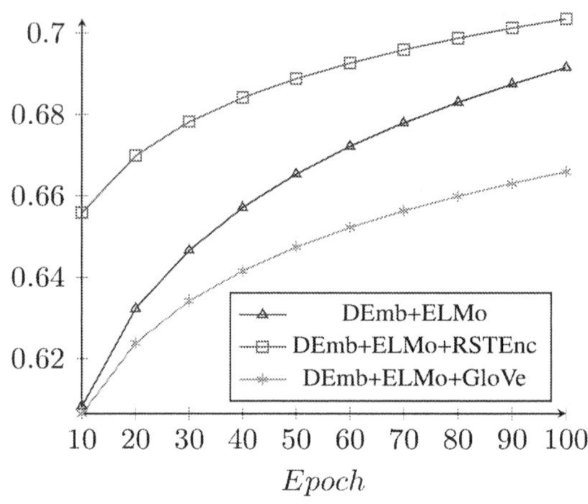

Figure 3: Trend lines for F1-measures in epochs 10-100 for AFu

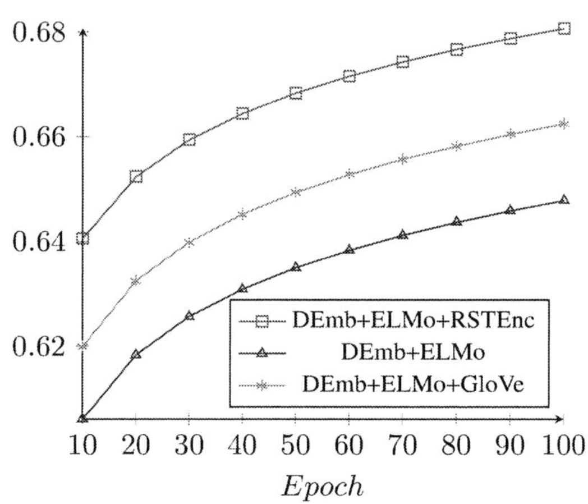

Figure 4: Trend lines for F1-measures in epochs 10-100 for ATy

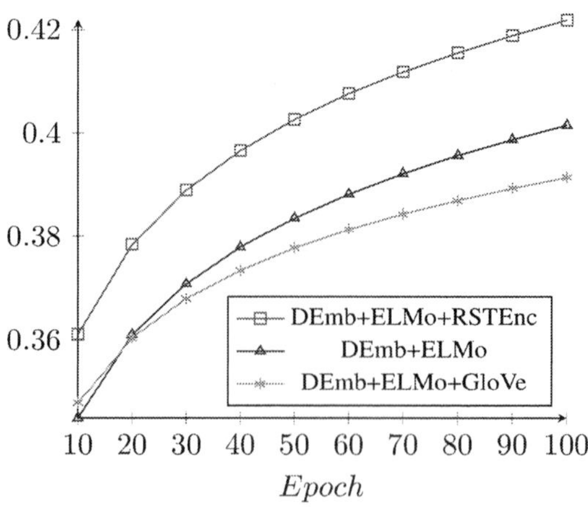

Figure 5: Trend lines for F1-measures in epochs 10-100 for APa

---

[11] https://allennlp.org/elmo

[12] A true positive is considered when both the boundary and the type of the entity match.

[13] The epochs before the 10th are not significant as the models have not had enough time to learn anything.

In order to determine whether the better performance of the RST encoders is due to the knowledge conveyed by the task-specific representations we conducted an additional experiment in which we concatenated 200-dimensional GloVe embeddings[14] (Pennington et al., 2014) ($\vec{g}$) obtaining 1524-dimension embeddings $[\vec{k}, \vec{e}, \vec{g}]$ used as input of each of the argument mining models. In this case, the results obtained are mixed, with an increase in performance of 0.02 F1 points in average–for the epochs 10 to 100–for ATy, a worse performance of 0.01 F1 points for AFu and no difference in performance for APa. The models with the GloVe embeddings (*DEmb+ELMo+GloVe*) have, therefore, worse performances in average of 0.04, 0.02 and 0.02 F1 points for AFu, ATy and APa with respect to the models that include the embeddings obtained by means of the RST encoders.

Figures 3, 4 and 5 show the trend lines of F1-measures obtained with the different models for the epochs 10 to 100 for the AFu, ATy and APa tasks, respectively. The graphs show that the models with information from the RST encoders not only learn better the argument mining tasks but they also do it in less time with respect to the other settings.

These results support out initial hypothesis in the sense that transferring discourse knowledge by means of representations learned in discourse parsing tasks can contribute to improve the performance of argument mining models trained with a rather small number of instances.

5 Acceptance prediction experiment

As a pilot application we explore the possibility of predicting the acceptance/rejection of papers in computer science conferences[15] based on the annotations generated by the best argument mining models of the experiments described in Section 4.

Quality assessment metrics that consider elements such as *clarity and simplicity, lack of redundancy and comprehensiveness* of scientific reporting have been developed for abstracts in other domains–in particular, in life sciences–(Timmer et al., 2003). These instruments were used in studies that show that abstracts with higher formal quality scores–as measured by human experts–are more frequently accepted for presentations in conferences (Timmer et al., 2001). We do not believe that these results can be directly extrapolated to the quality assessment of scientific abstracts in computer science, an area in which full manuscripts are most frequently considered for review and where abstracts have less fixed structures. Furthermore, clearer links between the formal quality of scientific reporting and the overall quality of research in computer science still need to be established. Considering all these limitations, we were interested in exploring whether the automatically identified argumentative structure of the abstracts could reflect some quality aspects of the full manuscripts and if this, in turn, could contribute to predict their acceptance in conferences in a specific research area in the field of computer science.

5.1 Dataset

As training set for the acceptance prediction experiment we use 117 abstracts of manuscripts submitted to the Compact Deep Neural Network Representation with Industrial Applications (CDNNRIA) and the Interpretability and Robustness for Audio, Speech and Language (IRASL) workshops held in the context of the Thirty-second Conference on Neural Information Processing Systems (NIPS 2018). As test set we use 30 abstracts of manuscripts submitted to the Sixth International Conference on Learning Representations (ICLR 2018). All of the abstracts were collected from the OpenReviews website (Soergel et al., 2013).[16]

The distribution of accepted/rejected papers in the training and test sets is shown in Table 3

Set	Conference	Accepted	Rejected
Train	*CDNNRIA*	35	23
Train	*IRASL*	30	29
		55	52
Test	*ICLR*	15	15

Table 3: Accepted/rejected papers in training and test sets

5.2 Experimental setup

The CDNNRIA, IRASL and ICLR abstracts are used as input to the AFu, ATy and APa models

---

[14]We used the 6 billion tokens versions trained with Wikipedia 2014 and Gigaword 5 available at `https://nlp.stanford.edu/projects/glove/`

[15]In particular, in the areas of neural-based systems and its applications to speech and language.

[16]`https://openreview.net/`

described in Section 4 obtaining sequences of argumentative units, types and parent attachments. These sequences are then used as features to train and evaluate a binary classifier aimed at predicting the acceptance or rejection of the corresponding papers. Table 4 shows sample training/test instances. As the number of argumentative units identified in each abstract might differ we use padding values (*nofunc*, *notype* and *100* for AFu, ATy and APa, respectively) to generate training and test instances with a fixed number of features (equal to three times the maximum number of argumentative units identified in the dataset).

x_1	x_2	...	x_n
none	*additional*	...	*support*
support	*support*	...	*none*
...	...	...	...
support	*nofunc*	...	*nofunc*
proposal	*assertion*	...	*assertion*
result	*assertion*	...	*proposal*
...	...	...	...
observation	*notype*	...	*notype*
0	*1*	...	*1*
1	*1*	...	*0*
...	...	...	...
-5	*100*	...	*100*

y_1	y_2	...	y_n
REJECT	ACCEPT		ACCEPT

Table 4: Example of input instances to the classifier

Considering that we are dealing with a small set of features with a reduced number of potential values for each one, we use a decision tree algorithm for our pilot classification experiment. In addition to the training and evaluation speed of the algorithm we consider that the higher interpretability of the results–by examining the decision points–can also contribute to assess to what degree the different elements of the predicted argumentative structure are used in the classification. We use Weka's implementation of the C4.5 algorithm (Quinlan, 1993) (J48) with default parameters with the exception of the confidence factor used for pruning the tree, which was selected evaluating the different models obtained against a random split of 20% of the test set used for validation.[17] As the training set is not perfectly

balanced, we pre-process the data with Weka's ClassBalancer algorithm, which assigns weights to each instance so that each class has the same total weight.

5.3 Results

The classifier trained with the argumentative units and relations extracted from the CDNNRIA/IRASL abstracts has a performance of 0.67 F1-score when evaluated with the training set obtained from processing the ICLR abstracts,[18] 0.17 F1 points above a random binary classification in a balanced set. As expected, the main decision points in the tree correspond, broadly, to those attributes that are also ranked higher when measuring their contribution to reduce the entropy with respect to the class.[19] Observing these features, we can see that the most relevant decision elements are the parent attachment of first argumentative unit, the argumentative functions of the first two units and the argumentative type of the first unit. Also relevant are the features that mark the end of the sequences of argumentative types and functions for the majority of the instances. This means that the number of identified units also have a relevant role in the predictions. However, the number of units by themselves is not a good predictor of the abstract's class. In fact, executing the same experiment but replacing the non-padding values for function, type and attachment for fixed values we obtain an F1-measure of 0.59 due, in particular, to a higher number of false negatives (accepted papers classified as rejected).

Features	P	R	F1
Arg. units alone	0.67	0.53	0.59
Arg. units with types, functions and parents	0.67	0.67	**0.67**

Table 5: Precision, recall and F1-measures for the acceptance prediction classifiers with and without fine-grained argumentative information

6 Conclusions and future work

In this work we explored the potential of leveraging existing discourse-annotated corpora to im-

---

[17] `weka.classifiers.trees.J48 -C0.6 -M2`

[18] 20 of the abstracts were correctly classified and ten were mis-classified: five as false positives and five as false negatives

[19] As calculated by means of Weka's InfoGainAttributeEval algorithm.

prove the performance of fine-grained argument mining models trained with a limited number of examples. In order to test our hypothesis, we proposed an annotation scheme and used it to enrich, with a new layer of argumentative structures, a subset of a corpus previously annotated with discourse-level units and relations. Promising results are obtained by implementing an inductive transfer learning method in which contextualized representations obtained by means of encoders trained with discourse parsing tasks are used as input of argument mining models. As a potential application of the annotations produced by the argument mining models, we implemented a simple classifier aimed at predicting the potential acceptance/rejection of computer science papers according to the argumentative structure of their abstracts. The results of these preliminary experiments are auspicious and motivate us to continue working in this area. As a first step in this direction, we plan to extend the coverage of the argumentative layer of annotations to the full SciDTB corpus. We expect this to become a valuable resource in argument mining research in scientific texts which, as mentioned, has been identified as a particularly challenging domain.

The obtained results open several paths up for additional research, including the implementation of other transfer learning approaches–e.g., multi-task learning settings[20]–as well as other neural architectures–including attention-based architectures, which have proven to achieve good results in argument mining tasks (Stab et al., 2018). As mentioned in Section 3.1, we are also interested in exploring the possibility of leveraging other existing tools and resources to facilitate the automatic identification of argumentative structures and relations, such as corpora annotated with different schema–including variants of CoreSC and AZ. We also intend to expand our acceptance prediction experiments using the PeerRead dataset (Kang et al., 2018),[21] which has a greater coverage than the NIPS and ICLR subsets that we used in our experiments. This dataset contains, in addition to the acceptance/rejection decisions, scores for different aspects of the papers–including *substance* and *clarity*, among others–, which would allow us to explore in more depth whether the ar-

gumentative structure of the abstracts–and, potentially, other sections–relate to more specific quality aspects of the manuscripts.

Acknowledgments

This work is (partly) supported by the Spanish Government under the María de Maeztu Units of Excellence Programme (MDM-2015-0502).

References

Or Biran and Owen Rambow. 2011. Identifying justifications in written dialogs by classifying text as argumentative. *International Journal of Semantic Computing*, 5(04):363–381.

Lutz Bornmann and Rüdiger Mutz. 2015. Growth rates of modern science: A bibliometric analysis based on the number of publications and cited references. *Journal of the Association for Information Science and Technology*, 66(11):2215–2222.

Elena Cabrio, Sara Tonelli, and Serena Villata. 2013. From discourse analysis to argumentation schemes and back: Relations and differences. In *International Workshop on Computational Logic in Multi-Agent Systems*, pages 1–17. Springer.

Steffen Eger, Johannes Daxenberger, and Iryna Gurevych. 2017. Neural end-to-end learning for computational argumentation mining. In *Proceedings of the 55th Annual Meeting of the Association for Computational Linguistics (ACL 2017)*, volume Volume 1: Long Papers, pages (11–22). Association for Computational Linguistics.

Valéria D. Feltrim, Simone Teufel, Maria Graças V. das Nunes, and Sandra M. Aluísio. 2006. *Argumentative Zoning Applied to Critiquing Novices' Scientific Abstracts*, pages 233–246. Springer Netherlands, Dordrecht.

Beatriz Fisas, Francesco Ronzano, and Horacio Saggion. 2016. A multi-layered annotated corpus of scientific papers. In *LREC*.

Nancy Green. 2015. Identifying argumentation schemes in genetics research articles. In *Proceedings of the 2nd Workshop on Argumentation Mining*, pages 12–21.

Ivan Habernal, Judith Eckle-Kohler, and Iryna Gurevych. 2014. Argumentation mining on the web from information seeking perspective. In *Proceedings of the Workshop on Frontiers and Connections between Argumentation Theory and Natural Language Processing, Forlì-Cesena, Italy, July 21-25, 2014*.

Ken Hyland. 1998. *Hedging in scientific research articles*, volume 54 of *Pragmatics Beyond New Series*. John Benjamins Publishing.

---

[20]We conducted preliminary experiments in this area with mixed results, so we plan to continue investigating this approach in order to clarify its true potential.

[21]https://github.com/allenai/PeerRead

Dongyeop Kang, Waleed Ammar, Bhavana Dalvi, Madeleine van Zuylen, Sebastian Kohlmeier, Eduard Hovy, and Roy Schwartz. 2018. A dataset of peer reviews (PeerRead): Collection, insights and NLP applications. In *Proceedings of the 2018 Conference of the North American Chapter of the Association for Computational Linguistics: Human Language Technologies (NAACL 2018)*, New Orleans, Louisiana. Association for Computational Linguistics.

Christian Kirschner, Judith Eckle-Kohler, and Iryna Gurevych. 2015. Linking the thoughts: Analysis of argumentation structures in scientific publications. In *Proceedings of the 2nd Workshop on Argumentation Mining*, pages 1–11.

Alexandros Komninos and Suresh Manandhar. 2016. Dependency-based embeddings for sentence classification tasks. In *Proceedings of the 2016 conference of the North American Chapter of the Association for Computational Linguistics: Human language technologies (NAACL 2016)*, pages 1490–1500.

Anne Lauscher, Goran Glavaš, and Kai Eckert. 2018a. ArguminSci: A tool for analyzing argumentation and rhetorical aspects in scientific writing. In *Proceedings of the 5th Workshop on Argument Mining (ArgMining2018)*, pages 22–28.

Anne Lauscher, Goran Glavaš, and Simone Paolo Ponzetto. 2018b. An argument-annotated corpus of scientific publications. In *Proceedings of the 5th Workshop on Argument Mining (ArgMining2018)*, pages 40–46.

Sujian Li, Liang Wang, Ziqiang Cao, and Wenjie Li. 2014. Text-level discourse dependency parsing. In *Proceedings of the 52nd Annual Meeting of the Association for Computational Linguistics (ACL 2014) (Volume 1: Long Papers)*, volume 1, pages 25–35.

Maria Liakata, Shyamasree Saha, Simon Dobnik, Colin Batchelor, and Dietrich Rebholz-Schuhmann. 2012. Automatic recognition of conceptualization zones in scientific articles and two life science applications. *Bioinformatics*, 28(7):991–1000.

Maria Liakata, Simone Teufel, Advaith Siddharthan, and Colin Batchelor. 2010. Corpora for the conceptualisation and zoning of scientific papers.

Marco Lippi and Paolo Torroni. 2016. Argumentation mining: State of the art and emerging trends. *ACM Transactions on Internet Technology (TOIT)*, 16(2):10.

William C Mann, CMIM Matthiessen, and Sandra A Thompson. 1992. Rhetorical structure theory and text analysis. *Discourse description: Diverse linguistic analyses of a fund-raising text*, pages 39–78.

Raquel Mochales and Marie-Francine Moens. 2011. Argumentation mining. *Artificial Intelligence and Law*, 19(1):1–22.

Mathieu Morey, Philippe Muller, and Nicholas Asher. 2017. How much progress have we made on RST discourse parsing? a replication study of recent results on the RST-DT. In *Proceedings of the 2017 Conference on Empirical Methods in Natural Language Processing (EMNLP 2017)*, pages 1319–1324, Copenhagen, Denmark. Association for Computational Linguistics.

Sinno Jialin Pan and Qiang Yang. 2010. A survey on transfer learning. *IEEE Transactions on knowledge and data engineering*, 22(10):1345–1359.

Andreas Peldszus and Manfred Stede. 2015a. An annotated corpus of argumentative microtexts. In *Proceedings of the First Conference on Argumentation, Lisbon, Portugal*.

Andreas Peldszus and Manfred Stede. 2015b. Joint prediction in MST-style discourse parsing for argumentation mining. In *Proceedings of the 2015 Conference on Empirical Methods in Natural Language Processing (EMNLP 2015)*, pages 938–948.

Andreas Peldszus and Manfred Stede. 2016. Rhetorical structure and argumentation structure in monologue text. In *Proceedings of the Third Workshop on Argument Mining (ArgMining2016)*, pages 103–112.

Jeffrey Pennington, Richard Socher, and Christopher Manning. 2014. GloVe: Global vectors for word representation. In *Proceedings of the 2014 Conference on Empirical Methods in Natural Language Processing (EMNLP 2014)*, pages 1532–1543.

Matthew E Peters, Mark Neumann, Mohit Iyyer, Matt Gardner, Christopher Clark, Kenton Lee, and Luke Zettlemoyer. 2018. Deep contextualized word representations. *arXiv preprint arXiv:1802.05365*.

J. Ross Quinlan. 1993. *C4.5: Programs for Machine Learning*. Morgan Kaufmann Publishers Inc., San Francisco, CA, USA.

Dragomir R Radev, Pradeep Muthukrishnan, Vahed Qazvinian, and Amjad Abu-Jbara. 2013. The ACL Anthology Network corpus. *Language Resources and Evaluation*, 47(4):919–944.

Nils Reimers and Iryna Gurevych. 2017. Reporting score distributions makes a difference: Performance study of LSTM-networks for sequence tagging. *arXiv preprint arXiv:1707.09861*.

David Soergel, Adam Saunders, and Andrew McCallum. 2013. Open scholarship and peer review: a time for experimentation. In *ICML Workshop on Peer Reviewing and Publishing Models (PEER)*.

Jonathan Sonntag and Manfred Stede. 2014. GraPAT: A tool for graph annotations. In *LREC*, pages 4147–4151.

Christian Stab and Iryna Gurevych. 2017. Parsing argumentation structures in persuasive essays. *Computational Linguistics*, 43(3):619–659.

Christian Stab, Christian Kirschner, Judith Eckle-Kohler, and Iryna Gurevych. 2014. Argumentation mining in persuasive essays and scientific articles from the discourse structure perspective. In *Proceedings of the Workshop on Frontiers and Connections between Argumentation Theory and Natural Language Processing, Forlì-Cesena, Italy, July 21-25, 2014*, pages 21–25.

Christian Stab, Tristan Miller, Benjamin Schiller, Pranav Rai, and Iryna Gurevych. 2018. Cross-topic argument mining from heterogeneous sources. In *Proceedings of the 2018 Conference on Empirical Methods in Natural Language Processing (EMNLP 2018)*, pages 3664–3674.

Manfred Stede, Stergos D Afantenos, Andreas Peldszus, Nicholas Asher, and Jérémy Perret. 2016. Parallel discourse annotations on a corpus of short texts. In *LREC*.

Simone Teufel, Advaith Siddharthan, and Colin Batchelor. 2009. Towards discipline-independent argumentative zoning: Evidence from chemistry and computational linguistics. In *Proceedings of the 2009 Conference on Empirical Methods in Natural Language Processing (EMNLP 2009) (Volume 3)*, pages 1493–1502. Association for Computational Linguistics.

Simone Teufel et al. 1999. *Argumentative zoning: Information extraction from scientific text*. Ph.D. thesis, University of Edinburgh.

Antje Timmer, Robert J Hilsden, and Lloyd R Sutherland. 2001. Determinants of abstract acceptance for the digestive diseases week–a cross sectional study. *BMC medical research methodology*, 1(1):13.

Antje Timmer, Lloyd R Sutherland, and Robert J Hilsden. 2003. Development and evaluation of a quality score for abstracts. *BMC medical research methodology*, 3(1):2.

Irvin Vargas-Campos and Fernando Alva-Manchego. 2016. Sciesp: Structural analysis of abstracts written in spanish. *Computación y Sistemas*, 20(3):551–558.

Henning Wachsmuth, Nona Naderi, Yufang Hou, Yonatan Bilu, Vinodkumar Prabhakaran, Tim Alberdingk Thijm, Graeme Hirst, and Benno Stein. 2017. Computational argumentation quality assessment in natural language. In *Proceedings of the 15th Conference of the European Chapter of the Association for Computational Linguistics (ACL 2017) (Volume 1: Long Papers)*, pages 176–187.

Douglas N Walton and David N Walton. 1989. *Informal logic: A handbook for critical argument*. Cambridge University Press.

An Yang and Sujian Li. 2018. SciDTB: Discourse dependency TreeBank for scientific abstracts. In *Proceedings of the 56th Annual Meeting of the Association for Computational Linguistics (ACL 2018) (Volume 2: Short Papers)*, pages 444–449, Melbourne, Australia. Association for Computational Linguistics.

Longkai Zhang and Houfeng Wang. 2014. Go climb a dependency tree and correct the grammatical errors. In *Proceedings of the 2014 Conference on Empirical Methods in Natural Language Processing (EMNLP 2014)*, pages 266–277, Doha, Qatar. Association for Computational Linguistics.

The Swedish PoliGraph:
A Semantic Graph for Argument Mining of Swedish Parliamentary Data

Stian Rødven Eide

Språkbanken Text
Department of Swedish
University of Gothenburg
`stian.rodven.eide@svenska.gu.se`

Abstract

As part of a larger project on argument mining of Swedish parliamentary data, we have created a semantic graph that, together with named entity recognition and resolution (NER), should make it easier to establish connections between arguments in a given debate. The graph is essentially a semantic database that keeps track of Members of Parliament (MPs), in particular their presence in the parliament and activity in debates, but also party affiliation and participation in commissions. The hope is that the Swedish PoliGraph will enable us to perform named entity resolution on debates in the Swedish parliament with a high accuracy, with the aim of determining to whom an argument is directed.

1 Introduction

While argument mining still is a young task in the field of computational linguistics, it has received much attention during the last five years. Parliamentary data is not only an ideal application of this, but also often a treasure trove of training data, given its standardised language and detailed accompanying metadata. Debates from the Swedish parliament, which will be the main focus for this project, are available from 1971 until the present date, with particularly detailed metadata present from 1993 and onward. The ultimate task of our project is to evaluate and develop tools for argument mining on these debates. As a first step, we have created the Swedish PoliGraph, a semantic graph to aid us in achieving our goal. Following the completion of this graph, we will use it to improve upon methods for NER that, in turn, can assist in determining the structure of discourse present in the various debates in the Swedish parliament.

2 About the Swedish Parliamentary Data

Coinciding with the ratification of *Lag (2010:566) om vidareutnyttjande av handlingar från den offentliga förvaltningen*, a law commonly known as *PSI-lagen* 're-use of Public Sector Information', *Riksdagens öppna data* 'parliamentary open data', from here on abbreviated as RÖD) was published in 2010. A massive collection of structured content from the databases of the Swedish parliament, RÖD is continuously updated, both with new data and with the gaps in older data filled in.

The available data is sorted into five categories: Documents, MPs, voting results, speeches and calendar. Of these, the documents constitute the largest category, with a substantial amount of data from 1971 and onward. The categories for MPs and voting results consist mostly of metadata, while speeches are transcripts of both addresses and replies, accompanied by extensive metadata, starting from 1993.[1]

In addition to their availability through a well documented API, the data can be downloaded in several formats, including HTML, plain text, CSV, XML, JSON and SQL.

For the initial stages of this project, we choose to focus on the speeches category (*anföranden* in Swedish), as this dataset is relatively consistent, fairly complete and contains the most metadata. Once we have developed our methods for argument mining, we can extend the data to include older protocols from debates dating back to 1971. A *speech* in this context refers to an entry in a debate, and the term will be used in this sense throughout the paper.

---

[1]An exhaustive description of the various available datasets cannot be given in this paper. The documents category in particular contains 40 different types of documents. Please see the RÖD website at `https://data.riksdagen.se/` and Riksdagen's page for descriptions of the various document types at `https://www.riksdagen.se/sv/Dokument-Lagar/`.

Proceedings of the 6th Workshop on Argument Mining, pages 52–57
Florence, Italy, August 1, 2019. ©2019 Association for Computational Linguistics

3 Development Details

3.1 The RÖD Documents

After removing a small number of ill-formed documents, we ended up with 325 202 speeches in our dataset. Starting with the downloads from RÖD in JSON format, each speech is one document, and constitutes one entry in a debate in the Swedish parliament. Most debates are on specific propositions from either the government, parliamentarians or commissions, though there are also weekly meetings in the parliament where MPs can address ministers directly with questions. Debates usually end with a voting session, the details of which are stored in a different dataset. At a later stage, we will combine our argument analysis with the votes in order to better understand the relationship between debates and the resulting votes.

3.2 Speeches

A typical speech document contains the metadata as outlined in table 1. Of particular importance here is *dok_id*, which designates the meeting in question, *anforande_nummer*, referring to the number of this speech in the chronological order of speeches during that meeting, and *rel_dok_id*, which is the ID of the proposition that is being debated. In order to map a single debate, we therefore need to:

1. Find all speeches with a given *rel_dok_id*.
2. Determine the meeting(s) this was debated in.
3. Establish the chronological order of the speeches during these meetings.
4. Analyse each speech and attempt to determine which previous speech or speeches (if any) was/were addressed or argued against.

3.3 Members of Parliament

For the Swedish PoliGraph, we have combined the speech information with metadata from the MP category, which includes basic biographical information as well as a complete history of their roles in the parliament. Such roles are usually their time working as an MP and commission work, but also longer sick leave is listed here as well as their substitutes in those cases. In addition to the essential identifiers "name" and "party", mappings are also created to MP's Wikidata-IDs and their listed name there, which sometimes provide more detail than the names as they are stored in RÖD.

The roles of MPs are generally described in terms of positions, where each assignment (or leave from that assignment) is stored as a factual predicate with eight arguments:

1. MP-ID
   A unique ID for each MP.
2. Agency code
   An identifying code for the agency. This can be ambiguous, as parties and commissions sometimes use the same identifier.
3. Role
   The MP's role in the agency, e.g. parliamentarian, commission chair or substitute.
4. From
   Starting date of the position.
5. To
   End date of the position.
6. Type
   The type of position, usually either "kammaruppdrag" for the parliament or "uppdrag" for commission work.
7. Uppdrag
   The info here varies. For commission work and other extraparliamentary duties, it contains the full name of the commission or equivalent. For extended leave, it lists the name of substitutes.
8. Status
   The MP's presence or absence during the given period.

Property	Description
dok_hangar_id	Internal document ID
dok_id	Meeting + speech no.
dok_titel	Protocol title
dok_rm	Parliamentary year
dok_nummer	Number of meeting
dok_datum	Date of speech
avsnittsrubrik	Topic title
underrubrik	Topic subtitle
kammaraktivitet	Type of debate
anforande_id	Unique speech ID
anforande_nummer	Speech number in debate
talare	Speaker name
parti	Speaker party
anforandetext	Full speech text
intressent_id	Speaker's ID
rel_dok_id	Document being debated
replik	Speech type
systemdatum	Date of publishing

Table 1: A typical speech document.

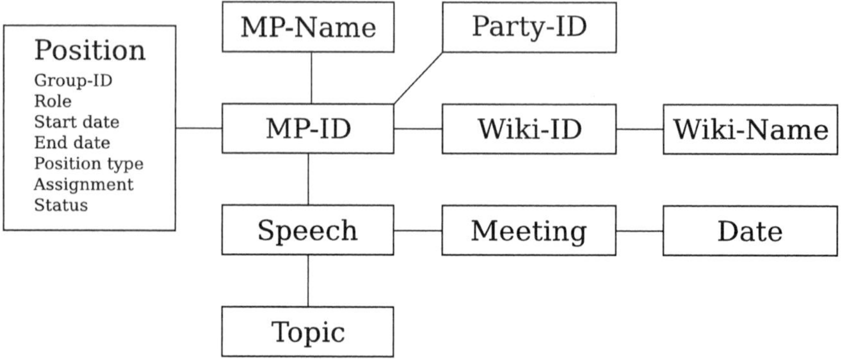

Figure 1: A semantic graph of Swedish MPs and debates.

3.4 Implementation

For our rendering of these data as a semantic graph, we chose to create a deductive database in SWI-Prolog, and combine it with the Pengines framework in order to offer web access. Prolog's modular nature allows for very quick prototyping and makes it easy to combine existing rules instead of writing complicated queries such as would be required with SQL or SPARQL. With Pengines, web access is offered simultaneously through a web interface and RPC (Remote Procedure Call) commands passed directly to the server from any Prolog client (Lager and Wielemaker, 2014).

Our Prolog database ended up consisting of a number of files, each mapping identifiers and properties to each other. In order to make NER as accurate as possible, we created mappings to MPs' names both as they are listed in the Swedish parliament and how they appear on Wikipedia. This, of course, includes a mapping between unique MP IDs in the parliament and their respective Wikidata-ID, which can potentially be of use for further integration with other analytical tools. For MPs, we also created a file listing their party affiliation that probably will be a necessary step in resolving name ambiguity, as well the previously mentioned position file that details their formal time in parliament and and activity in various commissions. Finally, we have two files that map meetings to dates and debate topics, respectively. An approximation of the resulting graph can be seen in figure 1.[2] The edges should be read as *has* or *is*, with either MP-ID or the node closest to it as the subject.

____
[2] An approximation in the sense that Prolog predicates can have any number of arguments. The Speech and Meeting nodes are for instance mapped to MP-ID and each other in the same predicate.

4 Usage Details

The Swedish PoliGraph is available to use and download from `https://spraakbanken.` `gu.se/poligraph/` under a Creative Commons Attribution licence.[3] We ask that this paper be cited in any published work using the code or the graph.

4.1 Rule Construction

In contrast to relational database queries, Prolog queries are largely dependent on rule construction. For the Swedish PoliGraph, we have created a small set of specialised rules for the purpose of disambiguating names and titles that specifically refer to MPs. A Prolog rule is essentially a list of predicates that must be true in order to satisfy a query. These predicates can be either facts or other rules. Any argument can be substituted with a variable that will, when queried, provide any answer for which that predicate would be true. To give an example, a rule stating that a given politician was an elected and working MP on a given date would be:

```
was_in_rd(Name, Date) :-
    rid_sname(Rid, Name),
    position(Rid,'kam',_,From,Tom,_,_,Status),
    Date >= From,
    Date =< Tom,
    Status \= 'Ledig'.
```

In somewhat clearer English, this rule states that: A person with a given *Name* was an elected and working MP on a given *Date* **IF** there exists a mapping from that name to an MP-ID **AND** that MP-ID had a position in *kam* (eng: the parliament) in that period **AND** their status in that time was not *Ledig* (eng: away).

____
[3] `https://creativecommons.org/licenses/` `by/4.0/`

4.2 Using the Swedish PoliGraph

There are three ways of using the Swedish Poli-Graph: (1) local querying with SWI-Prolog; (2) remote querying with SWI-Prolog and Pengines; and (3) via the web interface. Of these, the latter will necessarily be more limited in functionality than the other two, since a practically usable web interface will not be able to reproduce the flexibility that Prolog queries provide.

4.2.1 Local Querying

A central feature of Prolog as a programming language is its *declarative* nature. A Prolog program consists of facts and rules, and are usually interacted with in terms of queries, not unlike relational databases. For the Swedish PoliGraph, we have defined a number of predicates that can be queried directly, although it is also possible for a user to define new predicates extending or combining the existent ones.

In order to start using the Swedish PoliGraph locally, start SWI-Prolog and load the main program file with `[poligraph]`. There you will be able to query both the basic facts and the more complex rules. Note that for any argument, you can use either a quoted string or a number to search for an exact match, or use an upper-case string for a variable. Some simple examples are as follows:

```
/* ID of any MP with last name 'Löfven' */
?- rid_lname(Rid,'Löfven').
Rid = 218878014918.

/* Wikidata-ID for an MP-ID */
?- rid_wid(218878014918, Wid).
Wid = 'Q2740012'.

/* Party affiliation for an MP-ID */
?- rid_parti(218878014918, Party).
Party = 'S'.
```

The main predicate, however, is constructed for the following purpose: We have a speech, in which a name is mentioned. In order to resolve the name, we wish to see who by that name was talking previously in the same debate. Preferably we know both the meeting number (*dok_id*) and the topic (*rel_dok_id*). As an example, in a debate on 2016-12-12 on the topic of communication infrastructure, MP Teres Lindberg mentioned an Erik Ottoson in her speech, which was the 75th speech in that debate. Querying our program, we get the MP-ID, party affiliation and speech number(s) for that person's earlier participation in the debate:

```
?- had_previous_anf('Erik Ottoson', Rid, Anf, Party,
     'H401TU1', 'H40944', 75, _).
Rid = 832311880029,
Anf = 74,
Party = 'M' ;
```

```
Rid = 832311880029,
Anf = 72,
Party = 'M' ;
```

In more complex cases, a speaker may not provide the full name of the person they refer to, but rather just their last name or a phrase that only includes their party affiliation. We can then use the same predicate, retrieving the same information plus any additional matches. Where there exists ambiguity in the results, such as several people with the same last name or party affiliation, we can apply simple heuristics, e.g. the last speech before the current speaker's, to identify our target.

In a given query, any of the information we provide can be substituted with a variable, or vice versa. This means that we can get all speeches from a given party in a given debate by using variables for everything except Party and Topic:

```
?- had_anf(Name, Rid, Anf, 'S', 'H401TU1', Meeting).
Name = 'Lindberg',
Rid = 559925283228,
Anf = 73,
Meeting = 'H40944' ;
Name = 'Johansson',
Rid = 691264514114,
Anf = 63,
Meeting = 'H40944' ;
```

A complete list of currently defined predicates can be seen in table 2.

4.2.2 Remote Querying with Pengines

By using the Pengines library for SWI-Prolog, the Swedish PoliGraph can be queried remotely. This works essentially the same as local querying, except that the query is wrapped in a predicate `pengine_rpc/3`.[4] The predicate takes three arguments: The URL of the Pengines server, the predicate you wish to run and a list of options, which must include the name of the application on the server. Submitting our previous example over `pengine_rpc/3` would look like this:

```
?- pengine_rpc(
     'https://spraakbanken.gu.se/poligraph/',
     rid_lname(Rid,'Löfven'),
     [application(poligraph)]
).
```

Pengines also allows for several other options, such as specifying which information should be transferred between the client and the server and passing user-created predicates to be used in the query. For details on these options, we refer to Lager and Wielemaker (2014) and the official Pengines documentation[5].

---

[4]The trailing /3 is a Prolog convention to show the arity of a predicate.

[5]`http://www.swi-prolog.org/pldoc/package/pengines.html`

Predicate	Description
`rid_sname/2`	Maps an MP-ID to that person's sorting name, e.g. 'Löfven,Stefan'
`rid_wname/2`	Maps an MP-ID to that person's Wikipedia name, e.g. 'Stefan Löfven'
`rid_lname/2`	Maps an MP-ID to that person's last name
`rid_fname/2`	Maps an MP-ID to that person's first name
`rid_name/2`	Maps an MP-ID to any of the names above
`rid_wid/2`	Maps an MP-ID to that person's Wikidata-ID
`rid_party/2`	Maps an MP-ID to that person's party affiliation
`position/8`	See section 3.3 for details
`anforande/3`	Maps a speech to a meeting number (dok_id) and an MP-ID
`dokid_date/2`	Maps a meeting number (dok_id) to its date
`meet_anf_topic/3`	Maps a topic to a meeting number (dok_id) and a speech number
`had_previous_anf/8`	Matches previous speeches. See section 4.2.1 for details
`had_anf/6`	Gives speeches with topic, speaker, speech number, party and dok_id
`had_anf/4`	Gives the name, ID and party affiliation for all speeches on a given date
`was_in_rd/3`	Who was in the parliament in a given period
`was_mp/3`	Who was an elected MP (non-minister) in a given period
`was_minister/3`	Who was a minister in a given period
`was_ledig/3`	Who was on leave from the parliament in a given period
`has_position/3`	A simplification of position/8 – Matches MP's to their assignments

Table 2: A list of currently defined predicates.

4.2.3 The Web Interface

The web interface is by necessity simplified and only allows for a few selected queries. As such it is primarily intended for demonstration purposes, but it can also be used for qualitative research.

5 Related Work

While argumentation mining is a recent field of study where little has been done on parliamentary data (see e.g. Lippi and Torroni, 2016 for a good overview), semantic networks are almost as old as computers themselves, starting with a linguistic application by the Cambridge Language Research Unit in 1956 (Lehmann and Rodin, 1992). An essential part of the semantic web, there now exist large-scale semantic graphs on most subjects, the most comprehensive project being the Wikipedia-sourced DBpedia (Lehmann et al., 2014). For parliamentary data, the situation has improved over the last few years, and with the increasing implementation of public open data policies we can expect to see much further work in that domain. To our knowledge, the largest project for creating a semantic network from parliamentary data was Talk of Europe, which resulted in the LinkedEP Dataset (Hollink et al., 2017), covering all plenary debates held in the European Parliament between July 1999 and July 2017 (van Aggelen et al., 2017), as well as biographical information about the members of parliament sourced from Høyland

et al. (2009). We have also seen this inspire national efforts such as Talk of Norway (Lapponi et al., 2018), while several earlier projects are mentioned by Van Aggelen et al. (2017).

6 Conclusions and Future Work

We have created the Swedish PoliGraph specifically for named entity resolution and argumentation mining, and hope that it will prove fruitful to that end. Our next step will be NER, and while the current version of the graph is tailored for this, future needs may encourage us to augment it with further metadata, e.g. as additional features to be used in argumentation mining.

We also hope that this graph can be useful outside of our planned scope. The Swedish PoliGraph is both detailed and flexible enough that it can purposefully serve any project dealing with Swedish MPs and debates, be it academic, educational or journalistic.

Acknowledgments

The work presented here has been partly supported by an infrastructure grant to Språkbanken Text, University of Gothenburg, for contributing to building and operating a national e-infrastructure funded jointly by the Swedish Research Council (under contract no. 2017-00626) and the participating institutions. Thanks also to the reviewers for their constructive comments.

References

Astrid van Aggelen, Laura Hollink, Max Kemman, Martijn Kleppe, and Henri Beunders. 2017. The debates of the European parliament as linked open data. *Semantic Web*, 8(2):271–281.

Laura Hollink, Astrid van Aggelen, Henri Beunders, Martijn Kleppe, Max Kemman, and Jacco van Ossenbruggen. 2017. Talk of Europe – the debates of the European parliament as linked open data.

Bjørn Høyland, Indraneel Sircar, and Simon Hix. 2009. Forum section: An automated database of the European parliament. *European Union Politics*, 10(1):143–152.

Torbjörn Lager and Jan Wielemaker. 2014. Pengines: Web logic programming made easy. *TPLP*, 14(4-5):539–552.

Emanuele Lapponi, Martin G. Søyland, Erik Velldal, and Stephan Oepen. 2018. The talk of Norway: a richly annotated corpus of the Norwegian parliament, 1998–2016. *Language Resources and Evaluation*, 52(3):873–893.

Fritz Lehmann and Ervin Y Rodin. 1992. *Semantic networks in artificial intelligence*, volume 2. Pergamon Press, Oxford, UK.

Jens Lehmann, Robert Isele, Max Jakob, Anja Jentzsch, Dimitris Kontokostas, Pablo Mendes, Sebastian Hellmann, Mohamed Morsey, Patrick Van Kleef, Sören Auer, and Christian Bizer. 2014. DBpedia – a large-scale, multilingual knowledge base extracted from Wikipedia. *Semantic Web Journal*, 6.

Marco Lippi and Paolo Torroni. 2016. Argumentation mining: State of the art and emerging trends. *ACM Trans. Internet Technol.*, 16(2):10:1–10:25.

Towards Effective Rebuttal:
Listening Comprehension using Corpus-Wide Claim Mining

Tamar Lavee,* Matan Orbach*, Lili Kotlerman, Yoav Kantor, Shai Gretz,
Lena Dankin, Michal Jacovi, Yonatan Bilu, Ranit Aharonov and Noam Slonim
IBM Research

Abstract

Engaging in a live debate requires, among other things, the ability to effectively rebut arguments claimed by your opponent. In particular, this requires identifying these arguments. Here, we suggest doing so by automatically mining claims from a corpus of news articles containing billions of sentences, and searching for them in a given speech. This raises the question of whether such claims indeed correspond to those made in spoken speeches. To this end, we collected a large dataset of 400 speeches in English discussing 200 controversial topics, mined claims for each topic, and asked annotators to identify the mined claims mentioned in each speech. Results show that in the vast majority of speeches debaters indeed make use of such claims. In addition, we present several baselines for the automatic detection of mined claims in speeches, forming the basis for future work. All collected data is freely available for research.

1   Introduction

Project Debater[1] is a system designed to engage in a full live debate with expert human debaters. One of the major challenges in such a debate is listening to a several-minute long speech delivered by your opponent, identifying the main arguments, and rebutting them with effective persuasive counter arguments. This work focuses on the former, namely, automatically identifying arguments mentioned in opponent speeches.

One of the fundamental capabilities developed in Debater is the automatic mining of claims (Levy et al., 2014) – general, concise statements that directly support or contest a given topic – from a large text corpus. It allows Debater to present high-quality content supporting its side within its generated speeches. Our approach utilizes this capability for a different purpose: claims mined *from the opposing side* are searched for in a given opponent speech.

The implicit assumption in this approach is that mined claims would be often said by human opponents. This is far from trivial, since mined content from a large text corpus is not guaranteed to provide enough coverage over arguments made by individual human debaters. To assess this, we collected a large and varied dataset of recorded speeches discussing controversial topics, along with an annotation specifying which mined claims are mentioned in each speech.

Annotation results show our approach obtains good coverage, thus making the task of *claim matching* – automatically identifying given claims in speeches – interesting in the context of *mined* claims. Using the collected data, several claim matching baselines are examined, forming the basis for future work in this direction.

The main contributions of this paper are: (i) a recorded dataset of 400 speeches discussing 200 controversial topics, along with mined claims for each topic; (ii) an annotation specifying the claims mentioned in each speech; (iii) baselines for matching mined claims to speeches. All collected data is freely available for further research[2].

2   Related Work

(Mirkin et al., 2018b) recently presented a dataset similar to the one we collected in the context of Machine Listening Comprehension (MLC) over argumentative content. Instead of using mined claims, they extracted lists of potential arguments from iDebate[3], a manually curated high-quality database containing arguments for controversial

---

* These authors equally contributed to this work.

[1] `www.research.ibm.com/`
`artificial-intelligence/project-debater`

[2] `https://www.research.ibm.com/haifa/`
`dept/vst/debating_data.shtml`

[3] `https://idebate.org/debatabase`

Proceedings of the 6th Workshop on Argument Mining, pages 58–66
Florence, Italy, August 1, 2019. ©2019 Association for Computational Linguistics

topics. A major drawback of such an approach is topic coverage – any topic not included in the database cannot be handled. Another limitation is that argument lists from iDebate are short, each typically contains only 3 or 4 arguments from each side.

MLC has been recently gaining attention, and there are several new interesting works and datasets (Lee et al., 2018b,a; Ünlü et al., 2019). Other tasks are often phrased as a collection of test questions, which can be multiple choice (Tseng et al., 2016; Fang et al., 2016) or require, for example, identifying an entity mentioned by the speaker (Surdeanu et al., 2006; Comas et al., 2010).

Methods for detecting claims in given texts have been applied to various argumentative domains (e.g. by Palau and Moens (2011); Stab and Gurevych (2017); Habernal and Gurevych (2017)). While such tools may be applied to opponent speeches, a major difference in our setting is that it involves *spoken* rather than *written* language. Spoken spontaneous speeches often contain disfluencies such as breaks, repetitions, or other irregularities, and therefore claims detected in spoken content are likely to contain them as well. In addition, since the opponent speech audio is transcribed into text using an Automatic Speech Recognition (ASR) system, its errors propagate to detected claims. This is a crucial point for Debater – since a desired rebuttal in live debates typically includes a quote of the argument made by the opponent. Thus, any single disfluency or ASR error in a detected claim prevents its actual use.

3 Data

Motions As in Mirkin et al. (2018b), we manually curated a list of 200 controversial topics - referred to as motions, as in formal parliamentary proposals. Each motion focuses on a single Wikipedia concept, and is phrased similarly to parliamentary motions, e.g. *We should introduce compulsory voting*.

Speeches For each motion we recorded two argumentative speeches *contesting* it, as described in Mirkin et al. (2018b), producing a total of 400 speeches. Our choice of recording speeches contesting (rather than supporting) the motion is arbitrary, and all methods described henceforth would work similarly on speeches recorded for the other side. The dataset format follows the one described in Mirkin et al. (2018a). Each speech is associated

with a corresponding audio file, an automatic transcription of it[4], and a manually-transcribed "reference" text. Speeches were recorded by 9 expert debaters. On average, a speech contains 29 sentences and 748 tokens. The average ASR word error rate, computed by comparing to the manual transcripts, is 7.07%.

Mining Claims Figure 1 illustrates the suggested mined–claims based rebuttal generation pipeline. Following is a brief description of the existing components which perform claim mining. The rest of this work focuses on the subsequent component which identifies mentioned claims in speeches.

Processing starts from a large corpus of news articles containing billions of sentences. Given a controversial topic, several queries are applied, retrieving sentences which potentially contain claims that are relevant to the topic. Query results are then ranked by a neural-model trained to detect sentences containing claims (similarly to Levy et al. (2017, 2018)[5]). Top-ranked sentences are passed to a boundary detection component, responsible for finding the exact span of each claim within each sentence (Levy et al., 2014). Lastly, the stance of each claim towards the topic is detected using the method of Bar-Haim et al. (2017). Used models are tuned towards precision, aimed at obtaining a set of coherent, grammatically–correct claims from the opponent side, which can then be directly quoted in a live debate.

Prior to claim matching, mined claims are filtered, aiming to focus on those with a higher chance of obtaining a successful match. This included removing claims containing: (i) more than 10 tokens, since longer claims are less concise and may contain more than a single idea; (ii) named entities (found with Stanford NER (Finkel et al., 2005)), other than the topic itself, assuming they are too specific; (iii) unresolved demonstratives, which may hint to an incoherent sentence or an error in boundary detection.

The released dataset includes all output from these components, as well as a complete labeling indicating which texts are erroneously predicted to be claims, and what is the correct stance of all valid claims. The percentage of mined texts which are both labeled as claims and have a correctly

---

[4]See details in Section 5.

[5]We note that, as opposed to cited work, the corpus used here is not Wikipedia.

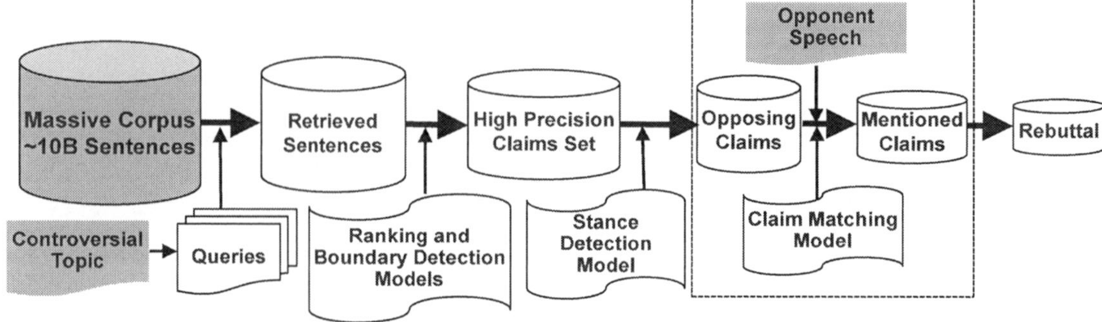

Figure 1: The suggested architecture for mined–claims based rebuttal generation. System inputs are depicted with a gray background. The focus of this work is marked on the right: detecting mentioned claims in opponents speeches. Preceding existing components are shortly described in Section 3. The entire pipeline starts from billions of sentences, and its final goal is producing few high quality rebuttals opposing the opponent speech.

identified stance is 86%.

Topic coverage Claim mining yielded, on average, 12.2 claims for each speech, suggesting match-candidates for 93.5% of the motions in our data. This shows the potentially high coverage of using mined claims. In contrast, only 39% of these motions have candidate iDebate arguments present in the dataset of Mirkin et al. (2018b).

4 Annotation

Next, we assessed whether mined claims are mentioned in recorded speeches through annotation. In case mined claims do occur in many speeches, the collected labels would form a dataset which can be used to develop algorithms for identifying mined claims in speeches.

In our annotation scheme, each question included a speech followed by a list of mined claims, and we asked to mark those claims which were mentioned by the speaker. Speeches were given in both text (manual transcription) and audio formats, to allow for listening, reading, or both. The length of each claim list was limited to at most 20 claims. Longer lists were split into multiple questions for the same speech.

Initially the task allowed for two labels: *Mentioned* or *Not mentioned*, yet error analysis showed major disagreements on claims alluded to, but not explicitly stated, in a speech. Example 1 illustrates this for the claim *compulsory voting is undemocratic*. Some annotators considered such cases as mentioned, while others disagreed. Thus, we modified the task to include three labels (*Explicit, Implicit, Not mentioned*), and provided detailed examples in the guidelines. Example 1 further

shows an explicit mention of the same claim[6].

Example 1 (Implicit / explicit mentions)
Claim: *Compulsory voting is undemocratic*

Implicit *...people have a right to not vote ... that's the way that rights work ... if you think that there is literally any reason a person might not want to vote ... you should ensure that that person is not penalized for not voting...*

Explicit *...it might be preferable if everyone voted, but it is undemocratic to force everyone to vote.*

Quality control Annotation of each question is time-consuming, since it requires going over a whole speech, and a list of claims. Combined with the amount of questions, we resorted to working with a crowd-sourcing platform[7], to make annotation practical. This required close monitoring and the removal of unreliable annotators. For quality control, we placed "test" claims among real mined claims, either using claims from different motions, expecting a negative answer, or by using claims unanimously labeled as mentioned for the same speech in previous rounds, expecting a positive label (explicit or implicit). We then defined thresholds on the accuracy of labeling of these test claims, and on the agreement of an annotator with its peers, disqualifying those who did not meet them. In addition, good annotators were awarded bonus payments, in order to keep them engaged. Each question was answered by seven annotators.

Annotation results A claim is considered as *mentioned* in a speech when a majority of anno-

---

[6]Full annotation guidelines, including more examples, are provided in the Appendix.

[7]Figure-Eight: www.figure-eight.com

tators marked it as either an explicit or an implicit mention. A mentioned claim is an *explicit* mention when its explicit answer count is strictly larger than its implicit answer count. Otherwise, it is an *implicit* mention.

Overall, annotation of all 400 speeches and their mined claims amounted to 4,882 speech–claim pairs. Of these, 34.7% were annotated as claims mentioned in the speech. Only 5.6% are explicit mentions, testifying to the difficulty of the matching task.

On average, there were 4.2 mentioned claims in every speech. 82.5% of the labels were agreed on by at least 5 out of the 7 annotators. The percentage of claims mentioned at least once is 44.8%, and in 87.3% of speeches at least one claim is mentioned (6.5% of speeches had no mined claims).

Annotation Quality To estimate inter-annotator agreement, we focus on annotators with a significant contribution, selecting those who have answered more than 20 common questions with each of at least 5 different peers. A per-annotator agreement score is defined by averaging Cohen's Kappa (Cohen, 1960) calculated with each peer. The final agreement score is the average of all annotators agreement scores.

Considering two labels (mentioned or not), agreement was 0.44. Mirkin et al. (2018b) reported a score of 0.5 on a similar annotation scheme performed by expert annotators. The difference is potentially due to the use of crowd, and the larger group of annotators taking part.

Note the applicability of chance-adjusted agreement scores to the crowd has been questioned, in particular for tasks within the argumentation domain (Passonneau and Carpenter, 2014; Habernal and Gurevych, 2016). Our test claims allow further validation of annotation quality, since their answers are known a-priory. The average annotator error rate on those test claims is low: 7.8%.

5   Evaluation

Annotation confirmed our hypothesis that claims mined from a corpus are indeed mentioned, or are at least alluded to, in spontaneous speeches on controversial topics. On average, of the 12.2 claims mined for each speech, about a third were annotated as mentioned. We now present several baselines for identifying those mentioned claims, using the collected data.

Speech pre–processing An input audio speech is automatically transcribed into text using IBM Watson ASR[8]. The text is then segmented to sentences as in Pahuja et al. (2017).

Next, given a claim, semantically similar sentences are identified. Each sentence is represented using a 200-dimensional vector constructed by: removing stopwords; representing remaining words using word2vec (*w2v*) (Mikolov et al., 2013) word embeddings learned over Wikipedia; computing a weighted average of those word embeddings using tf-idf weights (idf values are counted when considering each Wikipedia sentence as a document). The claim is represented similarly, and its semantic similarity to a given sentence is computed using the cosine similarity between their vector representations. All sentences with low similarity to the claim are ignored (using a fixed threshold).

Remaining sentences are scored by the harmonic mean (*HM*) of three additional semantic similarity measures, and the top-K ranked sentence are selected (we experiment with K $\in$ $\{1, 3, 5\}$). These features are:
– *Concept Coverage*: The fraction of Wikipedia concepts identified in the claim, found within the sentence.
– *Parse Pairs*: The parse trees of the claim and the sentence are obtained using Stanford parser (Socher et al., 2013). Then, pairwise edge similarity is defined to be the harmonic mean of the cosine similarities computed between the two parent word embeddings and the two child word embeddings. Each edge in the claim parse tree is scored using its maximal similarity to an edge from the sentence parse tree. Averaging these scores yields the final feature score.
– *Explicit Semantic Analysis* (Gabrilovich and Markovitch, 2007): Cosine similarity computed between vector representations of the claim and sentence over the Wikipedia concepts space.

Methods Following sentence selection, three methods are considered for scoring a speech and a claim:
HM: Averaging the selected sentences *HM* scores.
NN: Using a Siamese Network (Bromley et al., 1993), containing K instances of the same subnetwork: Each pair of a selected sentence and the claim is embedded with a BiLSTM, followed by

---

[8]`www.ibm.com/watson/services/`
`speech-to-text`

an attention layer, a fully connected layer, and finally a *softmax* layer which yields a score for the pair. The network outputs the maximum score of these K sub-networks.

LR: calculating 23 similarity measures between each selected sentence and the claim. For each measure, the average over the K selected sentences is taken. These averages are used as features for training a logistic regression classifier. Following is a brief description of the different groups of similarity measures we used.

– *w2v-based similarities* (5 features): Computing pairwise word similarities using the cosine similarity of the corresponding word embeddings, and applying several aggregation options.

– *Parse tree similarities* (6 features): Computing the parse tree of the claim and the sentence, and calculating similarities between different elements of those trees, similarly to the *Parse Pairs* feature described above.

– *Part of speech (POS) similarities* (5 features): Identifying tokens with a specific POS tag in the texts, and computing either the fraction of such tokens from one text which appear in the other, or otherwise aggregating w2v-based cosine similarities between these tokens in several ways.

– *Wikipedia concepts similarities* (2 features): The fraction of Wikipedia concepts from the claim which are present in the sentence, and vice versa.

– *Lexical similarities* (5 features): n-grams are extracted from the two texts in various settings (e.g. with or without lemmatization, or using different values of n). Then, each n-gram from the claim is scored by its maximal similarity to sentence n-grams (using a w2v-based similarity, with tf/idf weights). The feature values is the average of these scores.

Training and test sets   The data was randomly split into a *train* and *test* sets, equal in size. Each contains 100 motions and 200 speeches. The number of labeled speech-claim pairs is 2,456 in *train* and 2,426 in *test*.

Model selection as well as hyper-parameters tuning, such as the selection of K, are performed on *train* (using cross validation for *LR* and *NN*). Different configuration are ranked according to their Area Under the ROC Curve (AUC) measure.

Results   The AUC score of both *LR* and *NN* on *train*, for various values of K, was no higher than 0.57. In contrast, all *HM* configurations achieved

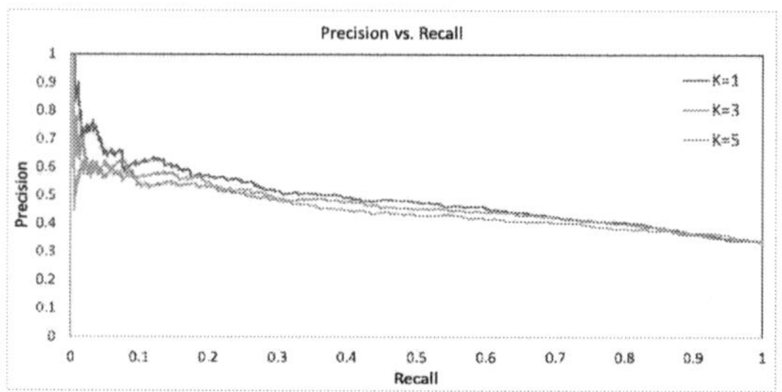

Figure 2: Precision-Recall curves for the top-3 claim matching configurations (all using *HM*) on *test*.

AUC higher than 0.62. We therefore focus on this method, though it is interesting, in future work, to improve the supervised methods or understand why they work somewhat poorly. Figure 2 shows precision-recall curves for *HM* and the different values of K on *test*. The different plots are comparable, yet there is a slight advantage to K = 1 for applications valuing precision over recall.

6   Conclusions and Future Work

We addressed the task of identifying arguments claimed in spoken argumentative content. Our suggested approach utilized claims mined from a large text corpora. The collected labeled data show these claims do cover, in most cases, arguments made by expert debaters. This confirms this is a valid approach for solving this task.

Interestingly, most claims are made implicitly, suggesting that assertion of claims often involves high lexical variability and expression of ideas across multiple (not always consecutive) sentences. This poses a challenge for automatic claim matching methods, as made evident by the baselines discussed here.

Successfully identifying arguments made by opponents forms the basis for an effective rebuttal. Our work leaves open the question of how to construct such rebuttals once a claim has been matched. This would be an interesting research direction for future work.

7   Acknowledgments

We are thankful to the debaters and annotators who took part in the creation of this dataset. We thank George Taylor and the entire Figure-Eight team for their continuous support during the annotation process.

References

Roy Bar-Haim, Indrajit Bhattacharya, Francesco Dinuzzo, Amrita Saha, and Noam Slonim. 2017. Stance classification of context-dependent claims. In *Proceedings of the 15th Conference of the European Chapter of the Association for Computational Linguistics: Volume 1, Long Papers*, pages 251–261, Valencia, Spain. Association for Computational Linguistics.

Jane Bromley, Isabelle Guyon, Yann LeCun, Eduard Säckinger, and Roopak Shah. 1993. Signature verification using a "siamese" time delay neural network. In *Proceedings of the 6th International Conference on Neural Information Processing Systems*, NIPS'93, pages 737–744, San Francisco, CA, USA. Morgan Kaufmann Publishers Inc.

Jacob Cohen. 1960. A Coefficient of Agreement for Nominal Scales. *Educational and Psychological Measurement*, 20(1):37–46.

Pere Comas, Jordi Turmo, and Lluís Màrquez. 2010. Using dependency parsing and machine learning for factoid question answering on spoken documents. In *INTERSPEECH 2010, 11th Annual Conference of the International Speech Communication Association, Makuhari, Chiba, Japan, September 26-30, 2010*, pages 1265–1268.

Wei Fang, Juei-Yang Hsu, Hung-yi Lee, and Lin-Shan Lee. 2016. Hierarchical attention model for improved machine comprehension of spoken content. In *2016 IEEE Spoken Language Technology Workshop, SLT 2016, San Diego, CA, USA, December 13-16, 2016*, pages 232–238.

Jenny Rose Finkel, Trond Grenager, and Christopher Manning. 2005. Incorporating non-local information into information extraction systems by gibbs sampling. In *Proceedings of the 43rd Annual Meeting on Association for Computational Linguistics*, ACL '05, pages 363–370, Stroudsburg, PA, USA. Association for Computational Linguistics.

Evgeniy Gabrilovich and Shaul Markovitch. 2007. Computing semantic relatedness using wikipedia-based explicit semantic analysis. In *IJCAI 2007, Proceedings of the 20th International Joint Conference on Artificial Intelligence, Hyderabad, India, January 6-12, 2007*, pages 1606–1611.

Ivan Habernal and Iryna Gurevych. 2016. Which argument is more convincing? analyzing and predicting convincingness of web arguments using bidirectional lstm. In *Proceedings of the 54th Annual Meeting of the Association for Computational Linguistics (Volume 1: Long Papers)*, volume 1, pages 1589–1599.

Ivan Habernal and Iryna Gurevych. 2017. Argumentation mining in user-generated web discourse. *Computational Linguistics*, 43(1):125–179.

Chia-Hsuan Lee, Shang-Ming Wang, Huan-Cheng Chang, and Hung-Yi Lee. 2018a. ODSQA: Open-Domain Spoken Question Answering Dataset. In *2018 IEEE Spoken Language Technology Workshop (SLT)*, pages 949–956. IEEE.

Chia-Hsuan Lee, Szu-Lin Wu, Chi-Liang Liu, and Hung-yi Lee. 2018b. Spoken SQuAD: A Study of Mitigating the Impact of Speech Recognition Errors on Listening Comprehension. In *Proceedings of Interspeech*.

Ran Levy, Yonatan Bilu, Daniel Hershcovich, Ehud Aharoni, and Noam Slonim. 2014. Context dependent claim detection. In *Proceedings of COLING 2014, the 25th International Conference on Computational Linguistics: Technical Papers*, pages 1489–1500. Dublin City University and Association for Computational Linguistics.

Ran Levy, Ben Bogin, Shai Gretz, Ranit Aharonov, and Noam Slonim. 2018. Towards an argumentative content search engine using weak supervision. In *Proceedings of the 27th International Conference on Computational Linguistics*, pages 2066–2081. Association for Computational Linguistics.

Ran Levy, Shai Gretz, Benjamin Sznajder, Shay Hummel, Ranit Aharonov, and Noam Slonim. 2017. Unsupervised corpus-wide claim detection. In *Proceedings of the 4th Workshop on Argument Mining, ArgMining@EMNLP 2017, Copenhagen, Denmark, September 8, 2017*, pages 79–84.

Tomas Mikolov, Kai Chen, Greg Corrado, and Jeffrey Dean. 2013. Efficient estimation of word representations in vector space. *CoRR*, abs/1301.3781.

Shachar Mirkin, Michal Jacovi, Tamar Lavee, Hong-Kwang Kuo, Samuel Thomas, Leslie Sager, Lili Kotlerman, Elad Venezian, and Noam Slonim. 2018a. A recorded debating dataset. In *Proceedings of LREC*.

Shachar Mirkin, Guy Moshkowich, Matan Orbach, Lili Kotlerman, Yoav Kantor, Tamar Lavee, Michal Jacovi, Yonatan Bilu, Ranit Aharonov, and Noam Slonim. 2018b. Listening comprehension over argumentative content. In *Proceedings of the 2018 Conference on Empirical Methods in Natural Language Processing*, pages 719–724. Association for Computational Linguistics.

Vardaan Pahuja, Anirban Laha, Shachar Mirkin, Vikas Raykar, Lili Kotlerman, and Guy Lev. 2017. Joint Learning of Correlated Sequence Labelling Tasks Using Bidirectional Recurrent Neural Networks. *Proceedings of Interspeech*.

Raquel Mochales Palau and Marie-Francine Moens. 2011. Argumentation mining. *Artif. Intell. Law*, 19(1):1–22.

Rebecca J Passonneau and Bob Carpenter. 2014. The benefits of a model of annotation. *Transactions of the Association for Computational Linguistics*, 2:311–326.

Richard Socher, John Bauer, Christopher D Manning, et al. 2013. Parsing with compositional vector grammars. In *Proceedings of the 51st Annual Meeting of the Association for Computational Linguistics (Volume 1: Long Papers)*, volume 1, pages 455–465.

Christian Stab and Iryna Gurevych. 2017. Parsing argumentation structures in persuasive essays. *Computational Linguistics*, 43(3):619–659.

Mihai Surdeanu, David Dominguez-Sal, and Pere Comas. 2006. Design and performance analysis of a factoid question answering system for spontaneous speech transcriptions. In *INTERSPEECH 2006 - IC-SLP, Ninth International Conference on Spoken Language Processing, Pittsburgh, PA, USA, September 17-21, 2006*.

Bo-Hsiang Tseng, Sheng-Syun Shen, Hung-Yi Lee, and Lin-Shan Lee. 2016. Towards Machine Comprehension of Spoken Content: Initial TOEFL Listening Comprehension Test by Machine. In *Proceedings of Interspeech*.

Merve Ünlü, Ebru Arisoy, and Murat Saraçlar. 2019. Question answering for spoken lecture processing. In *ICASSP 2019-2019 IEEE International Conference on Acoustics, Speech and Signal Processing (ICASSP)*, pages 7365–7369. IEEE.

Following are the guidelines used in the annotation of mined claims to recorded speeches.

Overview

In the following task you are given a speech that contests a controversial topic. You are asked to listen to the speech and/or read the transcription, then decide whether a list of potentially related claims were mentioned by the speaker explicitly, implicitly, or not at all.

Steps

- **Listen** to the speech and/or read the transcription of the speech. Note: some speeches are transcribed automatically and may contain errors.

- **Review** the list of possibly relevant claims. Note: few of the claims might not be full sentences. Please do your best to "complete" them to claims in a common-sense manner. If the claim doesn't make any sense, select "Not mentioned".

- **Decide** based on the speech only whether the speaker agrees with each claim, and choose the appropriate answer:

    - Agree - Explicitly
    - Agree - Implicitly
    - Not Mentioned

Rules & Tips

You should ask yourself whether the statement *"The speaker argued that <claim>"* is valid or not. Note, this statement can be valid even if the speaker was stating the claim using a somewhat different phrasing in her/his speech.

Examples

Agree - Explicitly

The claim was mentioned by the speaker, but perhaps phrased differently.

- If the speaker said: *organic food is simply healthier* then she explicitly agrees with the claim **organic food products are better in health**.

- If in a speech about the topic "We should ban boxing" the speaker said: *we think regulation is simply better in this instance than a ban* then she explicitly agrees with the claim **We should not ban boxing altogether, just regulate it**.

Agree - Implicitly

The claim was not mentioned by the speaker but it is clearly implied from the speech, and we know for sure that the speaker agrees with the claim.

The claim will usually be implied in one of the following ways:

- The claim is a generalization of a claim mentioned by the speaker.

    If the speaker said: *we allow people to make these decisions even if they might be physically bad for them* then she implicitly agrees with the claim **People should have the right to choose what to do with their bodies**.

- The claim summarizes an argument made by the speaker.

    If the speaker said: *It's essential that something is done to ensure that people don't have dental problems later in life. Water fluoridation is so cheap it's almost free. There are no proven side effects, the FDA and comparable groups in Europe have done lots and lots of tests and found that water fluoridation is actually a net health good, that there's no real risk to it* then she implicitly agrees with the claim **water fluoridation is safe and effective**.

- The claim can be deduced from an argument made by the speaker.

    If the speaker said *without the needle exchange program people are still going to do heroin or other kinds of drugs anyway with dirty or less safe needles. This does lead to things like HIV getting transmitted, it leads to other diseases as well, being more likely to get transmitted* then she implicitly agrees that **needle exchange programs could reduce the spread of disease**.

The text itself must contain some indication of the implied claim. Don't choose this option if you need to make an extra logical step to conclude that the speaker agrees with the claim. For example, if the speaker said *International aid has problems, but is still valuable*, then you should not conclude that she agrees with the claim **We should fix international aid, and not get rid of it** since she did not argue that the problems should be fixed.

Not Mentioned

The claim is not part of the speech.

For example, if the speaker said *and, yes, feminism has its flaws in the status quo ... but it can be reformed, and the tenets of equality that feminism stands for ... those tenets certainly should not be abandoned, and feminism has done a fantastic job, both historically and in the modern day, of championing those tenets.* then it can not be inferred that she agrees with the claim **We should try to fix the issues with feminism because people support it**. Although she suggests to fix the issues with feminism, she does not claim that people support it.

IMPORTANT NOTE: Your answers will be reviewed after the job is complete. We trust you to perform the task thoroughly, while carefully following the guidelines. Once your answers are determined as acceptable per our review, you might receive a bonus. Note that the bonus is given to contributors who complete at least 5 pages per job, and a higher bonus may be given to contributors who complete at least 50 pages.

Lexicon Guided Attentive Neural Network Model for Argument Mining

Jian-Fu Lin,[1] Kuo Yu Huang,[1] Hen-Hsen Huang,[2,3] Hsin-Hsi Chen[1,3]

[1] Department of Computer Science and Information Engineering,
National Taiwan University, Taiwan
[2] Department of Computer Science, National Chengchi University, Taiwan
[3] MOST Joint Research Center for AI Technology and All Vista Healthcare, Taiwan
{cflin,kyhuang}@nlg.csie.ntu.edu.tw,
hhhuang@nccu.edu.tw, hhchen@ntu.edu.tw

Abstract

Identification of argumentative components is an important stage of argument mining. Lexicon information is reported as one of the most frequently used features in the argument mining research. In this paper, we propose a methodology to integrate lexicon information into a neural network model by attention mechanism. We conduct experiments on the UKP dataset, which is collected from heterogeneous sources and contains several text types, e.g., microblog, Wikipedia, and news. We explore lexicons from various application scenarios such as sentiment analysis and emotion detection. We also compare the experimental results of leveraging different lexicons.

1 Introduction

Argument Mining (AM) is an emerging research area that has drawn more and more attention since around 2010. Recently, Project Debater from IBM has shown such an AI machine supported by argument mining techniques can do well at arguing. The task of AM can be divided into a few stages: (1) Extracting argumentative components from large texts, i.e., boundary detection or segmentation; (2) Classifying the extracted components into classes. In general, an argumentative component can be categorized into "Claim", which usually contains conclusions and stance toward the given topic, or "Premise", which contains reasoning or evidence used to support or attack a claim; (3) Predicting the relations between the identified argumentative components, i.e., supporting and attacking (Cabrio and Villata, 2018). Some works also consider more complex relations such as recursively support/attack the relations themselves rather than merely build relations between components (Peldszus and Stede, 2013).

Argument detection and classification can improve legal reasoning (Moens et al., 2007), policy

formulation (Florou et al., 2013), and persuasive writing (Stab and Gurevych, 2014). In this paper, we focus on mining argumentative components from a large collection of documents and further classifying them into roles of support/opposition. Our model is based on the recurrent neural network (RNN) , which has been widely used in natural language processing tasks (Cho et al., 2014). With the help of the attention mechanism (Bahdanau et al., 2015), RNN can further attend on the key information.

We propose a novel attention mechanism that is guided by argumentative lexicon information. Lexicon information is reported as one kind of the most frequently used features in argument mining (Cabrio and Villata, 2018). Previous works on AM have tried to integrate lexical features into the learning models (Levy et al., 2017; Nguyen and Litman, 2015; Rinott et al., 2015). These lexicons are mostly composed by human beings or derived by hand-crafted rules, and result in domain-specificity. That is, it may fail to be used for other domains. In the contrast of scarcity of general lexicon for AM, lexical resources are abundant in other fields like sentiment analysis, opinion mining, and emotion detection (Hu and Liu, 2004; Mohammad and Turney, 2013; Kiritchenko and Mohammad, 2016). As a more general domain, AM may get the benefits of not only in-domain lexicon, but also out-domain lexicons.

The contribution of this work is two-fold: (1) We propose an attention mechanism to leverage lexicon information. (2) In the face of the scarcity of argument lexicon, we explore several different types of lexicons to verify whether outside resources are useful for AM tasks.

The rest of this paper is organized as follows. Section 2 summarizes related works about AM. The dataset and linguistic resources used for experiments are shown in Section 3. We introduce

67

Proceedings of the 6th Workshop on Argument Mining, pages 67–73
Florence, Italy, August 1, 2019. ©2019 Association for Computational Linguistics

our model in Section 4 and show the experimental results in Section 5. We also look into the errors made by our best model in Section 6. Section 7 makes a discussion on experimental results and concludes this work.

2 Related Works

Neural networks have been used in varieties of AM tasks. To improve the vanilla LSTM model, Stab et al. (2018a) use attention mechanism to fuse topic and sentence information together. In the work of Laha and Raykar (2016), they present several bi-sequence classification models on different datasets. However, rather than using some sophisticated architecture such as attention, it considers only different concatenation or condition method on the output of LSTM. Eger et al. (2017) propose an end-to-end training model to mining argument structure, identifying argument components.

Besides syntactic and positional information, lexical information is also reported as one of the most used features in argument mining task (Cabrio and Villata, 2018). In some similar research fields such as sentiment analysis and emotion mining, a number of works have been proposed to combine lexical information with the NN models. Teng et al. (2016) use lexical scores as the weights and do the weighted sum over the outputs of the LSTM model, in order to derive the sentence scores. Zou et al. (2018) determines attention weights using lexicon labels, which lead the model to focus on the lexicon words. Bar-Haim et al. (2017) proposes an idea of expanding lexicons to improve stance classifying task.

However, in AM, seldom works directly combine lexicon with models. By using discourse feature, Levy et al. (2018) generates weak labels and use weak supervision. Shnarch et al. (2018) also present a methodology to blend such weak labeled data with high quality but scarce labeled data for AM. Al-Khatib et al. (2016) consider the distant supervision method. Most of these works use the end-to-end training paradigm with the outside resources only for generating the weak label, which may not fully leverage the information of the lexicons.

3 Resources

In this section, we introduce the dataset used to evaluate the performance of our proposed model. Besides, we describe each lexicon in brief and show how to perform the data preprocessing.

3.1 Data

We conduct the experiments on the dataset released by Stab et al. (2018b).[1] The dataset includes 25,492 sentences over eight topics that are randomly selected from an online list of controversial topics.[2] The selected topics, which are considered as queries, are used to retrieve documents from heterogeneous sources via the Google search engine. Among these sentences, 4,944 of them are supporting arguments, 6,195 are opposing arguments, and 14,353 are non-argument sentences. This dataset is commonly used for sentential argument identification task. Levy et al. (2018) collect a dataset with around 1.5 million sentences over 150 topics from Wikipedia. However, only 2,500 of them are labeled. It may not be sufficient for training a model, especially for neural network models.

The definition of argumentative components differs from dataset to dataset. In the dataset used in this work, an argumentative component is a span of text with reasoning or evidence, which is able to either support or oppose a topic (Stab et al., 2018b).

3.2 Lexicon resource

To improve the baseline model, we consider several existing lexicons across different domains. We first explore the claim lexicon that is built for argument mining task (Levy et al., 2017). We also include the lexicon resources often used in sentiment analysis (Hu and Liu, 2004) and emotion detection (Mohammad and Turney, 2013). We postulate that the resources for these application scenarios may have the potential for argument mining. We further develop a model based on the general purpose lexicon, WordNet (Miller, 1995).

These resources are applied in different ways. We use the claim lexicon (Levy et al., 2017), the sentiment lexicon (Hu and Liu, 2004), and the emotion lexicon (Mohammad and Turney, 2013) to extract critical words from the i-th input sentence $\mathcal{C}_i$, forming a sentence $\mathcal{A}_i$. In contrast, we consult WordNet (Miller, 1995) to expand the short topic $\mathcal{T}_i$ into the corresponding $\mathcal{A}_i$.

---

[1] https://www.informatik.tu-darmstadt.de/ukp/research_6/data

[2] https://www.procon.org/, https://www.questia.com/library/controversial-topics

Claim Lexicon. The claim lexicon is a lexicon containing words with argumentative characteristics. Levy et al. (2017) use the appearance of the term "that" as a weak signal of sentences containing argumentative components. After collecting nearly 1.86M sentences, they compute the prior probability of the term "that" $P(that)$ occurring in a sentence, and the probabilities $P(that|w_i)$, where $P(that|w_i)$ denotes the probability of a sentence having the term "that" and the word w_i is in the suffix after the main concept (i.e. the target entity in a controversial topic), given the sentence containing w_i. Those words with a probability $P(that|w_i) > P(that)$ are included in their proposed claim lexicon, resulting a lexicon with around 600 claim words. The lexicon was then used for designing sentence pattern rules called claim sentence query (CSQ). They believe the claim lexicon can help detect sentences containing argument.

Sentiment Lexicon. Hu and Liu (2004) built a sentiment lexicon that contains around 6,800 words. Each word is labeled as negative and/or positive. We construct an additional sentence $\mathcal{A}$ by extracting the words that are in both sentiment lexicon and the input sentence $\mathcal{C}$, regardless whether they are positive or negative.

Emotion Lexicon. The emotion lexicon built by Mohammad and Turney (2013) contains around 14,200 words. Each word in the lexicon is given eight emotion labels. An emotion in the lexicon could be one of eight emotions, including anger, anticipation, disgust, fear, joy, sadness, surprise, and trust. The labels are defined as follows:

$$label(w_i, e_j) = \begin{cases} 1, & \text{if } w_i \text{ associated with } e_j \\ 0, & \text{otherwise} \end{cases}$$

Where w_i is a word, and e_j is one of the eight emotions. In the experiment, we select the words that have at least one emotion labeled as 1, resulting a list of 6,468 words. We then use this list to create an additional sentence $\mathcal{A}$ from the input sentence $\mathcal{C}$.

WordNet. To expand a topic $\mathcal{T}$ composed of words $w_1^{\mathcal{T}}, w_2^{\mathcal{T}}, ..., w_K^{\mathcal{T}}$, we expand each of the words in it. For each word $w_i^{\mathcal{T}}$, we use WordNet (Miller, 1995) to find its corresponding synonyms. We then put the found synonyms together, forming an additional sentence $\mathcal{A}$, an expanded version of topic $\mathcal{T}$.

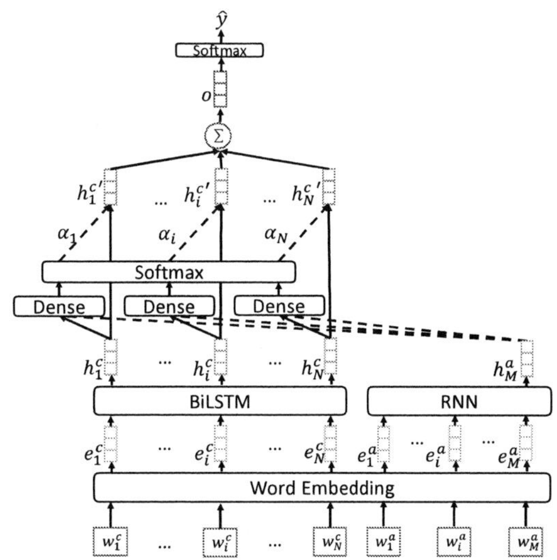

Figure 1: The architecture of Lexicon Guided Attentive Neural Network Model

4 Model

This section describes the development of the baseline model and the proposed model. To identify sentence-level argumentative components, the model is given a sentence $\mathcal{C}$, which contains a sequence of words $w_1^c, w_2^c, ..., w_N^c$ and a topic $\mathcal{T}$ with words $w_1^{\mathcal{T}}, w_2^{\mathcal{T}}, ..., w_K^{\mathcal{T}}$. The input word sequence is then encoded as a sequence of word embeddings via the GloVe word vectors. The pre-trained word vectors with the dimension of 100 released by Pennington et al. (2014) are used. Based on the given input, the model makes a prediction $\hat{y}$ for the given sentence, i.e., classifying it as *supporting argument*, *opposing argument*, or *non-argument*. For comparison, we implement a baseline model with the vanilla bidirectional LSTM (BiLSTM).

In order to exploit the linguistic knowledge, Lei et al. (2018) highlight the sentiment words of the input sentence, computing attention weight for each word with them. By integrating the sentiment lexicon into the neural network model, the work successfully improves the performance in sentiment analysis. This work proposes a model that integrates an outside lexicon resource into attention mechanism (Vaswani et al., 2017). For each input sentence, we compose an additional sentence $\mathcal{A}$, which contains words $w_1^a, w_2^a, ..., w_M^a$ based on the given lexicon. The additional sentence $\mathcal{A}$ is then forwarded to the embedding layer together with input sentence $\mathcal{C}$. The output of

model	F_1	P_{arg+}	P_{arg-}	R_{arg+}	R_{arg-}
BiLSTM	$.5337 \pm .0123$	$.4521 \pm .0391$	$.4832 \pm .0393$	$.2911 \pm .1139$	$.4816 \pm .1276$
ClaimLex*	$.5684 \pm .0222$	$.4736 \pm .0322$	$.5075 \pm .0450$	$\mathbf{.3756} \pm .1072$	$.5011 \pm .0854$
SentimentLex*	$.5718 \pm .0165$	$\mathbf{.4937} \pm .0365$	$.5125 \pm .0414$	$.3590 \pm .1043$	$.5240 \pm .0889$
EmotionLex*	$.5695 \pm .0129$	$.4920 \pm .0369$	$.5036 \pm .0356$	$.3524 \pm .0861$	$\mathbf{.5264} \pm .1006$
WordNet*	$\mathbf{.5788} \pm .0142$	$.4846 \pm .0292$	$\mathbf{.5191} \pm .0376$	$.3724 \pm .0818$	$.5235 \pm .0772$

Table 1: The results of the baseline model and the proposed model with different lexicon resources. The highest score of each column is highlighted in bold font.

embedding layer is the sequences $e_1^c, e_2^c, ..., e_N^c$ and $e_1^a, e_2^a, ..., e_M^a$, representing the embedded sentences $\mathcal{C}$ and $\mathcal{A}$, respectively. Then, e_i^c is fed into BiLSTM and results in h_i^c at the corresponding time step. As for $\mathcal{A}$, we add an RNN to collect its information and take the output h_M^a at the last time step as its representation. Though Lei et al. (2018) use an LSTM to encode the sentimental sentences, we do not follow their approach. In our work, the simple RNN outperforms the LSTM in the preliminary experiments.

The attention weight of the i-th word (i.e. α_i) is determined by the concatenation of the output of the BiLSTM h_i^c and the output of the RNN (i.e. h_M^a), which is given the additional sentence $\mathcal{A}$ as the input:

$$\alpha_i = \frac{exp(\sigma([h_i^c; h_M^a]))}{\sum_{i=1}^N exp(\sigma([h_i^c; h_M^a]))} \quad (1)$$

where α_i indicates the attention weight of i-th word of the input sentence, and $[h_i^c; h_M^a]$ indicates the concatenation of i-th hidden state and the RNN output state. The scoring function $\sigma(\cdot)$ is designed as:

$$\sigma([h_i^c; h_M^a]) = tanh(W_c[h_i^c; h_M^a]) \quad (2)$$

where W_c indicates trainable parameters.

All the weighted hidden states are then summed up, and connected to a fully connected layer for the final prediction:

$$o = \sum_{i=1}^N h_i^{c'} \quad (3)$$

$$h_i^{c'} = \alpha_i h_i^c \quad (4)$$

Figure 1 illustrates the architecture of our model.

5   Experiments

Because most of the lengths of input sentences are less than 60 and most of the lengths of additional sentences $\mathcal{A}$ are less than 20, we truncate them into lengths of 60 and 20 respectively. The dataset has 25,492 sentences in total. We conduct 5-fold cross validation for evaluating our model.

To evaluate our approaches, we report the average macro F_1 as ternary setting, precision and recall of predicting supporting arguments (P_{arg+}, R_{arg+}), and precision and recall of predicting opposing arguments (P_{arg-}, R_{arg-}). We run paired t-test for each proposed model in comparison with the baseline model, and mark the models having statistical significance (i.e. p-value < 0.05) with a wildcard. As the result shown in Table 1, we can observe that the proposed models benefit from the information from the adopted lexicons, improving the performance of argumentative components identification. The best model, which uses WordNet to expand topic $\mathcal{T}$, outperforms the baseline model by 4.5 percentage in F_1. The proposed model with the lowest F_1 score (i.e. ClaimLex) still outperforms the baseline by 3.4 percentage. Furthermore, the best performance reported by Stab et al. (2018b) on the same dataset is 0.4285 in macro F_1, which is the result of only incorporating topic information into their models. This shows the impact of the lexicon information.

However, we can also observe that the result of integrating claim lexicon (Levy et al., 2017) is out of our expectation though it is a resource for argument mining. Possible reasons are figured out as follows. Firstly, the lexicon is built based on a strong assumption, i.e., the present of the term "that" indicates a high probability of the occurrence of argumentative components. Secondly, the lexicon has only 586 words, indicating a very small coverage with the whole vocabulary. Thirdly, the lexicon built from the sentences across 100 different topics contains a number of domain-specific words such as "LGBTQ" and "militarily". Highlighting of these domain-specific words may cause noise when the topic is unrelated to them.

	Topic	Sentence	Prediction	Annotation
S1	death penalty	Advocates of death penalty cite examples on how imposing the death sentence or abolishing it have affected crime rate.	attack	support
S2	death penalty	Pain of Death: Executing a person can be quick and painless, or executing a person can be slow and painful.	support	non-arg
S3	gun control	If you can get to the phone to call 911, if you are strong enough to hold off your attacker until the police arrive, and if you can wait 15 minutes in the city or 45 minutes in the country for law enforcement to arrive while you struggle with the intruder, then you might make it.	support	attack
S4	cloning	Our of respect for human clones (human beings in every respect), a ban on human cloning should be opposed.	support	attack
S5	gun control	We should have more of it!	non-arg	support

Table 2: The examples that our best model fails to correctly predict. The sentences predicted/annotated as non-argumentative ones are abbreviated to *non-arg*.

6 Error Analysis

To know better what kind of sentence would mislead our model to make wrong predictions, we randomly sample the sentences with error from our best model, i.e., lexicon-guided attentive neural network model with WordNet. After looking into these errors, we find that the causes of a wrong prediction can be briefly categorized into the following cases. Some illustrations of the errors are listed in Table 2: (1) The sentences that have ambiguous words or state an open question can easily lead our model to predict the sentences' labels from non-argumentative to argumentative, or predict the labels from one stance, i.e., supporting or attacking, to the other. For example, both *"imposing"* and *"abolishing"* are shown in S1, which may cause the model to fails on correctly detecting the stances. S2 states an open question on the influence of death penalty, but the model mistakes it for an argumentative sentence; (2) When arguing over an issue, people may use irony to attack the opposite stance. Such statement may mislead the model, as S3 has shown; (3) We also find that our model may predict wrongly with the appearance of double negation. The part of the sentence S4, *"a ban on human cloning should be opposed"*, conveys the supporting stance with a double negative statement. With a limited amount of training data, the model may not be able to comprehend relatively complicated syntax.

On the other hand, some examples in the dataset may have been wrongly annotated. According to Stab et al. (2018b), arguments are defined as a span of text having reasoning or evidence that can be used to support or oppose a topic. S5 does explicitly declare its supporting stance, but nevertheless has no reasoning or evidence.

7 Conclusion

In this work, we propose a novel approach to leverage the lexicon from both in-domain and out-of-domain sources for the task of argumentative component mining. We explore several sources from different application scenarios, from claim lexicon (Levy et al., 2017) to other domain resources such as sentiment analysis (Hu and Liu, 2004), emotion detection (Mohammad and Turney, 2013), and the general domain lexicon resource (Miller, 1995). Experimental results confirm the effectiveness of the integration of lexicon information. The scarcity of the resources in argument mining is also highlighted in the discussion.

Acknowledgments

This research was partially supported by Ministry of Science and Technology, Taiwan, under grants MOST-106-2923-E-002-012-MY3, MOST-107-2634-F-002-011-, MOST-108-2634-F-002-008-.

References

Khalid Al-Khatib, Henning Wachsmuth, Matthias Hagen, Jonas Köhler, and Benno Stein. 2016. Cross-domain mining of argumentative text through distant supervision. In *Proceedings of the 2016 Conference of the North American Chapter of the Association for Computational Linguistics: Human Language Technologies*, pages 1395–1404, San Diego, California. Association for Computational Linguistics.

Dzmitry Bahdanau, Kyunghyun Cho, and Yoshua Bengio. 2015. Neural machine translation by jointly learning to align and translate. *CoRR*, abs/1409.0473.

Roy Bar-Haim, Lilach Edelstein, Charles Jochim, and Noam Slonim. 2017. Improving claim stance classification with lexical knowledge expansion and context utilization. In *Proceedings of the 4th Workshop on Argument Mining*, pages 32–38, Copenhagen, Denmark. Association for Computational Linguistics.

Elena Cabrio and Serena Villata. 2018. Five years of argument mining: a data-driven analysis. In *Proceedings of the Twenty-Seventh International Joint Conference on Artificial Intelligence, IJCAI-18*, pages 5427–5433. International Joint Conferences on Artificial Intelligence Organization.

Kyunghyun Cho, Bart van Merrienboer, Caglar Gulcehre, Dzmitry Bahdanau, Fethi Bougares, Holger Schwenk, and Yoshua Bengio. 2014. Learning phrase representations using rnn encoder–decoder for statistical machine translation. In *Proceedings of the 2014 Conference on Empirical Methods in Natural Language Processing (EMNLP)*, pages 1724–1734, Doha, Qatar. Association for Computational Linguistics.

Steffen Eger, Johannes Daxenberger, and Iryna Gurevych. 2017. Neural end-to-end learning for computational argumentation mining. In *Proceedings of the 55th Annual Meeting of the Association for Computational Linguistics (ACL 2017)*, volume Volume 1: Long Papers, pages (11–22). Association for Computational Linguistics.

Eirini Florou, Stasinos Konstantopoulos, Antonis Koukourikos, and Pythagoras Karampiperis. 2013. Argument extraction for supporting public policy formulation. In *Proceedings of the 7th Workshop on Language Technology for Cultural Heritage, Social Sciences, and Humanities*, pages 49–54.

Minqing Hu and Bing Liu. 2004. Mining and summarizing customer reviews. In *Proceedings of the Tenth ACM SIGKDD International Conference on Knowledge Discovery and Data Mining*, KDD '04, pages 168–177, New York, NY, USA. ACM.

Svetlana Kiritchenko and Saif Mohammad. 2016. The effect of negators, modals, and degree adverbs on sentiment composition. In *Proceedings of the 7th Workshop on Computational Approaches to Subjectivity, Sentiment and Social Media Analysis*, pages 43–52, San Diego, California. Association for Computational Linguistics.

Anirban Laha and Vikas Raykar. 2016. An empirical evaluation of various deep learning architectures for bi-sequence classification tasks. In *Proceedings of COLING 2016, the 26th International Conference on Computational Linguistics: Technical Papers*, pages 2762–2773, Osaka, Japan. The COLING 2016 Organizing Committee.

Zeyang Lei, Yujiu Yang, and Min Yang. 2018. Sentiment lexicon enhanced attention-based lstm for sentiment classification.

Ran Levy, Ben Bogin, Shai Gretz, Ranit Aharonov, and Noam Slonim. 2018. Towards an argumentative content search engine using weak supervision. In *Proceedings of the 27th International Conference on Computational Linguistics*, pages 2066–2081, Santa Fe, New Mexico, USA. Association for Computational Linguistics.

Ran Levy, Shai Gretz, Benjamin Sznajder, Shay Hummel, Ranit Aharonov, and Noam Slonim. 2017. Unsupervised corpus–wide claim detection. In *Proceedings of the 4th Workshop on Argument Mining*, pages 79–84, Copenhagen, Denmark. Association for Computational Linguistics.

George A. Miller. 1995. Wordnet: A lexical database for english. *Commun. ACM*, 38(11):39–41.

Marie-Francine Moens, Erik Boiy, Raquel Mochales Palau, and Chris Reed. 2007. Automatic detection of arguments in legal texts. In *Proceedings of the 11th International Conference on Artificial Intelligence and Law*, ICAIL '07, pages 225–230, New York, NY, USA. ACM.

Saif M. Mohammad and Peter D. Turney. 2013. Crowdsourcing a word-emotion association lexicon. 29(3):436–465.

Huy Nguyen and Diane Litman. 2015. Extracting argument and domain words for identifying argument components in texts. In *Proceedings of the 2nd Workshop on Argumentation Mining*, pages 22–28, Denver, CO. Association for Computational Linguistics.

Andreas Peldszus and Manfred Stede. 2013. From argument diagrams to argumentation mining in texts: A survey. *Int. J. Cogn. Inform. Nat. Intell.*, 7(1):1–31.

Jeffrey Pennington, Richard Socher, and Christopher D. Manning. 2014. Glove: Global vectors for word representation. In *Empirical Methods in Natural Language Processing (EMNLP)*, pages 1532–1543.

Ruty Rinott, Lena Dankin, Carlos Alzate Perez, Mitesh M. Khapra, Ehud Aharoni, and Noam Slonim. 2015. Show me your evidence - an automatic method for context dependent evidence detection. In *Proceedings of the 2015 Conference on Empirical Methods in Natural Language Processing*, pages 440–450, Lisbon, Portugal. Association for Computational Linguistics.

Eyal Shnarch, Carlos Alzate, Lena Dankin, Martin Gleize, Yufang Hou, Leshem Choshen, Ranit Aharonov, and Noam Slonim. 2018. Will it blend? blending weak and strong labeled data in a neural network for argumentation mining. In *Proceedings of the 56th Annual Meeting of the Association for Computational Linguistics (Volume 2: Short Papers)*, pages 599–605, Melbourne, Australia. Association for Computational Linguistics.

Christian Stab and Iryna Gurevych. 2014. Annotating argument components and relations in persuasive essays. In *Proceedings of COLING 2014, the 25th International Conference on Computational Linguistics: Technical Papers*, pages 1501–1510.

Christian Stab, Tristan Miller, and Iryna Gurevych. 2018a. Cross-topic argument mining from heterogeneous sources using attention-based neural networks. *arXiv preprint arXiv:1802.05758*.

Christian Stab, Tristan Miller, Benjamin Schiller, Pranav Rai, and Iryna Gurevych. 2018b. Crosstopic argument mining from heterogeneous sources. In *Proceedings of the 2018 Conference on Empirical Methods in Natural Language Processing*, pages 3664–3674, Brussels, Belgium. Association for Computational Linguistics.

Zhiyang Teng, Duy Tin Vo, and Yue Zhang. 2016. Context-sensitive lexicon features for neural sentiment analysis. In *Proceedings of the 2016 Conference on Empirical Methods in Natural Language Processing*, pages 1629–1638, Austin, Texas. Association for Computational Linguistics.

Ashish Vaswani, Noam Shazeer, Niki Parmar, Jakob Uszkoreit, Llion Jones, Aidan N Gomez, Ł ukasz Kaiser, and Illia Polosukhin. 2017. Attention is all you need. In I. Guyon, U. V. Luxburg, S. Bengio, H. Wallach, R. Fergus, S. Vishwanathan, and R. Garnett, editors, *Advances in Neural Information Processing Systems 30*, pages 5998–6008. Curran Associates, Inc.

Yicheng Zou, Tao Gui, Qi Zhang, and Xuanjing Huang. 2018. A lexicon-based supervised attention model for neural sentiment analysis. In *Proceedings of the 27th International Conference on Computational Linguistics*, pages 868–877, Santa Fe, New Mexico, USA. Association for Computational Linguistics.

Is It Worth the Attention?
A Comparative Evaluation of Attention Layers for
Argument Unit Segmentation

Maximilian Spliethöver[*] and **Jonas Klaff**[*] and **Hendrik Heuer**
University of Bremen
Bibliothekstraße 1, 28359 Bremen, Germany
{mspl, joklaff, hheuer}@uni-bremen.de

Abstract

Attention mechanisms have seen some success for natural language processing downstream tasks in recent years and generated new state-of-the-art results. A thorough evaluation of the attention mechanism for the task of Argumentation Mining is missing. With this paper, we report a comparative evaluation of attention layers in combination with a bidirectional long short-term memory network, which is the current state-of-the-art approach for the unit segmentation task. We also compare sentence-level contextualized word embeddings to pre-generated ones. Our findings suggest that for this task, the additional attention layer does not improve the performance. In most cases, contextualized embeddings do also not show an improvement on the score achieved by pre-defined embeddings.

1 Introduction

Argumentation Mining (AM) is increasingly applied in different fields of research like fake-news detection (Cabrio and Villata, 2018) and political argumentation and network analysis (Haunss et al.).

One crucial part of the AM pipeline is to segment written text into argumentative and non-argumentative units. Recent research in the area of unit segmentation (Eger et al., 2017; Ajjour et al., 2017) has lead to promising results with F1-scores of up to 0.90 for in-domain segmentation (Eger et al., 2017). Nevertheless, there is still a need for more robust approaches.

Given the recent progress of attention-based models in Neural Machine Translation (NMT) (Bahdanau et al., 2014; Vaswani et al., 2017), this paper evaluates the effectiveness of seperate attention layers for the task of argumentative unit segmentation. The idea of the attention layers added to the recurrent networks is to preprocess the input data and enable the model to prioritize those parts of the input sequence that are important for the current prediction (Bahdanau et al., 2014). This can be achieved by learning additional parameters during the training of the model. With the additional information gained, the model learns a better internal representation which improves performance.

Additionally, we evaluate the impact of contextualized distributed term representations (also referred to as word embeddings hereinafter) on all our models. The goal of word embeddings is to represent a word as a high-dimensional vector that encodes its approximate meaning. This vector will be generated by a model trained on a language modeling task, like next-word prediction (Mikolov et al., 2013), for a given text corpus. The representation is based on the word's surrounding context in the corpus. Words with a similar semantic meaning should then also have similar vector representations, as measured by their distance in the vector space (Sahlgren, 2005, 2006; Firth, 1957; Heuer, 2015). Different methods to pre-compute the embeddings include word2vec (Mikolov et al., 2013), FastText (Bojanowski et al., 2017) and GloVe (Pennington et al., 2014). To make use of the capabilities of pre-trained Language Models (LMs), such as BERT (Devlin et al., 2018) or Flair (Akbik et al., 2018), we evaluate how well their semantic representations perform, by using contextualized word embeddings. Those are, in contrast to previously mentioned methods, specific to the context of the word in the input sequence. One major benefit is the fact that the time-consuming feature engineering could become obsolete since the features are implicitly encoded in the word embeddings. Furthermore, a better semantic representation of the input could lead to better generalization capabilities of the model and, therefore, to

---

[*] The first two authors contributed equally. Their listing order is random.

Proceedings of the 6th Workshop on Argument Mining, pages 74–82
Florence, Italy, August 1, 2019. ©2019 Association for Computational Linguistics

better cross-domain performance.

This paper answers the following research questions, which will help to assess the importance of the attention layers and contextualized word embeddings for the argument unit segmentation task:

- **RQ1:** To what extent can seperate attention layers help the model focus on the, for the task of unit segmentation relevant, sequence parts and how much do they influence the predictions?

- **RQ2:** What is the impact of contextualized distributed term representations like BERT (Devlin et al., 2018) and Flair (Akbik et al., 2018) on the task of unit segmentation and do they improve upon pre-defined representations like GloVe?

The contributions of this paper are as follows: first, we present and evaluate new attention-based architectures for the task of argumentative text segmentation. Second, we review the effectiveness of recently proposed contextualized word embedding approaches in regard to AM. We will continue by presenting the previous work on this specific task, followed by a description of the different architectures used, the data set and the generation of the word embeddings. Afterwards, we will report the results, followed by a discussion and the limitations. We will finish with a conclusion and an outlook on possible future work.

2   Related Work

Attention mechanisms have long been utilized in deep neural networks. Some of its roots are in the salient region detection for the processing of images (Itti et al., 1998), which takes inspiration from human perception. The main idea is to focus the attention of the underlying network on points-of-interest in the input that are often surrounded by irrelevant parts (Mnih et al., 2014). This allows the model to put more weight on the important chunks. While earlier salient detectors were task-specific, newer approaches (e.g. Mnih et al., 2014) can be adapted to different tasks, like image description generation (Xu et al., 2015), and allow for the parameters of the attention to be tuned during the training. These additional tasks include sequence processing and the application of such networks to different areas of Natural Language Processing (NLP). One of the first use-cases for attention mechanisms in the field of NLP was machine translation. Bahdanau et al. (2014) utilized the attention to improve their NMT model. Vaswani et al. (2017) achieved new State-of-the-Art (sota) results by presenting an encoder-decoder architecture that is based on the attention mechanism, only adding a position-wise feed-forward network and normalizations in between. Devlin et al. (2018) picked up on the encoder part of this architecture to pre-train a bidirectional LM. After fine-tuning, they achieved a new sota performance on different downstream NLP tasks like part-of-speech tagging and questions-answering.

A possible way of posing the unit segmentation as NLP task is a token-based sequence labeling (Stab, 2017). While Tobias et al. (2018) used non-recurrent classifiers to approach this problem, others mostly applied recurrent networks to the task of unit boundary prediction. For example, Eger et al. (2017) reported different long short-term memory (LSTM) (Hochreiter and Schmidhuber, 1997) architectures. Further, Ajjour et al. (2017) proposed a setup with three bidirectional LSTMs (Bi-LSTMs) (Schuster and Paliwal, 1997) in total as their best solution. While the first two of them are fully connected and work on word embeddings and task-specific features respectively, the intention for the third is to take the output of the first two as input and learn to correct their errors. Even though the third Bi-LSTM did not improve on the F1-score metric, it did succeed in resolving some of the wrong consecutive token predictions, without worsening the final results.

To the best of the authors' knowledge, the attention mechanism has not been widely utilized for the task of argumentative unit segmentation. Stab et al. (2018) integrated the attention mechanism directly into their Bi-LSTM by calculating it at each time step t to evaluate the importance of the current hidden state h_t. To do that, they employed additive attention. A similar approach has been applied by Morio and Fujita (2018) for a three-label classification task (claim, premise or non-argumentative).

While a direct integration of the attention mechanism is able to take the previous state of the Bi-LSTM into the calculation, it seems less trivial to implement with the current available programming frameworks. In contrast, the approach presented in this paper uses attention as a separate layer that encodes all sequences before they are fed into a Bi-LSTM. This might enable the recurrent parts of the network to learn from better representations that are specific to the task they were trained on. The aim is further to evaluate the possible applications of attention layers for the task of sequence segmentation and token classification. A recurrent architecture (Ajjour et al., 2017) is compared to multiple modified versions that utilize the aforementioned attention mechanism.

In order to derive a representation of the input text that better resembles the context of the input for a specific task, several approaches have been presented. Akbik et al. (2018), for example, pre-train a character-level Bi-LSTM to predict the next character for a given text corpus. The pre-trained model is able to derive contextualized word embeddings by additionally utilizing the input sequence for a specific task. This allows the system to encode the preceding and following words of the given input sequence into the word representation. In comparison to that, the pre-trained BERT-LM utilizes stacked attention layers (Vaswani et al., 2017). By feeding a sequence into it and extracting the output of the last layer for each token, the idea is to implicitly use the attention mechanism to derive a better representation for every token. As is the case for the character-wise LM from Akbik et al. (2018), the BERT embeddings are contextualized by the whole input sequence of the specific task.

This paper will compare the two contextualized approaches described above with the pre-defined GloVe (Pennington et al., 2014) embeddings in the light of their usefulness for AM. The goal is to encode the features necessary to detect arguments by utilizing the context of a sentence.

3 Methodology

This paper evaluates different machine learning architectures with attention layers for the task of AM, and more specifically unit segmentation. The problem is framed as a multi-class token labeling task, in which each token is assigned one of three labels. A (B) label denotes that the token is at the beginning of an argumentative unit, an (I) label that it lies inside a unit and an (O) label that the token is not part of a unit. This framework has been applied previously for the same task (Stab, 2017; Eger et al., 2017; Ajjour et al., 2017).

The architectures proposed in this section build on Ajjour et al. (2017), omitting the second Bi-LSTM, which was used to process features other than word embeddings (see section 3.3). They are further being modified by adding attention layers at different positions. The goal is to reuse existing approaches and possibly enhance their ability to model long-range dependencies. Additionally, a simpler architecture, consisting of a single Bi-LSTM paired with an attention layer, is built and evaluated with the aim of reduced complexity.

In order to answer the second research question, this paper reports results in combination with improved input embeddings, in order to evaluate their effectiveness and impact on the AM downstream task.

All models are compared to the modified re-implementation of the architecture, which is defined as the baseline architecture.

3.1 Models

In order to evaluate the attention mechanisms, different architectures based on previous AM literature are implemented. The attention layer is added at different positions in the network.

All models were implemented using Python and the Keras framework with a TensorFlow backend. For the self-attention and multi-head attention layers, an existing implementation is used (HG, 2018a,b). The difference between the two is that the multi-head attention divides the input into multiple chunks and each head therefore works on a different vector subspace (Vaswani et al., 2017), while the self-attention works on the whole input sequence. This is supposed to allow the head to focus on specific features of the input. In this case, the self-attention layers use additive attention, while the multi-head attention layers use scaled dot-product attention, with the latter following the implementation of Vaswani et al. (2017).

Baseline re-implementation The baseline model from Ajjour et al. (2017) uses a total of three Bi-LSTMs (two of them fully connected) to assign labels to tokens (see Figure 1a). The re-implementation does not include the two fully connected Bi-LSTMs but instead uses only a single one that works on the word embeddings (see Figure 1b). Due to the fact that the second Bi-LSTM in the first layer is only used to encode the non-semantic features like part-of-speech tags and discourse marker labels, it is omitted in the re-implementation. Hereafter, we will refer

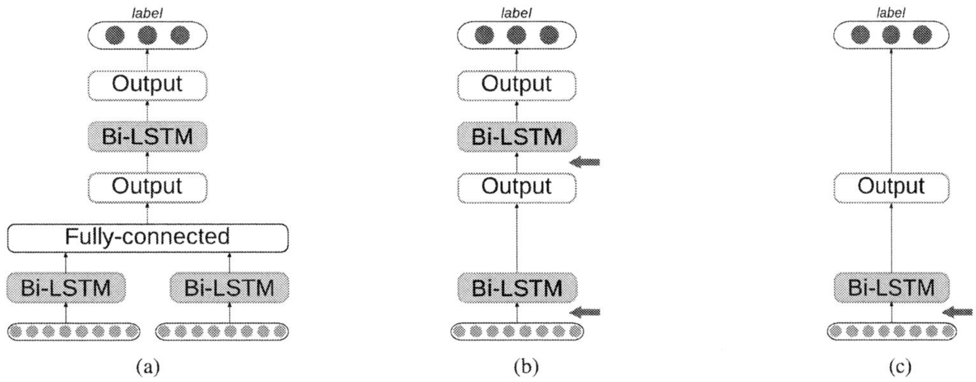

Figure 1: *(a)* The original baseline architecture as reported by Ajjour et al. (2017). *(b)* The modified baseline architecture without the second input Bi-LSTM. The bold arrows show the positions at which the additional attention layers are added to build the **Baseline**$_{+input}$ and **Baseline**$_{+error}$ architectures. *(c)* The **Bi-LSTM** architecture incorporates only one Bi-LSTM. The bold arrow shows the position at which the additional attention layer is added to build the **Bi-LSTM**$_{+input}$ architecture.

to this model as **Baseline**. Also, the batch size was increased from 8 to 64, compared to the original implementation, as a trade-off between convergence time and the model's generalization performance (Keskar et al., 2016). Nevertheless, this model achieves comparable scores to the ones presented in the original paper. The slightly lower performance can probably be attributed to implementation details.

Baseline$_{+input}$ **and Baseline**$_{+error}$ For both variations, the architecture shown in in Figure 1b was used as a basis. Multi-head-attention layers are added at different positions in the network. The number of attention heads depends on the dimension of the embedding vectors. For the GloVe (300 dimensions) and the BERT (3072 dimensions) embeddings, six heads are used, while the Flair (4196 dimensions) embeddings require four heads. Both numbers were the largest divisor for the respective input vector size that worked inside the computational boundaries available. In the first model, an attention layer was added before the first Bi-LSTM in an attempt to apply a relevance score directly to the tokens, in order to better capture dependencies of the input sequence. This model will be referred to as **Baseline**$_{+input}$. The second variation adds the attention layer after the first and before the second Bi-LSTM, which will be called **Baseline**$_{+error}$. According to Ajjour et al. (2017), the latter Bi-LSTM is used to correct the errors of the first one. The attention layer should be able to support the model in the error correction process. In contrast to the first approach, this does

not change the input data, but only works on the output of the first Bi-LSTM.

Bi-LSTM and Bi-LSTM$_{+input}$ To decrease the complexity of the architecture, two additional models with a single Bi-LSTM are trained. The first variant has no attention layer, while the second one utilized the same input attention described above (see Figure 1c). They will be refered to as **Bi-LSTM** and **Bi-LSTM**$_{+input}$ respectively. Both architectures use a self-attention mechanism instead of the above-mentioned multi-head-attention, due to better results in preliminary tests.

3.2   Data

The different architectures were trained and evaluated on the "Argument annotated Essays (version 2)" corpus (also referred to as Persuasive Essays corpus) (Stab and Gurevych, 2017). It was utilized for the same task in previous literature (Ajjour et al., 2017; Eger et al., 2017).

The corpus, compiled for parsing argumentative structures in written text, consists of a random sample of 402 student essays. The annotation scheme includes the argumentative units and the relations between them, as well as the major claim and stance of the author towards a specific topic. The texts were annotated by non-professionals, labeling the boundary of each argumentative unit alongside the unit type. A type can either be major-claim, claim or premise. For the unit segmentation task, the corpus is labeled by treating major claims, claims, and premises as argumentative units[1]. For comparability reasons in the evaluation process, the models are trained and tested with the train-test-split defined by Stab and Gurevych (2017). The development set was composed of the last 20 percent of the training set and shuffled before use.

3.3 Features

For each token, a set of three different embeddings is generated and compared regarding their capability as standalone input features. The resulting weighted F1-score is then used as a proxy for measuring the usefulness of the generated text-representation in light of this specific downstream task.

In combination with the re-implemented architecture, the word embeddings approach GloVe (Pennington et al., 2014), trained on 6 billion tokens, serves as the baseline.

As a first approach to enhance the performance, the GloVe embeddings are stacked with the character-based Flair embeddings (Akbik et al., 2018), which are generated by a Bi-LSTM model. Akbik et al. (2018) argue that the resulting embeddings are contextualized, since the LM was trained to predict the most probable next character and therefore to encode the context of the whole sequence.

Similar to that, we also compare contextualized BERT-embeddings as standalone features (Devlin et al., 2018). An increased performance is expected because of the pre-training procedure of the LM. The BERT-LM was trained to predict a (randomly masked) word by utilizing the context of its appearance, as well as on next sentence prediction. Due to its sota performance for both, token-level and sentence-level tasks, the authors of this paper argue that the derived representations are well suited for the task of unit segmentation. Also, the representation fits the needs of the inter-token and sentence dependencies of the task. It is expected that this enables the model to better grasp the notion or pattern of an argument. Both contextualized embeddings are generated using the Flair library (Zalando Research, 2018).

For the of the BERT-embeddings the "bert-base-uncased" LM, consisting of 12-layers and pre-trained on lowercased data, is used. At the time

Model	GloVe	BERT	Flair
Baseline	0.86	0.83	**0.87**
Baseline$_{+input}$	**0.85**	0.68	0.67
Baseline$_{+error}$	0.67	**0.68**	0.67
Bi-LSTM	**0.86**	0.86	0.86
Bi-LSTM$_{+input}$	**0.84**	0.83	0.81

Table 1: The weighted F1-scores for the **Baseline** and all four variations. Results are shown per variation and embedding. Each row shows the performance of one architecture with different word embeddings as input vector. The highest score for each architecture is marked in bold.

of writing, the Flair library extracts the representations for the first subword token from the last four layers of the pre-trained BERT model. The subtoken embeddings is then used as representation for the whole token. Features specifically engineered for this task are not included in the input, following the argumentation of Eger et al. (2017) that they will probably not be generalizable to different data sets.

4 Results

We evaluate the performance of all architectures on the Persuasive Essays data set detailed above. The models are re-initialized after every evaluation and do not share any weights. This allows us to answer the first research question of whether additional attention layers have a positive impact on the prediction quality.

To answer the second research question, we re-run each training, replacing the GloVe embeddings with BERT and Flair embeddings. Both contextualized embedding methods are tested separately. We contextualize the tokens on the sentence level since the BERT model (Devlin et al., 2018) only allows for a maximum input length of 512 characters. This makes document-level or paragraph-level embeddings impractical for the data set.

As a performance measure, we report the weighted F1-score instead of the macro F1-score, since it takes the imbalance of the samples per label into account.

For our re-implementation of the baseline, we are able to approximately reproduce the results reported by Ajjour et al. (2017). Additionally, we can verify that there is no major change in the performance when adding a second Bi-LSTM to the network (compare results for **Bi-LSTM** and **Baseline** in Table 1).

4.1 Attention Layers

The results of the token classification task are presented in Table 1. Generally speaking, the added attention encodings do not improve upon the original architecture's performance, no matter at which position they are added. Architectures with an input attention encoding, namely **Baseline**$_{+input}$ and **Bi-LSTM**$_{+input}$, do achieve similar performances compared to their respective baseline. But the F1-score performance is in strong contrast to the generalization error, which is in most cases lower for the **Baseline** model.

The **Baseline**$_{+error}$ architecture, on the other hand, which is supposed to help the second Bi-LSTM in the network to correct the errors made by the first one, performs worse across all tests. For the Flair embeddings, this results in a 0.20 points performance drop in the F1-score measure.

4.2 Contextualized Word Embeddings

The results for the enhanced word embedding evaluations are reported in Table 1. In some cases, the models utilizing the word embeddings generated by the BERT-LM achieve a lower performance score than the other embeddings. This drop is most noticeable for the **Baseline**$_{+input}$ model, while the performance for the **Bi-LSTM**$_{+input}$ decreases only slightly. The **Baseline**$_{+error}$ model is able to achieve results that outperform both, GloVe and Flair embeddings.

Compared to the GloVe vectors, the models trained on the Flair embeddings mostly lose in F1-score performance as well. For example, the **Baseline**$_{+input}$ model drops by 0.18. On the other hand, the **Baseline** model is able to slightly improve upon the GloVe score using the Flair embeddings, achieving a final score of 0.87, which also marks the best overall score in our testings.

An interesting observation is the fact that the enhanced embeddings seem to increase the generalization error (compare Figure 2). The **Baseline** model trained on the GloVe embeddings, for example, shows a difference in the final validation and training loss of around 0.17 and increases for the BERT and Flair embeddings to roughly 0.60 and 0.48, respectively.

5 Discussion

Given the experimental results, we discuss the resulting implications for our two research questions and conclude this section by presenting some limitations.

5.1 Attention Layers

Our results suggest that the attention encoding does not increase the performance of the model, as we hypothesized above. This is true for both, the input and the error encoding. A potential explanation is the fact that we use the attention mechanism as an additional layer to encode the input. Other approaches, like Morio and Fujita (2018) or Stab et al. (2018), incorporate it into the Bi-LSTM architecture and calculate the weight of the hidden states at every time step.

While the performance does not decrease meaningfully for the **Baseline**$_{+input}$ and **Bi-LSTM**$_{+input}$ models (using the GloVe embeddings as features), it does for the error encoding **Baseline**$_{+error}$ model. This drop might be explained by the vector space the attention mechanism is working on. Due to its small size of only four features, it is unlikely that the resulting vector has a meaningful encoding.

A deeper inspection of the output values from the different layers in the network and how they influence the overall classification task might give more insight into the cause of the problem.

5.2 Contextualized Word Embeddings

For most of the tests we conduct, the contextualized embedding approaches do not improve upon the GloVe embeddings. This is especially true for the architectures that include an attention layer, which does not seem to be able to handle the encoding of high dimensional vectors very well. The results further suggest that the amount of neurons in the Bi-LSTMs is not an issue in this case, since the **Baseline** model achieves comparable results across all three embeddings.

A potential way to improve the results of the enhanced embeddings is to contextualize them on the paragraph level. While we contextualize them on a sentence level, the dependencies between arguments might span over multiple sentences, sometimes even a paragraph, as described by Stab and Gurevych (2017) for the Persuasive Essays data set. Following this reasoning, one might think that a document level contextualization makes sense

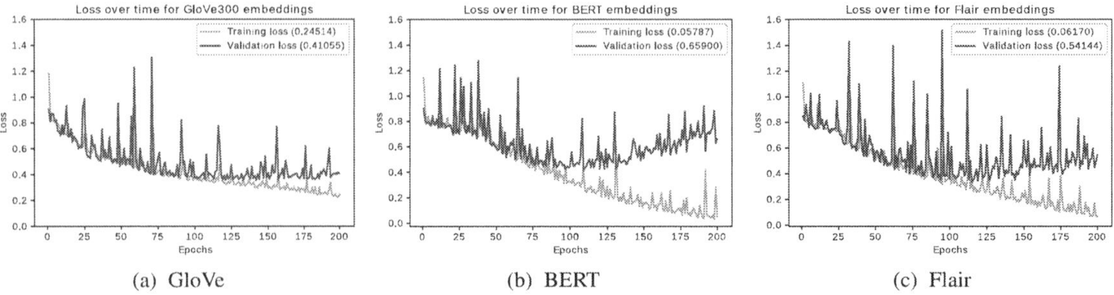

Figure 2: The loss curves of the **Baseline** architecture using different input embeddings. Figure *(a)* shows the training process of the model using the GloVe embeddings, while the model in Figure *(b)* used the BERT embeddings and Figure *(c)* the Flair embeddings. The orange line shows the training loss, the green line the validation loss.

and adds even more information to the embedding. For the task of AM, however, we argue against this for two reasons. First, argumentative units usually do not span over the whole document and it might include additional counter-arguments (Stab and Gurevych, 2017). The contextualization would most likely cause a lot of noise and make the vector less useful. Also, depending on the size of the document, the size of the vector might be too small to hold the contextual information of the full document. Second, the model trained on such embeddings would probably not generalize very well. An argumentative document can be written in different formats with different purposes, like an essay, a speech or a newspaper article. Contextualizing the embeddings on the document level might then also encode the structure of the text and decrease the cross-domain applicability of the model. However, further research is needed.

5.3 Limitations

The results we report and analyze above are the networks' performance as validated on the data splits provided by Stab and Gurevych (2017). Due to time and resource restrictions, we evaluate the results after a single training run and perform neither an averaging over multiple runs nor any cross-validation. Both could lead to more robust results. As another consequence of the above-mentioned restrictions, we are also not able to test the model's generalization capabilities on different data sets.

For the learning rate, we perform only a basic Bayesian hyperparameter optimization (Snoek et al., 2012) with four iterations per model. These limitations are especially important for the variations of the **Baseline** architecture, since the performed changes to the architecture, even though

rather small, entail the need for independently tuned hyperparameters.

Furthermore, an additional evaluation of the different contextualization levels for the embeddings could provide a clearer picture of how much the results actually improve, compared to non-contextualized methods.

6 Conclusion

Recent improvements in utilizing contextual information for sequence processing had a big impact on the area of NLP, namely advances of attention architectures and contextualized word embeddings. For example, the Transformer architecture (Vaswani et al., 2017) employs attention to achieve sota scores on different NLP tasks. Further, the Flair model (Akbik et al., 2018) incorporates character-wise context to generate enhanced word representations.

In this paper, we report on the usefulness of these two approaches for the task of AM. First, we are able to show that an attention layer as additional encoding of the input does not improve upon the current sota approach of a Bi-LSTM. Additionally, the attention mechanism seems to fail for a low-dimensional vector space. Second, we present the impact of contextualized word embeddings for AM. Although the Flair embeddings slightly improve upon the performance of the GloVe embeddings for the **Baseline** architecture, we can not confirm any advantage over non-contextualized embeddings.

6.1 Future Work

A first extension of this work could be a proper hyperparameter optimization for the attention-based models. Second, we plan to explore an attempt to fine-tune solely attention based pre-trained models like BERT (Devlin et al., 2018) to domain-specific data. Recent research by Howard and Ruder (2018) in transfer-learning for NLP has shown great improvement for several NLP-downstream tasks, while reducing the needed amount of labeled training data.

Third, we contextualize the embeddings on the sentence level only. According to Stab and Gurevych (2017), arguments can sometimes span over multiple sentences. Therefore, the contextualization of the embeddings could be extended to a paragraph level, in order to make use of possible inter-dependencies within it. Additionally, a fine-tuning approach of the underlying LMs to the AM task could further enhance the embeddings.

Acknowledgments

We thank our three anonymous reviewers, as well as Laura Spillner, for their valuable feedback and helpful suggestions on earlier drafts of this paper. We also thank Andreas Breiter for early feedback on the approach and supervising the research-based learning project CoVis of the University of Bremen, which enabled us to work on this paper, as well as the rest of the master's project CoVis.

References

Yamen Ajjour, Wei-Fan Chen, Johannes Kiesel, Henning Wachsmuth, and Benno Stein. 2017. Unit Segmentation of Argumentative Texts. In *Proceedings of the 4th Workshop on Argument Mining*, pages 118–128, Copenhagen, Denmark. Association for Computational Linguistics.

Alan Akbik, Duncan Blythe, and Roland Vollgraf. 2018. Contextual String Embeddings for Sequence Labeling. In *Proceedings of the 27th International Conference on Computational Linguistics*, pages 1638–1649, Santa Fe, New Mexico, USA. Association for Computational Linguistics.

Dzmitry Bahdanau, Kyunghyun Cho, and Yoshua Bengio. 2014. Neural Machine Translation by Jointly Learning to Align and Translate. arXiv: 1409.0473.

Piotr Bojanowski, Edouard Grave, Armand Joulin, and Tomas Mikolov. 2017. Enriching Word Vectors with Subword Information. *Transactions of the Association for Computational Linguistics*, 5:135–146.

Elena Cabrio and Serena Villata. 2018. Five Years of Argument Mining: a Data-driven Analysis. In *Proceedings of the Twenty-Seventh International Joint Conference on Artificial Intelligence*, pages 5427–5433, Stockholm, Sweden. International Joint Conferences on Artificial Intelligence Organization.

Jacob Devlin, Ming-Wei Chang, Kenton Lee, and Kristina Toutanova. 2018. BERT: Pre-training of Deep Bidirectional Transformers for Language Understanding. arXiv: 1810.04805.

Steffen Eger, Johannes Daxenberger, and Iryna Gurevych. 2017. Neural End-to-End Learning for Computational Argumentation Mining. In *Proceedings of the 55th Annual Meeting of the Association for Computational Linguistics (Volume 1: Long Papers)*, pages 11–22, Vancouver, Canada. Association for Computational Linguistics.

J. R. Firth. 1957. A synopsis of linguistic theory 1930-55. pages 1–32.

Sebastian Haunss, Jonas Kuhn, Sebastian Padó, and Nico Blokker. MARDY: Modeling ARgumentation DYnamics in Political Discourse. `https://www.socium.uni-bremen.de/projekte/?proj=570&print=1`, last accessed: 2019-06-04, 16:48UTC+2.

Hendrik Heuer. 2015. Semantic and stylistic text analysis and text summary evaluation. Master thesis.

Zhao HG. 2018a. Attention mechanism for processing sequential data that considers the context for each timestamp. `https://github.com/CyberZHG/keras-self-attention`, last accessed: 2019-05-01, 21:39UTC+2.

Zhao HG. 2018b. A wrapper layer for stacking layers horizontally. `https://github.com/CyberZHG/keras-multi-head`, last accessed: 2019-05-01, 21:40UTC+2.

Sepp Hochreiter and Jürgen Schmidhuber. 1997. Long Short-Term Memory. *Neural Computation*, 9(8):1735–1780.

Jeremy Howard and Sebastian Ruder. 2018. Universal Language Model Fine-tuning for Text Classification. In *Proceedings of the 56th Annual Meeting of the Association for Computational Linguistics (Volume 1: Long Papers)*, pages 328–339, Melbourne, Australia. Association for Computational Linguistics.

Laurent Itti, Christof Koch, and Ernst Niebur. 1998. A model of saliency-based visual attention for rapid scene analysis. *IEEE Transactions on Pattern Analysis and Machine Intelligence*, 20(11):1254–1259.

Nitish Shirish Keskar, Dheevatsa Mudigere, Jorge Nocedal, Mikhail Smelyanskiy, and Ping Tak Peter Tang. 2016. On Large-Batch Training for Deep Learning: Generalization Gap and Sharp Minima. arXiv: 1609.04836.

Tomas Mikolov, Kai Chen, Greg Corrado, and Jeffrey Dean. 2013. Efficient Estimation of Word Representations in Vector Space. arXiv: 1301.3781.

Volodymyr Mnih, Nicolas Heess, Alex Graves, and Koray Kavukcuoglu. 2014. Recurrent Models of Visual Attention. arXiv: 1406.6247.

Gaku Morio and Katsuhide Fujita. 2018. End-to-End Argument Mining for Discussion Threads Based on Parallel Constrained Pointer Architecture. In *Proceedings of the 5th Workshop on Argument Mining*, pages 11–21, Brussels, Belgium. Association for Computational Linguistics.

Jeffrey Pennington, Richard Socher, and Christopher Manning. 2014. Glove: Global Vectors for Word Representation. In *Proceedings of the 2014 Conference on Empirical Methods in Natural Language Processing (EMNLP)*, pages 1532–1543, Doha, Qatar. Association for Computational Linguistics.

Magnus Sahlgren. 2005. An introduction to random indexing. In *Methods and applications of semantic indexing workshop at the 7th international conference on terminology and knowledge engineering*, volume 5. TKE.

Magnus Sahlgren. 2006. *The Word-Space Model: using distributional analysis to represent syntagmatic and paradigmatic relations between words in high-dimensional vector spaces*. Ph.D. thesis, Stockholm University.

Mike Schuster and Kuldip K. Paliwal. 1997. Bidirectional recurrent neural networks. *IEEE Trans. Signal Processing*, 45:2673–2681.

Jasper Snoek, Hugo Larochelle, and Ryan P Adams. 2012. Practical Bayesian Optimization of Machine Learning Algorithms. In F. Pereira, C. J. C. Burges, L. Bottou, and K. Q. Weinberger, editors, *Advances in Neural Information Processing Systems 25*, pages 2951–2959. Curran Associates, Inc.

Christian Stab and Iryna Gurevych. 2017. Parsing Argumentation Structures in Persuasive Essays. *Computational Linguistics*, 43(3):619–659.

Christian Stab, Tristan Miller, Benjamin Schiller, Pranav Rai, and Iryna Gurevych. 2018. Cross-topic Argument Mining from Heterogeneous Sources. In *Proceedings of the 2018 Conference on Empirical Methods in Natural Language Processing*, pages 3664–3674. Association for Computational Linguistics. Event-place: Brussels, Belgium.

Christian Matthias Edwin Stab. 2017. *Argumentative Writing Support by means of Natural Language Processing*. Ph.D. thesis, Technische Universität Darmstadt, Darmstadt.

Mayer Tobias, Cabrio Elena, Lippi Marco, Torroni Paolo, and Villata Serena. 2018. Argument Mining on Clinical Trials. *Frontiers in Artificial Intelligence and Applications*, pages 137–148.

Ashish Vaswani, Noam Shazeer, Niki Parmar, Jakob Uszkoreit, Llion Jones, Aidan N. Gomez, Lukasz Kaiser, and Illia Polosukhin. 2017. Attention is All You Need. In *Proceedings of the 31st International Conference on Neural Information Processing Systems*, NIPS'17, pages 6000–6010, USA. Curran Associates Inc. Event-place: Long Beach, California, USA.

Kelvin Xu, Jimmy Ba, Ryan Kiros, Kyunghyun Cho, Aaron Courville, Ruslan Salakhudinov, Rich Zemel, and Yoshua Bengio. 2015. Show, Attend and Tell: Neural Image Caption Generation with Visual Attention. In *Proceedings of the 32nd International Conference on Machine Learning*, volume 37 of *Proceedings of Machine Learning Research*, pages 2048–2057, Lille, France. PMLR.

Zalando Research. 2018. A very simple framework for state-of-the-art Natural Language Processing (NLP). `https://github.com/zalandoresearch/flair`, last accessed: 2019-05-01, 21:39UTC+2.

Argument Component Classification by Relation Identification by Neural Network and TextRank

Mamoru Deguchi
University of Tokyo
deguchi-mamoru@graco.c.u-tokyo.ac.jp

Kazunori Yamaguchi
University of Tokyo
yamaguch@graco.c.u-tokyo.ac.jp

Abstract

In recent years, argumentation mining, which automatically extracts the structure of argumentation from unstructured documents such as essays and debates, is gaining attention. For argumentation mining applications, argument-component classification is an important subtask.

The existing methods can be classified into supervised methods and unsupervised methods. Many existing supervised methods use a classifier to identify the roles of argument components, such as " claim " or " premise " , but many of them use information of a single sentence without relying on the whole document. On the other hand, existing unsupervised document classification has the advantage of being able to use the whole document, but accuracy of these methods is not so high.

In this paper, we propose a method for argument-component classification that combines relation identification by neural networks and TextRank to integrate relation informations (i.e. the strength of the relation). This method can use argumentation-specific knowledge by employing supervised learning on a corpus while maintaining the advantage of using the whole document.

Experiments on two corpora, one consisting of student essays and the other of Wikipedia articles, show the effectiveness of this method.

1 Introduction

In recent years, argumentation mining, which automatically extracts the structure of argumentation from unstructured documents such as essays and debates, is gaining attention.

Argumentation mining consists of the following four subtasks (Potash et al., 2017).

1. Extracting the argument component (AC for short) from a given document (component idenfication).

2. Assigning a label such as claim or premise to each AC (component classification).

3. Determining whether each pair of ACs is related or not (relation identification).

4. Assigning a label such as attack or support to the related pairs of ACs (relation classification).

We focus on component classification. Generally, an AC is classified as a claim or a premise. A claim is the conclusion of an argument, and a premise is an assumption or reason to induce the conclusion.

In this paper, we propose a method that can be applied to new domains of argumentation with little cost.

Previous methods of component classification can be classified as supervised document classification and unsupervised document classification using topic models or TextRank, a ranking algorithm. Many existing methods of supervised document classication perform classication using a single sentence without relying on the whole document. Existing unsupervised document classification has the advantage of being able to use the whole document, but it can not use argumentation specific knowledge, such as the fact that "therefore" relates a conclusion with its reason.

In this paper, we propose a framework for component classification using the argumentation-specific knowledge by employing supervised learning on a corpus while maintaining the advantage of using the whole document.

The research on component classification has been done on various domains of argumentation. (Levy et al., 2014) proposed a method to extract from a Wikipedia artitle a sentence including Context Dependent Claim (CDC) that directly supports the topic of the article by combining context-

Proceedings of the 6th Workshop on Argument Mining, pages 83–91
Florence, Italy, August 1, 2019. ©2019 Association for Computational Linguistics

free and context-dependent features such as the cosine similarity between the topic of the article and the sentence. (Lippi and Torroni, 2015) proposed a method to extract a CDC from a sentence using a support-vector machine (SVM) with Tree Kernels on the phrase structure of the sentence. As for student essays, (Stab and Gurevych, 2014) proposed a method to classify a sentence as a major claim, claim, or premise using an SVM on the basis of features such as the position of the AC in a paragraph and a clue expression. However, these methods have a disadvantage in that new features must be developed in order to apply said methods to a new domain of argumentation.

(Daxenberger et al., 2017) proposed a method to extract claims in various domains of argumentation using a recurrent neural network (RNN) and convolutional neural network (CNN). These are methods for classifying a sentence, so they cannot use information outside of the sentence. This is a significant disadvantage for these methods in component classification because the role of an AC is determined relatively to those of other ACs in the document. For example, the probability that an AC is a claim is higher if the AC is supported by some premises. Thus, using the relation of an AC to other ACs is important when classifying the AC.

Some researchers have tried to improve the performance of component classification by employing the relation information between ACs. In (Stab and Gurevych, 2017), the results of component classification and relation identification are combined to improve both of their performances using integer programming. In this method, the cost to apply a new domain of argumentation is high because hand-crafted features are highly dependent on the domain of argumentation such as the position of AC in the argumentation or a clue expression.

In (Potash et al., 2017), component classification and relation identification between ACs are performed simultaneously using a PointerNet neural network. This improves the classification performance. In this research, the dependency relation is limited to within a paragraph, and the whole document cannot be used.

There is also research on component classification using unsupervised learning. (Ferrara et al., 2017) proposed a method to extract a sentence including AC, extract a major claim (the standpoint of the author for the topic of an es-

say), and classify ACs using a topic model. In (Petasis and Karkaletsis, 2016), sentences including a major claim and a claim are extracted by ranking the sentences using the TextRank (Mihalcea and Tarau, 2004) on the basis of the similarity of sentences. These studies use relations among ACs in a document and are not dependent on the domain of argumentation. However, these methods are not highly accurate.

In this paper, we propose a neural network to evaluate the probability of there being a relation between ACs and to rank ACs using TextRank on the basis of probability.

Our method uses argumentation-specific knowledge for relation identification between ACs, and the results are used for component classification. The argumentation-specific knowledge is extracted by a neural network from a small corpus. Thus, this method can be applied to various domains of argumentation with little cost. We applied the proposed method to two domains of argumentation and had positive results.

2 Previous Methods

2.1 Component Classification using TextRank

In this section, we explain what TextRank is and discuss previous methods of component classification using TextRank.

TextRank is a PageRank-based ranking algorithm applied to natural language processing. It has been used for keyword extraction and extraneous document summarization. In TextRank, a document is represented by a weighted directed graph with a fragment of a text such as a sentence, phrase, or word as a node; a metric between two nodes are used as a weight on the edge between the nodes. From this directed graph, a recurrent equation is generated and its solution is used to determine the rank of the nodes.

For example, suppose that a weighted direct graph $G = (S, E)$ is obtained from a document $D = \{S_1, ..., S_n\}$. Here, $E \subseteq S \times S$ and E_{ij} $(1 \leq i, j \leq n)$ are a directed edge from sentence S_i to sentence S_j. For a directed edge E_{ij}, a metric $w(S_i, S_j)$ from a sentence S_i to S_i is used as the weight of the edge. Then, $WS(S_i)$ determined by Eq. 2 is used as the score of the sentence S_i.

$$W(S_i, S_j) = \frac{w(S_i, S_j)}{\sum_{S_k \in Out(S_i)} w(S_i, S_k)} \qquad (1)$$

$$WS(S_i) = (1-d)+d* \sum_{S_j \in In(S_i)} W(S_j, S_i) \cdot WS(S_j) \quad (2)$$

$In(S_i)$ is the set of sentences that have an outgoing edge to the sentence S_i, and $Out(S_j)$ is the set of sentences that have an incoming edge from S_j. d is a hyperparameter (random surfer rate) taking a value between 0 and 1. In the previous work (Petasis and Karkaletsis, 2016; Ferrara et al., 2017), the term frequency inverse document frequency (TFIDF) cosine similarity between sentences S_i and S_i was used as $w(S_i, S_j)$. In (Petasis and Karkaletsis, 2016), the score was determined for each sentence, and the method was evaluated correct if the top one or two sentences according to the score includes the target major claim or claim.

2.2 Relation Identification between Argument Components

In this section, we give an overview of research on relation identification between ACs. (Stab and Gurevych, 2017) performed a binary classification of whether or not there is a relation between two ACs using SVM on the basis of features extracted from ACs in the domain of student essays. (Nguyen and Litman, 2016) performed a classification of the relation between ACs using features obtained from the information around the AC as well as the features obtained from the AC itself. (Rinott et al., 2015) classified evidence (claim dependent evidence: CDE) into Study, Expert, and Anecdotal in accordance with their properties in Wikipedia articles of a random topic, and then extracted CDE of each Claim using a combination of logistic regression (LR) classifiers. In these studies, features used for classification have to be prepared by hand, so these methods have the disadvantage of a high cost to develop the features.

(Cocarascu and Toni, 2017) classified the relation between ACs with neural networks using a corpus they developed.

In this paper, we propose a method that can be applied to various domains of argumentation with little cost. We think that preparing a small corpus with labels is acceptable for better accuracy, but developing new features is too costly because for developing new features, skills on feature enginering as well as knowledge on the domaim of argument are required. For these reasons, we employ a novel neural network to determine the probability that an AC is related to other ACs as in the ap-

proach of (Cocarascu and Toni, 2017), use probability as the weight for TextRank, and use the score of the AC as the likelihood that the AC is major claim or claim.

3 Proposed Method

In this section, we explain our approach. Section 3.1 explains the neural network we use to identify the relations between ACs. Section 3.2 explains a method for extracting claims by applying the TextRank algorithm to the identified relation.

3.1 Relation Identification

We use a neural network for identifying the relations between ACs. The neural network is used to convert an AC into a single sentence vector and to output the probability that there exists a relation between a pair of ACs using the vectors of the ACs. The neural network consists of

1. a neural network to convert an AC into a single sentence vector, and

2. a neural network to assess the relatedness of the vectors of two ACs.

We tested long short-term memory (LSTM) and a CNN for Step 1. In Step 2, we tested the following two methods to combine the vectors of two documents obtained in Step 1. In the first method, we concatenated the two vectors and fed them to the fully connected layer. In the second method, we fed the two vectors as a sequence to LSTM, and the hidden units of LSTM were concatenated and sent to the fully connected layer.

We evaluated the neural networks on the basis of their performance when combined with TextRank. Figure 1 shows the neural network that obtained the best performance.

The input to the neural network is a pair consisting of $AC_i = (w_1, w_2, ...w_k)$ and $AC_j = (w'_1, w'_2, ...w'_{k'})$, where w_l is a word in an AC and k and k' is the length of the AC_i and AC_j. AC_i and AC_j are converted into word vectors $V_i = (v_1, v_2, ...v_k)$ and $V_j = (v'_1, v'_2, ...v'_{k'})$ in the embedding layer. v_l is a word vector for a word w_l. They are transformed by LSTM to make sentence vectors V_{AC_i} and V_{AC_j}. V_{AC_i} and V_{AC_j} are concatenated and sent to the next LSTM layers. Then, hidden state of each timesteps of LSTM layer are concatenated and sent to the next dense layers. Finally, the softmax function produces the estimated probability of the relation of the pair.

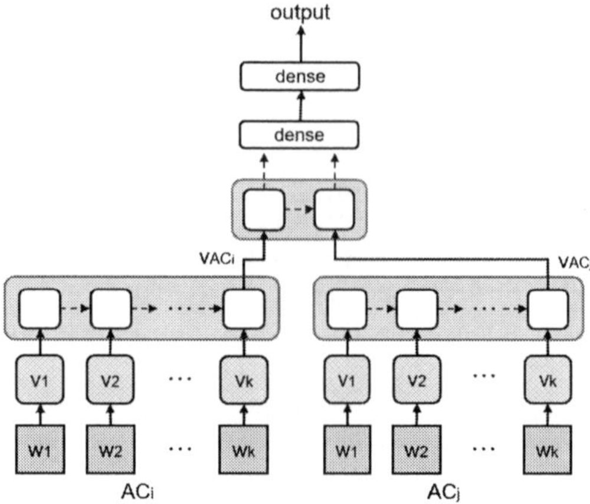

Figure 1: Proposed neural network for relation identi-fication: LSTM and dense network

If there is a relation between AC_i and AC_j, we denote the pair as $link$, and otherwise as $nolink$.

3.2 TextRank for Argument Mining

The relation identifier in Section 3.1 yields the probability $P(link|S_i, S_j)$ from AC_i to AC_j. We use this estimated probability $P(link|S_i, S_j)$ as $w(S_i, S_j)$ in Eq. 1. Because there is no ground to determine $w(S_i, S_i)$, we empirically set $w(S_i, S_i)$ to 1.

4 Experiment

In this section, we explain the corpus we use, ex-perimental setting, and results.

4.1 Data

We used two copora in this experiment, one consisting of student essays and the other of Wikipedia articles.

4.1.1 Student Essay

(Stab and Gurevych, 2017) distributed an-notated student essays in English extracted from the online forum essayforum.com at https://www.informatik.tu-darmstadt.de/ (Argument Annotated Essays (version 2)). The annotation consists of classification labels of the ACs and the relations among the ACs. We call this corpus "Student Essay." The basic figures of Student Essay are shown in Table 1.

As for the classification, ACs are classified as major claims, claims, and premises. A major claim shows the standpoint of the author on the topic of the essay. A claim supports or attacks the major claim. A premise is an assumption or a rea-son in an argument and supports or attacks a claim or another premise.

Regarding relations between ACs, the relation between claims is generally marked as for or against and that between premises as support or attack. In this paper, however, we do not use these types of relation (i.e. for, against, support, or at-tack). Rather, if there exists a relation of any type between a pair of ACs, we consider the pair as a positive example. Other pairs of ACs could serve as negative examples. However, the number of such negative examples is much larger than that of positive examples. In addition, most of the neg-ative example AC pairs are irrelevant to learning. Thus, we used only the reverse pairs (i.e. major claim and claim, major claim and premise, and claim and premise) as negative examples.

4.1.2 Wikipedia Article

(Aharoni et al., 2014) distributed annotated Wikipedia articles[1] with the topic labels, claim (CDC), and context dependent evidence (CDE). A topic is a short statement of the subject of an article. CDC is a statement supporting or attacking the topic that is directly related to a main claim of the article. CDE is a text fragment directly supporting some CDC under the topic of the article. We call this corpus "Wikipedia Article." The basic figures of Wikipedia Article are shown in Table 2.

CDE can be classified as Study, Expert, and Anecdotal according to the type of evidence. Study is CDE backed by quantitative analysis. Ex-pert is CDE backed by an expert (person or orga-nization). Anecdotal is CDE backed by an event or example. In this experiment, if CDC and CDE in an article were related, we used the pair as a positive example. Otherwise, they were used as a negative example. We did not use the different types of CDE.

Table 1: Student Essay

essay	Type of AC			Relation	
	MajorClaim	Claim	Premise	link	nolink
402	751	1506	3832	6673	91798

4.2 Proposed Method

In this section, we explain the experimen-tal details of the proposed method. For

---

[1] http://www.research.ibm.com/haifa/dept/vst/debating_data.shtml

Table 2: Wikipedia Article

essay	Type of AC		Relation	
	CDC	CDE	link	nolink
102	350	795	1291	31634

word vectors, we used pretrained word vectors with 300 dimensions available at https://code.google.com/archive/p/word2vec/.

The neural network was implemented in Keras[2].

For Student Essay, we used the following settings. LSTM had 64 units. The fully connected layer had 64 units with a dropout rate of 0.5. A sigmoid function was used in the output layer. Binary cross-entropy was used as the loss function. The batch size was 128. Early stopping was employed using validation loss. The longest AC consisted of 67 words with 7238 words in vocabulary. We employed five-fold cross validation for testing. Ten percent of the training data was used as validation data.

For Wikipedia Article, we used the following settings. LSTM had 32 units. The fully connected layer had 64 units with a dropout rate of 0.3. A sigmoid function was used in the output layer. Binary cross-entropy was used as the loss function. The batch size was 128. Early stopping was employed using validation loss. The longest AC was 254 words with 6412 words in vocabulary. We employed ten-fold cross validation for testing because the data size of Wikipedia Article is smaller than that of Student Essay. Ten percent of the training data was used as validation data.

The hyperparameter d of TextRank was set 0.85 throughtout the experiments.

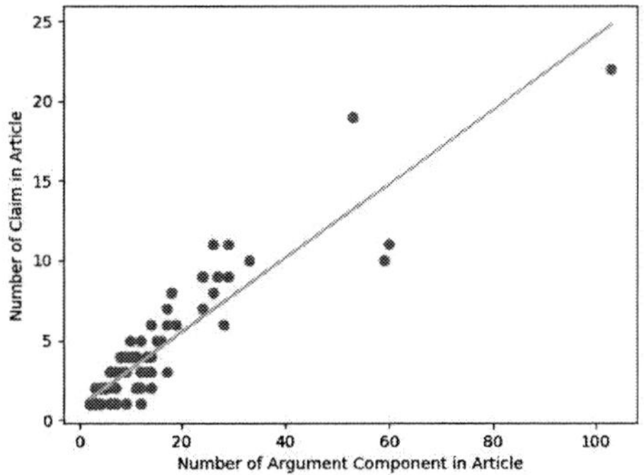

Figure 2: The Number of ACs vs. That of Claims in Wikipedia Article

---

[2]https://keras.io/

4.3 Previous Work: TextRank-TFIDF and TextRank-W2V

Here, we explain the similarities used in TextRank for comparison. For the similarity of TFIDF, we used the TFIDF vectors as used in (Petasis and Karkaletsis, 2016). We call this TextRank with the TFIDF cosine similarity "TextRank-TFIDF".

For the similarity of word2vec, we used the vector obtained by averaging the vectors of words in a sentence. For the word vectors, we used pre-trained Word2Vec with 300 dimensions at https://code.google.com/archive/p/word2vec/. We call TextRank with the word2vec consine similarity "TextRank-W2V".

4.4 Previous Work: Supervised Component Classification

Here, we explain the detail of supervised component classification for comparison. Because Student Essay has major claims and claims, we constructed two classifiers: the one which detects only major claims and another which detects all claims (including the major claims). For the classifier, we used a neural network classifier. As for the neural networks, we tested LSTM, bidirectional LSTM (biLSTM), and CNN. The input to the network was a sequence of AC word vectors. The output was whether the input AC is major claim (claim) or not. We used the following settings. LSTM and biLSTM had 64 units. The fully connected layer had 64 units with dropout rate 0.5. A sigmoid function was used in the output layer. The binary crossentropy was used as the loss function. The CNN had the kernel sizes 3, 4, and 5. The number of filters was 64. The max pooling had poolsize 2. The fully connected layer had 64 units with dropout rate 0.5. A sigmoid function was used in the output layer. Binary crossentropy was used as the loss function.

To discriminate major claims, claims, and premises, we used three-way classification. For three-way classification, we employed the softmax function. For the loss, we used categorical cross entropy.

We employed five-fold cross validation for testing. Ten percent of the training data was used as validation data for early stopping.

For word vectors, we used the pre-trained Word2Vec with 300 dimensions available at https://code.google.com/archive/p/word2vec/.

Table 3: Results of Claim Detection using TextRank in Student Essay

evaluation metrics	total	TextRank-TFIDF		TextRank-W2V		Our Model	
		correct essay	accuracy	correct essay	accuracy	correct essay	accuracy
MajorClaim@1	402	116	0.289	79	0.197	218	**0.542**
MajorClaim@2	402	173	0.430	128	0.318	282	**0.701**
MajorClaim@3	402	215	0.535	176	0.438	326	**0.811**
Claim@1	402	252	0.627	198	0.493	319	**0.794**
Claim@2	402	330	0.821	291	0.724	372	**0.925**
Claim@3	402	361	0.898	337	0.838	392	**0.975**

Table 4: Results of Claim detection using TextRank in Wikipedia Article

evaluation metrics	total	TextRank-TFIDF		TextRank-W2V		Our Model	
		correct essay	accuracy	correct essay	accuracy	correct essay	accuracy
Claim@1	104	13	0.125	2	0.019	101	**0.971**
Claim@2	104	44	0.423	30	0.288	103	**0.990**

Table 5: Averaged Rank of Major Claim, Claim, and Premise in Student Essay

Component Type	TextRank-TFIDF	TextRank-W2V	Our Model
MajorClaim	6.397	7.071	**3.883**
Claim	7.609	8.050	**6.664**
Premise	9.399	9.093	**10.263**

Table 6: Average Rank of Claim and Premise in Wikipedia Article

Component Type	TextRank-TFIDF	TextRank-W2V	Our Model
Claim	17.162	17.780	**4.747**
Premise	14.368	14.089	**19.959**

Table 7: Precision and Recall detecting Claim in Student Essay

Method	Precision	Recall	F-Score
Claim@1	**0.794**	0.146	0.247
Claim@2	0.748	0.276	0.403
Claim@3	0.715	0.395	0.509
Claim@6	0.602	0.661	0.630
Claim@7	0.571	**0.731**	**0.641**
LSTM	0.60	0.62	0.61
BiLSTM	0.57	0.61	0.59
CNN	0.58	0.58	0.58

Table 8: Precision and Recall detecting Major Claim in Student Essay

Method	Precision	Recall	F-Score
MajorClaim@1	**0.542**	0.298	0.384
MajorClaim@2	0.437	0.472	0.454
MajorClaim@3	0.371	**0.602**	**0.458**
LSTM	0.44	0.39	0.41
BiLSTM	0.49	0.35	0.41
CNN	0.49	0.31	0.38

4.5 Evaluation Method

For the comparison between our method and TextRank-TFIDF/TextRank-W2V, we used Claim@k and MajorClaim@k as evaluation metrics. In MajorClaim@k, the result is considered correct if the top k according to the ranking includes the target major claim. In Claim@k, the result is considered correct if the top k according to the ranking includes the target claim and major claim. In Student Essay, MajorClaim@k and Claim@k were evalueted for $k = 1, 2, 3$. Wikipedia Article does not include major claim, so the evaluation was done only for Claim@k. The number of ACs varies significantly, and the minimum is 2, so we report Claim@k for $k = 2$ to evaluate all the ACs. The number of articles that had two ACs was 24 out of 102. This means that these 24 articles are considered correct regardless of the output of the classifier when evaluating at Claim@2. So we should be careful that there is possibility of overestimation.

For component classification, we employed the precision, recall, and F-score as evaluation metrics that are often used in text classification. Our method obtains a rank of the ACs. For comparison, we set a threshold; if the rank was higher than the threshold, we considered the AC to be a major claim or claim. We used 1-3 as the threshold for Student Essay.

The number of ACs varies more for Wikipedia Article, ranging from a minimum of 2 to maximum of 103, with an average of 11.12. Thus, if we were to employ a small, fixed threshold, the recall would get smaller for an article with many ACs. In order to resolve this problem, we employed a linear regression to predict the number of claims from the number of ACs and used the prediction as a threshold. We call this "@adaptive." For the regression on Wikipedia Article, the regression coefficient was 0.232, and the intercept was 0.873 with R-squared as 0.846. The fitted line is drawn

Table 9: Precision and Recall detecting Claim in Wikipedia Corpus

Method	Precision	Recall	F-Score
Claim@adaptive	0.832	0.875	0.853
Claim@1	**0.971**	0.554	0.706
Claim@2	0.788	0.734	0.760
LSTM	0.89	**0.97**	**0.93**
BiLSTM	0.92	0.86	0.90
CNN	0.94	0.91	**0.93**

in Fig. 2.

For Student Essay, we evaluated a case wherein only major claims is considered and one wherein both major claims and claims are considered.

4.6 Experimental Result and Discussion

Tables 3 and 4 show the results using our method and TextRank-TFIDF/TextRank-W2V to Student Essay and Wikipedia Article.

For Student Essay, our proposed method outperformed the previous TextRank-TFIDF/TextRank-W2V. In particular, our method achieved 0.542, which is significantly better than the 0.289 of TextRank-TFIDF, for major claims.

Simply employing word vectors alone did not improve the performance; MajorClaim@1 was 0.197 for TextRank-W2V while it was 0.289 for TextRank-TFIDF.

Table 5 shows the averaged rank of major claims, claims and premises. For TextRank-TFIDF/TextRank-W2V, the difference in the averaged ranks for major claims, claims, premises is small, and they are not well separated. In our proposed method, the averaged ranks of major claims, claims, and premises are 3.883, 6.664, and 10.263, respectively, and they are well articulated. For Wikipedia Article, our method correctly assigns a higher rank to claims while TextRank-TFIDF/TextRank-W2V incorrectly assign a higher rank to premises.

Tables 7, 8, and 9 show the result of comparison of our method to the neural network classifiers. Our method ranks ACs into specified types of AC: major claim, claim, or premise for Student Essay. Because the neural network classifiers are classifiers, in order to make a comparison, we set a threshold on the rank to make classification. For Wikipedia Article, because the number of ACs varies, we use an adaptive threshold explained in Section 4.5.

For Student Essay, our method was the best in F-Score for major claim with 3 as the threshold,

Table 10: F-Score of three-way Classification of MajorClaim, Claim, and Premise of Student Essay

Method	MajorClaim	Claim	Premise
LSTM	0.37	0.34	0.75
BiLSTM	0.27	0.22	0.76
CNN	0.33	0.30	0.75

Table 11: Confusion Matrix of three-way Classification of MajorClaim, Claim, and Premise using LSTM of Student Essay for 20% test set of Table 1

	MajorClaim	Claim	Premise
MajorClaim	44	44	71
Claim	18	96	201
Premise	19	113	612

and also for claim with 7 as seen in Tables 7 and 8. This shows the effectiveness of our method for classifying AC into major claim and claim.

For Student Essay, our method is better than the neural network classifier. Table 10 shows the F-score for three-way classifier. In this table, LSTM and biLSTM are slightly better than CNN, but the difference is small. It is notable that the score is high for premise, but it is low for major claim and claim. Table 11 shows the confusion matrix for LSTM. The table shows this more clearly. Our method is effective for discriminating major claim and claim because major claim and claim are separated by ranking,

For Wikipedia Article, the neural network classifier marked better F-Scores. This can be understood that the argumentation structure of Wikipedia Article is more controlled and can be extracted just by the neural network classifier. We show the confusion matrix for LSTM of Wikipedia Article at Table 12.

However our method is better than the neural network classifier in the precision of @1 in Table 9. If one want to find out not all the claim but main claim, our method can serve better.

In summary, our method outperformed the previous methods for Student Essay. For Wikipedia Article, our method was slightly worse than the neural network classifiers.

5 Conclusion and Future Work

In this paper, we proposed a method to classify claim (major claim) by the combination of the neural network to determine the relation between ACs and TextRank to integrate the relation information to rank claim (major claim) higher. The

Table 12: Confusion Matrix of Classification of Claim, and Premise using LSTM of Wikipedia Article for 20% test set of Table 2

	Claim	Premise
Claim	70	2
Premise	9	151

experiments on Student Essay and Wikipedia Article show that the proposed method performed better in major claim and claim classification compared with TextRank with unsupervised similarity measure. This shows the effectiveness of utilizing the relation between ACs. Compared with the neural network classifier, the proposed method performed better for Student Essay, and not better in F-Score but better in precision for Wikipedia Article. Thus, if we need more precision such as the case that we want to find out only claim, the proposed method has an advantage. In addition, the proposed method performed well for a rather complex argument structure such as major claim, claim, and premise utilizing the ranking produced by the method. In summary, the proposed method performed well for multiple corpora with different argument structures and varying number of ACs.

We are going to use word vectors using the contextual information to improve the relation identification and also test other ranking algorithms such as RankNet (Burges et al., 2005) and ListNet (Cao et al., 2007).

References

Ehud Aharoni, Anatoly Polnarov, Tamar Lavee, Daniel Hershcovich, Ran Levy, Ruty Rinott, Dan Gutfreund, and Noam Slonim. 2014. A benchmark dataset for automatic detection of claims and evidence in the context of controversial topics. In *Proceedings of the First Workshop on Argumentation Mining*, pages 64–68, Baltimore, Maryland. Association for Computational Linguistics.

Chris Burges, Tal Shaked, Erin Renshaw, Ari Lazier, Matt Deeds, Nicole Hamilton, and Greg Hullender. 2005. Learning to rank using gradient descent. In *Proceedings of the 22Nd International Conference on Machine Learning*, ICML '05, pages 89–96, New York, NY, USA. ACM.

Zhe Cao, Tao Qin, Tie-Yan Liu, Ming-Feng Tsai, and Hang Li. 2007. Learning to rank: From pairwise approach to listwise approach. In *Proceedings of the 24th International Conference on Machine Learning*, ICML '07, pages 129–136, New York, NY, USA. ACM.

Oana Cocarascu and Francesca Toni. 2017. Identifying attack and support argumentative relations using deep learning. In *Proceedings of the 2017 Conference on Empirical Methods in Natural Language Processing*, pages 1374–1379, Copenhagen, Denmark. Association for Computational Linguistics.

Johannes Daxenberger, Steffen Eger, Ivan Habernal, Christian Stab, and Iryna Gurevych. 2017. What is the essence of a claim? cross-domain claim identification. In *Proceedings of the 2017 Conference on Empirical Methods in Natural Language Processing*, pages 2055–2066, Copenhagen, Denmark. Association for Computational Linguistics.

Alfio Ferrara, Stefano Montanelli, and Georgios Petasis. 2017. Unsupervised detection of argumentative units though topic modeling techniques. In *Proceedings of the 4th Workshop on Argument Mining*, pages 97–107, Copenhagen, Denmark. Association for Computational Linguistics.

Ran Levy, Yonatan Bilu, Daniel Hershcovich, Ehud Aharoni, and Noam Slonim. 2014. Context dependent claim detection. In *Proceedings of COLING 2014, the 25th International Conference on Computational Linguistics: Technical Papers*, pages 1489–1500, Dublin, Ireland. Dublin City University and Association for Computational Linguistics.

Marco Lippi and Paolo Torroni. 2015. Context-independent claim detection for argument mining. In *Proceedings of the 24th International Conference on Artificial Intelligence*, IJCAI'15, pages 185–191. AAAI Press.

Rada Mihalcea and Paul Tarau. 2004. Textrank: Bringing order into text. In *Proceedings of EMNLP 2004*, pages 404–411, Barcelona, Spain. Association for Computational Linguistics.

Huy Nguyen and Diane Litman. 2016. Context-aware argumentative relation mining. In *Proceedings of the 54th Annual Meeting of the Association for Computational Linguistics (Volume 1: Long Papers)*, pages 1127–1137, Berlin, Germany. Association for Computational Linguistics.

Georgios Petasis and Vangelis Karkaletsis. 2016. Identifying argument components through textrank. In *Proceedings of the Third Workshop on Argument Mining (ArgMining2016)*, pages 94–102, Berlin, Germany. Association for Computational Linguistics.

Peter Potash, Alexey Romanov, and Anna Rumshisky. 2017. Here's my point: Joint pointer architecture for argument mining. In *Proceedings of the 2017 Conference on Empirical Methods in Natural Language Processing*, pages 1364–1373, Copenhagen, Denmark. Association for Computational Linguistics.

Ruty Rinott, Lena Dankin, Carlos Alzate Perez, Mitesh M. Khapra, Ehud Aharoni, and Noam Slonim. 2015. Show me your evidence - an automatic method for context dependent evidence detection. In *Proceedings of the 2015 Conference on Empirical Methods in Natural Language Processing*, pages 440–450, Lisbon, Portugal. Association for Computational Linguistics.

Christian Stab and Iryna Gurevych. 2014. Identifying argumentative discourse structures in persuasive essays. In *EMNLP*, pages 46–56.

Christian Stab and Iryna Gurevych. 2017. Parsing argumentation structures in persuasive essays. *Computational Linguistics*, 43(3):619–659.

Argumentative Evidences Classification and Argument Scheme Detection Using Tree Kernels

Davide Liga

CIRSFID

Alma Mater Studiorum - University of Bologna

Via Galliera, 3 - 40121, Bologna, Italy

`davide.liga2@unibo.it`

Abstract

The purpose of this study is to deploy a novel methodology for classifying different argumentative support (supporting *evidences*) in arguments, without considering the context. The proposed methodology is based on the idea that the use of Tree Kernel algorithms can be a good way to discriminate between different types of argumentative stances without the need of highly engineered features. This can be useful in different Argumentation Mining sub-tasks. This work provides an example of classifier built using a Tree Kernel method, which can discriminate between different kinds of argumentative support with a high accuracy. The ability to distinguish different kinds of support is, in fact, a key step toward Argument Scheme classification.

1 Introduction to the Argument Mining Pipeline

Argument Mining (AM) is a field of growing interest in the scientific community and a growing number of works have been written about this topic in the last few years (Cabrio and Villata, 2018; Lippi and Torroni, 2015). Since it is a relatively young research domain, its specific target area is huge and its taxonomy is relatively flexible, for example *Argument Mining* and *Argumentation Mining* are used interchangeably. In spite of this flexibility, it is possible to define a unique and broad target, which is the extraction of argumentative units and their relations from data.

Another characteristic of AM is its close connection with other domains such as Knowledge Representation and Reasoning, Computational Argumentation, Information Extraction, Opinion Mining, Human-Computer Interaction. Also, there is a strong relation between AM and Natural Language Processing (NLP), since language is the means by which humans express arguments.

Habernal et al. (2014) noticed a relation between Opinion Mining (also known as Sentiment Analysis) and Argument Mining. The former aims to detect *what* people say, the latter wants to understand *why*. For this reason, Lippi and Torroni (2015) consider AM as an evolution of Opinion Mining in terms of targets.

Being AM a multifaceted problem, it can be useful to imagine it as a pipeline (with much research focused on one or more of the involved steps). For example, Lippi and Torroni (2015) described it as a three-steps process, from a Machine Learning perspective. The first step is to discriminate between argumentative and non-argumentative data; the second step is to detect argument boundaries; the third step is to predict the relations between arguments or between argumentative components. The second and third step are strictly dependent on the underlying argumentative model (the most frequently used is the claim/premise model described in Walton et al., 2008, while another frequent choice is the model proposed by Toulmin, 2003). Cabrio and Villata (2018) proposed a simpler two-step pipeline, where the first phase is the identification of arguments and the second step is the prediction of argument relations. In this case, the first step involves not only the classification argumentative vs non-argumentative, but also the sub-tasks of identifying arguments components (claims, premises, etc.) and their boundaries. While, the second step comprises predicting the heterogeneous nature of argument relations (e.g., *supports*, *attacks*) and the links between evidences (premises) and claims (conclusions). For the purposes of this paper, this two-step pipeline will be considered.

In an ideal AM pipeline, after having detected the argumentative units, their relations (e.g., premises, conclusions) and the nature of their relations (e.g., support, attack), the further step is to fit

Proceedings of the 6th Workshop on Argument Mining, pages 92–97

Florence, Italy, August 1, 2019. ©2019 Association for Computational Linguistics

this argumentative map into a suitable Argument Scheme (e.g., argument from Expert Opinion, argument from Example).

To do so it is necessary to develop classifiers able to discriminate between different kinds of argumentative evidences. This work is an attempt to give a contribution to the achievement of this sub-task of the pipeline, finding a working methodology to discriminate between different types of support prepositions (or *evidence*), since being able to classify different kind of support is a crucial aspect when dealing with the classification of Argument Schemes.

In particular, the proposed methodology is based on the use of Tree Kernels (TKs).

2 Related Works

This work presents an approach for classifying evidence typology within arguments using Tree Kernels (TKs, described in Moschitti, 2006) with the aim to facilitate the detection of Argument Schemes. TKs have already been used successfully in several NLP-related works, for example in semantic role labelling (Moschitti et al., 2008), metaphor identification (Hovy et al., 2013) and question answering (Filice and Moschitti, 2018). However, the application of TK in the domain of AM has been relatively limited compared to other methodologies mostly that are dependent on highly engineered feature sets. One of the first use in Argumentation Mining was proposed by Rooney et al. (2012), who simply employed sequences of Part-of-Speech tags. At that moment, however, the Argumentation Mining community was still too young. Some years later, Lippi and Torroni (2015) suggested to exploit the potentialities of TKs for detecting arguments (the first step in the Argument Mining pipeline) and presented a promising tool for automatically extract arguments from text (Lippi and Torroni, 2016). Interestingly, TKs have been used to specific domains: Mayer et al. (2018) exploited them for an AM approach related to Clinical Trials, while promising results have been achieved also in the legal domain (Lippi et al., 2015, 2018). TKs have also been used in (Wachsmuth et al., 2017) for analyzing the similarities between argumentative structures, thus focusing not on the level of the sentences (step one), but on the level of the argumentative relations (step two of the Argument Mining pipeline).

To the best of our knowledge, this is the first attempt to use TKs in the very last part of the Argument Mining pipeline. In fact, the approach presented here aims to differentiate different kinds of evidences (or *premises*), which is an important sub-task when trying to detect the most suitable Argumentative Scheme.

Other studies tried to classify arguments by scheme using different approaches. For example, Feng and Hirst (2011) created a complex pipeline of classifiers that achieved and accuracy ranging from 63 to 91% in one-against-others classification and 80-94% in pairwise classification. In another study Lawrence and Reed (2016) achieved a similar result, with F-scores ranging from 0.78 to 0.91. However, these two works employed a set of highly engineered features, which is exactly what this study wants to avoid.

3 Tree Kernels Methods

From a very general perspective, a classification problem can be considered as an attempt to learn a function f able to map in the best way an input space $\mathcal{X}$ to an output space $\mathcal{Y}$, where the former is the initial vector space and the latter is the set of target labels. While in many cases the input space is composed of simple features such as Bag-of-Words or n-grams occurrences, sometimes highly engineered (and costly) features are needed, especially when dealing with complex classification problems like those typically encountered in the AM pipeline. TK methods can solve the problem of costly engineered features, embedding in the input space $\mathcal{X}$ more complex structural information (e.g., graphs, trees) without creating *ad-hoc* features. In other words, sentences can be converted into tree representations and their similarity can be calculated by considering the number of common substructures (fragments).

Kernel machines classifiers, such as support-vector machine (SVM), have been widely used in classification problems. A kernel can be considered as a *similarity measure* that is able to map the inputs of an original vector space $\mathcal{X}$ into an high-dimensional feature space $\mathcal{V}$ *implicitly*, which is to say without the need to calculate the coordinates of data in the new space. More specifically, a kernel $k(\mathbf{x}, \mathbf{x}')$ (where $\mathbf{x}$ and $\mathbf{x}'$ belong to the input space $\mathcal{X}$ and represent the labelled and unlabelled input respectively) can be represented as an inner product in a high-dimensional space $\mathcal{V}$. In this regard, the kernel can be considered as a mapping $\varphi : \mathcal{X} \to \mathcal{V}$ where φ is an implicit mapping. The kernel function can be thus represented as:

$$k(\mathbf{x}, \mathbf{x}') = \langle \varphi(\mathbf{x}), \varphi(\mathbf{x}') \rangle_{\mathcal{V}} \qquad (1)$$

Where $\langle ., . \rangle_{\mathcal{V}}$ must necessarily be an inner product.

Given a training dataset of n examples $\{(\mathbf{x}_i, y_i)\}_{i=1}^{n}$, where $i \in \{c_1, c_2\}$ with c_1 and c_2 being the specific classes of a binary classification, the final classifier $\hat{y} \in \{c_1, c_2\}$ can be calculated using the above-mentioned kernel function in the following way:

$$\hat{y} = \sum_{i=1}^{n} w_i y_i k(\mathbf{x}_i, \mathbf{x}') \qquad (2)$$

Or:

$$\hat{y} = \sum_{i=1}^{n} w_i y_i \varphi(\mathbf{x}) . \varphi(\mathbf{x}') \qquad (3)$$

Where w_i are the weights learned by the trained algorithm.

A TK can be considered a *similarity measure* able to evaluate the differences between two trees. Before selecting the appropriate TK function, two important steps should be considered: choosing the type of tree representation and the type of fragments. In this work, sentences have been converted into Grammatical Relation Centered Tree (GRCT) representations, which involves PoS-Tag units and lexical terms. While their structures have been divided into Partial Trees (PTs) fragments (Moschitti, 2006), where each node is composed of any possible sub-tree, partial or not, providing a higher generalization. A description of various kind of tree representations can be found in Croce et al. (2011b), while a brief description of tree fragments can be found in Nguyen et al. (2009) and Moschitti (2006).

In this case, the PTK can be expressed using the following equation (Moschitti, 2006):

$$K(T_1, T_2) = \sum_{n_1 \in N_{T_1}} \sum_{n_2 \in N_{T_2}} \Delta(n_1, n_2) \qquad (4)$$

Where T_1 and T_2 are the two trees whose similarity should be evaluated, N_{T_1} and N_{T_2} are their respective set of nodes, and $\Delta(n_1, n_2)$ represent the number of common fragments in n_1 and n_2 (Moschitti, 2006).

DS1	n.	DS2	n.
Expert/testimony	372	Expert/testimony	311
Study/statistics	281	Study/statistics	258
Total	653	**Total**	569

Table 1: Number of sentences in the two datasets, grouped by category group.

4 The Use Case

Two important Argument Mining datasets have been considered, and they will be referred to as DS1 and DS2. The first one is taken from Al Khatibet al. (2016), while DS2 is from Aharoni et al. (2014). This work is "downstream" from these two previous works which interestingly contains arguments taken from several topics, facilitating the creation of a context-independent classifier.

Although these two datasets have been built for different tasks, they share a very similar labelling system. The two datasets, in fact, classify argumentative text depending on three common labels (i.e. Study/Statistics, Expert/Testimony, Anecdote). In this study, only the first two groups have been considered suitable for the final purpose of detecting evidence typology. The idea is to train a classifier to automatically recognize when a text is an evidence coming from *studies/statistics* and when it comes from an expert *opinion/testimony*.

Since the two datasets have been created for other purposes, there is a further layer of complexity. For example, DS1 was composed of very segmented data, and it was necessary to recompose segmented sentences. Moreover, even though the two datasets share a similar labelling system when referring to some evidence typology (especially anecdote, study/statistics and expert/testimony), they could assume a slightly different idea of what these labels actually describe. In spite of these problems, their combination can be a powerful set of data for our aims, and the results of this experiment seem to confirm this assumption.

As can be seen from Table 1, a total of 653 sentences have been extracted from DS1 (372 belonging to the group "expert/testimony" and 281 belonging to the group "study/statistics"). While 569 sentences have been extracted from DS2 (311 for the "expert/testimony" group, 258 for the "study/statistics" group).

After having extracted the sentences from DS1 and DS2, a Grammatical Relation Centered Tree (GRCT) representation was created for each sentence of the two datasets. Furthermore, a TFIDF

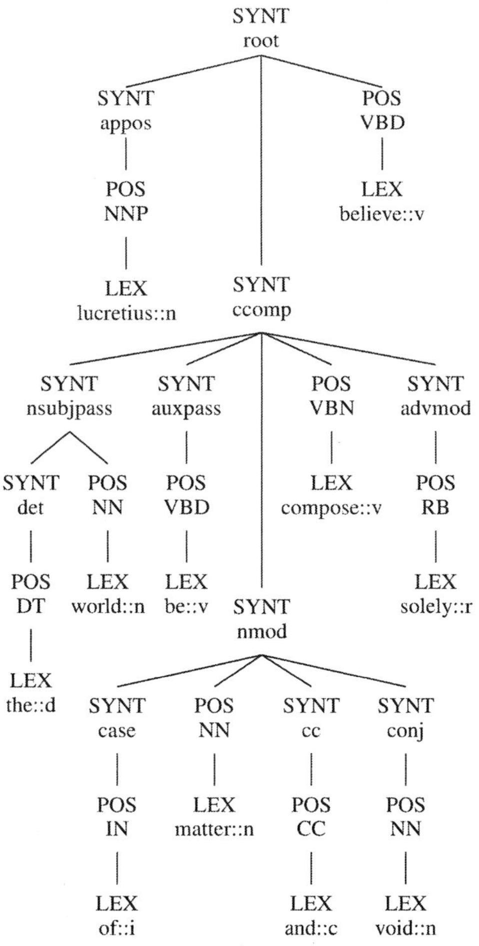

Figure 1: The GCRT representation for the sentence *"Lucretius believed the world was composed of matter and void"*

vectorialization has been applied to each dataset.

In other words, the sentences of the two datasets were converted into two kinds of "representation", with each labelled example having both a Grammatical Relation Centered Tree and a vector of TFIDF BoW, representing the features of the sentence.

For example, the sentence: *"Lucretius believed the world was composed of matter and void"* taken from DS2, can be represented as the GCRT in the Figure 1 and can have the following TFIDF vectorial representation:

```
the:0.0924 and:0.1237 of:0.1193
was:0.1095 believed:0.2526
world:0.1537 matter:0.2092
void:0.3157 composed:0.3020
```

The final classification algorithm was trained on

these two kinds of representations by using KeLP (Filice et al., 2015). Since KeLP allows to combine multiple kernel functions, the classification algorithm was built as a combination of a Linear Kernel and a Smoothed Partial Tree Kernel (SPTK) (Croce et al., 2011a), with the first kernel related to the TFIDF vectors and the second kernel related to the GRCT representations. More details on kernel combinations can be found in Shawe-Taylor and Cristianini (2004). However, to evaluate the contribution of TKs, the experiment was also performed by using just one of the two representations (SPTK or TFIDF).

More precisely, two groups of classifiers were trained following two different strategies. The classifiers of the first group were trained on the 653 instances of DS1, dividing it into two subsets of 458 and 195 instances, for training and test. The second group of classifiers was trained on the 569 instances of DS2, dividing it into two subsets of 399 and 170 sentences, for training and test. After having been trained and tested on its given dataset, each classifier has also been tested on the other dataset (DS2 for the first group, DS1 for the second group). In this way, the ability of classifiers to generalize can be evaluated.

Since each group has three classifiers (TFIDF, SPTK, and the combination SPTK+TFIDF), a total of six classifiers has been evaluated.

5 Results

The results can be seen in Table 2. To evaluate the performance of the two groups of classifiers, a simple "Majority" baseline was created. Interestingly, all classifiers outperformed the baseline in all metrics.

Overall, TKs (SPTKs, in this case) outperformed simple TFIDF in three cases out of four (the TFIDF of the first classifier is the only exception). It means that TKs can not only reach the performances of traditional features such as TFIDF, but also outperform them. Noticeably, the combination of TK and TFIDF has always performed better than simple TFIDF, which means that combining TKs and traditional features is a valid strategy to improve performances.

The classifiers of the first group had a good performance not only on the dataset they were trained on (DS1), but also on DS2. Noticeably, also the classifiers of the second group performed better on DS1.

BASELINE	DS1			DS2		
	P	R	F1	P	R	F1
Averages (macro)	0.28	0.50	**0.36**	0.27	0.50	**0.35**

GROUP 1	Performance on DS1								
	TFIDF			SPTK			SPTK+TFIDF		
	P	R	F1	P	R	F1	P	R	F1
Study	0.93	0.87	0.90	0.88	0.83	0.85	0.90	0.92	0.91
Expert	0.89	0.94	0.92	0.85	0.90	0.88	0.93	0.91	0.92
Average F1 (macro)	**0.91**			**0.87**			**0.92**		
	Performance on DS2								
Study	0.80	0.55	0.65	0.77	0.67	0.71	0.78	0.66	0.72
Expert	0.70	0.88	0.78	0.75	0.83	0.79	0.75	0.85	0.80
Average F1 (macro)	**0.72**			**0.75**			**0.76**		

GROUP 2	Performance on DS1								
	TFIDF			SPTK			SPTK+TFIDF		
	P	R	F1	P	R	F1	P	R	F1
Study	0.84	0.54	0.66	0.81	0.78	0.80	0.82	0.80	0.81
Expert	0.73	0.92	0.81	0.84	0.86	0.85	0.85	0.87	0.86
Average F1 (macro)	**0.74**			**0.82**			**0.84**		
	Performance on DS2								
Study	0.70	0.67	0.68	0.76	0.64	0.69	0.69	0.69	0.69
Expert	0.73	0.76	0.74	0.73	0.83	0.78	0.74	0.74	0.74
Average F1 (macro)	**0.71**			**0.73**			**0.72**		

Table 2: Results of the majority baseline and two groups of classifiers, reporting precision (P), recall (R) and F1.

6 Conclusion

The aim of this work is to show that it is possible to perform a fine-grain discrimination between different kinds of argumentative evidence by using TKs, without the need of using sophisticated feature vectors. The achieved classifier exploited the ability of Tree Kernels to calculate similarities between tree-structured sentences, considering the similarity of their fragments.

The experiment was performed on two famous Argument Mining datasets, which share a similar labelling system (they were referred to as DS1 and DS2). More specifically, two groups of classifiers were trained combining a SPTK related to the GCRT representations and a linear kernel related to the TFIDF-BoW vector representations. The first group of classifiers was trained on DS1, while the second was trained on DS2.

A possible improvement to this approach could be achieved by adding also n-grams to assess if they can offer a better representation of sentences. Moreover, it would be interesting to compare results from different kinds of tree representation to assess whether GRCTs are the best choice for this particular task.

One of the achievements of this study is the successful combination of two important datasets originally designed for other purposes.

Also, it is worth remarking that this study is context-independent and focused on the structures of argumentative evidences without considering the specific context in which arguments are placed.

Finally, the main achievement of this work is to show that TKs can differentiate between different kinds of supporting evidences with high performances, which can facilitate the discrimination among different Argument Schemes (e.g. Argument from Expert Opinion), a crucial sub-task in the Argumentation Mining pipeline.

Acknowledgments

The author would like to thank professor Monica Palmirani for her invaluable support and all the anonymous reviewers for their important feedback.

References

Ehud Aharoni, Anatoly Polnarov, Tamar Lavee, Daniel Hershcovich, Ran Levy, Ruty Rinott, Dan Gutfreund, and Noam Slonim. 2014. A benchmark dataset for automatic detection of claims and evidence in the context of controversial topics. In *Proceedings of the First Workshop on Argumentation Mining*, pages 64–68.

Khalid Al Khatib, Henning Wachsmuth, Johannes Kiesel, Matthias Hagen, and Benno Stein. 2016. A news editorial corpus for mining argumentation strategies. In *Proceedings of COLING 2016, the 26th International Conference on Computational Linguistics: Technical Papers*, pages 3433–3443.

Elena Cabrio and Serena Villata. 2018. Five years of argument mining: a data-driven analysis. In *IJCAI*, pages 5427–5433.

Danilo Croce, Alessandro Moschitti, and Roberto Basili. 2011a. Semantic convolution kernels over dependency trees: smoothed partial tree kernel. In *Proceedings of the 20th ACM international conference on Information and knowledge management*, pages 2013–2016. ACM.

Danilo Croce, Alessandro Moschitti, and Roberto Basili. 2011b. Structured lexical similarity via convolution kernels on dependency trees. In *Proceedings of the Conference on Empirical Methods in Natural Language Processing*, pages 1034–1046. Association for Computational Linguistics.

Vanessa Wei Feng and Graeme Hirst. 2011. Classifying arguments by scheme. In *Proceedings of the 49th annual meeting of the association for computational linguistics: Human language technologies*, pages 987–996.

Simone Filice, Giuseppe Castellucci, Danilo Croce, and Roberto Basili. 2015. Kelp: a kernel-based learning platform for natural language processing. *Proceedings of ACL-IJCNLP 2015 System Demonstrations*, pages 19–24.

Simone Filice and Alessandro Moschitti. 2018. Learning pairwise patterns in community question answering. *Intelligenza Artificiale*, 12(2):49–65.

Ivan Habernal, Judith Eckle-Kohler, and Iryna Gurevych. 2014. Argumentation mining on the web from information seeking perspective. In *ArgNLP*.

Dirk Hovy, Shashank Shrivastava, Sujay Kumar Jauhar, Mrinmaya Sachan, Kartik Goyal, Huying Li, Whitney Sanders, and Eduard Hovy. 2013. Identifying metaphorical word use with tree kernels. In *Proceedings of the First Workshop on Metaphor in NLP*, pages 52–57.

John Lawrence and Chris Reed. 2016. Argument mining using argumentation scheme structures. In *COMMA*, pages 379–390.

Marco Lippi, Francesca Lagioia, Giuseppe Contissa, Giovanni Sartor, and Paolo Torroni. 2015. Claim detection in judgments of the eu court of justice. In *AI Approaches to the Complexity of Legal Systems*, pages 513–527. Springer.

Marco Lippi, Przemysław Pałka, Giuseppe Contissa, Francesca Lagioia, Hans-Wolfgang Micklitz, Giovanni Sartor, and Paolo Torroni. 2018. Claudette: an automated detector of potentially unfair clauses in online terms of service. *Artificial Intelligence and Law*, pages 1–23.

Marco Lippi and Paolo Torroni. 2015. Argument mining: A machine learning perspective. In *International Workshop on Theory and Applications of Formal Argumentation*, pages 163–176. Springer.

Marco Lippi and Paolo Torroni. 2016. Margot: A web server for argumentation mining. *Expert Systems with Applications*, 65:292–303.

Tobias Mayer, Elena Cabrio, Marco Lippi, Paolo Torroni, and Serena Villata. 2018. Argument mining on clinical trials. *Computational Models of Argument: Proceedings of COMMA 2018*, 305:137.

Alessandro Moschitti. 2006. Efficient convolution kernels for dependency and constituent syntactic trees. In *European Conference on Machine Learning*, pages 318–329. Springer.

Alessandro Moschitti, Daniele Pighin, and Roberto Basili. 2008. Tree kernels for semantic role labeling. *Computational Linguistics*, 34(2):193–224.

Truc-Vien T Nguyen, Alessandro Moschitti, and Giuseppe Riccardi. 2009. Convolution kernels on constituent, dependency and sequential structures for relation extraction. In *Proceedings of the 2009 Conference on Empirical Methods in Natural Language Processing: Volume 3-Volume 3*, pages 1378–1387. Association for Computational Linguistics.

Niall Rooney, Hui Wang, and Fiona Browne. 2012. Applying kernel methods to argumentation mining. In *Twenty-Fifth International FLAIRS Conference*.

John Shawe-Taylor, Nello Cristianini, et al. 2004. *Kernel methods for pattern analysis*. Cambridge university press.

Stephen E Toulmin. 2003. *The uses of argument*. Cambridge university press.

Henning Wachsmuth, Giovanni Da San Martino, Dora Kiesel, and Benno Stein. 2017. The impact of modeling overall argumentation with tree kernels. In *Proceedings of the 2017 Conference on Empirical Methods in Natural Language Processing*, pages 2379–2389.

Douglas Walton, Christopher Reed, and Fabrizio Macagno. 2008. *Argumentation schemes*. Cambridge University Press.

The utility of discourse parsing features for predicting argumentation structure

Freya Hewett, Roshan Prakash Rane, Nina Harlacher, Manfred Stede

University of Potsdam, Germany

{hewett,rane,harlacher,stede@uni-potsdam.de}

Abstract

Research on argumentation mining from text has frequently discussed relationships to discourse parsing, but few empirical results are available so far. One corpus that has been annotated in parallel for argumentation structure and for discourse structure (RST, SDRT) are the 'argumentative microtexts' (Peldszus and Stede, 2016a). While results on perusing the gold RST annotations for predicting argumentation have been published (Peldszus and Stede, 2016b), the step to automatic discourse parsing has not yet been taken. In this paper, we run various discourse parsers (RST, PDTB) on the corpus, compare their results to the gold annotations (for RST) and then assess the contribution of automatically-derived discourse features for argumentation parsing. After reproducing the state-of-the-art Evidence Graph model from Afantenos et al. (2018) for the microtexts, we find that PDTB features can indeed improve its performance.

1 Introduction

The argumentative structure of texts, as captured, for instance, by schemata from Peldszus and Stede (2013) or Stab and Gurevych (2014), is represented by tree structures that suggest a certain similarity to accounts of discourse structure, such as in Rhetorical Structure Theory (Mann and Thompson, 1988) or Segmented Discourse Representation Theory (Asher and Lascarides, 2003). These approaches aim at accounting for the *coherence* of texts, which is clearly related – though not identical – to the structure of complex arguments. This is not a new observation (Habernal and Gurevych, 2017), but we are not aware of many empirically-grounded studies of the correspondences between the two realms. A corpus that facilitates such experiments is the 'argumentative microtext corpus' (Peldszus and Stede, 2016a), as it offers annotation not only for argumentation but also for discourse structure in terms of RST and SDRT. While there is evidence that RST trees can "in principle" be helpful for parsing the argumentation (based on the gold annotations; see Peldszus and Stede, 2016b), we are not aware of experiments which try to verify such effects with automatic parsers. Our work aims to bridge this gap. We use common parsers for RST and for Shallow Discourse Parsing (specifically the Penn Discourse Treebank, henceforth PDTB), run them on the microtexts, and first compare the RST output to the gold annotations, in order to assess the prospects of the idea. Having selected the most promising parsers, we then compute a set of features from their output and add them to a state-of-the-art implementation of argumentation parsing on the microtexts (Afantenos et al., 2018). The results indicate that the parsed PDTB features do in fact improve the accuracy of the argumentation annotation.

Section 2 discusses related work, and Section 3 describes the corpus and the discourse parsers we used. Initial analyses of parser results are given in Section 4, and the experiments on predicting argumentation structure are reported in Section 5. The paper closes with some conclusions in Section 6.

2 Related work

A number of researchers have studied connections between discourse structure and argumentation. Cabrio et al. (2013) look at the link between PDTB relations and the argumentation schemes from Walton et al. (2008). They find, for example, that the PDTB relation 'expansion' corresponds to the 'Argument by Example', which can be defined as when the second argument offers a summary or a conclusion based on the first argument. Generally, the presence of connectives or other discourse markers has often been employed

Proceedings of the 6th Workshop on Argument Mining, pages 98–103

Florence, Italy, August 1, 2019. ©2019 Association for Computational Linguistics

for detecting argument components and relations between them. Stab and Gurevych (2014) compile a list of 55 discourse markers which indicate argumentative discourse and use these as features to detect the argumentative role in German essays. Eckle-Kohler et al. (2015) instead look at German news items which are annotated with the argumentative roles 'claim' and 'premise' (with various sub-categories). They found that both single discourse markers and semantic groups of such markers occurred in significant correlation with claims or premises. Turning specifically to RST, Green (2010) proposes the ArgRST annotation scheme, which represents both argumentation and discourse analysis in the same structure. *Inter alia*, she finds parallels between the RST relation 'evidence' and the premise and claim of an argument.

Finally, Peldszus and Stede (2016b) present a qualitative study on the mapping from manual RST annotations to argumentation structure and also conduct experiments using a new feature set which is based exclusively on the gold RST annotation (of the 'microtext' corpus; see Section 3.1). These features include the position of the segment in the text, whether a segment has incoming or outgoing edges, and the type of RST relation between segments, amongst others. They showed that especially two subtasks of argumentation structure parsing in the microtexts (finding the central claim and the attachment point of segments) can clearly benefit from these features. Our project is a continuation of that study, as we essentially replicate the model, but use automatically parsed RST trees instead of the gold annotations, in order to assess a "real world" scenario.

3 Data and parsers

3.1 Argumentative microtexts

Part 1 of the microtexts corpus (Peldszus and Stede, 2016a) is a freely available[1] parallel corpus of 112 short texts with 576 argumentative segments. They were originally written in German and have been professionally translated to English, preserving the segmentation where possible. The texts have been collected in a controlled text generation experiment using a short instruction. All texts have been annotated with argumentation structure according to the scheme of Peldszus and Stede (2013), i.e., trees with one claim and support/attack relations between the segments. Fur-

thermore, various other layers of annotation have been produced, including RST trees (Stede et al., 2016). Later, Musi et al. (2018) conducted a study comparing the RST trees to annotations of argumentation schemes.

3.2 Argumentation parsing

Various researchers have used slightly different approaches to automatically parse the argumentation structure in the microtexts. Peldszus and Stede (2015) decompose the problem into the four subtasks of finding the central claim (*cc*) segment, and for each other segment its role (*ro*: proponent or opponent), its function (*fu*: support, rebut, undercut), and the segment it attaches to (*at*). They use a minimum spanning tree (MST) decoder on a so-called 'evidence graph' that combines the probabilities computed for the four subtasks. Stab and Gurevych (2016) achieved slightly better results for some subtasks using Integer Linear Programming. Potash et al. (2017) use a bidirectional LSTM encoder and achieve competitive results on the microtexts, but they solve only part of the problem (no support/attack distinction). Finally, Afantenos et al. (2018) compare ILP and MST by training a classifier for each subtask (*cc, ro, fu, at*) and use this combined distribution as input to the decoders. Their best model is a replication of the evidence graph model with MST decoding from Peldszus and Stede (2015) with some additional features, including discourse connectives for English. As this is this the model with best results for the complete problem, we will replicate it for our experiments.

3.3 Discourse parsing: first observations

We parsed a subset of the corpus with various parsers (Ji and Eisenstein, 2014; Feng and Hirst, 2014; Lin et al., 2014; Biran and McKeown, 2015), and after a manual analysis of the results, chose the systems of Feng and Hirst (2014) and Lin et al. (2014). These were used "out of the box", without having been trained on our data, to produce the automatic RST- and PDTB-parses for our study in a domain-independent way.

In a small pilot study, we compared the RST parser output to the gold argumentation structures for 10 texts of the corpus. We observed that the parser sometimes produced different segmentations, either combining segments, or using completely new boundaries. We also noted that the central claims matched the most-nuclear RST seg-

---

[1] http://angcl.ling.uni-potsdam.de/resources/argmicro.html

99

ment (for an explanation, see Section 4.1 below) in 50% of the graphs, and that 26 RST edges – out of 40 – corresponded to ARG edges. In these cases the relation labels were also coherent. For instance, the ARG relation *undercut* matched with the RST relation *concession* and *antithesis*, *support* corresponded with RST edges *explanation* and *cause*.

Likewise, for the 10 texts we checked the output of the PDTB parser and observed that again, the boundaries did not match in most cases. There were very few argumentation pairs that matched to the ARG edges, and the parser in general did not pick up on many relations, in particular implicit relations.

Due to the segment boundary mismatches we observed, we decided to use common pre-segmented text, taken from the gold-annotated corpus, as input to the parsers for all the following experiments. While this is in line with practices in related research, it has to be noted as a certain simplification of the "real world" scenario, as discourse- and argumentation parsing are not quite used out of the box anymore.

4 Quantitative analysis of parser output

In the next step, we turned to the full corpus of 112 texts. For quantitatively comparing our automatically-parsed texts to the gold-standard argumentative annotations of the microtexts, we first converted the tree structures to a dependency format, adapting the techniques described in Stede et al. (2016). These include converting multi-nuclear RST relations such as *joint* or *contrast* to nested binary relations by combining the sources of the relations. In a similar vein, *join* nodes in the ARG trees were converted to a *joint* edge between the two relevant segments, and *undercut* edges which target a relation between two edges were converted to target the source of the attacked relation. The PDTB parser output included relation predictions both within and across our pre-determined segments; for the purposes of this comparison we only considered the inter-segmental relations.

4.1 Central claims

The "most nuclear" (MN) segment in the RST structure can be identified by tracing down from the root node to the nucleus at each level, until reaching the lowest level (Marcu, 2000). We inter-preted this for our RST trees by defining the MN as the segment or group with no parent. If it is a group, the RST tree can have more than one MN. If the ARG CC matches any of these MNs then it counts as match. There were a total of 67 matches, which represents about 60% of the corpus. The corresponding figure for gold RST and ARG from (Peldszus and Stede, 2016b) is 85%. Considering there are 5 segments in each text on average, we see the automatic result as a quite promising score.

4.2 Common undirected edges

	reb	join	sup	und	link	exa	NONE
elaboration	22	23	88	6	4	3	115
same-unit	2	0	1	0	0	0	8
joint	2	13	1	1	10	0	32
contrast	7	2	3	28	0	0	19
temporal	0	0	0	0	0	0	1
evaluation	3	0	3	0	0	0	7
summary	0	0	0	0	0	0	1
explanation	1	1	8	1	0	1	7
cause	0	3	8	1	1	0	3
topic-comment	0	0	0	0	0	0	1
background	0	9	14	0	0	0	7
attribution	0	4	0	0	0	0	3
condition	0	14	0	0	0	0	0
enablement	0	1	1	0	0	0	0
manner-means	0	1	1	0	0	0	0
comparison	0	0	2	0	0	0	0
NONE	65	10	114	23	6	4	0

Table 1: Co-occurrence matrix of the RST (rows) and ARG (columns) relations of the matching edges in the converted annotations

	join	und	reb	sup	link	exa	NONE
Temporal.Synchrony	6	1	0	10	0	0	1
Expansion.Conjunction	3	0	2	0	2	0	24
Comparison.Contrast	0	21	5	0	0	0	18
Expansion.Alternative	0	0	1	0	0	0	0
Contingency.Cause	0	0	0	9	0	0	7
Expansion.Instantiation	0	0	0	0	0	1	0
Contingency.Condition	5	0	0	2	0	0	2
Temporal.Asynchronous	0	1	0	1	0	0	0
Comparison.Concession	1	0	2	0	0	0	1
NONE	61	25	71	189	10	2	0

Table 2: Co-occurrence matrix of the PDTB (rows) and ARG (columns) relations of the matching edges in the converted annotations

RST & ARG: Although a large amount of edges in one annotation had no corresponding edge in the other annotation, there are some similarities. *Contrast* maps to *undercut* 28 times, and *elaboration* is frequently mapped to *join*, *support*, which seems plausible, and *rebuttal* which seems less so.

PDTB & ARG: Although few edges matched (73), this is in part due to the fact that only a total of 176 PDTB relations were identified by the parser, in comparison to 547 relations in the ARG annotation. *Comparison.Contrast* maps to *undercut* 21 times and *Temporal.Synchrony* often maps to *join*, both of which seem to be a suitable mapping.

4.3 RST gold vs. parser

Besides comparing RST parses to argumentative structures, we were also interested in evaluating the RST parser on the microtexts, i.e., on their gold RST trees. To this end, we converted the gold annotations to a comparable format, which involved converting the 'span' relations (which were not present in the parser's output), adjusting the segment IDs so that they were in ascending order, and converting the more fine-grained relations to the smaller set used by the parser (using the taxonomy in Das and Taboada, 2014). We adapted the metrics to evaluate the parser output from those proposed by Joty et al. (2015); our results are given in Table 3.

	Span	Nuclearity	Relation
F1	0.338	0.264	0.115

Table 3: RST parser evaluation, with the categories used by Joty et al. (2015) and others.

5 Prediction experiments and results

Finally, we address the task of predicting the ARG structure with the help of discourse parser output. We extended the system of Afantenos et al. (2018) and started from the feature set used by Peldszus and Stede (2016b); our own new features, listed in Table 4, will be referred to as 'RST+' and 'PDTB' respectively. The task now is to assess their contribution in comparison to the 'Default' and 'RST' features from Peldszus and Stede (2016b) and to the best performing lexical, syntactic, semantic and discourse features used by Afantenos et al. (2018). In Table 5, which shows our results, the latter are labelled as '2018'.

We experimented with different combinations of the features on two different settings of the model: the simple relation set (*support* and *attack*); and the more fine-grained full relation set (*support, example, join, link, undercut* and *rebuttal*). We used the same train-test splits as in Peldszus and Stede (2015), which involved 10 iterations of 5-fold cross validation. The results for the full relation set were marginally better than those for the simple relations, aside from the *fu* classi-

PDTB parser output
1:[Intelligence services must urgently be regulated more tightly by parliament;] 2:[this should be clear to everyone after the disclosures of Edward Snowden.] 3:[Granted, those concern primarily the British and American intelligence services,][Comparison.Contrast] *4:[but the German services evidently do collaborate with them closely.] 5:[Their tools, data and expertise have been used to keep us under surveillance for a long time.]*

RST parser output

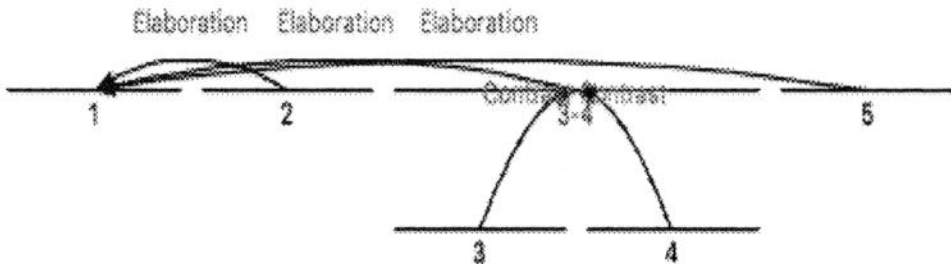

Best performing ARG model output
[2, 1, 'join'], [3, 1, 'rebut'], [4, 3, 'undercut'], [5, 1, 'support']

Gold ARG annotation
[2, 1, 'support'], [3, 2, 'undercut'], [4, 3, 'undercut'], [5, 4, 'support']

Figure 1: Parser and model output for microtext b005. The numbers refer to the segments. RST tree created using RSTTool (O'Donnell, 2000).

fier whose highest score, 0.750, was achieved with the combination of all features for the simple relations. Even though the statistical analysis of the PDTB output at first did not seem promising, the PDTB features did improve all classifiers' performances. The model's performance was best for the majority of classifiers with the features employed by Afantenos et al. (2018) in collaboration with our features for both settings. In particular, our model achieved promising improvements on the attachment and function classifiers.

For illustration, Figure 1 shows the various analyses for one text from the corpus.

6 Discussion and conclusion

In our study we experimented with using discourse parser output for argumentation mining, using pre-segmented text. We not only looked at RST features, which have already been used in related research, but also experimented with PDTB features. After experimenting with various available parsers, we selected one for RST and one for PDTB, converted their output for our corpus to a common format, and determined correlations. In a follow-up experiment, we used features from both discourse parsers for predicting the argumentation structure, based on a re-implementation of the system of Afantenos et al. (2018). Despite the fact

Feature description	Classifier	Tag
Absolute & relative no. of all children/parents and grandchildren/grandparents of segment	fu, ro	RST+
Relative no. of grandchildren/grandparents before & after the segment	fu, ro	RST+
Absolute & relative distance to parent and direction	at	RST+
Whether the segment is involved in a multi-nuclear relation	at	RST+
Whether segment has any PDTB connections to neighbouring segments	cc, fu, ro, at	PDTB
Count of incoming & outgoing PDTB connectives	cc, fu, ro	PDTB
Level one and two of the PDTB semantic relation	cc, fu, ro, at	PDTB
Raw text of PDTB connective	cc, fu, ro, at	PDTB

Table 4: Feature descriptions.

features	cc	ro	fu	at
Default features	0.722 (+/- 0.068)	0.467 (+/- 0.054)	0.224 (+/- 0.015)	0.673 (+/- 0.034)
Default, RST	0.729 (+/- 0.068)	0.600 (+/- 0.049)	0.278 (+/- 0.034)	0.680 (+/- 0.033)
Default, RST, RST+	0.732 (+/- 0.068)	0.582 (+/- 0.049)	0.305 (+/- 0.048)	0.685 (+/- 0.026)
Default, PDTB	0.771 (+/- 0.073)	0.720 (+/- 0.048)	0.420 (+/- 0.056)	0.691 (+/- 0.030)
Default, RST, RST+, PDTB	0.759 (+/- 0.078)	0.721 (+/- 0.045)	0.417 (+/- 0.050)	0.703 (+/- 0.031)
Default, 2018	**0.854 (+/- 0.057)**	**0.737 (+/- 0.052)**	0.444 (+/- 0.044)	0.720 (+/- 0.023)
Default, 2018, RST, RST+, PDTB	0.852 (+/- 0.054)	0.728 (+/- 0.056)	**0.461 (+/- 0.044)**	**0.732 (+/- 0.027)**

Table 5: Results for the full relation set with complex setting: macro-averaged F1 score, variance in parentheses, maximum is in bold for each classifier

that the PDTB parser only identified a relatively small amount of relations, and these did not map very well to the ARG annotation, the PDTB features still improved the results more than the RST features did (compare lines 2 and 4 to line 1 in Table 5). Combining both feature sets led to further improvements (lines 5, 7). We thus conclude that discourse parser features, and specifically PDTB features, add valuable information in particular for the classification of the function and attachment subtasks of ARG parsing, and could therefore be further explored and applied to other argumentative corpora.

Future work in this line of research includes a qualitative error analysis of the parsers' contributions to ARG parsing, and an ablation test for identifying the impact of the individual RST and PDTB features. Furthermore, recently a second part of the microtext corpus has been released (see website in footnote 1), which is larger than part 1 and would also warrant similar experiments. This would also be a test for the potential influence of the translation step (German to English) in creating part 1.

Acknowledgments

We thank the anonymous reviewers for their helpful comments on the earlier version of the paper.

References

Stergos Afantenos, Andreas Peldszus, and Manfred Stede. 2018. Comparing decoding mechanisms for parsing argumentative structures. *Argument and Computation*, 9(3):177–192.

Nicholas Asher and Alex Lascarides. 2003. *Logics of Conversation*. Cambridge University Press, Cambridge.

Or Biran and Kathleen McKeown. 2015. Pdtb discourse parsing as a tagging task: The two taggers approach. In *Proceedings of the 16th Annual Meeting of the Special Interest Group on Discourse and Dialogue (SIGDIAL 2015)*, pages 96–104.

Elena Cabrio, Sara Tonelli, and Serena Villata. 2013. From discourse analysis to argumentation schemes and back: Relations and differences. *Lecture Notes in Computer Science (Computational Logic in Multi-Agent Systems)*, 8143:1–17.

Debopam Das and Maite Taboada. 2014. *RST Signalling Corpus Annotation Manual*. Simon Fraser University.

Judith Eckle-Kohler, Roland Kluge, and Iryna Gurevych. 2015. On the role of discourse markers for discriminating claims and premises in argumentative discourse. In *Proceedings of the 2015 Conference on Empirical Methods in Natural Language Processing (EMNLP)*, pages 2236–2242.

Vanessa Wei Feng and Graeme Hirst. 2014. A linear-time bottom-up discourse parser with constraints and post-editing. In *Proceedings of the 52nd Annual Meeting of the Association for Computational Linguistics*, pages 511–521.

Nancy Green. 2010. Representation of argumentation in text with rhetorical structure theory. *Argumentation*, 24(2):181–196.

Ivan Habernal and Iryna Gurevych. 2017. Argumentation mining in user-generated web discourse. *Computational Linguistics*, 43(1):125–179.

Yangfeng Ji and Jacob Eisenstein. 2014. Representation learning for text-level discourse parsing. In *Proceedings of the 52nd Annual Meeting of the Association for Computational Linguistics*, pages 13–24.

Shafiq Joty, Giuseppe Carenini, and Raymond T. Ng. 2015. Codra: A novel discriminative framework for rhetorical analysis. *Computational Linguistics*, 41(3):385–435.

Ziheng Lin, Hwee Tou Nh, and Min-Yen Kan. 2014. A pdtb-styled end-to-end discourse parser. *Natural Language Engineering*, 20:151–184.

William Mann and Sandra Thompson. 1988. Rhetorical structure theory: Towards a functional theory of text organization. *TEXT*, 8:243–281.

Daniel Marcu. 2000. *The theory and practice of discourse parsing and summarization*. MIT Press, Cambridge/MA.

Elena Musi, Tariq Alhindi, Manfred Stede, Leonard Kriese, Smaranda Muresan, and Andrea Rocci. 2018. A multi-layer annotated corpus of argumentative text: From argument schemes to discourse relations. In *Proceedings of the 11h International Conference on Language Resources and Evaluation (LREC'18)*, Miyazaki, Japan.

Michael O'Donnell. 2000. Rsttool 2.4 a markup tool for rhetorical structure theory. In *Proceedings of the International Natural Language Generation Conference (INLG'2000)*, pages 253–256.

Andreas Peldszus and Manfred Stede. 2013. From argument diagrams to argumentation mining in texts. *International Journal of Cognitive Informatics and Natural Intelligence*, 7(1):1–31.

Andreas Peldszus and Manfred Stede. 2015. Joint prediction in mst-style discourse parsing for argumentation mining. In *Proceedings of the 2015 Conference on Empirical Methods in Natural Language Processing (EMNLP)*, pages 938–948.

Andreas Peldszus and Manfred Stede. 2016a. An annotated corpus of argumentative microtexts. In *Argumentation and Reasoned Action - Proceedings of the 1st European Conference on Argumentation 2*, pages 801–816.

Andreas Peldszus and Manfred Stede. 2016b. Rhetorical structure and argumentation structure in monologue text. In *Proceedings of the Third Workshop on Argument Mining (ArgMining2016)*, pages 103–112.

Peter Potash, Alexey Romanov, and Anna Rumshisky. 2017. Heres my point: Joint pointer architecture for argument mining. In *Proceedings of the 2017 Conference on Empirical Methods in Natural Language Processing (EMNLP)*, pages 1364–1373.

Christian Stab and Iryna Gurevych. 2014. Identifying argumentative discourse structures in persuasive essays. In *Proceedings of the 2014 Conference on Empirical Methods in Natural Language Processing (EMNLP)*, pages 46–56.

Christian Stab and Iryna Gurevych. 2016. Parsing argumentation structures in persuasive essays. *Computational Linguistics*, 43(3):619–660.

Manfred Stede, Stergos Afantenos, Andreas Peldszus, Nicholas Asher, and Jrmy Perret. 2016. Parallel discourse annotations on a corpus of short texts. In *Proceedings of the Ninth International Conference on Language Resources and Evaluation (LREC)*, pages 1051–1058.

Douglas Walton, C. Reed, and F. Macagno. 2008. *Argumentation Schemes*. Cambridge University Press, Cambridge.

Detecting Argumentative Discourse Acts with Linguistic Alignment

Timothy Niven and **Hung-Yu Kao**

Intelligent Knowledge Management Lab
Department of Computer Science and Information Engineering
National Cheng Kung University
Tainan, Taiwan
`tim.niven.public@gmail.com, hykao@mail.ncku.edu.tw`

Abstract

We report the results of preliminary investigations into the relationship between linguistic alignment and dialogical argumentation at the level of discourse acts. We annotated a proof of concept dataset with illocutions and transitions at the comment level based on Inference Anchoring Theory. We estimated linguistic alignment across discourse acts and found significant variation. Alignment features calculated at the dyad level are found to be useful for detecting a range of argumentative discourse acts.

1 Introduction

Argumentation mining remains a difficult problem for machines. Even for humans, understanding the substance of an argument can involve complex pragmatic interpretation (Cohen, 1987). Consider the reply of B in Figure 1. Absent broader conversational context, and perhaps knowledge of the background beliefs of B, it can be difficult to judge whether they are asking "which religions are correlated with increased life expectancy?" (pure questioning) or giving their opinion that "not just any religion is correlated with a longer life" (assertive questioning). Since only the latter is an argumentative discourse unit (ADU) (Stede, 2013), ambiguities like this therefore make it difficult to accurately identify the structure of argumentation.

In this work we investigate using a subtle yet robust signal to resolve such ambiguity: linguistic alignment. Alignment can be calculated in an unsupervised manner and does not require textual understanding. It is therefore well suited to our current technology as an extra pragmatic feature to assist dialogical argumentation mining. Our hypothesis is that, since alignment has been shown to relate to communication strategies (Doyle and Frank, 2016), different alignment effects will be

A: ...To be able to claim that life expectancy and health are tied to religion you have to rule out hundreds of other factors: diet; lifestyle; racial characteristics; genetic pre-disposition (religion tends to run in families) etc...

B: ...Can I just have ANY religion and have a longer life?

Figure 1: An example dyad from our dataset. Without disambiguating information it is hard to know if B's reply is pure or assertive questioning.

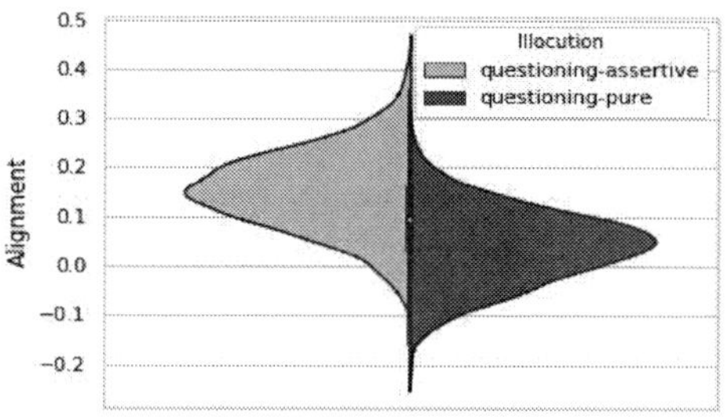

Figure 2: Posterior densities on alignment estimates for pure and assertive questioning in our dataset, indicating that alignment can help to disambiguate discourse acts.

observed over different argumentative discourse acts, providing signal for their detection. For example, Figure 2 shows our estimated posterior densities for alignment scores over pure and assertive questioning. On this basis, if B's comment in Figure 1 is accompanied by a significantly positive alignment score, we would be correct more often than not classifying it as assertive questioning.

In this preliminary work we aim to address the following questions:

1. Are the majority of argumentative discourse acts associated with significantly different alignment effects?

2. Are alignment features useful for detecting argumentative discourse acts?

Proceedings of the 6th Workshop on Argument Mining, pages 104–112
Florence, Italy, August 1, 2019. ©2019 Association for Computational Linguistics

2   Background and Related Work

Linguistic alignment is a form of communication accommodation (Giles et al., 1991) whereby speakers adapt their word choice to match their interlocutor (Niederhoffer and Pennebaker, 2002). It can be calculated as an increase in the probability of using a word category having just heard it, relative to a baseline usage rate. An example is given in Figure 3. Note that alignment is calculated over *non-content* word categories.[1] While content words are clearly set by the topic of conversation, the usage rates of particular non-content word categories has shown to be a robust measure of linguistic style (Pennebaker and King, 2000). Consistent with previous work, we focus on alignment over the Linguistic Inquiry and Word Count (LIWC) categories (Pennebaker et al., 2015), listed in Table 1.

Linguistic alignment is a robust phenomenon found in a variety of settings. It has been used to predict employment outcomes (Srivastava et al., 2018), romantic matches (Ireland et al., 2011), and performance at cooperative tasks (Fusaroli et al., 2012; Kacewicz et al., 2014). People have been found to align to power (Willemyns et al., 1997; Gnisci, 2005; Danescu-Niculescu-Mizil et al., 2011), to people they like (Bilous and Krauss, 1988; Natale, 1975), to in-group members (Shin and Doyle, 2018), and to people more central in social networks (Noble and Fernandez, 2015). The variety of these contexts suggest alignment is ubiquitous and modulated by a complex range of factors.

Some previous work bears on argumentation. Binarized alignment features indicating the presence of words from LIWC categories were found to improve the detection of disagreement in online comments (Rosenthal and McKeown, 2015). We utilize more robust calculation methods that account for baseline usage rates which thereby avoid mistaking similarity for alignment (Doyle et al., 2016). Accommodation of *body movements* was found to decrease in face-to-face argumentative conflict where interlocutors had fundamentally differing opinions (Paxton and Dale, 2013; Duran and Fusaroli, 2017). In contrast we are concerned with linguistic forms of alignment.

---

[1] Previous work has indicated the primacy of word-based over category-based alignment (Doyle and Frank, 2016). We leave investigation of alignment over words in argumentation to future work.

	B's reply	
A's message	has pronoun	no pronoun
has pronoun	8	2
no pronoun	5	5

Figure 3: Example of linguistic alignment using a binarized "by-message" calculation technique (Doyle and Frank, 2016). *B*'s baseline usage rate of pronouns is 0.5, coming from the bottom row. The top row shows the probability of *B* using a pronoun increases to 0.8 after seeing one in *A*'s message.

Category	Examples	Usage
Article	*a, the*	0.076
Certainty	*always, never*	0.016
Conjunction	*but, and, though*	0.060
Discrepancy	*should, would*	0.018
Negation	*not, never*	0.018
Preposition	*to, in, by, from*	0.137
Pronoun	*it, you*	0.108
Quantifier	*few, many*	0.025
Tentative	*maybe, perhaps*	0.030
Insight	*think, know, consider*	0.027
Causation	*because, effect, hence*	0.021

Table 1: LIWC dictionary categories we use, examples, and baseline production rates observed in our dataset of ~ 1.5 million comments on news articles.

We focus on the argumentative discourse acts of Inference Anchoring Theory (IAT) (Budzynska and Reed, 2011; Budzynska et al., 2016). IAT is well motivated theoretically, providing a principled way to relate dialogue to argument structure. As noted above, an utterance that has the surface form of a question may have different functions in an argument - asking for a reason, stating a belief, or both. The IAT framework is designed to make these crucial distinctions, and covers a comprehensive range of argumentative discourse acts.

Two previous datasets are similar to ours. The US 2016 Election Reddit corpus (Visser et al., 2019) comes from our target genre and is reliably annotated with IAT conventions. However, the content is restricted to a single topic. Furthermore, political group effects have already been demonstrated to influence alignment (Shin and Doyle, 2018). These considerations limit our ability to generalize using this dataset alone. The Internet Argument Corpus (Abbott et al., 2016), used in prior work on disagreement (Rosenthal and McKeown, 2015), is much larger than our current dataset, however the annotations do not cover the principled and comprehensive set of discourse acts that we require to support dialogical argumentation mining in general.

A: ... it is worth pointing out that other groups hold their own values above the law of the land. Traditional European-Australian culture values sticking by your mates and not dobbing on people well above law-abidance.

B: May i say that "Sticking by your mates'" is not cited as a religious law and people generally understand that "Sticking by your mates" will not protect you when Breaking the Law. ... There is a question about religious rights and my point was "Religious rights are a person's right as long it stays within our laws of our land.." Should we protect a person's right to be Religiously happy to stone a women to death for adultery or kill a person for blasphmey?

Figure 4: Annotating discourse acts across a message-reply pair. The blue text spans are *Asserting*. The red span is *Disagreeing*, which always crosses the comments - in this case attacking the inference in *A*. If *A* was the reply we would annotate the purple span as *Arguing*, as it offers a reason in support of the preceding assertion. In the reply, *Arguing* is provided by the green span, which is an instance of *Assertive Questioning*. Note that we only annotate what is in *B*. This pair is therefore annotated as: {*Asserting, Disagreeing, Assertive Questioning, Arguing*}.

3   Dataset

In this section we outline our annotation process. So far we have 800 message-reply pairs but annotated by just a single annotator. In future work we will scale up considerably with multiple annotators, and include Mandarin data for cross-linguistic comparison.

3.1   Source

We scraped ∼1.5M below the line comments from an academic news website, The Conversation,[2] covering all articles from its inception in 2011 to the end of 2017. In order to maximize the generalizabilty of our conclusions we selected comments covering a variety of topics. We also picked as evenly as possible from the continuum of controversiality, as measured by the proportion of deleted comments in each topic. More controversial topics are likely to see higher degrees of polarization, which should affect alignment across groups (Shin and Doyle, 2018). The most controversial topics we included are *climate change* and *immigration*. Among the least controversial are *agriculture* and *tax*.

Nevertheless this data source has its own peculiarities that attenuate liberal generalization. As the site is well moderated, comments are on topic and abusive comments are deleted, even if they also contain argumentative content. The messages are generally longer and less noisy than, for example, Twitter data. Moreover, many commenters are from research and academia. Therefore in general we see a high quality of writing, and of argumentation.

3.2   Annotation

The list of illocutions we chose to annotate are taken from Budzynska et al. (2016): *Asserting, Ironic Asserting, (Pure/Assertive/Rhetorical) Questioning, (Pure/Assertive/Rhetorical) Challenging, Conceding, Restating,* and *Non-Argumentative* (anything else). The transitions we consider follow IAT conventions. *Arguing* holds over two units, where a reason is offered as support for some proposition. *Disagreeing* occurs where an assertion conflicts with another. *Agreeing* is instantiated by phrases such as "I agree" and "Yeah."

Annotating *Rhetorical Questioning/Challenging* is the most difficult. As noted by Budzynska et al. (2016), there is no common specification for *Rhetorical Questioning*. We follow their definition, by which *Pure* and *Assertive Questioning/Challenging* ask for the speaker's opinion/evidence, and the *Assertive* and *Rhetorical* types communicate the speakers own opinion. Therefore the *Pure* varieties do not convey the speakers opinion, and the *Rhetorical* types do not expect a reply. Annotating *Rhetorical Questioning/Challenging* therefore requires a more complicated pragmatic judgment of the speaker's intention.

Our annotation scheme departs from previous work in that we only annotate at the comment and not the text segment level. Multiple annotations often apply to a single comment. An example is given in Figure 4. The text spans of the identified illocutions are highlighted and the transitions are indicated with arrows for clarity, but note that we did not annotate at that level.

---

[2]https://theconversation.com/global

Another difference from prior work relates to *Concessions*. Unlike Budzynska et al. (2016) we do not explicitly annotate the sub-type *Popular Concession* - where a speaker concedes in order to prepare the ground for disagreement. A potential confound with the annotation scheme described so far is ambiguous cases of *Agreeing* and *Disagreeing* in the same comment, which could be expected in a *Popular Concession*: "Yeah, I agree that X, but [counter-argument]." Because we are annotating at the level of the comment, we are able to distinguish these cases by considering combinations of discourse acts. A *Popular Concession* is distinguished by the presence of *Conceding* along with *Disagreeing*, optionally with *Agreeing*. A *Pure Concession* is then distinguished by the presence of *Conceding* and the absence of *Disagreeing*. We therefore do not need to rule that only one of *Agreeing* or *Disagreeing* can occur in a single comment.

We found that *Asserting* (627/800), *Arguing* (463/800), and *Disagreeing* (402/800) are by far the most common individually, and as a combination (339/800), reflecting the argumentative nature of our dataset. The distribution of comments over discourse acts is Zipfian. The lowest frequency discourse act is *Ironic Asserting*, which has only 12 annotations in our 800 comments.

4 Methodology

4.1 Alignment over Discourse Acts

To estimate alignment scores across discourse acts we parameterize the message and reply generation process as a hierarchy of normal distributions, following the word-based hierarchical alignment model (WHAM) (Doyle and Frank, 2016). Each message is treated as a bag of words and word category usage is modeled as a binomial draw. WHAM is based on the hierarchical alignment model (HAM) (Doyle et al., 2016), adapted by much other previous work (Doyle and Frank, 2016; Yurovsky et al., 2016; Doyle et al., 2017). WHAM's principal benefit over HAM is controlling for message length, which was shown to be important for accurate alignment calculation (Doyle and Frank, 2016). Our adaptation is shown in Figure 5. For further details of WHAM we refer the reader to the original work.

A key problem we need to address is our inability to aggregate counts over all messages in a conversation between two speakers (as in Figure 3).

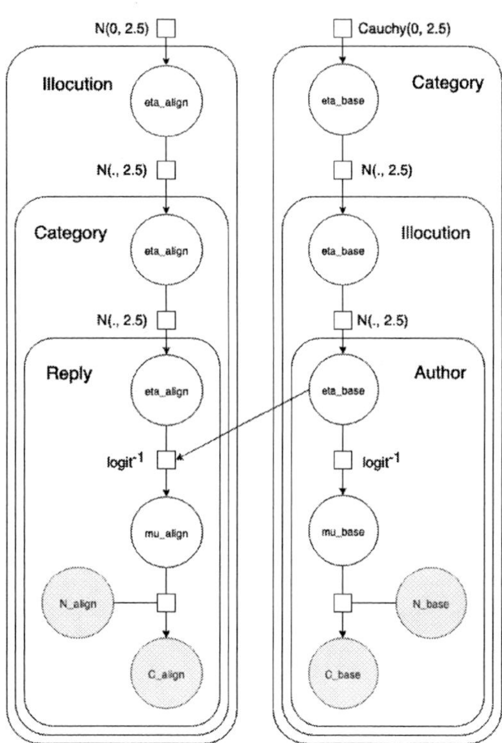

Figure 5: Our adaptation of WHAM (Doyle and Frank, 2016) for estimating alignment over argumentative discourse acts.

This is a virtue of the original WHAM model that provides more reliable alignment statistics. We cannot aggregate counts over multiple message-reply pairs since our target is the discourse acts in *individual* replies. However, we are helped somewhat by the long average comment length in our chosen genre ($\mu = 82.5$ words, $\sigma = 66.5$). The lowest baseline category usage rate is approximately 0.8% ($\mu = 3.6\%$, $\sigma = 2.2\%$). Therefore an average comment length gives us enough opportunity to see much of the effects of alignment on the binomial draw, but is likely to systematically underestimate alignment. In future work we will investigate this phenomenon with simulated data, and continue to search for a solution that makes better use of the statistics.

However, we can make more robust estimates of the baseline rate of word category usage by considering our entire dataset ($\sim$ 1.5 million comments). We have annotations for 261 authors. The most prolific author has $11,327$ comments. On average an author has 429 comments ($\sigma = 1,409$). For most authors we find multiple replies to comments that do not have each word category, making these statistics relatively reliable.

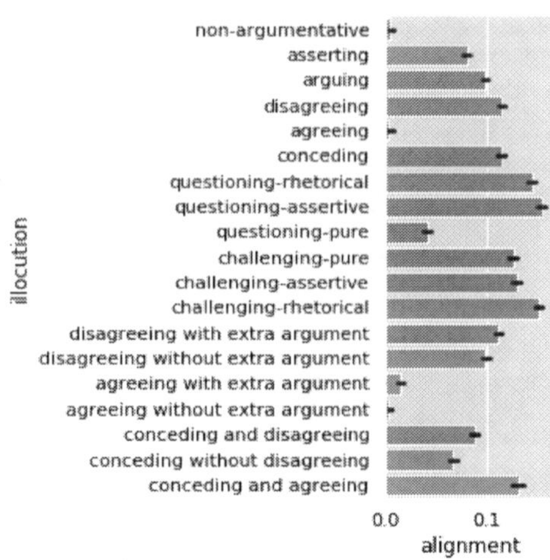

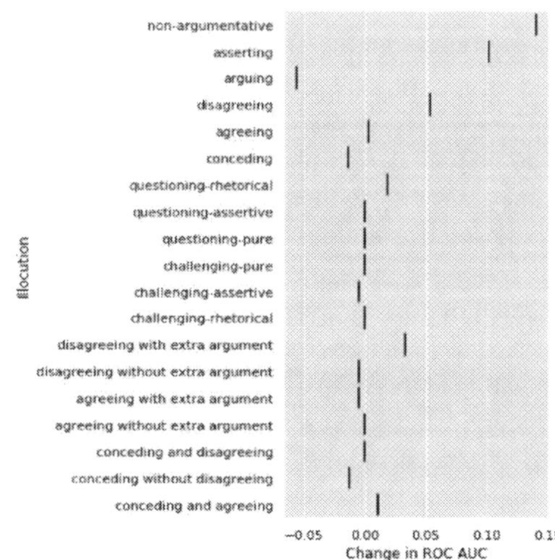

Figure 6: Alignment estimates over IAT discourse acts and combinations of interest. The error bars represent 95% highest posterior density.

Figure 7: ROC AUC Performance change from bag of GloVe vectors due to adding alignment features.

Bayesian posteriors for discourse act alignments are then estimated using Hamiltonian Monte Carlo, implemented with PyStan (Carpenter et al., 2017). We use $1,000$ iterations of No U-Turn Sampling, with 500 warmup iterations, and 3 chains. To address research question (1) we then compare the posterior densities of the last 500 samples from each chain, and look for significant differences in the means.

4.2 Alignment Over Comments

In this preliminary work, we use a simpler method for local alignment at the individual comment-reply level that we found effective. We utilize the author baselines calculated for each LIWC category from the entire dataset. Then, for each message and reply, we calculate the local change in logit space from the baseline to the observed usage rate, based on the binary criterion of whether the original message contained a word from the category. Formally, let the LIWC categories used in the first message be $\mathbb{C}_a$. For a LIWC category c, given the baseline logit space probability $\eta^{(c)}$ of the replier, and the observed usage rate r of words from category c in the reply, we calculate the alignment score as

$$s^{(c)} = \begin{cases} \mathrm{logit}(r) - \eta^{(c)} & c \in \mathbb{C}_a \\ 0 & \text{otherwise} \end{cases}$$

We clip these values to be in the range $[-5, 5]$

to avoid infinite values and floor effects - for example where the reply does not contain a word from c. This range is large enough to cover the size of alignment effects we observed. Following this calculation method we end up with an 11-dimensional vector of alignments over each LIWC category for each reply.

4.3 Detecting Argumentative Discourse Acts

To investigate our second preliminary research question we perform logistic regression for each annotated comment and each discourse act. Our baseline is a bag of GloVe vectors (Pennington et al., 2014). We use the 25-dimensional vectors trained on 27 billion tokens from a Twitter corpus. We concatenate the 11-dimensional alignment score vector to the bag of GloVe representation and look for an increase in performance. We randomly split the dataset into 600 training data points, and 200 for testing. We implement logistic regression with Scikit-learn (Pedregosa et al., 2011) and use the LBFGS solver. We set the maximum number of iterations to $10,000$ to allow enough exploration time. Because this is not a deterministic algorithm, we take the mean performance of 20 runs over different random seeds as the final result. As we are concerned with detection, and because the labels in each class are very imbalanced, our evaluation metric is ROC AUC.

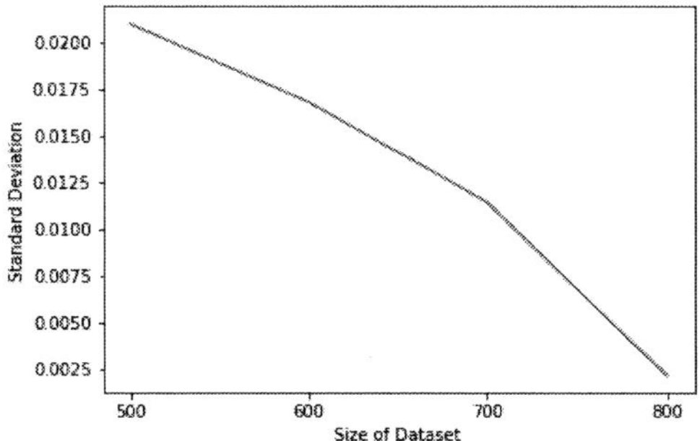

Figure 8: Mean of the standard deviation of parameter estimates as a function of dataset size. For each dataset size we fit the model 10 times with a different random seed.

5   Results and Discussion

All data and code to reproduce these results are available on Github.[3]

5.1   Alignment and Discourse Acts

Figure 6 shows the alignment estimates over our annotated discourse acts. Due the limitations of our data we limit our preliminary research question to whether these differences are significant. We conducted pairwise t-tests for the significance of the difference between the means of our alignment estimates for each discourse act. A clear majority were significant ($p >> 0.05$), with only 6.4% (22/342) insignificant. We therefore answer our first research question positively.

5.2   Detecting Discourse Acts

Figure 7 shows the change in ROC AUC of our logistic regression model with alignment features as compared to the baseline. In general alignment features are useful, with the net change over all discourse acts being positive. We therefore answer our second research question in the affirmative. However, arguing has taken an unexpected step backwards that requires further explanation. It could be a result of overfitting due to the small size of our dataset.

6   Reliability

Due to the limitations of our study we asked the question: how reliable are the alignment estimates presented here? We expect noise to come from three sources: (1) the small size of our dataset; (2) using a non-deterministic optimization algorithm;

(3) only having one annotator. We are unable to address (3) in the present work. However we investigated (1) and (2) by fitting our model 10 times with different random seeds for different dataset sizes (500, 600, 700, and 800 data points) and calculating the standard deviation in the estimated parameter means across the 10 runs. The results are given in Figure 8. We can see that by 800 data points the mean of the standard deviation has reduced significantly to around 0.002. Thus in the aggregate the parameters estimates appear to be converging already - although parameters with few data points still show larger variance. We clearly need more data for lower frequency discourse acts.

7   Conclusion and Future Work

We have reported what are likely to be robust results showing significant difference among alignment effects over argumentative discourse acts in a below the line comments genre. Comment level alignment features were shown to be useful for detecting argumentative discourse acts in the aggregate. Our study is limited by a small dataset, which is particularly felt for low frequency discourse acts, and an annotation scheme lacking multiple annotators. Therefore our immediate future work includes expanding our dataset and acquiring multiple annotations. We also plan to make our investigations more robust by including a cross-linguistic comparison with Mandarin data.

Although these results are not robust enough to draw more interesting conclusions about the observed patterns, we make one suggestive observation. Alignment appears higher for discourse acts that involve arguing. *Non-argumentative*, *Agreeing*, and *Pure Questioning* show no alignment effects. In general, *Arguing* and *Disagreeing* increase alignment. There is support in the previous literature for a view of alignment as modulated by engagement (Niederhoffer and Pennebaker, 2002). Our genre can be characterized as a clash of opinions. If engaging in debate is modulating alignment it would not be surprising if alignment effects were higher over argumentative discourse acts. We leave a thorough treatment of this question to future work.

We note that our agreement and disagreement estimates are at odds with previous work on body and head movement accommodation that showed alignment *decrease* with disagreement (Paxton and Dale, 2013; Duran and Fusaroli, 2017). There

---

[3]https://github.com/IKMLab/argalign1

are some considerations that may account for this discrepancy. Previous work (Doyle and Frank, 2016) showed that alignment was less pronounced in telephone than online textual conversation (Twitter). It was hypothesized that in the textual genre there is time to review the original message when composing a reply. There may also be time to reflect and choose a communication strategy. In face-to-face argumentation, on the other hand, one is forced to react in the moment, with far less time to prepare a considered response. Our tentative results appear to support a view alignment as modulated by *communication strategy* (Fusaroli et al., 2012).

We also need to apply our methods to existing datasets for comparison. In particular the US 2016 Election Reddit corpus (Visser et al., 2019) is already annotated with IAT discourse acts. The IAC should also be used to further investigate the relationship between alignment and disagreement, particularly as our finding appears to contradict previous results.

Our methods, particularly the calculation of local alignment in replying comments, can be sharpened, especially as the volume of data grows. We also note that in our dataset repliers often directly quote large portions of text in the original message. This may skew alignment calculations in these instances. We will apply a preprocessing step in future to control for this. Another peculiar feature of our genre is that comments are often directed to the broader audience. IAC is annotated with this aspect, and it will be important to investigate how this affects alignment. It may be worthwhile investigating methods that consider a broader context than the immediate message and reply. We also need to consider alignment over words as well as categories, particular as previous research showed alignment over words to be a more primary phenomenon (Doyle and Frank, 2016).

Other phenomenon have been proposed to modulate alignment in argumentation. It has been suggested that arguing a minority position may be accompanied by an increased need for persuasiveness (Pennebaker et al., 2003) (and therefore an increased usage of "causation" words). Argumentation schemes may also prove to modulate alignment. An argument from authority, for example as an eyewitness, could require a communicative strategy that sounds authoritative - having the power of knowledge. Previous results showed that power does not align but is aligned to. That would lead to the hypothesis that such an argument scheme should be correlated with a smaller or negative alignment effect. Modeling argument schemes directly may therefore help to improve the accuracy of argumentative alignment estimates.

Acknowledgements

We would like to thank the reviewers for their helpful comments.

References

Rob Abbott, Brian Ecker, Pranav Anand, and Marilyn A. Walker. 2016. Internet argument corpus 2.0: An sql schema for dialogic social media and the corpora to go with it. In *LREC*.

Frances R. Bilous and Robert M. Krauss. 1988. Dominance and accommodation in the conversational behaviours of same- and mixed-gender dyads. *Language & Communication*, 8(3):183 – 194. Special Issue Communicative Accomodation: Recent Developments.

Kasia Budzynska, Mathilde Janier, Chris Reed, and Patrick Saint-Dizier. 2016. Theoretical foundations for illocutionary structure parsing. *Journal of Argumentation and Computation*, 7(1):91–108. Thanks to IOS PRESS editor. The definitive version is available at http://www.iospress.nl/journal/argument-computation/. This papers appears in Volume 7 of Journal of Argumentation and Computation ISSN 1946-2166 The original PDF is available at: http://content.iospress.com/articles/argument-and-computation/aac005.

Katarzyna Budzynska and Chris Reed. 2011. Speech acts of argumentation: Inference anchors and peripheral cues in dialogue. In *Computational Models of Natural Argument*.

Bob Carpenter, Andrew Gelman, Matthew Hoffman, Daniel Lee, Ben Goodrich, Michael Betancourt, Marcus Brubaker, Jiqiang Guo, Peter Li, and Allen Riddell. 2017. Stan: A probabilistic programming language. *Journal of Statistical Software, Articles*, 76(1):1–32.

Robin Cohen. 1987. Analyzing the structure of argumentative discourse. *Computational Linguistics*, 13:11–24.

Cristian Danescu-Niculescu-Mizil, Lillian Lee, Bo Pang, and Jon M. Kleinberg. 2011. Echoes of power: Language effects and power differences in social interaction. *CoRR*, abs/1112.3670.

Gabriel Doyle and Michael C. Frank. 2016. Investigating the sources of linguistic alignment in conversation. In *Proceedings of the 54th Annual Meeting of the Association for Computational Linguistics (Volume 1: Long Papers)*, pages 526–536, Berlin, Germany. Association for Computational Linguistics.

Gabriel Doyle, Amir Goldberg, Sameer Srivastava, and Michael Frank. 2017. Alignment at work: Using language to distinguish the internalization and self-regulation components of cultural fit in organizations. In *Proceedings of the 55th Annual Meeting of the Association for Computational Linguistics (Volume 1: Long Papers)*, pages 603–612, Vancouver, Canada. Association for Computational Linguistics.

Gabriel Doyle, Dan Yurovsky, and Michael C. Frank. 2016. A robust framework for estimating linguistic alignment in twitter conversations. In *Proceedings of the 25th International Conference on World Wide Web*, WWW '16, pages 637–648, Republic and Canton of Geneva, Switzerland. International World Wide Web Conferences Steering Committee.

Nicholas D. Duran and Riccardo Fusaroli. 2017. Conversing with a devils advocate: Interpersonal coordination in deception and disagreement. *PLOS ONE*, 12(6):1–25.

Riccardo Fusaroli, Bahador Bahrami, Karsten Olsen, Andreas Roepstorff, Geraint Rees, Chris Frith, and Kristian Tyln. 2012. Coming to terms: Quantifying the benefits of linguistic coordination. *Psychological Science*, 23(8):931–939. PMID: 22810169.

Howard Giles, Nikolas Coupland, and Justine Coupland. 1991. *Accommodation theory: Communication, context, and consequence*, Studies in Emotion and Social Interaction, page 168. Cambridge University Press.

Augusto Gnisci. 2005. Sequential strategies of accommodation: a new method in courtroom. *The British journal of social psychology*, 44 Pt 4:621–43.

Molly E. Ireland, Richard B. Slatcher, Paul W. Eastwick, Lauren E. Scissors, Eli J. Finkel, and James W. Pennebaker. 2011. Language style matching predicts relationship initiation and stability. *Psychological Science*, 22(1):39–44. PMID: 21149854.

Ewa Kacewicz, James W. Pennebaker, Matthew Davis, Moongee Jeon, and Arthur C. Graesser. 2014. Pronoun use reflects standings in social hierarchies. *Journal of Language and Social Psychology*, 33(2):125–143.

Michael Natale. 1975. Convergence of mean vocal intensity in dyadic communication as a function of social desirability. *Journal of Personality and Social Psychology*, 32:790–804.

Kate G. Niederhoffer and James W. Pennebaker. 2002. Linguistic style matching in social interaction. *Journal of Language and Social Psychology*, 21(4):337–360.

Bill Noble and Raquel Fernandez. 2015. Centre stage: How social network position shapes linguistic coordination. In *Proceedings of the 6th Workshop on Cognitive Modeling and Computational Linguistics*, pages 29–38, Denver, Colorado. Association for Computational Linguistics.

Alexandra Paxton and Rick Dale. 2013. Argument disrupts interpersonal alignment. *Quarterly journal of experimental psychology (2006)*, 66:2092–102.

F. Pedregosa, G. Varoquaux, A. Gramfort, V. Michel, B. Thirion, O. Grisel, M. Blondel, P. Prettenhofer, R. Weiss, V. Dubourg, J. Vanderplas, A. Passos, D. Cournapeau, M. Brucher, M. Perrot, and E. Duchesnay. 2011. Scikit-learn: Machine learning in Python. *Journal of Machine Learning Research*, 12:2825–2830.

James Pennebaker, Ryan Boyd, Kayla Jordan, and Kate Blackburn. 2015. The development and psychometric properties of liwc2015.

James Pennebaker and Laura King. 2000. Linguistic styles: Language use as an individual difference. *Journal of personality and social psychology*, 77:1296–312.

James W. Pennebaker, Matthias R. Mehl, and Kate G. Niederhoffer. 2003. Psychological aspects of natural language use: Our words, our selves. *Annual Review of Psychology*, 54(1):547–577. PMID: 12185209.

Jeffrey Pennington, Richard Socher, and Christopher D. Manning. 2014. Glove: Global vectors for word representation. In *Empirical Methods in Natural Language Processing (EMNLP)*, pages 1532–1543.

Sara Rosenthal and Kathy McKeown. 2015. I couldn't agree more: The role of conversational structure in agreement and disagreement detection in online discussions. In *SIGDIAL Conference*.

Hagyeong Shin and Gabriel Doyle. 2018. Alignment, acceptance, and rejection of group identities in online political discourse. In *Proceedings of the 2018 Conference of the North American Chapter of the Association for Computational Linguistics: Student Research Workshop*, pages 1–8, New Orleans, Louisiana, USA. Association for Computational Linguistics.

Sameer B. Srivastava, Amir Goldberg, V. Govind Manian, and Christopher Potts. 2018. Enculturation trajectories: Language, cultural adaptation, and individual outcomes in organizations. *Management Science*, 64(3):1348–1364.

Manfred Stede. 2013. From argument diagrams to argumentation mining in texts:. *International Journal of Cognitive Informatics and Natural Intelligence*, 7:1–31.

Jacky Visser, Barbara Konat, Rory Duthie, Marcin Koszowy, Katarzyna Budzynska, and Chris Reed. 2019. Argumentation in the 2016 us presidential elections: annotated corpora of television debates and social media reaction. *Language Resources and Evaluation*.

Michael Willemyns, Cynthia Gallois, Victor J. Callan, and Jeffery Pittam. 1997. Accent accommodation in the job interview: Impact of interviewer accent and gender. *Journal of Language and Social Psychology*, 16(1):3–22.

Daniel Yurovsky, Gabriel Doyle, and Michael C. Frank. 2016. Linguistic input is tuned to children's developmental level. In *CogSci*.

Annotation of Rhetorical Moves in Biochemistry Articles

Mohammed Alliheedi
Al Baha University, KSA
University of Waterloo
Waterloo, Ontario, Canada
mallihee@uwaterloo.ca

Robert E. Mercer
Dept. of Computer Science
University of Western Ontario
London, Ontario, Canada
mercer@csd.uwo.ca

Robin Cohen
Dept. of Computer Science
University of Waterloo
Waterloo, Ontario, Canada
rcohen@uwaterloo.ca

Abstract

This paper focuses on the real world application of scientific writing and on determining rhetorical moves, an important step in establishing the argument structure of biomedical articles. Using the observation that the structure of scholarly writing in laboratory-based experimental sciences closely follows laboratory procedures, we examine most closely the Methods section of the texts and adopt an approach of identifying rhetorical moves that are procedure-oriented. We also propose a verb-centric frame semantics with an effective set of semantic roles in order to support the analysis. These components are designed to support a computational model that extends a promising proposal of appropriate rhetorical moves for this domain, but one which is merely descriptive. Our work also contributes to the understanding of argument-related annotation schemes. In particular, we conduct a detailed study with human annotators to confirm that our selection of semantic roles is effective in determining the underlying rhetorical structure of existing biomedical articles in an extensive dataset. The annotated dataset that we produce provides the important knowledge needed for our ultimate goal of analyzing biochemistry articles.

1 Introduction

Scientists must routinely review the scholarly literature in their fields to keep abreast of current advances and to retrieve information relevant to their research. However, the volume of online scientific literature is immense, and rapidly increasing. In the biomedical field, the National Center for Biotechnology Information (NCBI) developed a literature search engine, PubMed[1], to access various databases such as MEDLINE (journal citations and abstracts for biomedical literature), full-text life science e-journals, and online books. Between 2010 and 2018 PubMed repositories increased from more than 20 million citations for biomedical literature (Lu, 2011) to more than 28 million[2]. As a consequence, it has become extremely challenging for biomedical scientists to keep current with information in their fields. This challenge has attracted Natural Language Processing researchers to develop resources and automated tools for performing various tasks in Information Extraction and Text Mining using online corpora of biomedical articles, and thus enable biomedical researchers to better manage and exploit this volume of data (Hunter and Cohen, 2006).

The types of tasks currently handled by Biomedical Natural Language Processing (BioNLP) systems have generally been aimed at extracting very specific and limited information, for example, protein and gene names and relations (Cohen and Demner-Fushman, 2014), and so have been able to rely on relatively simple forms of information extraction. Although these approaches fulfil some information needs, more in-depth and comprehensive information contained in biomedical texts would be highly valuable to scientists. This type of information can enable validating scientific claims, tracing current research directions, reproducing scientific procedures, and so forth. Recently, a new and more challenging information extraction task has been introduced as a means of obtaining this type of information: identifying the argumentation structure in biomedical articles (e.g., (Green, 2014, 2015)).

The essence of argumentation can be considered as influencing others to gain their adherence to a particular idea (Perelman and Olbrechts-Tyteca, 1973). Arguments have an explicit logical structure, for example, claims that are backed with reasons, which in turn are supported by evidence,

---

[1] http://www.ncbi.nlm.nih.gov/pubmed

[2] http://www.ncbi.nlm.nih.gov/books/NBK3827/

113

Proceedings of the 6th Workshop on Argument Mining, pages 113–123
Florence, Italy, August 1, 2019. ©2019 Association for Computational Linguistics

leading to conclusions (Toulmin, 2003). Argumentation analysis is the recognition and identification of the different forms of argumentative structures in texts. Various studies have used recurrent patterns of text organization called *rhetorical moves* (i.e., text segments that are rhetorical and perform specific communicative goals) to analyze argumentative organization of texts manually (Swales, 1990) or automatically (Teufel and Moens, 2002). Swales' CARS model targets the Introduction section[3] of scientific articles. Teufel's interests are concentrated on rhetorical moves associated with defining the research space and suggesting the knowledge claims for computational linguistics and chemistry articles (Teufel, 2010). Kanoksilapatham (2003) adds to these works by providing the first comprehensive set of rhetorical moves for complete biochemistry articles.

With our long-term goal being analyzing argumentation in biochemistry articles, our mid-term research goal is to provide a computational model for Kanoksilapatham's descriptive rhetorical move taxonomy. Our research agenda is to design algorithms which would produce a representation of rhetorical moves in a biochemistry article and in this paper we outline the proposed semantic categories to be used, and discuss how we were able to guide human annotators to provide their interpretations of the analysis (to later be used as a gold standard in order to test our solutions).

Initially, our focus is on the Methods section of the taxonomy since this provides a description of the procedures followed in the experiment and the analysis of the results of the experiment thereby giving a framework for analyzing the moves in the remainder of the article. Because the experimental process is procedural, the moves tend to follow the verbs describing the steps in the experimental process. In other words, argumentation structure and scientific method both consist of rhetorical moves and experimental process, respectively. When a scientist describes her/his method in the writen article, it contains a list of experimental steps which are described by verbs (actions). These verbs evoke (initiate) the rhetorical moves in the writing. To understand the moves, we need information about the semantic roles associated with these procedural verbs. Two well known databases containing semantic role information, Framenet (Baker et al., 1998) and Verbnet (Schuler, 2005), do not provide the information appropriate for the verbs found in this scientific domain. Our goal is to provide FrameNet and VerbNet-like information for the specialized domain of biochemistry.

So, the focus of this paper is to introduce the semantic roles that we are proposing for this domain, some of which are the same as those normally found and some which are new and we suggest are required for this domain. With these semantic roles and the Methods section rhetorical moves, we have begun annotating a corpus of the Methods sections from biochemistry articles. The annotation consists of the semantic roles and the rhetorical moves associated with each verb.

The paper is structured as follows: First, an overview of some theoretical and computational approaches to argumentation are presented in Section 2. Then, our proposed approach to argumentation analysis is described in Section 3. Next, a description of our annotation scheme is given in Section 4. A description of an annotation study conducted along with the creation of a dataset is given in Section 5. Finally, the future work and a conclusion of this paper is given in Section 6.

2 Related Work

2.1 Theoretical Approaches to Rhetorical Moves and Argumentation

Swales (1990) proposed the Create-A-Research-Space (CARS) model that uses intuition about the argumentative structure of scientific research articles. Swales defined rhetorical moves as text segments that convey communicative goals. However, despite the widespread influence of the CARS model, some researchers observed two problems: (i) the inconsistent assignment of rhetorical moves to text segments because the identification of the rhetorical moves relies on overall text comprehension, and (ii) a lack of empirical validation of moves in linguistic terms (Kanoksilapatham, 2003).

To overcome these problems, Kanoksilapatham (2003) advanced Swales' approach to move analysis by developing a framework that combines his original CARS model with the use of Biber's (1991) multidimensional analysis to enrich the model with additional information about linguistic characteristics. Although Kanoksilapatham provides an extension to the Swales move analysis

---

[3]Experimental articles in the biomedical sciences are normally organized in the IMRaD style: Introduction, Methods, Results, and Discussion.

study and attempted a validation of these moves in biochemistry articles, she only provides a descriptive analysis about rhetorical moves without defining an explicit method for analyzing and recognizing these moves in texts.

2.2 Annotating Rhetorical Moves and Argumentation Schemes

Argumentative Zoning (AZ) was developed by Teufel and Moens (1999) to categorize sentences based on their contextual information (e.g., determining authorship of knowledge claims). The AZ scheme classifies sentences into seven categories including the ones from the CARS model (Swales, 1990). The data set consisted of 48 computational linguistic papers. Three annotators were involved in the study to extract sentences that fell into these seven categories. The results showed kappa scores of 83% and 82% between the annotators in the first and second schemes, respectively. The AZ scheme was later modified to suit the characteristics of biology articles (Mizuta et al., 2006). Furthermore, Teufel et al. (2009) and Teufel (2010) proposed a revised version of AZ to include more categories for annotating scientific articles such as chemistry. This revised version was planned to model all experimental sciences, which is challenging, since the style of scientific writing varies across disciplines. Most recently, Teufel (2015) has proposed a modified version of AZ to recognize rhetorical moves in scientific articles.

Liakata et al. (2012) developed an annotation scheme called Core Scientific Concepts (CoreSC) to classify sentences into scientific categories (e.g., "related to author's other work"). The authors use Machine Learning classifiers (i.e., Conditional Random Fields and Support Vector Machines) to automatically classify sentences into the CoreSC categories. The data set consisted of 265 biochemistry and chemistry articles. The authors were only able to achieve an accuracy around 50% in categorizing sentences in the appropriate CoreSC scientific categories indicating that this is a very difficult task.

Overall, these different approaches based on argumentation theories for analyzing and recognizing argumentative elements, including move analysis ((Kanoksilapatham, 2003) (Swales, 1990)), argumentative zoning (Teufel et al., 1999), and epistemic topoi (Gladkova, 2011), lacked a formal knowledge representation which could be used

computationally for in-depth argumentation analysis and mining.

Another problem in identifying argumentative elements is that relatively few biomedical related corpora annotated with argumentation structures currently exist for use in training or evaluating Machine Learning classifiers.[4] This has encouraged researchers to begin developing annotated corpora for use by the Computational Argumentation community ((Green, 2014, 2015), in particular).

Green (2014) proposed a plan for creating an annotated corpus of biomedical genetics research articles. Importantly, in justifying the need for such a corpus, Green strongly argued for domain knowledge as a requisite of argumentation recognition in the experimental sciences. Green (2015) specified a set of argumentation schemes for scientific claims in genetics research articles. The author used a corpus of unannotated genetics research articles, and identified the components (e.g., premises, conclusions) of an argument as well as its type of scheme. Overall, the author's ultimate goal for this initial study was to develop annotation guidelines for creating corpora for argumentation mining research.

None of these previous approaches to automated argumentation analysis and mining provided a formal knowledge representation that could be used in detecting and recognizing argumentative elements. We believe that developing a formal representational framework based on verb semantics in procedural scientific discourse will enable a more in-depth analysis of argumentative elements in a computationally feasible manner. We intend to provide such knowledge for the biochemistry domain to achieve this goal. This paper discusses the annotation of a corpus of biochemistry text, the first step in this longer term enterprise.

3 Procedurally Rhetorical Verb-centric Frame Semantics

In this research we will work on the biochemistry domain to develop a formal knowledge representation, *procedurally rhetorical verb-centric frame semantics*, that can be used for in-depth argumen-

---

[4] We note, however, increasing attention to this concern, with the design of such corpora as The Internet Argument Corpus (IAC) for research in political debates on internet forums (Walker et al., 2012) and the Dr. Inventor Multi-Layer Scientific Corpus (DRI) for computer graphics articles (Lauscher et al., 2018).

tation analysis, is computationally feasible to implement, and will enable argumentation mining of more-detailed scientific knowledge than is currently available. This will be an important step towards providing researchers in Computational Argumentation working in domains with similar discourse structure with a means of using and evaluating the metrics we will develop. To the best of our knowledge, no research has proposed or incorporated the idea of a semantic frame based on verb analysis to assist in the analysis of argumentation in biochemistry articles.

We have introduced various methods for detecting rhetorical moves in Section 2. We hypothesize that recognizing and detecting rhetorical moves would provide additional information to our framework of argumentation analysis. We also hypothesize that the Methods sections in biochemistry articles contain rhetorical moves which can be correlated with the author's experimental procedures. These moves can be used to determine salient information about the elements of the article's argumentative structure (e.g., premises) and can contribute to the overall understanding of the author's scientific claims. A key aspect of our hypothesis is that development of a frame-based knowledge representation can be based on the semantics of the verbs associated with these procedures. This representation can provide detailed knowledge for understanding these rhetorical moves, which will in turn facilitate analysis of argumentation structure. In other words, we propose that a *procedurally rhetorical verb-centric frame semantics* can be used to obtain a deeper analysis of sentence meaning than is currently the case with simple methods of Information Extraction (e.g., shallow syntactic pattern) and in a computationally feasible manner. Hence our focus on this critical section as a starting point for confirming the value of our chosen model for rhetorical moves and semantic roles.

Scientific argument[5] is defined as a process that scientists follow by using certain procedures to obtain empirical data which will either support or defeat their claims, hence leading to the intended conclusion. The strength of a scientific argument depends on its reproducibility and consistency. For a scientific argument to be strong, a scientist should identify and explain all the proce-

dures in their experiment, i.e., reproducibility, so that another researcher who follows the same procedures will reach the same conclusion, i.e., consistency. Thus, for a well-constructed scientific article, a scientist should expect the same conclusion if she follows the same procedures in the same sequence as described in the Methods section.

Scientific writing in the biochemistry domain has certain characteristics that made it ideal for our purposes. In this domain, experimental procedures describe the sequence of actions the biochemist performs to carry out an experiment to derive scientific conclusions, to demonstrate science experiments as can be seen in the experimental manuals (e.g., (Boyer, 2012; Sambrook and Russell, 2001)). Verbs play an essential role as indicators of these experimental procedures. These procedures can be viewed as corresponding to the elements of the scientific argumentation structure. For example, when examining a biological substance (e.g., a certain type of bacteria) in order to prove a hypothesis (e.g., this bacteria is correlated with a certain disease) the biochemist would perform a sequence of certain procedures to arrive at a conclusion. Essentially, biochemists create an argumentation framework through the scientific methodology they follow—how they perform their experiments is how they argue. We can observe that this genre— biochemistry articles—is procedure-oriented since the scientific procedures that are described are parallel to the scientific argumentation in the text. For example:

Example 1 *"Beads with bound proteins were washed six times (for 10 min under rotation at 4 C) with pulldown buffer and proteins harvested in SDS-sample buffer, separated by SDS-PAGE, and analyzed by autoradiography." (Ester and Uetz, 2008).*

In this example, the verbs "washed", "harvested", "separated", and "analyzed" are used to illustrate the procedure steps in sequential order. Such an experiment can be reproduced if one follows these steps.

Fillmore (1976) introduced the notion of frame semantics as a theory of meaning. A *semantic frame* is defined as 'any coherent individuatable perception, memory, experience, action or object' by Fillmore (1977), in other words, coherently structured concepts that are related to each other to represent a complete knowledge of world events or experiences. For example, to un-

---

[5]http://www.ces.fau.edu/nasa/introduction/scientific-inquiry/why-do-scientists-argue-and-challenge-each-others-results.php

derstand the word "buy", one would access the knowledge contained in the commercial transaction frame which includes words such as the person who buys the goods (buyer), the goods that are being sold (goods), the person who sells the goods (seller), and the currency that the buyer and seller agree on (money).

Following Fillmore's theory of frame semantics, FrameNet (Baker et al., 1998) was developed to create an online lexical resource for English. This framework includes more than 170,000 manually annotated sentences and 10,000 words. The computational linguistics community has been attracted to the concept of frame semantics and has developed computational resources using this concept, such as VerbNet (Schuler, 2005), an on-line verb lexicon for English and PropBank (Palmer et al., 2005), an annotated corpus with basic semantic propositions.

Following the notion of frame semantics, we propose to build a knowledge representation framework to analyze verbs in a procedure-oriented genre. Our concept of procedurally rhetorical verb-centric frame semantics is intended to address this lack of a formal framework by developing a computationally feasible knowledge representation that will enable argumentation analysis. The knowledge contained in the frame semantics will facilitate the extraction of elements of arguments, i.e., argumentation mining. To reiterate, our hypothesis is that procedurally rhetorical verb-centric frame semantics can provide a knowledge representation framework for analyzing and representing the meanings of the verbs used in biochemistry articles. In turn, these frames will facilitate the identification of argumentation structure in the discourse describing experimental procedures by highlighting the important steps in the experiment which are used to argue for the author's claims.

4 Annotation Scheme for Experimental Events

We have developed a new annotation scheme for identifying the structured representation of knowledge in a set of sentences describing the experimental procedures in the Method sections of biochemical articles. Several researchers have developed other forms of schemes (e.g., "bio-events" (Thompson et al., 2008)) to extract biological information (e.g., gene regulation). However, a bio-

event is different from our definition of an experimental event. On the one hand, a bio-event is concerned with detection of bio-molecular events within the biomedical literature, such as the identification of events that are related to given proteins (Thompson et al., 2008). In our case, an experimental event is concerned with processes and procedures that are used to investigate biological events. The experimental event is also concerned with the recognition of the biochemist's reasoning of standard biochemical procedures such as using certain instruments or specific biological materials. Our annotation scheme consists of two tiers of information. A *rhetorical move* is on the sentence or clause level while *semantic role* is on the word or phrase level. The following subsections describe these two tiers of information.

Annotators are allowed to select the text span for labeling units (e.g., rhetorical moves and semantic roles) with some constraints as follows:

1. For a sentence or clause to be qualified as a rhetorical move, it must include a main verb and stand on its own. For example:

   Example 2 *"Beads with bound proteins were **washed** six times (for 10 min under rotation at 4°C) with pulldown buffer ..." (Ester and Uetz, 2008).*

2. A sentence or clause that is qualified as a rhetorical move, it should have at least one or more semantic roles. Given the previous example, one could label the sentence as follows: - "Beads with bound proteins" as a *theme* - "were washed" as a *predicate*, - "six times", "for 10 min", "under rotation", and "at 4°C" as protocol-details (repetition, time, condition, and temperature respectively).

4.1 Annotation for Rhetorical Moves

We have developed a set of rhetorical moves following Kanoksilapatham's (2003; 2005) work. That is, we have adapted and modified some of Kanoksilapatham's moves, as well as adding new more fine-grained moves to our annotation scheme. In combination, there are four major rhetorical moves concerned with the Methods section in biochemistry articles as can be seen in Table 1.

The clause given in Example 2, which is part of a complete sentence that contains several verbs, should be labeled as "Description-of-method".

Move type	Definition
Description-of-method	Concerned with sentences that describe experimental events.
Appeal-to-authority	Concerned with sentences that discuss the use of well-established methods.
Background information	Concerned with all background information for the experimental events such as "method justification, comment, or observation, exclusion of data, approval of use of human tissue" as defined by Kanoksilapatham (2003).
Source-of-materials	Concerned with the use of certain biological materials in the experimental events.

Table 1: Rhetorical Moves in the Method Sections of Biochemistry Articles

Semantic role	Definition
Agent	Generally a human or an animate subject.
Patient	Participants that have undergone a process.
Predicate	A word that initiates the frame.
Theme	Participants in a location or undergoing a change of location.
Goal	Identifies a thing toward which an action is directed or a place to which something moves.
Factitive	A referent that results from the action or state identified by a verb.
Location	The physical place where the experiments took place.
Protocol-Detail:	
Time	Identifies the time or a duration of an experimental process.
Temperature	Identifies the temperature of an experimental process.
Condition	Identifies the condition of how an experimental process is performed.
Repetition	Identifies the number of times an experimental process is repeated.
Buffer	Identifies the buffer that was used in an experimental process.
Cofactor	Identifies the cofactor that was used in an experimental process.
Instrument:	
Change	Describes objects (or forces) that come in contact with an object and cause some change.
Measure	Describes an object or protocol that can measure another object(s).
Observe	Describes an object which can be used to observe another object(s).
Maintain	Describes an object or protocol which can be used to maintain the state of object(s).
Catalyst	Describes an object that can be used as a catalytic "facilitator" for an experimental event to occur.
Reference	Refers to a method or protocol that is being used.
Mathematical	Describes a mathematical or computational instrument

Table 2: Semantic Roles in the Annotation Scheme of our Experimental Event

4.2 Annotation for Semantic Roles

As described earlier, our experimental event scheme was inspired by the annotation scheme for bio-events (Thompson et al., 2011). We based our experimental event scheme for verb arguments on the inventory of semantic roles in VerbNet (Schuler, 2005) and modified and added new semantic roles to define our scheme. Our experimental event scheme includes: *Theme*, *Patient*, *Predicate*, *Agent*, *Location*, and *Goal*. The complete set of semantic roles and their definitions in our experimental event scheme is presented in Table 2.

Working with a biochemist, we have extended the VerbNet definition of the semantic role *Instrument* from simply "an object or force that comes in contact with an object and causes some change in them" (Schuler, 2005) to include a variety of sub-categories corresponding to various types of biological and man-made instruments used in a biochemistry laboratory. We have also added *Protocol detail* as a set of semantic roles that identify certain types of information about experimental processes such as time and temperature.

5 Annotation

5.1 Data Set

We have created a data set consisting of 105 text files. These files include only the Methods sections from biochemistry journal articles which were randomly selected from PubMed Central. To prepare the data set for our task, all files were converted to plain text files that included one sentence per line and all figures and tables were omitted. We have used this data set for our initial text analysis that we described in Section 3. We also extended our data set to include 3499 articles between the years 2013 to 2015 from the top nine journals in biochemistry (Cell, Genome Research, Molecular Cell, Molecular Biology and Evolution, Molecular Aspects of Medicine, Nature Medicine, Nature Methods, Nature Structural & Molecular Biology, and Nature Chemical Biology).

5.2 Annotation Guidelines

We have created guidelines for annotating the Methods section in biochemistry articles. The guidelines include a description and the necessary background information of the task. The guidelines also include examples for each type of semantic role and their occurrence in the text. A list of questions supplements the guidelines to help annotators classify each sentence into its proper category. This task is done for semantic role labeling at the word level and rhetorical move labeling at the sentence level. We further supplemented the guidelines with a list of common co-factors and buffers that are normally used in the experimental procedures. Essentially, each annotator is asked to read the guidelines and if at any point she/he has a question or needs clarification, we can illustrate by providing more examples. We set up a meeting with the annotators either by Skype or in person to answer their questions. In fact, the guidelines have been revised and updated several times to reflect the annotators' feedback.

Our plan is to hire experts in the biomedical domain to label the Methods section in all of the articles in our dataset using our annotation scheme. Due to resource limitations, only 5% of the total number of articles have been annotated by two annotators, to date. We have hired ten annotators with a variety of backgrounds (Biochemistry, Bioinformatics, Biology) and different academic levels ranging from Bachelor to PhD degree. The annotators have engaged in various training sessions that were led by the authors. We have provided different resources that can help and support the annotators in this project. These resources include frequent meetings, the annotation guidelines, a list of questions and answers about the annotation, our biochemistry expert (a PhD student working with us), and the use of web-based software called Slack[6] which allows annotators to post questions, comments, or illustrate an example from the data set. We have also created a demo video[7] that shows annotators step by step how to use the GATE tool[8] and how to use the schema to label texts. Annotators are asked to use the GATE tool as an interface which gives them access to our developed schema for the semantic roles.

Each article is labeled by two annotators. The labeling is done on a verb basis rather than a full-sentence basis. In other words, each sentence with more than one verb is divided into smaller text spans (Annotation Units (AUs)), which are composed of a verb and the text containing its semantic roles. The annotators identity the verb in that AU and label all associated semantic roles for that verb

---

[6]https://slack.com/

[7]The demo video and guidelines are available at https://uwaterloo.ca/scholar/mallihee/links/gate-annotation-demo-and-annotation-guidelines

[8]https://gate.ac.uk/

Configuration	Kappa score
Original annotation	61.3%
Theme combined with patient and all instrument roles combined	68.9%
Protocol details combined	71.6%
Adjudicated	93.6%

Table 3: Inter annotator agreement κ-score for semantic role labeling

within that AU. The annotators decide which constituent is a semantic role. Then, annotators label the entire AU with appropriate rhetorical moves. Each annotation is stored in an XML file. Figure 1 shows an example of some sentences annotated for both rhetorical moves and semantic roles.

5.3 Inter-annotator Agreement

Identification of semantic roles: We measured the inter-annotator agreement for semantic role labeling between the two annotations of the same article using the κ-score (Cohen, 1960). To have a matching label, both the semantic role category and the text span must be the same. Then, we measured the κ-score after the adjudication step which was done by one of the authors. The adjudication step's main goal is to resolve any disagreement in annotations (Palmer et al., 2005). We have also measured the kappa score for different configurations of the data set as shown in Table 3. "Original annotation" is the annotation that was provided by the annotators. "Theme combined with patient and all instrument roles combined" indicates theme and patient were combined as one role and all instrument subcategories were considered as one. "Protocol detail combined" indicates that in addition to the previous merging of semantic roles, all protocol detail subcategories were combined as one role. "Adjudicated" means that the disagreements in the original annotations were resolved and any missing semantic roles were added. All of the κ-scores in Table 3 are rated substantial (Landis and Koch, 1977; McHugh, 2012). The results are very promising.

Identification of rhetorical moves: We also measured the inter-annotator agreement for rhetorical move identification between the two annotations of each article using the κ-score. Here again, the rhetorical move and text span must be the same to be considered a match. As seen in Table 4, we

Configuration	Kappa score
Original	42.0%
Adjudicated	98.2%

Table 4: Inter annotator agreement κ-score for rhetorical move identification

have measured the kappa-score for two configurations. "Original" is the annotation provided by the annotators, while "Adjudicated" means that the disagreements in the original annotations were resolved. The Adjudicated step was done by one of the authors. The result, shown in Table 4, shows a moderate to almost perfect agreement (Landis and Koch, 1977; McHugh, 2012). We have calculated the confusion matrix for the original annotation of rhetorical moves. During our adjudication step, we noticed some commonly mislabeled instances by some annotators. For example:

Example 3 *"The hierarchical cluster analyses were performed in MATLAB (Release 2012a), and the bar graphs were produced in Microsoft Excel 2010." (Davies et al., 2015).*

This sentence should be labeled "Description-of-method" since it clearly describes steps of the authors' method, i.e., using tools to perform analyses and produce graphs. However, one annotator mislabeled it as "Appeal-to-authority".

Example 4 *"Constructs comprising new opsin sequences cloned in pMT4 were transiently transfected into Neuro-2a cells with GeneJuice reagent (Novagen), according to the manufacturer's instructions (for further information, see Supplemental Material)." (Davies et al., 2015).*

This sentence was labeled incorrectly as "Description-of-method" whereas it should be labeled as "Appeal-to-authority" since it refers to an "established" method. We have concluded that our annotation guidelines need to be updated to better aid our annotators to properly select the right rhetorical move for each candidate AU.

6 Conclusion and Future Work

In this paper, we have presented the semantic roles that we have suggested to be necessary for this scientific domain and which will be used in our annotation scheme. This Experimental Event Scheme, which is based on the proposed semantic roles, is the first step towards developing an automated rhetorical move analysis. We have also presented

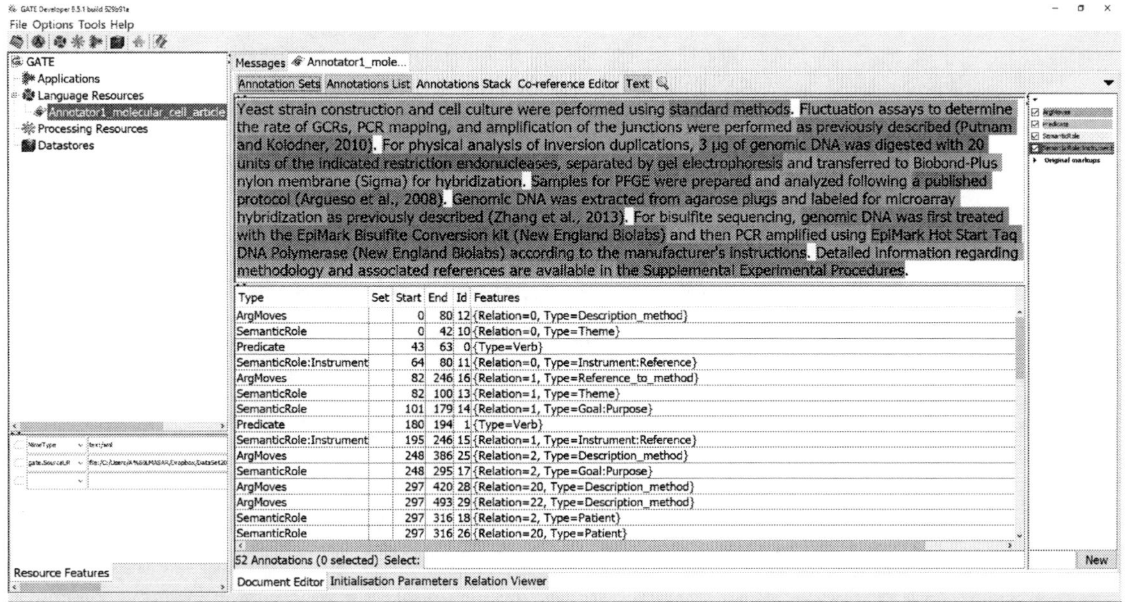

Figure 1: Snippet extracted from one article (Deng et al., 2015) of our annotated dataset showing the labelling of the rhetorical moves and semantic roles using the GATE tool.

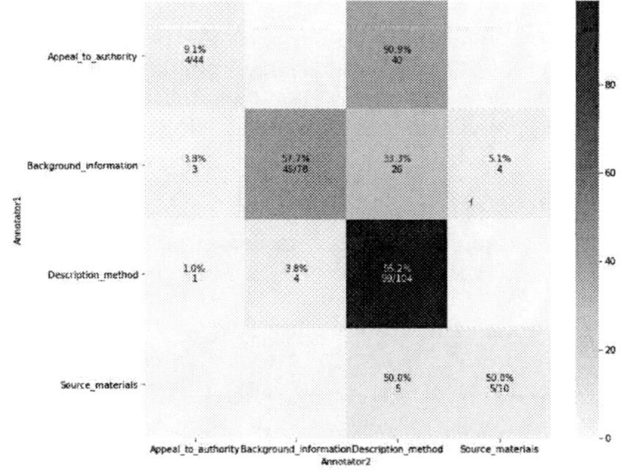

Figure 2: Confusion matrix for rhetorical move identification.

the most common rhetorical moves based on our observations of biochemistry procedures. We also have described our annotation study along with the dataset used. Ultimately, we aim to develop a framework to analyze argumentation structure in biochemistry procedures using the rhetorical moves.

We note that while there is substantial agreement among annotators in our results with respect to semantic roles, the agreement regarding rhetorical moves is more modest. One reason why this might be the case is the fact that the anno-tated dataset to date is relatively small and annotators might actually have more inherent insight into recognizing the differences between rhetorical moves. Since these moves have spans which range from clauses to full sentences, whereas semantic roles are confined to at most a few words, the guidelines for annotation that were developed focused more on this simpler case. We anticipate expanding these guidelines in order to improve inter-annotator agreement regarding rhetorical moves in the future.

As future work, in parallel with annotating the complete data set, we will develop a computational model to label the rhetorical moves for this domain. As well, from our experience with annotating the biochemistry articles with our experts, we recognized that not all of the information needed to interpret the move structure is available in the text. What is needed is an ontology that captures the knowledge that a working biochemist would have regarding biochemistry experimental procedures, especially the sequence of events that are normally undertaken in these procedures. We have begun building such an ontology and future development will involve some automation.

Acknowledgments This research was funded by Al Baha University and the University of Waterloo. We thank our annotators for their dedication to the annotation effort.

References

Collin F. Baker, Charles J. Fillmore, and John B. Lowe. 1998. The Berkeley FramNnet project. In *Proceedings of the 17th international conference on Computational linguistics-Volume 1*, pages 86–90. Association for Computational Linguistics.

Douglas Biber. 1991. *Variation across speech and writing*. Cambridge University Press.

Rodney F. Boyer. 2012. *Biochemistry Laboratory: Modern Theory and Techniques*. Prentice Hall.

Jacob Cohen. 1960. A coefficient of agreement for nominal scales. *Educational and psychological measurement*, 20(1):37–46.

Kevin Bretonnel Cohen and Dina Demner-Fushman. 2014. *Biomedical natural language processing*, volume 11. John Benjamins Publishing Company.

Wayne IL Davies, T Katherine Tamai, Lei Zheng, Josephine K Fu, Jason Rihel, Russell G Foster, David Whitmore, and Mark W Hankins. 2015. An extended family of novel vertebrate photopigments is widely expressed and displays a diversity of function. *Genome research*, 25(11):1666–1679.

Sarah K Deng, Yi Yin, Thomas D Petes, and Lorraine S Symington. 2015. Mre11-sae2 and rpa collaborate to prevent palindromic gene amplification. *Molecular cell*, 60(3):500–508.

Claudia Ester and Peter Uetz. 2008. The ff domains of yeast u1 snrnp protein prp40 mediate interactions with luc7 and snu71. *BMC biochemistry*, 9(1):29.

Charles J Fillmore. 1976. Frame semantics and the nature of language. *Annals of the New York Academy of Sciences*, 280(1):20–32.

Charles J Fillmore. 1977. Topics in lexical semantics. *Current issues in linguistic theory*, 76:138.

Olga Gladkova. 2011. *Identification of epistemic topoi in a corpus of biomedical research articles*. Ph.D. thesis, University of Waterloo.

Nancy Green. 2014. Towards creation of a corpus for argumentation mining the biomedical genetics research literature. In *Proceedings of the first workshop on argumentation mining*, pages 11–18.

Nancy Green. 2015. Identifying argumentation schemes in genetics research articles. In *Proceedings of the 2nd Workshop on Argumentation Mining*, pages 12–21.

Lawrence Hunter and K. Bretonnel Cohen. 2006. Biomedical language processing: What's beyond pubmed? *Molecular Cell*, 21(5):589–594.

Budsaba Kanoksilapatham. 2003. *A corpus-based investigation of scientific research articles: Linking move analysis with multidimensional analysis*. Ph.D. thesis, Georgetown University.

Budsaba Kanoksilapatham. 2005. Rhetorical structure of biochemistry research articles. *English for Specific Purposes*, 24(3):269–292.

J Richard Landis and Gary G Koch. 1977. The measurement of observer agreement for categorical data. *biometrics*, pages 159–174.

Anne Lauscher, Goran Glavaš, and Simone Paolo Ponzetto. 2018. An argument-annotated corpus of scientific publications. In *Proceedings of the 5th Workshop on Argument Mining*, pages 40–46, Brussels, Belgium. Association for Computational Linguistics.

Maria Liakata, Shyamasree Saha, Simon Dobnik, Colin Batchelor, and Dietrich Rebholz-Schuhmann. 2012. Automatic recognition of conceptualization zones in scientific articles and two life science applications. *Bioinformatics*, 28(7):991–1000.

Zhiyong Lu. 2011. Pubmed and beyond: a survey of web tools for searching biomedical literature. *Database*, 2011.

Mary L McHugh. 2012. Interrater reliability: the kappa statistic. *Biochemia medica: Biochemia medica*, 22(3):276–282.

Yoko Mizuta, Anna Korhonen, Tony Mullen, and Nigel Collier. 2006. Zone analysis in biology articles as a basis for information extraction. *International journal of medical informatics*, 75(6):468–487.

Martha Palmer, Daniel Gildea, and Paul Kingsbury. 2005. The proposition bank: An annotated corpus of semantic roles. *Computational linguistics*, 31(1):71–106.

C. Perelman and L. Olbrechts-Tyteca. 1973. *The New Rhetoric: A Treatise on Argumentation*. University of Notre Dame Press.

Joseph Sambrook and David W. Russell. 2001. *Molecular Cloning: A Laboratory Manual*. Cold Spring Harbor Laboratory Press.

Karin Kipper Schuler. 2005. *Verbnet: a broad-coverage, comprehensive verb lexicon*. Ph.D. thesis, University of Pennsylvania.

John Swales. 1990. *Genre analysis: English in academic and research settings*. Cambridge University Press.

S. Teufel. 2010. *The Structure of Scientific Articles: Applications to Citation Indexing and Summarization*. CSLI Studies in Computational. Center for the Study of Language and Information.

Simone Teufel. 2015. Scientific argumentation detection as limited-domain intention recognition. In *Proceedings of the Workshop on Frontiers and Connections between Argumentation Theory and Natural Language Processing*, volume 1341 of *CEUR Workshop Proceedings*, page 9pp.

Simone Teufel, Jean Carletta, and Marc Moens. 1999. An annotation scheme for discourse-level argumentation in research articles. In *Proceedings of the ninth conference on European chapter of the Association for Computational Linguistics*, pages 110–117. Association for Computational Linguistics.

Simone Teufel and Marc Moens. 2002. Summarizing scientific articles: experiments with relevance and rhetorical status. *Computational linguistics*, 28(4):409–445.

Simone Teufel, Advaith Siddharthan, and Colin Batchelor. 2009. Towards discipline-independent argumentative zoning: Evidence from chemistry and computational linguistics. In *Proceedings of the 2009 Conference on Empirical Methods in Natural Language Processing*, pages 1493–1502.

Paul Thompson, Philip Cotter, John McNaught, Sophia Ananiadou, Montemagni, Andrea Simonetta, Trabucco, and Giulia Venturi. 2008. Building a bio-event annotated corpus for the acquisition of semantic frames from biomedical corpora. In *Proceedings of the Sixth International Language Resources and Evaluation*. European Language Resources Association.

Paul Thompson, Raheel Nawaz, John McNaught, and Sophia Ananiadou. 2011. Enriching a biomedical event corpus with meta-knowledge annotation. *BMC Bioinformatics*, 12(1):393.

Stephen E Toulmin. 2003. *The uses of argument*. Cambridge university press.

Marilyn Walker, Jean Fox Tree, Pranav Anand, Rob Abbott, and Joseph King. 2012. A corpus for research on deliberation and debate. In *Proceedings of the Eighth International Conference on Language Resources and Evaluation (LREC-2012)*, pages 812–817, Istanbul, Turkey. European Language Resources Association (ELRA).

Evaluation of Scientific Elements for
Text Similarity in Biomedical Publications

Mariana Neves, Daniel Butzke, Barbara Grune
German Centre for the Protection of Laboratory Animals (Bf3R),
German Federal Institute for Risk Assessment (BfR)
Diedersdorfer Weg 1, 12277, Berlin, Germany
`mariana.lara-neves@bfr.bund.de`

Abstract

Rhetorical elements from scientific publications provide a more structured view of the document and allow algorithms to focus on particular parts of the text. We surveyed the literature for previously proposed schemes for rhetorical elements and present an overview of its current state of the art. We also searched for available tools using these schemes and applied four tools for our particular task of ranking biomedical abstracts based on text similarity. Comparison of the tools with two strong baselines shows that the predictions provided by the ArguminSci tool can support our use case of mining alternative methods for animal experiments.

1 Introduction

We aim to mine alternative methods to animal experiments from the biomedical literature. These are methods that address any of the so-called 3R principles of replacement (no animals at all or use of invertebrates over vertebrates), reduce (use of less animals), or refinement (cause less harm to animals) (Gruber and Hartung, 2004; Doke and Dhawale, 2015). For such complex natural language processing (NLP) applications, it is necessary to rely on appropriate tools to precisely understand the text and better find the potential relevant documents. The rhetorical elements, such as zones or particular entities, can support NLP algorithms by focusing on the relevant elements of the text (Mann and Thompson, 1987).

Given a certain document that describes an animal experiment for a certain research goal, hereafter called input document, we would like to find potential publications, hereafter called candidate documents, that describe an alternative method for the same research goal. Thus, some of the scientific elements should be similar between input and candidate documents, e.g. research goals and outcomes, while some others should be different, e.g. methods. Finding an alternative method to animal experiment requires two tasks: (a) performing a text similarity task with respect to some aspects of the publication, and (b) precisely understanding the proposed method with respect to the 3R principles. Therefore, the extraction of rhetorical elements has the potential to boost performance for these tasks.

Previous works have proposed many schemes for rhetorical elements in scientific publication, as reviewed in Webber et al. (2012). In a more recent survey, Nasar et al. (2018) present a good overview on both metadata and schemes for scientific articles. On the one hand, many of these schemes are not supported by an annotated corpus for training suitable information extraction tools. On the other hand, some tools based on these schemes are readily available for use.

We surveyed published schemes for rhetorical elements, whether focused on the biomedical domain or not, and we present a short overview on these. For those schemes for which we could find available tools, the latter was used to process a collection of 562 biomedical abstracts. We performed a comparison of the output (rhetorical elements) from the tools in the scope of a text similarity task on a manually annotated dataset. In this work, we limited our evaluation for text similarity but did not address whether the proposed methods comply with the 3R principles.

In summary, the contributions of this work are the following: (a) a short survey on existing schemes and corpora for rhetorical elements in scientific publications; (b) the identification of the schemes for which available tools are readily available for use; and (c) the evaluation of the available tools on a biomedical use case for text similarity. The next section presents a survey on

Proceedings of the 6th Workshop on Argument Mining, pages 124–135
Florence, Italy, August 1, 2019. ©2019 Association for Computational Linguistics

the available schemes, followed by the methodology that we propose to compare the tools in the scope of text similarity. We present the results in Section 4 and our discussion in Section 5.

2 Schemes for Rhetorical Elements

We classified the schemes according to the annotation level they address, either on the sentence, entity or relation-level. We present a summary of all schemes that we found, but give a more detailed description for (selected) schemes for which an annotated corpus is available (cf. Table 1).

2.1 Sentence-level Schemes

Many schemes model scientific elements on the level of sentences or phrases, i.e., for document zoning. It consists of splitting the publications (whether abstracts or full texts) on zones according to its scientific content, e.g. introduction, methods, results. Shimbo et al. (2003) proposed five categories and used structured abstracts from Medline while Hirohata et al. (2008) suggested four zoning categories. Further, Mullen et al. (2005) proposed a schema in which labels are grouped in three groups. Agarwal and Yu (2009) defined four categories (IMRAD schema) and manually annotated 148 articles, which was also used by Varga et al. (2012) for the annotation of more than 1,000 biomedical articles. Ruch et al. (2007) also annotated and tried machine learning in biomedical abstracts. However, none of the above data seems to be available for use, but we found many schemes with available corpora:

AZ (Teufel and Moens, 2002). The Argumentative Zoning (AZ) schema was first proposed by Teufel and Moens (2002) and an annotated corpus is freely available for download[1]. The schema is composed of seven rhetorical categories and the corresponding corpus contains 80 articles on computational linguistics. Teufel et al. (2009) extended the schema to 11 categories (the AZ-II schema), applied it to chemistry papers, and later compared it to the CoreSC schema (Liakata et al., 2010).[2] Later, Kovačević et al. (2012) annotated 110 articles in computational linguistics with a modified version of the AZ labels. Mizuta et al. (2006) also adapted the AZ schema to biomedicine by annotating 20 full-text articles.

Guo et al. (2010) compared three zoning schemes in abstracts, including a reduced version of the AZ schema composed of seven categories, and annotated 1,000 abstracts with these schemes.[3]

CoreSC (Liakata et al., 2010). This schema consists of three layers of labels and the corresponding ART corpus[4] is composed of 225 full texts. The corpus and schema were used in Guo et al. (2010) (just the first layer) and in Liakata et al. (2012a) for two life sciences applications, while Liakata et al. (2012b) compared it to a schema for biomedical events and developed the the SAPIENTA software[5].

Dr. Inventor (Ronzano and Saggion, 2015; Fisas et al., 2015). The Dr. Inventor Framework proposes five categories and annotated 40 Computer Graphics papers, the so-called Dr. Inventor Rhetorically Annotated Corpus. Later, they also annotated another layer for citation purposes (Fisas et al., 2016). An extension of this schema with argumentative components and relations was recently published (Lauscher et al., 2018b), along with a tool for the prediction of the scientific elements (Lauscher et al., 2018a).

MAZEA (Dayrell et al., 2012). This schema considers six categories and the corpus was annotated for 645 abstracts from Physical Sciences and Engineering and Life and Health Sciences.[6] A Web application is available for tagging abstracts.

PIBOSO (Kim et al., 2011). It was designed for the clinical domain and proposes six categories of a modified version of the PICO criteria. It was used for the ALTA-NICTA shared task[7] and recent works using this corpus include Hassanzadeh et al. (2014) and Jin and Szolovits (2018). The latter relies on deep learning methods and the implementation is readily available.

PubMed RCT (Dernoncourt and Lee, 2017). It is a collection that includes two corpora of 20,000 and 200,000 medical abstracts annotated

---

[1] https://www.cl.cam.ac.uk/~sht25/AZ_corpus.html

[2] However, the AZ-II corpus was not found.

[3] However, the URL informed in a later publication (Guo et al., 2013) no longer exists.

[4] https://www.aber.ac.uk/en/cs/research/cb/projects/art/art-corpus/

[5] http://www.sapientaproject.com/software

[6] http://www.nilc.icmc.usp.br/mazea-web/downloads.php

[7] https://www.kaggle.com/c/alta-nicta-challenge2

	Tools	Categories	Corpora	Topic
Sentence/Phrase	AZ	AIM, TEXTUAL, OWN, BACKGROUND, CONTRAST, BASIC, OTHER	80 (Teufel and Moens, 2002) and 20 (Mizuta et al., 2006)	CL, bio
	CoreSC	[Level 1] Hypothesis, Motivation, Background, Goal, Object, Method, Experiment, Model, Observation, Result, Conclusion	225 (Liakata et al., 2010)	chem
	Dr. Inventor	Approach, Challenge, Background, Outcomes, Future Work	40 (Ronzano and Saggion, 2015)	CG
	MAZEA	background, gap, purpose, method, result, conclusion	645 abstracts (Dayrell et al., 2012)	phy, eng, LS
	PIBOSO	Population, Intervention, Background, Outcome, Study Design, Other	1,000 abstracts (Kim et al., 2011)	bio
	PubMedRCT	background, objective, method, result, conclusion	20,000 and 200,000 abstracts (Dernoncourt and Lee, 2017)	bio
	Wilbur	FOCUS, POLARITY, CERTAINTY, EVIDENCE, DIRECTIONALITY	10,000 sentences (Shatkay et al., 2008)	bio
Ent.	ScienceIE	Task, Process, Material	500 (Augenstein et al., 2017)	CS
Relation	Gábor	USAGE, RESULT, MODEL, PART_WHOLE, TOPIC, COMPARISON	500 abstracts (Gábor et al., 2018)	CL
	SciDTB	[Coarse level] Attribution, Background, Cause-effect, Comparison, Condition, Contrast, Elaboration, Enablement, Evaluation, Explain, Joint, Manner-means, Progression, Same-unit, Summary, Temporal	798 abstracts (Yang and Li, 2018)	CL
Hybrid	Green	[Levels 1-3] 1. Causation, 1.1 One Group, 1.1.1 Agreement Arguments, 1.1.2 Eliminate Candidates, 1.1.3 Explanation-Based, 1.2 Two Group, 1.2.1 Difference, 1.2.2 Analogy (Causal), 1.2.3 Explanation-Based, 2. Other, 2.1 Classification, 2.2 Confirmation	one (Green, 2018)	bio

Table 1: Summary of the selected schemes and corresponding categories, size of the annotated corpora, and topic of the latter. Only the categories from the certain levels were shown for some schemes with various layers. Numbers or the corpora refer to full-text documents, unless otherwise stated. Regarding the topics, "CL" stands for computational linguistics, "bio" for biomedicine, "chem" for chemistry, "CG" for Computer Graphics, "phy" for Physics, "eng" for Engineering, "LS" for Life Sciences, and "CS" for Computer Science.

with five categories. The corpus is freely available[8] as well as at least two tools for its detection, namely the one from Jin and Szolovits (2018) (cf. PIBOSO above) and one based on AllenNLP (Achakulvisut et al., 2018).

Wilbur (Wilbur et al., 2006). It consists of a schema developed for biomedical articles on five dimensions. Later, the authors annotated 10,000 sentences from full-text publications (Shatkay et al., 2008), which was made available after a detailed analysis (Rzhetsky et al., 2009).[9] The annotation are on the level of fragments, which usually correspond to either the sentences or phrases.

2.2 Entity-level Schemes

Entity-level schemes aim at annotating the elements on the level of entities. Gupta and Manning (2011) proposed a simple schema based on three concepts and labeled 474 abstracts of computational linguistics. More recently, Jung (2017) defined five entity types and annotated 1,000 articles about information and communication technology (ICT) and chemical engineering. Blake (2010) also proposed a schema based on various levels of evidence (implicit and explicit claims) and annotated 29 full-text biomedical articles. However, none of the above data seems to be available but we found one schema with annotated corpus:

ScienceIE (Augenstein et al., 2017). This schema proposes three elements on the entity level as well as the annotation of keyphrases. The corpus contains 500 articles about Computer Science, Material Sciences and Physics, which were split into training, development and test datasets and used for the a SemEval task in 2017. We found the implementation from two of the participants on the shared task, namely (Prasad and Kan, 2017) and (Eger et al., 2017).

2.3 Relation-level Schemes

Previous work also considered schemes that consider relations between scientific elements. Prasad et al. (2011) defined eight discourse relations in the Biomedical Discourse Relation Bank (Bio-DRB) and annotated 24 articles from the GENIA corpus, which was later used in a couple of works (Ramesh and Yu, 2010; Polepalli Ramesh et al.,

2012). Tateisi et al. (2013) defined 16 relations and annotated 30 articles, while Meyers et al. (2014) proposed five relations and sub-relations with which they annotated 200 biomedical articles. However, none of the data above seems to be available, but we found corpora for the following two schemes:

Gábor (Gábor et al., 2016) It is a schema in the form of an ontology of 18 relations for the scientific literature, besides three more general relations. Six of these relations were recently addressed in the SemEval'18 Task 7, for which annotated data is available (Gábor et al., 2018). For sub-task 2 in SemEval'18 Task 7, the code from the team that obtained the best scores in this task is available (Luan et al., 2018).

SciDTB (Yang and Li, 2018). It is a discourse treebank for scientific articles that includes 17 coarse-grained and 26 fine-grained relation types. They annotated 798 abstracts from the ACL Anthology that are available for download.[10]

2.4 Hybrid Schemes

Hybrid schemes contain labels which cover more than one of the levels above. Tateisi et al. (2016) created an ontology of entities and relations and annotated 400 abstracts about computational linguistic. However, we found only one hybrid schema for which annotated data is available:

Green (Green, 2018). It is schema of 15 arguments annotated for one single article from the biomedical domain. The schema includes both entities and relations that are organized in a short taxonomy. Both schema and the annotated article are available.[11]

3 Methods

We evaluated tools that consider some of the schemes that we found (cf. Section 2) for the task of text similarity in the scope of our use case of mining alternative methods for animal experiments. In this section we described the data and the tools that we used as well as the evaluation methodology.

3.1 Data

We evaluated the selected schemes and tools for the task of text similarity. For this purpose, we

---

[8]https://github.com/
Franck-Dernoncourt/pubmed-rct
[9]https://doi.org/10.1371/journal.pcbi.
1000391.s002

[10]https://github.com/PKU-TANGENT/SciDTB
[11]https://github.com/greennl/BIO-Arg

model our problem as the following: given an input document that describes an animal experiment, we would like to mine similar candidate documents that are potential alternatives to animal testing. Our definition of similarity requires that both input and candidate documents should have similar research goal and comparable outcomes. However, the methods in the input document should be substantial different from those in the candidate documents. Therefore, we aim to compare input and candidate documents based on certain rhetorical elements as opposed to using the whole text.

Our evaluation datasets consist of seven input documents from Medline whose identifiers (PMIDs) are 11489449, 11932745, 16192371, 16850029, 19735549, 21494637 and 24204323. For each input document, we collected the top 200 documents (titles and abstracts) retrieved from PubMed's "similar articles" functionality. On one hand, the candidate documents are already very similar to the input document. On the other hand, the list of candidates returned by PubMed does not consider our definition of similarity.

In order to build a suitable test set for our use case, a biomedical researcher manually validated at least the top 100 documents with regards to three degrees of similarity: very similar, similar and not similar. These three labels only consider the similarity of the research goals of each pair of abstracts (input vs. candidate documents) but do not address the 3R principles. Some documents were ignored because either they were only partially similar or because no decision could be made only based on the title and the abstract.

After manual validation by the expert, our seven datasets encompass a total of 562 publications (titles and abstracts). Figure 1 illustrates the distribution of the labels for each input document. Only four from the seven input documents had very similar publications (from only 2 to 8 of them), while similar ones (from only 4 to 19) could be found for all of them. However, the non similar publications are still the largest part (from 56 to 76) of the list. The annotated data is available for download [12].

Some of the tools that we compared require some linguistic information not originally included in our documents, such as sentences and tokens. We utilized syntok[13] for both sentence splitting and tokenization to build input data for one of

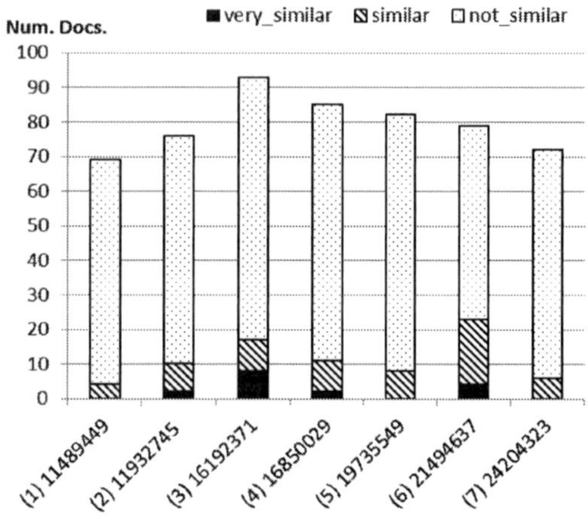

Figure 1: Number of documents according to the degree of similarity to the input document. The number of the dataset (1-7) is shown before the PMID.

the tools, namely, Prasad and Kan (2017).

3.2 Tools

We found a few available tools that address some of schemes discussed in Section 2. However, we had dismiss some of them due to various problems.

We experienced many problems with the TensorFlow library while trying the tool[14] developed by (Eger et al., 2017) for the ScienceIE schema. The tool seems to require a version of the library that it is no longer available and we could not resolve this issue not even after contacting the tool's developers. We also dismissed the tool[15] from Jin and Szolovits (2018) for the PIBOSO and PubMedRCT schemes. The installation worked but we were not able to train it due to memory problems. Finally, we did not try the tool[16] from Luan et al. (2018) since it addresses a relation-based schema (Gábor) that requires pre-tagged entities. Using named entities provided by other tools would probably add too much noise to the experiment. Finally, we had to dismiss the SAPIENTA tool (Liakata et al., 2012b) because it only allows uploading documents one by one to the Web application and we could not overcome this problem. We describe below the four tools that we

---

[12]https://github.com/mariananeves/
scientific-elements-text-similarity
[13]https://github.com/fnl/syntok

[14]https://github.com/UKPLab/
semeval2017-scienceie
[15]https://github.com/jind11/
HSLN-Joint-Sentence-Classification
[16]https://bitbucket.org/luanyi/
semeval2018/src/master/

tried for the extraction of rhetorical elements. Examples for the sentence-based (zones) and entity-based annotations are shown in Figure 2. We released in the GitHub repository the annotations extracted by the tools in the JSON format supported by the TextAE tool[17].

Achakulvisut et al.[18] (Achakulvisut et al., 2018) (PubMedRCT schema). It addresses the PubMed RCT schema, thus provides predictions for five zoning labels, namely, "Background", "Objective", "Method", "Results" and "Conclusions". We utilized the pre-trained models for Conditional Random Fields (CRF) as provided by the tool. Given that there is no publication, it is not clear what methods are behind the available models, but probably CRF.

ArguminSci[19] (Lauscher et al., 2018a) (Dr. Inventor schema extended). ArguminSci is available both for download as well as on-line (Web application). It provides predictions for five schemes but we considered only the "Discourse Role Classification (DRC)" whose labels are "Background", "Challenge", "Approach", "Outcome" and "Future Work". ArguminSci's models are based on bidirectional recurrent networks with long short-term memory cells (Bi-LSTMs) and we utilized the command line version of the tool.

MAZEA tool[20] and schema (Dayrell et al., 2012). The tool addresses six categories, namely, "Background", "Gap", "Purpose", "Method", "Result" and "Conclusion". It is currently not available for download but only as a Web tool that requires to manually upload each document individually. However, the developers kindly processed our documents locally and sent the predictions back to us. The tool utilizes machine learning algorithms, such as Support Vector Machines (SVM) and Decision Trees.

Prasad and Kan[21] (Prasad and Kan, 2017) (ScienceIE schema). It addresses the three labels for entities from the ScienceIE schema, namely, "Task", "Process" and "Material". From the

repository, we utilized the scripts for feature processing and the template to train the model with CRF++[22]. We had to correct the provided template in order to successfully train the system. The entity recognition approach is based on various features and uses the CRF algorithm.

3.3 Evaluation

We evaluated the tools for the task of text similarity. Therefore, we calculated the similarity between the input and candidate documents, either based on the whole text or on selected rhetorical elements as provided by the tools. When utilizing the output from the various tools, we built a pseudo-document based either on the sentences or entities that we obtained. For the zoning tools, we concatenated the sentences to form a single text, while we printed the entities (one per line) for the entity-based predictions. Similarly, when evaluating combination of various labels, we concatenated the text from various labels into a single file.

We performed text similarity using the TextFlow tool (Mrabet et al., 2017) and utilized these similarity scores to rank the candidate documents. Subsequently, we evaluated the ranked list with regard the metrics of precision, recall and f-score at rank 10, i.e. P@10, R@10 and F@10. P@10 is the rate of correct positive candidate documents in the top 10 highest ranked documents, i.e. $P@10 = \frac{TP@10}{10}$. The R@10 corresponds to the rate of positives candidate documents in the top 10 over the total of all positive instances, i.e. $R@10 = \frac{TP@10}{Num.Positive}$. Finally, the F@10 is the harmonic average of the P@10 and R@10 above, i.e. $F@10 = \frac{2*P@10*R@10}{P@10+R@10}$.

We considered as positive examples all those publications manually classified by our expert as "very similar" or "similar". Given the few of these instances in our datasets, we decided to make no distinction between both categories. As a result, the number of positive examples for the input documents in Figure 1 are 4, 10, 16, 11, 8, 23 and 6, respectively. We evaluated at rank 10 due to the reason that only two datasets have more than 20 positive instances, while only two of them over 10 positive instances. For datasets which contain more than 10 positive examples, we considered the number of positive instances to be equal to 10 in the equation of R@10. For the final comparison between the various tools and baselines, we per-

---

[17] http://textae.pubannotation.org/

[18] https://github.com/titipata/detecting-scientific-claim

[19] https://github.com/anlausch/ArguminSci

[20] http://www.nilc.icmc.usp.br/mazea-web/

[21] https://github.com/animeshprasad/science_ie

[22] https://taku910.github.io/crfpp/

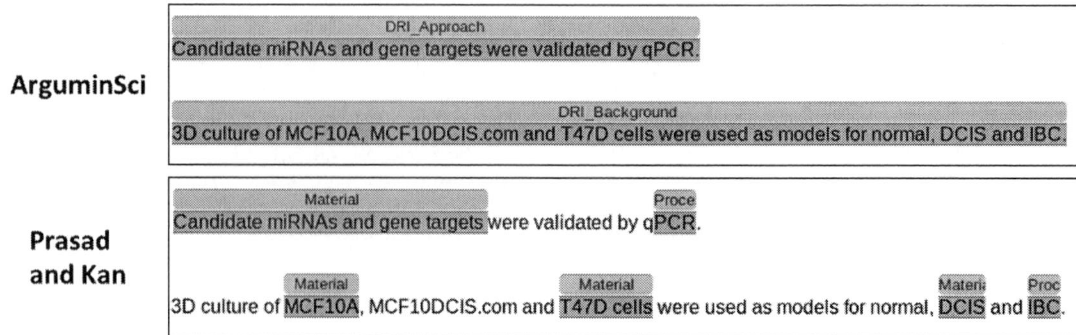

Figure 2: Visualization in the TextAE tool of the annotations provided by two of the tools that we used.

formed an average of the metrics over the seven datasets.

We defined two baselines for comparison: (i) the original order of the candidate documents as returned by PubMed's "similar articles" functionality; and (ii) string similarity based on the whole text (title and abstract) without any pre-processing on the text. For the first baseline, we searched in PubMed for each of the seven PMIDs and downloaded the list of the top 100 similar articles (stand of March 13th, 2019). Given that the current list of similar articles might include citations not present at the time when our corpus was annotated, we dismissed any document not included in our dataset when calculating the above metrics, i.e., we did not consider them as false positives.

4   Results

We compared the tools based on the metrics of P@10, R@10 and F@10 that assess the performance of the various tools for the ranking task. We performed a total of 38 experiments which includes the four tools and baselines, as well as some combinations of selected labels from the tools. The combination of labels were decided based on the performance of the single labels and on our understanding of which labels are more relevant for our use case. Table 2 presents the results for our two baselines and the best results for each tool. In the following we specify the labels that obtained the best results:

- Achakulvisut et al: the combination of all labels, i.e. "Background-Conclusions-Methods-Objective-Results"

- ArguminSci: two combinations of labels were equally good: "Background-Challenge-

Tools	P@10	R@10	F@10
PubMed	0.30	0.33	0.31
Title+Abstract	0.43	0.51	0.45
Achakulvisut et al	0.44	0.52	0.47
ArguminSci	0.47	0.56	0.50
MAZEA	0.4	0.47	0.42
Prasad and Kan	0.44	0.54	0.47
Min score	0.14	0.16	0.15
Max score	0.83	1.0	0.90

Table 2: Summary of the results from the two baselines (two first rows) and when using the selected tools. The maximum scores represent the maximum value of P@10, R@10 and F@10 that could have been obtained by any of the approaches. The minimum scores are the ones obtained when randomly selecting 10 candidates in each dataset, averaged over 1,000 experiments.

Outcome" and "Background-Challenge-Outcome-FutureWork".

- MAZEA: the combination "Method-Result".

- Prasad and Kan: the combination "Process-Material".

For our datasets, all approaches using rhetorical tools obtained a better performance than the baseline from PubMed. Further, three tools scored higher than our strong baseline that uses TextFlow over the whole text (titles and abstracts). Two of the tools (Achakulvisut et al and ArguminSci) address zoning èlements while one of them (Prasad and Kan) returns entity-level annotations. However, none of the tools scored close the maximum possible scores. Given that we do not have at least 10 positive instances ("very similar" or "similar") for some of our input documents, our maximum P@10 is of 0.83 instead of 1.0.

The three zoning tools rely on labels that can

Tools	Labels	P@10	R@10	F@10
Achakulvisut	Background	0.28	0.32	0.30
	Objective	0.33	0.41	0.35
	Methods	0.31	0.40	0.34
	Results	0.20	0.25	0.22
	Conclusions	0.23	0.26	0.24
ArguminSci	Background	0.23	0.25	0.24
	Challenge	0.23	0.26	0.24
	Approach	0.26	0.32	0.28
	Outcome	0.41	0.50	0.44
	Future Work	0.33	0.41	0.35
MAZEA	Background	0.24	0.28	0.25
	Purpose	0.24	0.25	0.25
	Method	0.30	0.37	0.32
	Result	0.28	0.32	0.30
	Conclusion	0.23	0.30	0.25
Prasad	Process	0.37	0.48	0.40
	Material	0.31	0.35	0.33
	Task	0.28	0.36	0.31

Table 3: Performance of the single labels in the re-ranking task.

be mapped to one another, as shown by the order of their labels in Table 3. When examining the performance of single labels, only the "Outcome" label from ArguminSci tool could perform close our strong baseline.

The labels that we expected to be more relevant, i.e. the ones more related to the background and outcome sections and less with the methods section, did not always perform better in the ranking task. For instance, the F@10 obtained by the label "Approach" from ArguminSci performed slightly better (0.28) than the "Background" (0.24) and "Challenge" (0.24) labels. Similarly, the label "Method" from MAZEA performed better (0.32) than "Background" (0.25) and "Purpose" (0.25) sections. We wonder whether the good performance of methods-related labels were actually due to mistakes in the classification performed by the tools.

Our experiments showed that a combination of labels always performed better than the single ones, while some combinations of labels performed better than others (cf. Figure 3). We could not find any difference in the text similarity scores (as computed by TextFlow) when considering different order of the same labels in the concatenation of the text.

5 Discussion

We carried out a total of 38 experiments that involved diverse tools, single labels and combination of various labels. We ran an error analysis to learn more about the false negatives and false positives that we obtained.

At least one positive document was missed by any of the tools, i.e. was not placed among the top 10 positions. Many of the documents that we missed are certainly due to the limitation of considering only the top 10 highest ranked positions. However, none of the experiments obtained a recall of 1.0. The highest recall that we obtained was 0.9 for the dataset 3 (16192371) using the ArguminSci tool and either the single label "Outcome" or the combination of labels "Challenge-Outcome-FutureWork".

On one hand, five documents were missed by all experiments (38 times), namely, candidate documents "19155551", "29133591", "21362567", "19667187" and "26047474" from datasets 3, 5, 6, 6, and 7, respectively. On the other hand, the candidate document "25174890" from dataset 6 was the least missed one: only by three experiments. A total of 333 documents were wrongly classified as positive, i.e. were placed among the top 10 ones, by any of the 38 experiments. No candidate document was mistakenly classified by all approaches, but the more frequent ones were: "21501651" (27 times) and "23571276" (25 times), both from dataset 4, and "11494364" (25 times) from dataset 7. Our expert checked again the labels assigned to the top FPs and FNs above described and confirmed that their labels are correct and that the documents have been wrongly classified by the corresponding approaches.

Our experiments have shown that many of the tools can indeed support our use case, specially when compared to the original list provided by PubMed. Regarding the integration of these tools into a workflow, one of the tools is currently not available (MAZEA), while all the others need some adaptations to be used in real-life applications. With respect to the methods behind the tools, ArguminSci, which is based on LSTM, performed slightly better than the ones based on CRF (Achakulvisut et al, Prasad and Kan) and superior than the machine learning algorithms in MAZEA. However, we did not evaluate the predictions made by the tools, but only their impact in a specific text similarity task.

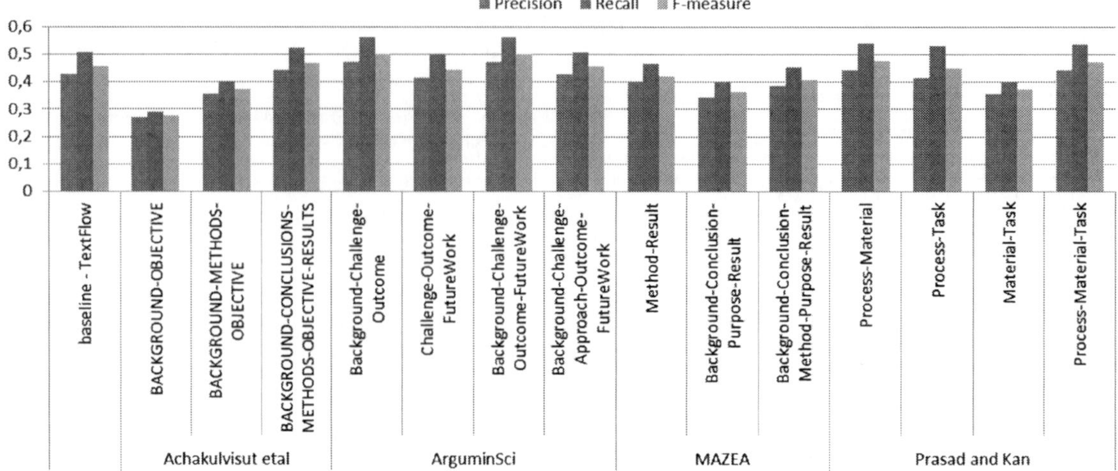

Figure 3: Comparison to the baselines of various combinations of labels as provided by the tools.

We expected that the best performing tools would be the ones that utilized corpora specifically built for the biomedical domain. From the tools that we evaluated, only Achakulvisut et al and MAZEA were specifically trained on documents from the biomedical or health domains. Nevertheless, ArguminSci, the best performing one, was trained on documents from computer graphics while and Prasad and Kan utilizes documents about computational linguistics.

We also investigated whether there was any impact of the document type in the corpora, i.e. either full texts or only abstracts, on the performance of the corresponding tools. However, we did not observe any clear association between these two aspects. While the best performing tool (ArguminSci) was trained on full texts, Achakulvisut et al utilizes only Medline abstracts. Similar to ArguminSci, the tool from Prasad and Kan is also based on full text documents.

We carried out experiments with various tools but limited to a very specific use case. Even though our datasets contains a reasonable number of documents (562), the similarity of the candidate documents was computed with respect to only seven input documents, and datasets were annotated by only one annotator. Further, we only considered titles and abstracts in our evaluation, while some tools were trained on full-text documents. Previous work has already shown the differences of information and performance of NLP tools in biomedical abstracts and full texts (Verspoor et al., 2012; Mons et al., 2004). Our future work will ad-

dress many aspects: (i) use of full texts; (ii) improvement of the datasets with additional annotators; (iii) estimation of the compliance with the 3R principles by a candidate document, in addition to the calculation of similarity; (iv) evaluation of the relation-based tool (Luan et al., 2018) and the one for which we experienced memory problems (Jin and Szolovits, 2018); and (v) evaluation of other schemes (e.g. Wilbur et al. (2006)) for which an implementation is currently not available.

6   Conclusions

We surveyed schemes that model scientific elements in publications and selected four schemes for which we could find an available tool. We utilized the predictions from these tools for assessing the text similarity between documents and further ranking them in the scope of mining alternative methods to animal testing. Our experiments show that a considerable improvement can be obtained when using ArguminSci, with respect to the original ranking returned by PubMed and to the strong baseline that we considered. However, there is still much room for improvement given that the obtained scores are still far below the possible maximum values.

Acknowledgments

We would like to thank Arnaldo Candido Junior and Sandra Maria Aluísio from the MAZEA tool for kindly processing our documents. We also would like to thank Animesh Prasad and Min-Yen Kan for their support when using their tool.

References

Titipat Achakulvisut, Chandra Bhagavatula, Daniel E Acuna, and Konrad P Kording. 2018. Claim extraction for scientific publications. `https://github.com/titipata/detecting-scientific-claim`.

Shashank Agarwal and Hong Yu. 2009. Automatically classifying sentences in full-text biomedical articles into introduction, methods, results and discussion. *Summit on Translat Bioinforma*, 2009:6–10. Amias2009-6[PII].

Isabelle Augenstein, Mrinal Das, Sebastian Riedel, Lakshmi Vikraman, and Andrew McCallum. 2017. Semeval 2017 Task 10: ScienceIE - Extracting Keyphrases and Relations from Scientific Publications. In *Proceedings of the 11th International Workshop on Semantic Evaluation (SemEval-2017)*, pages 546–555, Vancouver, Canada. Association for Computational Linguistics.

Catherine Blake. 2010. Beyond genes, proteins, and abstracts: Identifying scientific claims from full-text biomedical articles. *Journal of Biomedical Informatics*, 43(2):173 – 189.

Carmen Dayrell, Arnaldo Candido Jr., Gabriel Lima, Danilo Machado Jr., Ann Copestake, Valria Feltrim, Stella Tagnin, and Sandra Aluisio. 2012. Rhetorical move detection in english abstracts: Multi-label sentence classifiers and their annotated corpora. In *Proceedings of the Eight International Conference on Language Resources and Evaluation (LREC'12)*, Istanbul, Turkey. European Language Resources Association (ELRA).

Franck Dernoncourt and Ji Young Lee. 2017. Pubmed 200k rct: a dataset for sequential sentence classification in medical abstracts. In *Proceedings of the Eighth International Joint Conference on Natural Language Processing (Volume 2: Short Papers)*, pages 308–313. Asian Federation of Natural Language Processing.

Sonali K. Doke and Shashikant C. Dhawale. 2015. Alternatives to animal testing: A review. *Saudi Pharmaceutical Journal*, 23(3):223 – 229.

Steffen Eger, Erik-Lân Do Dinh, Ilia Kuznetsov, Masoud Kiaeeha, and Iryna Gurevych. 2017. Eelection at semeval-2017 task 10: Ensemble of neural learners for keyphrase classification. In *Proceedings of the 11th International Workshop on Semantic Evaluation (SemEval-2017)*, pages 942–946. Association for Computational Linguistics.

Beatriz Fisas, Francesco Ronzano, and Horacio Saggion. 2016. A multi-layered annotated corpus of scientific papers. In *Proceedings of the Tenth International Conference on Language Resources and Evaluation (LREC 2016)*, Paris, France. European Language Resources Association (ELRA).

Beatriz Fisas, Horacio Saggion, and Francesco Ronzano. 2015. On the discoursive structure of computer graphics research papers. In *Proceedings of The 9th Linguistic Annotation Workshop*, pages 42–51, Denver, Colorado, USA. Association for Computational Linguistics.

Kata Gábor, Davide Buscaldi, Anne-Kathrin Schumann, Behrang QasemiZadeh, Haïfa Zargayouna, and Thierry Charnois. 2018. Semeval-2018 Task 7: Semantic relation extraction and classification in scientific papers. In *Proceedings of International Workshop on Semantic Evaluation (SemEval-2018)*, New Orleans, LA, USA.

Kata Gábor, Haifa Zargayouna, Davide Buscaldi, Isabelle Tellier, and Thierry Charnois. 2016. Semantic annotation of the acl anthology corpus for the automatic analysis of scientific literature. In *Proceedings of the Tenth International Conference on Language Resources and Evaluation (LREC 2016)*, Paris, France. European Language Resources Association (ELRA).

Nancy Green. 2018. Proposed method for annotation of scientific arguments in terms of semantic relations and argument schemes. In *Proceedings of the 5th Workshop on Argument Mining*, pages 105–110. Association for Computational Linguistics.

Franz P Gruber and Thomas Hartung. 2004. Alternatives to animal experimentation in basic research. *ALTEX*, 21 Suppl 1:331.

Yufan Guo, Anna Korhonen, Maria Liakata, Ilona Silins Karolinska, Lin Sun, and Ulla Stenius. 2010. Identifying the information structure of scientific abstracts: An investigation of three different schemes. In *Proceedings of the 2010 Workshop on Biomedical Natural Language Processing*, BioNLP '10, pages 99–107, Stroudsburg, PA, USA. Association for Computational Linguistics.

Yufan Guo, Ilona Silins, Ulla Stenius, and Anna Korhonen. 2013. Active learning-based information structure analysis of full scientific articles and two applications for biomedical literature review. *Bioinformatics*, 29(11):1440–1447.

Sonal Gupta and Christopher D. Manning. 2011. Analyzing the dynamics of research by extracting key aspects of scientific papers. In *In Proceedings of IJCNLP*.

Hamed Hassanzadeh, Tudor Groza, and Jane Hunter. 2014. Identifying scientific artefacts in biomedical literature: The evidence based medicine use case. *Journal of Biomedical Informatics*, 49:159 – 170.

Kenji Hirohata, Naoaki Okazaki, Sophia Ananiadou, and Mitsuru Ishizuka. 2008. Identifying sections in scientific abstracts using conditional random fields. In *In Proc. of the IJCNLP 2008*.

Di Jin and Peter Szolovits. 2018. Hierarchical neural networks for sequential sentence classification in medical scientific abstracts. In *Proceedings of the 2018 Conference on Empirical Methods in Natural Language Processing*, pages 3100–3109. Association for Computational Linguistics.

Yuchul Jung. 2017. A semantic annotation framework for scientific publications. *Quality & Quantity*, 51(3):1009–1025.

Su Nam Kim, David Martinez, Lawrence Cavedon, and Lars Yencken. 2011. Automatic classification of sentences to support evidence based medicine. *BMC Bioinformatics*, 12(2):S5.

Aleksandar Kovačević, Zora Konjović, Branko Milosavljević, and Goran Nenadic. 2012. Mining methodologies from nlp publications: A case study in automatic terminology recognition. *Computer Speech & Language*, 26(2):105 – 126.

Anne Lauscher, Goran Glavaš, and Kai Eckert. 2018a. Arguminsci: A tool for analyzing argumentation and rhetorical aspects in scientific writing. In *Proceedings of the 5th Workshop on Argument Mining*, pages 22–28. Association for Computational Linguistics.

Anne Lauscher, Goran Glavaš, and Simone Paolo Ponzetto. 2018b. An argument-annotated corpus of scientific publications. In *Proceedings of the 5th Workshop on Argument Mining*, pages 40–46. Association for Computational Linguistics.

Maria Liakata, Shyamasree Saha, Simon Dobnik, Colin Batchelor, and Dietrich Rebholz-Schuhmann. 2012a. Automatic recognition of conceptualization zones in scientific articles and two life science applications. *Bioinformatics*, 28(7):991–1000.

Maria Liakata, Simone Teufel, Advaith Siddharthan, and Colin Batchelor. 2010. Corpora for the conceptualisation and zoning of scientific papers. In *Proceedings of the Seventh International Conference on Language Resources and Evaluation (LREC'10)*, Valletta, Malta. European Language Resources Association (ELRA).

Maria Liakata, Paul Thompson, Anita de Waard, Raheel Nawaz, Henk Pander Maat, and Sophia Ananiadou. 2012b. A three-way perspective on scientific discourse annotation for knowledge extraction. In *Proceedings of the Workshop on Detecting Structure in Scholarly Discourse*, ACL '12, pages 37–46, Stroudsburg, PA, USA. Association for Computational Linguistics.

Yi Luan, Mari Ostendorf, and Hannaneh Hajishirzi. 2018. The uwnlp system at semeval-2018 task 7: Neural relation extraction model with selectively incorporated concept embeddings. In *Proceedings of The 12th International Workshop on Semantic Evaluation*, pages 788–792. Association for Computational Linguistics.

William C. Mann and Sandra A. Thompson. 1987. *Rhetorical Structure Theory: Description and Construction of Text Structures*. Springer Netherlands, Dordrecht.

Adam Meyers, Giancarlo Lee, Angus Grieve-Smith, Yifan He, and Harriet Taber. 2014. Annotating relations in scientific articles. In *Proceedings of the Ninth International Conference on Language Resources and Evaluation (LREC'14)*, Reykjavik, Iceland. European Language Resources Association (ELRA).

Yoko Mizuta, Anna Korhonen, Tony Mullen, and Nigel Collier. 2006. Zone analysis in biology articles as a basis for information extraction. *International Journal of Medical Informatics*, 75(6):468 – 487. Recent Advances in Natural Language Processing for Biomedical Applications Special Issue.

B. Mons, B. J. A. Schijvenaars, C. C. van der Eijk, E. M. van Mulligen, J. A. Kors, M. Weeber, M. J. Schuemie, and R. Jelier. 2004. Distribution of information in biomedical abstracts and full-text publications. *Bioinformatics*, 20(16):2597–2604.

Yassine Mrabet, Halil Kilicoglu, and Dina Demner-Fushman. 2017. Textflow: A text similarity measure based on continuous sequences. In *Proceedings of the 55th Annual Meeting of the Association for Computational Linguistics (Volume 1: Long Papers)*, pages 763–772. Association for Computational Linguistics.

Tony Mullen, Yoko Mizuta, and Nigel Collier. 2005. A baseline feature set for learning rhetorical zones using full articles in the biomedical domain. *SIGKDD Explor. Newsl.*, 7(1):52–58.

Zara Nasar, Syed Waqar Jaffry, and Muhammad Kamran Malik. 2018. Information extraction from scientific articles: a survey. *Scientometrics*.

Balaji Polepalli Ramesh, Rashmi Prasad, Tim Miller, Brian Harrington, and Hong Yu. 2012. Automatic discourse connective detection in biomedical text. *Journal of the American Medical Informatics Association*, 19(5):800–808.

Animesh Prasad and Min-Yen Kan. 2017. Wing-nus at semeval-2017 task 10: Keyphrase extraction and classification as joint sequence labeling. In *Proceedings of the 11th International Workshop on Semantic Evaluation (SemEval-2017)*, pages 972–976, Vancouver, Canada. Association for Computational Linguistics.

Rashmi Prasad, Susan McRoy, Nadya Frid, Aravind Joshi, and Hong Yu. 2011. The biomedical discourse relation bank. *BMC Bioinformatics*, 12(1):188.

Balaji Polepalli Ramesh and Hong Yu. 2010. Identifying discourse connectives in biomedical text. *AMIA Annu Symp Proc*, 2010:657–661. Amia-2010_sympproc_0657[PII].

134

Francesco Ronzano and Horacio Saggion. 2015. Dr. inventor framework: Extracting structured information from scientific publications. In *Discovery Science*, pages 209–220, Cham. Springer International Publishing.

Patrick Ruch, Celia Boyer, Christine Chichester, Imad Tbahriti, Antoine Geissbhler, Paul Fabry, Julien Gobeill, Violaine Pillet, Dietrich Rebholz-Schuhmann, Christian Lovis, and Anne-Lise Veuthey. 2007. Using argumentation to extract key sentences from biomedical abstracts. *International Journal of Medical Informatics*, 76(2):195 – 200. Connecting Medical Informatics and Bio-Informatics - MIE 2005.

Andrey Rzhetsky, Hagit Shatkay, and W. John Wilbur. 2009. How to get the most out of your curation effort. *PLOS Computational Biology*, 5(5):1–13.

Hagit Shatkay, Fengxia Pan, Andrey Rzhetsky, and W. John Wilbur. 2008. Multi-dimensional classification of biomedical text: Toward automated, practical provision of high-utility text to diverse users. *Bioinformatics*, 24(18):2086–2093.

Masashi Shimbo, Takahiro Yamasaki, and Yuji Matsumoto. 2003. Using sectioning information for text retrieval: a case study with the medline abstracts. In *Proceedings of Second International Workshop on Active Mining (AM'03)*, pages 32–41.

Yuka Tateisi, Tomoko Ohta, Sampo Pyysalo, Yusuke Miyao, and Akiko Aizawa. 2016. Typed entity and relation annotation on computer science papers. In *Proceedings of the Tenth International Conference on Language Resources and Evaluation (LREC 2016)*, Paris, France. European Language Resources Association (ELRA).

Yuka Tateisi, Yo Shidahara, Yusuke Miyao, and Akiko Aizawa. 2013. Relation annotation for understanding research papers. In *LAW@ACL*.

Simone Teufel and Marc Moens. 2002. Summarizing scientific articles: Experiments with relevance and rhetorical status. *Comput. Linguist.*, 28(4):409–445.

Simone Teufel, Advaith Siddharthan, and Colin Batchelor. 2009. Towards discipline-independent argumentative zoning: Evidence from chemistry and computational linguistics. In *Proceedings of the 2009 Conference on Empirical Methods in Natural Language Processing: Volume 3 - Volume 3*, EMNLP '09, pages 1493–1502, Stroudsburg, PA, USA. Association for Computational Linguistics.

Andrea Varga, Daniel Preotiuc-Pietro, and Fabio Ciravegna. 2012. Unsupervised document zone identification using probabilistic graphical models. In *Proceedings of the Eight International Conference on Language Resources and Evaluation (LREC'12)*, Istanbul, Turkey. European Language Resources Association (ELRA).

Karin Verspoor, Kevin Bretonnel Cohen, Arrick Lanfranchi, Colin Warner, Helen L. Johnson, Christophe Roeder, Jinho D. Choi, Christopher Funk, Yuriy Malenkiy, Miriam Eckert, Nianwen Xue, William A. Baumgartner, Michael Bada, Martha Palmer, and Lawrence E. Hunter. 2012. A corpus of full-text journal articles is a robust evaluation tool for revealing differences in performance of biomedical natural language processing tools. *BMC Bioinformatics*, 13(1):207.

Bonnie Webber, Markus Egg, and Valia Kordoni. 2012. Discourse structure and language technology. *Natural Language Engineering*, 18(4):437490.

W. John Wilbur, Andrey Rzhetsky, and Hagit Shatkay. 2006. New directions in biomedical text annotation: definitions, guidelines and corpus construction. *BMC Bioinformatics*, 7(1):356.

An Yang and Sujian Li. 2018. SciDTB: Discourse dependency treebank for scientific abstracts. In *Proceedings of the 56th Annual Meeting of the Association for Computational Linguistics (Volume 2: Short Papers)*, pages 444–449. Association for Computational Linguistics.

Categorizing Comparative Sentences

Alexander Panchenko[⋆,‡]**, Alexander Bondarenko**[†]**, Mirco Franzek**[‡]**,
Matthias Hagen**[†]**, and Chris Biemann**[‡]

[⋆]Skolkovo Institute of Science and Technology, Moscow, Russia
[‡]Language Technology Group, Universität Hamburg, Hamburg, Germany
[†]Big Data Analytics Group, Martin-Luther Universität Halle-Wittenberg, Halle, Germany

Abstract

We tackle the tasks of automatically identifying comparative sentences and categorizing the intended preference (e.g., "Python has better NLP libraries than MATLAB" → Python, better, MATLAB). To this end, we manually annotate 7,199 sentences for 217 distinct target item pairs from several domains (27% of the sentences contain an oriented comparison in the sense of "better" or "worse"). A gradient boosting model based on pre-trained sentence embeddings reaches an F1 score of 85% in our experimental evaluation. The model can be used to extract comparative sentences for pro/con argumentation in comparative / argument search engines or debating technologies.

1 Introduction

Everyone faces choice problems on a daily basis: from choosing between products (e.g., which camera to buy), to more generic preferences for all kinds of things: cities to visit, universities to study at, or even programming languages to use. Informed choices need to be based on a comparison and objective argumentation to favor one of the candidates. Often, people seek support from other people—for instance, a lot of questions like "How does X compare to Y?" are asked on question answering platforms.

The Web also contains pages about comparing various objects: Specialized web resources systematize human experts results for domain-specific comparisons (for insurances, cameras, restaurants, hotels, etc.) while systems like WolframAlpha aim at providing comparative functionality across domains. Still, such pages and systems usually suffer from coverage issues relying on structured databases as the only source of information ignoring the rich textual content available on the web.

No system is currently able to satisfy open-domain comparative information needs with sufficient coverage and explanations of the compared items' relative qualities. Indeed, information retrieval systems and web search engines are able to directly answer many factoid questions (one-boxes, direct answers, etc.) but do not yet treat comparative information needs any different than standard queries. Search engines show the default "ten blue links" for many comparative information needs even though a direct answer enriched by pro/cons for the different options might be the much more helpful result.

One reason might be that despite the wealth of comparisons on the web with argumentative explanations, there is still no widespread technology for its extraction. In this work, we propose the first steps towards closing this gap by proposing classifiers to identify and to categorize comparative sentences.

The task of identifying and categorizing comparative sentences is to decide for a given sentence whether it compares at least two items and, if so, which item "wins" the comparison. For instance, given the sentence *Python is better suited for data analysis than MATLAB due to the many available deep learning libraries*, the system should categorize it as comparative and that it favors Python (Python "wins" over MATLAB). Identifying and categorizing comparative sentences can be viewed as a sub-task of argumentation mining (Lippi and Torroni, 2016) in the sense that detected comparative sentences (and probably also their context sentences) can support pro/con analyses for two or more items. Such comparative pro/cons might be used to trigger reactions in debates (one advantage of some item can be countered by some advantage of the other item, etc.) or they can form the basis for answering comparative information needs submitted to argument search engines.

Proceedings of the 6th Workshop on Argument Mining, pages 136–145
Florence, Italy, August 1, 2019. ©2019 Association for Computational Linguistics

Our main contributions are two-fold:

1. We release CompSent-19, a new corpus consisting of 7,199 sentences containing item pairs (27% of the sentences are tagged as comparative and annotated with a preference);

2. We present an experimental study of supervised classifiers and a strong rule-based baseline from prior work.

The new CompSent-19 corpus,[1] pre-trained sentence categorization models, and our source codes[2] are publicly available online.

2 Related Work

A number of online comparison portals like GoCompare or Compare.com provide access to structured databases where products of the same class can be ranked along with their aspects. Other systems like Diffen.com and Versus.com try to compare any pair of items on arbitrary properties. They reach high coverage through the integration of a large number of structured resources such as databases and semi-structured resources like Wikipedia, but still list aspects side by side without providing further verbal explanations—none of the portals aim at extracting comparisons from text. Promising data sources for textual comparisons are question answering portals like Quora or Yahoo! Answers that contain a lot of "How does X compare to Y?"-questions with human answers but the web itself is an even larger source of textual comparisons.

Mining and categorizing comparative sentences from the web could support search engines in answering comparative queries (with potential argumentation justifying the preference in the mined sentence itself or in its context) but also has opinion mining (Ganapathibhotla and Liu, 2008) as another important application. Still, previous work on recognizing comparative sentences has mostly been conducted in the biomedical domain. For instance, Fiszman et al. (2007) identify sentences explicitly comparing elements of drug therapy via manually developed comparative and direction patterns informed by a lot of domain knowledge. Later, Park and Blake (2012) trained a high-precision Bayesian Network classifier for toxicol-

ogy publications that used lexical clues (comparatives and domain-specific vocabulary) but also paths between comparison targets in dependency parses. More recently, Gupta et al. (2017) described a system for the biomedical domain that also combines manually collected patterns for lexical matches and dependency parses in order to identify comparison targets and comparison type using the as gradable, non-gradable, superlative-taxonomy of Jindal and Liu (2006).

Developing a system for mining comparative sentences (with potential argumentation support for a preference) from the web might utilize specialized jargon like hashtags for argumentative tweets (Dusmanu et al., 2017) but at the same time faces the challenges recognized for general web argument mining (Šnajder, 2017): web text is typically not well formulated, misses argument structures, and contains poorly formulated claims. In contrast to the use of dependency parses for mining comparative sentences in the biomedical domain, such syntactic features are often impossible to derive for noisy web text and were even shown to not really help in identifying argument structures from well-formulated texts like persuasive essays or Wikipedia articles (Aker et al., 2017; Stab and Gurevych, 2014); simpler structural features such as punctuation subsumed syntactic features in the above studies.

The role of discourse markers in the identification of claims and premises was discussed by Eckle-Kohler et al. (2015), who found such markers to be moderately useful for identifying argumentative sentences. Also Daxenberger et al. (2017) noted that claims share lexical clues across different datasets. They also concluded from their experiments that typical argumentation mining datasets were too small to unleash the power of recent DNN-based classifiers; methods based on feature engineering still worked best.

3 Dataset

As there is no large publicly available cross-domain dataset for comparative argument mining, we create one composed of sentences annotated with markers BETTER (the first item is better or "wins") / WORSE (the first item is worse or "looses") or NONE (the sentence does not contain a comparison of the target items). The BETTER-sentences represent a pro argument in favor of the first compared item (or a con argument for the sec-

---

ond item) while the roles are exchanged for the WORSE-sentences.

In our dataset, we aim to minimize domain-specific biases to rather capture the nature of comparison and not the nature of particular domains. We thus decided to control the specificity of domains via the selection of the comparison targets. We hypothesized and could confirm in preliminary experiments that comparison targets usually have a common hypernym (i.e., they are instances of the same class), which we utilize for the selection of the compared item pairs.

The most specific domain we choose is *Computer Science* with comparison targets like programming languages, database products and technology standards such as Bluetooth or Ethernet. Many computer science concepts can be compared objectively (e.g., via transmission speed or suitability for certain applications). The comparison targets were manually extracted from Wikipedia "List of"-articles that cover computer science. In the annotation process, annotators were asked to label sentences from this domain only if they had some basic knowledge in computer science.

The second, broader domain is *Brands*. It contains items of various types (e.g., cars, electronics, or food). As brands are present in everyday life, we assume basically anyone to be able to label sentences containing well-known brands such as Coca-Cola or Mercedes. Again, target items for this domain were manually extracted from Wikipedia "List of"-articles.

The third *Random* domain is not restricted to any topic. For each of 24 randomly selected seed words,[3] 10 similar words were collected based on the distributional similarity JoBimText API (Biemann and Riedl, 2013).

Especially for brands and computer science, the resulting item lists were large (4,493 in brands and 1,339 in computer science). In a manual inspection, low-frequency and ambiguous items were removed (e.g., the computer science concepts "RAID" (a hardware concept) and "Unity" (a game engine) are also regularly used nouns). The remaining items were combined into pairs. For each item type (seed Wikipedia list or seed word), all possible item combinations were created. These pairs were then used to mine sentences

containing both items from a web-scale corpus.

Our sentence source is the publicly available index of the DepCC (Panchenko et al., 2018), an index of more then 14 billion dependency-parsed English sentences from the Common Crawl filtered for duplicates. This index was queried for sentences containing both items in each target pair. For 90% of the pairs, we also added frequent comparative cue words[4] to the query in order to bias the results towards actual comparative sentences but at the same time also allow for comparisons that do not contain any of the anticipated cues. This focused querying was necessary as a random sampling would have resulted in only a very tiny fraction of comparative sentences. Note that even sentences containing a cue word do not necessarily express a comparison between the desired targets (e.g., dog vs. cat: He's the best pet that you can get, *better* than a dog or cat). It is thus especially crucial to enable a classifier to learn not to rely on the presence of the cue words only (which is very likely in a random sample of sentences with very few comparisons). For our dataset, we keep target pairs with at least 100 retrieved sentences.

From all sentences for the target pairs, we randomly sampled 2,500 instances in each category as potential candidates for a crowd-sourced annotation that we conducted on the Figure Eight platform in several small batches. Each sentence was annotated by at least five trusted workers. Of all annotated sentences, 71% received unanimous votes, and at least 4 out of 5 workers agreed for over 85%, at least 4 out of 5 workers agreed.

Our final Comparative Sentences Corpus 2019 (CompSent-19) is formed by the 7,199 sentences for 271 distinct item pairs that remained after removing the 301 sentences with an annotation confidence below 50%, a Figure-Eight-internal measure combining annotator trust and voting. Table 1 shows example sentences with their annotation while Table 2 outlines the corpus characteristics. Only a 27%-minority of the sentences are annotated as comparative (despite the selection bias with comparative cue words); in 70% of these, the favored item is named first.

---

[3]Created using randomlists.com: book, car, carpenter, cellphone, Christmas, coffee, cork, Florida, hamster, hiking, Hoover, Metallica, NBC, Netflix, ninja, pencil, salad, soccer, Starbucks, sword, Tolkien, wine, wood, XBox, Yale.

[4]Better, easier, faster, nicer, wiser, cooler, decent, safer, superior, solid, terrific, worse, harder, slower, poorly, uglier, poorer, lousy, nastier, inferior, mediocre.

Table 1: Examples sentences for the three domains with their annotated comparative label (the **first item** is BETTER/WORSE/NONE than the second item (note that the item order matters).

Domain	Sentence	Label
CompSci	This time **Windows 8** was roughly 8 percent slower than Windows 7.	WORSE
CompSci	I've concluded that it is better to use **Python** for scripting rather than Bash.	BETTER
Brands	These include **Motorola**, Samsung and Nokia.	NONE
Brands	**Honda** quality has gone downhill, Hyundai or Ford is a much better value.	WORSE
Random	Right now, I think **tennis** is easier than baseball.	BETTER
Random	I've grown older and wiser and avoid the **pasta** and bread like the plague.	NONE

Table 2: Characteristics of our CompSent-19 dataset.

Domain	Label			Total
	BETTER	WORSE	NONE	
CompSci	581	248	1,596	2,425
Brands	404	167	1,764	2,335
Random	379	178	1,882	2,439
Total	1,364	593	5,242	7,199

4 Supervised Categorization of Comparative Sentences

We split the 7,199 sentences of our CompSent-19 corpus into an 80% training set (5,759 sentences: 4,194 NONE, 1,091 BETTER, and 474 WORSE) and a 20% held-out set. During development, the experiments were evaluated on the training set using stratified 5-fold cross-validation; the held-out set was only used for the final evaluation. If not stated otherwise, scikit-learn (Pedregosa et al., 2011) was used to perform feature processing, classification, and evaluation.

4.1 Preprocessing

A first preprocessing step decides if the full sentence or only a part of it should be used for feature computation. Each sentence is considered to consist of three parts: the *beginning part* are all words before the first comparison target, the *ending part* are all words after the second comparison target, and the *middle part* are all words between the targets. Different combinations of partial sentence representations were used in our classification experiments.

The second preprocessing step is carried out to examine the importance of the lexicalized comparison targets for the classification. The targets either stay untouched, are removed, or replaced using two different replacement strategies. In the first variant, both targets are replaced by the term ITEM (*oblivious replacement*). In the second variant, the first object was replaced by ITEM_A and the second by ITEM_B (*distinct replacement*).

4.2 Supervised Classification Models

We compare 13 models ranging from the lower-capacity linear models, such as Logistic Regression, Naïve Bayes, and SVMs with various kernels to high-capacity ones based on decision trees and their ensembles such as Random Forest, Extra Trees, and Gradient Boosting relying on decision trees. Implementation-wise, twelve of the tested models are available via scikit-learn, while for XGBoost we used the implementation of Chen and Guestrin (2016). Apart from XGBoost and the Extra Trees Classifier, all models have been used in previous argumentation mining studies.

4.3 Sentence Representations

We study the classification performance impact of various feature types.

Bag of Words and Bag of Ngrams   The bag-of-words (BOW) model is a simple vector representation of text documents. All distinct words from the corpus form the vocabulary V. Typically, a document d is represented by a V-dimensional vector $\mathbf{d}$ (Salton et al., 1975). When comparing different classification models, we use BOW with binary weights as a baseline but also try extensions like tf- or tf-idf-weigthing and bag of token n-grams. In general, BOW models have a rather high representation length while being rather sparse at the same time (many 0 feature scores).

Part-of-speech (POS) n-grams   Another vector representation is formed by the frequencies of the 500 most frequent POS bi-, tri and four-grams.[5]

---

[5]Using spaCy's POS tagger:spacy.io/api/annotation#pos-tagging.

Contains JJR A Boolean feature capturing the presence of a JJR POS tag (comparative adjective).

Word Embeddings We rely on GloVe (Pennington et al., 2014) embeddings of size 300 to create a dense, low-dimension vector representation of a sentence.[6] We average all word vectors of a sentence, representing it by kind of a centroid word—a simple method shown to be effective for several tasks (Wieting et al., 2016).

Sentence Embeddings Bags of words and average word embeddings lose sequence information, which intuitively should help for (directed) comparison extraction. Sentence embeddings aim to learn representations for spans of text instead of single words by taking sequence information into account. Several methods like FastSent (Hill et al., 2016) or SkipTought (Kiros et al., 2015) have been proposed to create sentence embeddings. We use InferSent (Conneau et al., 2017) that learns sentence embeddings similar to word embeddings. A neural network is trained on the Stanford Natural Language Inference (SNLI) dataset (Bowman et al., 2015) containing 570,000 English sentence pairs (each labelled as entailment, contradiction, or neutral). InferSent combines the embeddings u and v of the two sentences from a sentence pair into one feature vector (containing the concatenation, the element-wise product, and the element-wise difference of u and v), that is then fed into a fully connected layer and a softmax layer. We use the pre-trained embeddings in our experiments.[7]

Dependency-based Features The HypeNet method to detect hypernym relations between words (Shwartz et al., 2016) combines distributional and dependency path-based methods to create a vector representation for word pairs. The LexNet generalization of HypeNet encodes tries to capture multiple semantic relationships between two words also using dependency path information (Shwartz and Dagan, 2016). Since dependency paths have been one of the major sources for comparison extraction in related work from the biomedical domain (see Section 2), we also include two LexNet-based features in our experiments.

LexNet (original) In the original LexNet paper, an LSTM (Hochreiter and Schmidhuber,

---

[6]Using spaCy's `en_core_web_lg` model: spacy.io/models/en#section-en_core_web_lg.

[7]github.com/facebookresearch/InferSent

1997) is used to create path embeddings out of the string paths. Since the details of the LSTM encoder are not mentioned, we tested different architectures and hyper-parameters and achieved the best results with one LSTM layer with 200 neurons, batch size of 128, RMSprop with learning rate 0.01 and 150 epochs, and max pooling with a pool size of 2. A Keras embedding layer is used to create word embeddings of length 100 for the string path components.

In the original study, paths were restricted to a length of four with the first comparison target having to be reachable from the lowest common head of the two targets by following left edges only, the second one by following right edges. With this LexNet (original) restriction, a path was found for only 1,519 of our 5,759 training sentences.

LexNet (customized) To overcome the LexNet (original) coverage issue, we relaxed the restriction by extending the maximal path length to 16 and ignoring edge directions. With this second LexNet (customized) setup, for only 399 training sentences no path was found (assigned to the artificial NOPATH).

5   Experiments

We conduct classification experiments using several machine learning approaches and representations and analyse the results. We use common performance metrics: precision, recall and F1 per each class and micro-averaged when reporting overall results.

5.1   Impact of Classification Models

To identify the best classification algorithm, we used a fixed baseline set of feature representations: a sparse bag-of-words model with binary weights computed on the whole sentence (see Section 4.3). We used F1 score to measure the models performance.

Tree-based methods and linear models worked well. Support Vector Machines with non-linear kernels assigned NONE to all sentences. As XGBoost and Logistic Regression achieved high F1 scores (see Figure 1), no further investigations on the performance of other algorithms were done. A set of hyper-parameters for XGBoost was tested using exhaustive grid search and randomized search but with no significant performance increase. For the futher experiments, we selected XGBoost with 1,000 estimators. The main idea

Figure 1: Impact of classification models: F1 scores on 5-fold cross validation of various classification algorithms based on a baseline binary bag-of-words representation. The black bars show the standard deviation.

behind boosting is to fit weak learners (i.e., classifiers only performing slightly better than random guessing) sequentially on modified versions of the data subsequently combining them to produce the final prediction. The *XGBoost* boosting method used here is *gradient boosting* (Friedman, 2001) with *decision trees* as learners. In gradient boosting, G_{m+1} is fitted on the residuals of G_m. Thus, each following tree tries to improve on the training examples on which the previous learner was weak.

In our experiments, we also tried various neural classification models based on neural network, such as recurrent neural networks, e.g. LSTM (Hochreiter and Schmidhuber, 1997) and simpler feed-forward architectures. However, none of them worked better than the simpler classifiers presented in this paper. We attribute this to the size of our training dataset.

5.2 Impact of Feature Representations

The classification results of the best-performing feature configurations in our three-class scenario are presented in Figure 2. Each feature was tested and evaluated using five stratified folds. The black bars show the standard deviation. All scores were calculated with scikit-learn's metric module. All features except for the LexNet (original) used the middle part of the sentence and left the objects untouched. In the LexNet features, the comparison targets were replaced with *OBJECT_A* and *OBJECT_B*, whereas LexNet (original) used the full sentence.

Table 3: Performance (F1) of the best classifier-based model compared to the rule-based baseline.

Model	BETTER	WORSE	NONE	**ALL**
Rule-based Baseline	0.65	**0.44**	0.90	0.82
InferSent+XGBoost	**0.75**	0.43	**0.92**	**0.85**

The best single feature (InferSent of the text between objects) yields an overall F1 score 3 points above the baseline with known compared objects positions. The worst single feature (LexNet (original)) scores 12 points below the baseline (see Section 5.3). Bag-of-Unigrams (F1 score 0.848) and InferSent (F1 score 0.842) deliver roughly equal results.

Despite the fact that only 1,519 sentences got a path embedding for LexNet (original), the feature is able to predict some sentences correctly (F1 score of 0.75 on this subset). This indicates that this feature setup is reasonable and would probably work well if it had a higher coverage.

To our surprise, combining feature representations did not help, i.e., we were not able to exceed over the score of the single best representation (InferSent on the sentence middle part) in any setup, which is why we do not report results on combinations.

Using the full sentence worked second best. Adding the beginning and/or ending part of the sentence did not increase the F1 score at all, no matter if the same or other representation type than the one for the middle part is used. Using the beginning and ending part alone never resulted in an F1 score above the baseline. Similarly, replacing or removing the objects did not increase the score significantly. In most cases, the difference in the F1 score between no replacement/removal and the best replacement/removal strategy was only reflected in the third or fourth decimal place. Hence, the actual objects are not important at all for the classification, which hints at the domain-independence of the dataset. This is also supported by the fact that adding the word vectors of the comparison targets as features did not increase the result in any configuration.

An interesting observation is that the simple

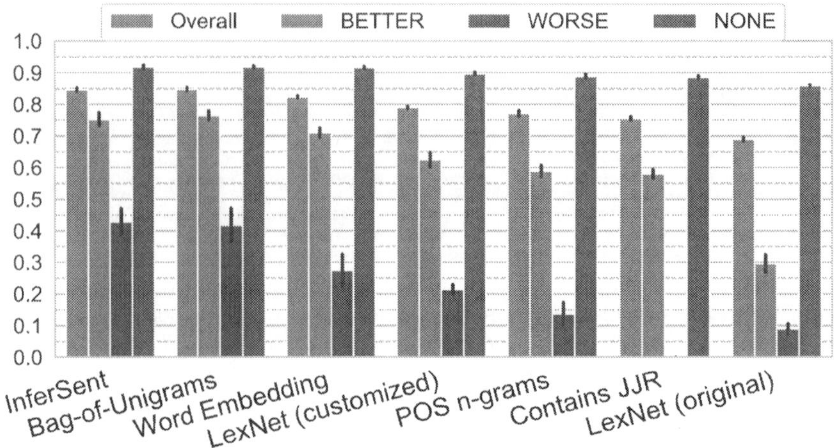

Figure 2: Impact of feature representation: F1 scores of sentence classification model based on XGBoost. The black bars indicate the standard deviation in the 5-fold cross validation.

bag-of-words model performs equal to or better than the majority of the more complex models in this setup.

5.3 Comparison to a Rule-based Baseline

As a rule-based baseline, we adapt the closest classification approach to ours introduced by Ganapathibhotla and Liu (2008). Given a comparative sentence and a pair of the objects being compared, the model decides which one is superior based on the author's opinion. It distinguishes two types of comparatives: opinionated (with explicit preference: *better*, *worse*, etc.) and with context-dependent opinions (implicit preference: *lower*, *higher*, etc.). Classification is performed based on the list of the opinion words considering an opinion orientation borrowed from the work by Hu and Liu (2004). However, our task is different in two aspects. First, we classify sentences in three not two classes. Second, we identify a comparison direction, i.e., infer a superior object, in a single sentence (and not an overall subjective opinion) without having access to additional context assuming extraction of the objective information. As the authors did not share their code and data, we fetched comparative adjectives and adverbs from open language learning web resources, e.g., sparklebox.co.uk. Then we manually organized them in two lists indicating whether the sentence's left-hand located object superior to the right-hand (*better*, *cheaper*, *easier*, etc.) one or not (*worse*, *harder*, *lower*, etc.). We classify sentences containing a keyword from the first list

Table 4: Cross-domain evaluation in terms of total F1 for all classes (best results per row in bold).

Train \ Test	CompSci	Brands	Random
CompSci	0.82	**0.84**	**0.84**
Brands	0.76	**0.83**	**0.83**
Random	0.79	0.84	**0.86**

(74 words in total) as BETTER, from the second list (63 words) as WORSE and NONE with no keywords found. We added negation rules to invert the label if the keyword is preceded by *not* or the second compared object by *but*.

A comparison of the best statistical classifier with this rule-based baseline is presented in Table 3. The statistical model substantially outperforms the rule-based baseline for the BETTER and NONE classes while being comparable for the WORSE class. The overall improvement of the statistical model over the rule-based approach is about 3 points in terms of F1 score (0.85 as the best achieved performance). Furthermore, note that reported performance of the rule-based model could be a bit inflated as building of the dataset involved the use of similar cue words as those used in this baseline (cf. Section 3) even though these cue word lists were build independently.

5.4 Cross-domain Evaluation

Table 4 presents results of a cross-domain evaluation of our models. As one can observe our model shows remarkably high cross-domain transfer with some out-of-domain combinations outperforming

Table 5: Examples of XGBoost errors with the InferSent features. Confidence shows the confidence of the annotators and is calculated as (judgments for majority class) / (total judgments).

	Sentence	Predicted	Gold	Confidence
1	Is **Python** better than **Perl**?	BETTER	NONE	0.6
2	Is **Microsoft** better because of **Apple**?	BETTER	NONE	1.0
3	**Microsoft** is the devil but **Sony** truly isn't any better.	WORSE	NONE	1.0
4	**Python** is much better suited as a "glue" language, while **Java** is better characterized as a low-level implementation language.	BETTER	NONE	1.0
5	Its Azure PaaS/IaaS platform hasn't overtaken **Amazon** yet in market share, but **Microsoft** has enjoyed nine straight quarters of growth at 10 percent or better	NONE	WORSE	1.0
6	arrrggghh...**Python** is a terrible language - only **Perl** sucks worse.	WORSE	BETTER	1.0
7	Good to see again a **Renault** ahead of a **Ferrari**.	NONE	BETTER	1.0

in-domain training, e.g., CompSci-Brands. While a substantial drop is observed for a few other domain pairs, e.g., Random-CompSci, the performance is still well above the majority class baseline suggesting that some knowledge transfer happened even in these cases and comparative argumentation is not highly domain-dependent.

Similarly, we applied the rule-based baseline to three domains independently and obtained F1 of 0.80 for CompSci, 0.81 for Brands and 0.84 for Random domains.

5.5 Error Analysis

The WORSE appeared to be the hardest class to recognize: 1,311 sentences were incorrectly classified. We look at comparing the performance of InferSent and LexNet (customized) thoroughly. Both features caused the same errors on 607 sentences. The InferSent feature made 220 additional errors, while the LexNet feature made 484. Surprisingly, the majority of errors was made on sentences with a high annotation confidence: 425 of the shared errors were made on sentences with a confidence of one. InferSent made 156 errors on highly confident sentences, while LexNet made 356. Examples of errors made by the InferSent feature are presented in Table 5.

The first two sentences look comparative, but they are questions. Despite annotation of questions as NONE as explicitly stated in the guidelines, InferSent frequently classified questions as comparative. Sentences three and four are comparative, but they have no clear "winner" of the comparison. The guidelines instructs that only sentences with obvious "winners" should be labeled with BETTER or WORSE. InferSent was not able to learn this restriction. Sentence six has three negative words in it. Sentence seven is hard to classify, as it does not contain any comparative cue word.

The LexNet feature made errors in fairly simple sentences like *Right now Apple is worse than Microsoft ever was*. While InferSent's errors can be coarsely grouped, the errors made by LexNet seem to be more random. We assume that the amount of training data for the neural network encoder is not sufficiently large. However, the overall result of LexNet indicates that the encoder trained on more data would likely yield satisfactory results. The performance for LexNet path embeddings shows that this is a reasonable way to encode sentences. The original setup found only paths for 26% of the sentences, yet it yielded an F1 score 8 points above the baseline. The customization made it even more powerful. While we expected that a combination of LexNet features and one of the other features like InferSent would be beneficial, as they encode different information (lexical and syntactical), this turned out to be not the case.

We explain the relatively low performance of all models on the WORSE class by the fact that people tend to more often refer to use lexical BETTER-constructions (when the firstly mentioned compared object is favored) than WORSE-constructions, similarly to many opinion mining datasets, where the positive class is observed more frequently. Besides, the tested models do not use explicit representations of negations, which may lead to a confusion of the BETTER and WORSE classes.

6 Conclusion

We tackle the task of identifying comparative sentences and categorizing the contained preference. Comparisons are a special kind of argumentative premise and can be deployed in constructing pro/con argumentation to support an informed choice. As our contributions, we (1) create the CompSent-19 corpus of 7,199 sentences from diverse domains (27% of the sentences being comparative and having an annotated preference direction), and (2) we evaluate several feature-based supervised approaches on our new corpus.

In our experiments, it turned out that the words between two compared items in a sentence are the most important for detecting comparisons and categorizing the preference direction.

The best classifier has already been integrated in a system that is able to efficiently mine comparative sentences from web-scale sources and to identify the direction of the comparisons: CAM—the comparative argumentative machine Schildwächter et al. (2019). CAM mines sentences from the web-scale Common Crawl and uses them to argumentatively compare objects specified by a user (e.g., whether Python is better than MATLAB for NLP).[8]

Promising directions for future work are exploiting neural classification approaches, integrating features based on contextualized word representations (Peters et al., 2018; Devlin et al., 2018), and better handling direction shifters like negations and complex implicit syntactic comparative constructions.

Acknowledgments

This work has been supported by the Deutsche Forschungsgemeinschaft (DFG) within the project "Argumentation in Comparative Question Answering (ACQuA)" (grant BI 1544/7-1 and HA 5851/2-1) that is part of the Priority Program "Robust Argumentation Machines (RATIO)" (SPP-1999).

References

Ahmet Aker, Alfred Sliwa, Yuan Ma, Ruishen Lui, Niravkumar Borad, Seyedeh Ziyaei, and Mina Ghobadi. 2017. What works and what does not: Classifier and feature analysis for argument mining. In *Proceedings of the 4th Workshop on Argument Mining*, pages 91–96, Copenhagen, Denmark. Association for Confutational Linguinics.

Chris Biemann and Martin Riedl. 2013. Text: now in 2D! A framework for lexical expansion with contextual similarity. *Journal of Language Modelling*, 1(1):55–95.

Samuel R. Bowman, Gabor Angeli, Christopher Potts, and Christopher D. Manning. 2015. A large annotated corpus for learning natural language inference. In *Proceedings of the 2015 Conference on Empirical Methods in Natural Language Processing (EMNLP)*, pages 632–642, Lisbon, Portugal. Association for Computational Linguistics.

Tianqi Chen and Carlos Guestrin. 2016. XGBoost: A Scalable Tree Boosting System. In *Proceedings of the 22Nd ACM SIGKDD International Conference on Knowledge Discovery and Data Mining*, KDD '16, pages 785–794, San Francisco, California, USA. ACM.

Alexis Conneau, Douwe Kiela, Holger Schwenk, Loïc Barrault, and Antoine Bordes. 2017. Supervised learning of universal sentence representations from natural language inference data. In *Proceedings of the 2017 Conference on Empirical Methods in Natural Language Processing*, pages 670–680, Copenhagen, Denmark. Association for Computational Linguistics.

Johannes Daxenberger, Steffen Eger, Ivan Habernal, Christian Stab, and Iryna Gurevych. 2017. What is the essence of a claim? cross-domain claim identification. In *Proceedings of the 2017 Conference on Empirical Methods in Natural Language Processing*, pages 2055–2066, Copenhagen, Denmark. Association for Computational Linguistics.

Jacob Devlin, Ming-Wei Chang, Kenton Lee, and Kristina Toutanova. 2018. BERT: Pre-training of deep bidirectional transformers for language understanding. *arXiv preprint arXiv:1810.04805*.

Mihai Dusmanu, Elena Cabrio, and Serena Villata. 2017. Argument mining on twitter: Arguments, facts and sources. In *Proceedings of the 2017 Conference on Empirical Methods in Natural Language Processing*, pages 2317–2322, Copenhagen, Denmark. Association for Computational Linguistics.

Judith Eckle-Kohler, Roland Kluge, and Iryna Gurevych. 2015. On the role of discourse markers for discriminating claims and premises in argumentative discourse. In *Proceedings of the 2015 Conference on Empirical Methods in Natural Language Processing*, pages 2236–2242, Lisbon, Portugal. Association for Computational Linguistics.

Marcelo Fiszman, Dina Demner-Fushman, Francois M. Lang, Philip Goetz, and Thomas C. Rindflesch. 2007. Interpreting comparative constructions in biomedical text. In *Proceedings of the Workshop on BioNLP 2007: Biological, Translational, and Clinical Language Processing*, pages 137–144, Prague, Czech Republic. Association for Computational Linguistics.

Jerome H. Friedman. 2001. Greedy function approximation: a gradient boosting machine. *Annals of statistics*, pages 1189–1232.

Murthy Ganapathibhotla and Bing Liu. 2008. Mining opinions in comparative sentences. In *Proceedings of the 22nd International Conference on Computational Linguistics (Coling 2008)*, pages 241–248,

---

[8]ltdemos.informatik.uni-hamburg.de/cam/

Manchester, UK. Coling 2008 Organizing Committee.

Samir Gupta, A.S.M. Ashique Mahmood, Karen Ross, Cathy Wu, and K. Vijay-Shanker. 2017. Identifying comparative structures in biomedical text. In *BioNLP 2017*, pages 206–215, Vancouver, BC, Canada,. Association for Computational Linguistics.

Felix Hill, Kyunghyun Cho, and Anna Korhonen. 2016. Learning distributed representations of sentences from unlabelled data. In *Proceedings of the 2016 Conference of the North American Chapter of the Association for Computational Linguistics: Human Language Technologies*, pages 1367–1377, San Diego, CA, USA. Association for Computational Linguistics.

Sepp Hochreiter and Jürgen Schmidhuber. 1997. Long short-term memory. *Neural computation*, 9(8):1735–1780.

Minqing Hu and Bing Liu. 2004. Mining and summarizing customer reviews. In *Proceedings of the Tenth ACM SIGKDD International Conference on Knowledge Discovery and Data Mining, Seattle, Washington, USA, August 22-25, 2004*, pages 168–177.

Nitin Jindal and Bing Liu. 2006. Mining comparative sentences and relations. In *Proceedings of the 21st National Conference on Artificial Intelligence - Volume 2*, AAAI'06, pages 1331–1336, Boston, MA, USA. AAAI Press.

Ryan Kiros, Yukun Zhu, Ruslan R Salakhutdinov, Richard Zemel, Raquel Urtasun, Antonio Torralba, and Sanja Fidler. 2015. Skip-thought vectors. In *Advances in Neural Information Processing Systems 28*, pages 3294–3302, Montréal, MN, Canada. Curran Associates, Inc.

Marco Lippi and Paolo Torroni. 2016. Argumentation mining: State of the art and emerging trends. *ACM Trans. Internet Technol.*, 16(2):10:1–10:25.

Alexander Panchenko, Eugen Ruppert, Stefano Faralli, Simone P. Ponzetto, and Chris Biemann. 2018. Building a web-scale dependency-parsed corpus from CommonCrawl. In *Proceedings of the Eleventh International Conference on Language Resources and Evaluation (LREC 2018)*, Miyazaki, Japan. European Language Resources Association (ELRA).

Dae Hoon Park and Catherine Blake. 2012. Identifying comparative claim sentences in full-text scientific articles. In *Proceedings of the Workshop on Detecting Structure in Scholarly Discourse*, pages 1–9, Jeju Island, Korea. Association for Computational Linguistics.

Fabian Pedregosa, Gaël Varoquaux, Alexandre Gramfort, Vincent Michel, Bertrand Thirion, Olivier Grisel, Mathieu Blondel, Peter Prettenhofer, Ron Weiss, Vincent Dubourg, Jake Vanderplas, Alexandre Passos, David Cournapeau, Matthieu Brucher, Matthieu Perrot, and Edouard Duchesnay. 2011. Scikit-learn: Machine learning in Python. *Journal of Machine Learning Research*, 12:2825–2830.

Jeffrey Pennington, Richard Socher, and Christopher D. Manning. 2014. Glove: Global vectors for word representation. In *Proceedings of the 2014 Conference on Empirical Methods in Natural Language Processing (EMNLP)*, pages 1532–1543, Doha, Qatar. Association for Computational Linguistics.

Matthew Peters, Mark Neumann, Mohit Iyyer, Matt Gardner, Christopher Clark, Kenton Lee, and Luke Zettlemoyer. 2018. Deep contextualized word representations. In *Proceedings of the 2018 Conference of the North American Chapter of the Association for Computational Linguistics: Human Language Technologies, Volume 1 (Long Papers)*, pages 2227–2237, New Orleans, LA, USA. Association for Computational Linguistics.

Gerard M. Salton, Andrew Wong, and Chungshu Yang. 1975. A vector space model for automatic indexing. *Commun. ACM*, 18(11):613–620.

Matthias Schildwächter, Alexander Bondarenko, Julian Zenker, Matthias Hagen, Chris Biemann, and Alexander Panchenko. 2019. Answering comparative questions: Better than ten-blue-links? In *Proceeding of 2019 Conference on Human Information Interaction and Retrieval (CHIIR '19)*, Glasgow, United Kingdom.

Vered Shwartz and Ido Dagan. 2016. The roles of path-based and distributional information in recognizing lexical semantic relations. *CoRR*, abs/1608.05014.

Vered Shwartz, Yoav Goldberg, and Ido Dagan. 2016. Improving hypernymy detection with an integrated path-based and distributional method. In *Proceedings of the 54th Annual Meeting of the Association for Computational Linguistics (Volume 1: Long Papers)*, pages 2389–2398, Berlin, Germany. Association for Computational Linguistics.

Jan Šnajder. 2017. Social media argumentation mining: The quest for deliberateness in raucousness. *CoRR*, abs/1701.00168.

Christian Stab and Iryna Gurevych. 2014. Identifying argumentative discourse structures in persuasive essays. In *Proceedings of the 2014 Conference on Empirical Methods in Natural Language Processing (EMNLP)*, pages 46–56, Doha, Qatar. Association for Computational Linguistics.

John Wieting, Mohit Bansal, Kevin Gimpel, and Karen Livescu. 2016. Towards universal paraphrastic sentence embeddings. In *Proceedings of the 6th International Conference on Learning Representations*, Vancouver, BC, Canada.

Ranking Passages for Argument Convincingness

Peter Potash, Adam Ferguson, Timothy J. Hazen
Microsoft Research Montreal
{pepotash,adfergus,tihazen}@microsoft.com

Abstract

In data ranking applications, pairwise annotation is often more consistent than cardinal annotation for learning ranking models. We examine this in a case study on ranking text passages for argument convincingness. Our task is to choose text passages that provide the highest-quality, most-convincing arguments for opposing sides of a topic. Using data from a deployed system within the Bing search engine, we construct a pairwise-labeled dataset for argument convincingness that is substantially more comprehensive in topical coverage compared to existing public resources. We detail the process of extracting topical passages for queries submitted to a search engine, creating annotated sets of passages aligned to different stances on a topic, and assessing argument convincingness of passages using pairwise annotation. Using a state-of-the-art convincingness model, we evaluate several methods for using pairwise-annotated data examples to train models for ranking passages. Our results show pairwise training outperforms training that regresses to a target score for each passage. Our results also show a simple 'win-rate' score is a better regression target than the previously proposed page-rank target. Lastly, addressing the need to filter noisy crowd-sourced annotations when constructing a dataset, we show that filtering for transitivity within pairwise annotations is more effective than filtering based on annotation confidence measures for individual examples.

1   Introduction

In online searches, results are typically presented to users ranked only by the relevancy of the results to the query. Search engines typically learn such relevancy through the positive reinforcement of user clicks. However, when queries address topics with multiple perspectives, some of which may be polarizing and divisive, search result click-through may reinforce biases of users contributing to the digital filter bubble or echo chamber phenomena (Barberá et al., 2015; Vaccari, 2013; Jamieson and Cappella, 2008; Wallsten, 2005).

To counter the filter bubble effect, search engines may seek to actively provide diverse results to topical queries (Yom-Tov et al., 2014), or even explicitly present arguments on different sides of an issue (Stab et al., 2018). In such scenarios, it is desirable to not only consider the relevancy of the diverse search results, but also their quality and convincingness. In our work, we seek to rank a collection of text passages by their argument convincingness, for use in Bing's multi-perspective search feature that presents arguments on different sides of a topical issue requested by a search query. An example of our use case and the goal of the model we aim to construct are presented in Table 1.

Habernal and Gurevych (2016) formally introduced the task of predicting argument convincingness to the language processing community by providing the first annotated corpus[1] (the UKP dataset), as well as providing initial experimental results on the dataset. The UKP dataset is annotated in a pairwise fashion: given two arguments with the same stance toward an issue, label which argument is more convincing. The implementation of pairwise annotation for this dataset is theoretically and practically grounded.

Motivated by the pioneering work of Thurstone (1927), pairwise labeling is a popular method for annotating items for attribute value (Heldsinger

---

[1] Although the ChangeMyView (CMV) (Tan et al., 2016) dataset had been published several months earlier, we believe the argumentation involved in the CMV dataset is more along the lines of debate and persuasion because commentators are trying to rebut the initial opinions and assertions made by the original poster. The same also holds for the dataset from Durmus and Cardie (2018).

Proceedings of the 6th Workshop on Argument Mining, pages 146–155
Florence, Italy, August 1, 2019. ©2019 Association for Computational Linguistics

Query: reasons why nafta is good	
Passages with a "Pro" stance	**Passages with a "Con" stance**
Candidate 1: NAFTA has six advantages. First, it quadrupled trade between Canada, Mexico, and the United States. That's because the agreement eliminated tariffs. Trade increased to $1.14 trillion in 2015. Second, it lowered prices. The United States imports Mexican oil for less than before the agreement.	**Candidate 1:** Is NAFTA a Bad Deal? The North American Free Trade Agreement (NAFTA) has come under fire recently, with some labeling it a disaster and claiming that it is the driving force behind the relocation of American firms like Ford Motor Company to Mexico.
Candidate 2: Because it helps in political interests. NAFTA is meant to lower tariffs and therefore create pro business alliances between the three signing nations. This allows for the U.S. to buy products cheaper from Canada and tears down the barriers to trade such as tariffs fees etc.	**Candidate 2:** Best Answer: see... the problem is... people who support NAFTA only compare it to either all out free trade... or no trade. trade is good and needed... but that doesn't mean it has to be, or should be FREE trade... so stop with these false comparisons of we have to trade...

Table 1: The table above shows the use-case for a ranking model for convincingness. Suppose a user has typed the query 'reasons why nafta is good'. Normally, this query will elicit links to texts that reflect only a positive stance toward the 'nafta' issue. Alternatively, a system can be designed to show arguments from *both* sides of the issue. In our system, we seek to select and present one passage to show for each side of the issue. Given passages that have been mapped to the pro and con sides of the issue, we will use our model to choose the best passage to show for each side of the issue. The above example illustrates a situation with two passage candidates for each of the pro/con sides, and our model needs to choose the most convincing one to display for each side.

and Humphry, 2010; Loewen et al., 2012). Recently, Shah et al. (2014) have conducted a suite of annotation experiments in order to empirically validate the belief that pairwise annotation is faster and more accurate than cardinal annotation for comparative tasks[2]. This paper presents a practical case study of a scenario where we have annotated data in a pairwise fashion and wish to train a model for ranking purposes.

The base model we use for predicting argument convincingness is an extension of the sum-of-embeddings model proposed by Potash et al. (2017). Our base model records state-of-the-art performance on the ranking subtask from the UKP dataset. Building on the base model, we explain two primary methods for going from pairwise data to a general ranking model: 1) Train a model that independently produces scores for each passage using a pairwise training paradigm to minimize a cross entropy objective function; 2) Assign real-valued scores to each passage, and train a model with a regression objective function to minimize the model's error against these scores. The second approach requires a method to pre-generate the real-valued passage scores used as the regression targets using only pairwise annotations. Towards this secondary goal, we test two approaches: 1) Following Habernal and Gurevych (2016), we generate PageRank (PR) (Page et al., 1999) scores using directed graphs derived from the labeled pairs; 2) We compute a simple 'Win-Rate' (WR) percentage based on how often a passage is rated more convincing against its competitor passages.

In order to test the robustness of the proposed techniques for using pairwise-labeled data to create a ranking model, we construct a new dataset for convincingness with a superior coverage of topics compared to the UKP dataset, which only has passages for 16 topics and roughly 1k total passages. In comparison, our dataset covers 3,234 topics, with roughly 30k total passages. The results of experiments on the large-scale dataset show that the best method for training a ranking model is to use the pairwise labels directly. Secondly, regarding the regression-based models, regressing to WR is better than PR, and even competitive with pairwise training. Finally, filtering data based on label confidence can actually hurt performance, although it can be beneficial to weight a pairwise model based on label confidence. Alternatively, removing query-passage sets where cycles appear

---

[2]In cardinal annotation, each individual example is assigned a score from a scale to signify the intensity of a given attributed being annotated.

in the directed graphs induced by the labels of passage pairs is a preferred method for data-filtering in our case study.

2   Related Work

In terms of predicting argument convincingness, only four authors have published results on the UKP dataset (Habernal and Gurevych, 2016; Chalaguine and Schulz, 2017; Potash et al., 2017; Simpson and Gurevych, 2018), with Potash et al. (2017) and Simpson and Gurevych (2018) posting state-of-the-art results on the pairwise classification[3] and ranking tasks, respectively. Simpson and Gurevych's model uses Gaussian Process Preference Learning (Chu and Ghahramani, 2005), which learns a mapping from input passage representations to real-valued scores.

Related to our use of label confidence to weight training examples, solving problems in NLP with models that leverage annotator agreement/confidence has previously been explored. Plank et al. (2014) and Alonso et al. (2015) use the information from individual annotations on examples to improve sequential (part-of-speech tagging) and structural (dependency parsing) tasks. Previously, Beigman and Klebanov (2009) had shown theoretically that noise from ambiguously-annotated examples are more harmful to certain learning models, namely the Voting Perceptron algorithm (Freund and Schapire, 1999).

Lastly, methods for ranking from pairs is a relevant research area for our work. Chen et al. (2013) adopt an active learning framework for the popular Bradley-Terry model (Bradley and Terry, 1952) in order to minimize the amount of annotations required to train a ranking model from pairwise data. Negahban et al. (2016) propose an algorithm, Rank Centrality, that works on a graph induced by pairwise annotations where node scores come from their stationary probability under a random walk. Chen and Suh (2015) improve upon Rank Centrality by introducing an algorithm that is specifically intended to recover the top k rankings via spectral initialization and continued refinement over the pairs with a maximum likelihood estimation.

---

[3]See Section 4.1 for more details of this model, as it is the basis for our approach for modeling argument convincingness. Moreover, the model from Simpson and Gurevych was not yet public as we were developing our model.

3   Dataset

Throughout the paper, we will refer to elements of our dataset using terms that form a hierarchy. At the top level, we use the term *topic*. A topic is an idea/issue devoid of a specific stance/assertion. Examples of topics are "coffee", "nafta", "margarine", and "fluoride". Within each topic are *queries*, which are search statements/questions that possess a specific thesis/stance with regard to its topic. For the topic "coffee", a query may be "is coffee good for you", which takes as the assertion: "coffee is good for you". An alternative query may be "is coffee bad for you". The third element of the hierarchy is a *passage*. A passage exists with respect to a query, and argues the position that is present in a query. Each query has multiple passages, all with the same stance toward a topic. In this section we describe the process of going from raw search data to a cleaned and annotated dataset with passages of the same topic and stance annotated for argument convincingness. The reason we want to have data annotated in this manner is it reflects the context in which we would plan to use the proposed model: we make the assumption that the input passages to be ranked are all on the same side of a stance related to a given issue, which, in a practical scenario, has been dealt with by upstream processing.

3.1   Dataset Creation

In order to test the utility of a convincingness model over a large variety of topics we created a dataset with larger topical coverage compared to the UKP data. We seeded the process with data collected for Bing's multi-perspective search feature, which was designed to show two short passages arguing for opposing stances of an issue expressed by a user query submitted to the system (e.g., "is coffee good for you"). The dataset consists of *topic, query, passage* triples. Each query conveys a *pro* or *con* sentiment for the expressed topic. Multiple potential passages are matched with each topic based on the Bing search engine's relevancy rankings with each passage assigned to the *pro* or *con* side of the topic based on a sentiment analysis classifier trained for the task. The passages themselves are snippets of text that have been scraped from the Web. For each query in a triplet, we have also automatically determined a paired query expressing the opposing stance (e.g., "is coffee bad for you") which we use to help

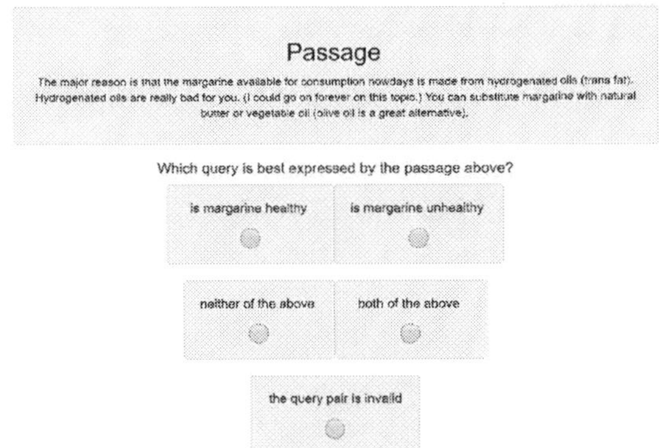

Figure 1: For stance annotation, workers are presented with a passage and a query pair, where each query is meant to reflect either a positive or negative stance toward an issue. The worker must choose which query best aligns with the passage.

validate the stance of passages as detailed below. The initial seed set contained 95,318 triples across 18,864 unique queries covering 3,439 topics. The initial annotations of the pro/con stances of queries and passages of the data available from the pre-existing system were created using automatic means (e.g., a sentiment analysis model) and were hence errorful. Additionally, no assessment of the convincingness of the passages had been conducted. Thus, we performed a two-stage manual annotation process on the dataset to (1) generate ground truth stance labels for query/passage pairs, and (2) generate pairwise convincingness assessments of passages associated with the same topic and stance.

3.2 Stance Annotation

Passage stance was determined by crowd workers judging which query from a positive-negative pair best aligns with a given passage. Workers also had the option of labeling that neither query aligns (i.e., the passage does not express a specific stance), or that both queries align with the passage (i.e., the passage provides arguments for both sides of the issue). To ensure that the query pairs themselves are valid, a fifth option specifying invalidity was provided for instances when a query is off-topic from the passage, is ambiguous in meaning, expresses multiple stances, or if both queries hold the same stance. Figure 1 shows the stance annotation layout. The goal of stance annotation is to identify pairs of passages that argue the same stance on a topic, as expressed by a query.

To contribute to the dataset, workers first had to read accompanying guidelines and examples then pass a qualification test with a grade of 70%. This test consisted of ten judgements made on passages pre-determined to represent two of each of the five available options. Feedback on the correct option was given after each judgement. If workers failed the initial qualifying set, they were provided with a second attempt on ten new instances to encourage learning and skill development.

Qualified workers who later hit an average speed less than six seconds per judgement[4], compared to the overall average of 16 seconds, or who had a low agreement score with other annotators, were removed from the task and their work was re-assigned to others. To prevent worker fatigue and ensure a wide breadth of participation, individual workers were prohibited from performing more than 10% of the available annotations tasks. The average number of annotations provided per worker was 1,178. Using this approach, each raw data point was annotated three times from a pool of 223 workers. The process yielded a total of 71,840 passage pairs associated with the same stance on the same topic.

3.3 Convincingness Annotation

Comparisons on passage convincingness are performed by workers judging which passage, from a pair with the same stance toward an issue, is more convincing. Refer to Figure 2 for the layout of the convincingness annotation. Workers are provided with tips on how to determine convincingness, such as evaluating topic deviation, use of facts, and citation of authority figures. To force workers to make a decision, workers were not given the option to rate the passages as equally convincing. Workers are instructed to consider the passage coherency and writing quality in the event of a tie in convincingness. Each of the 71,840 passage pairs identified during the stance annotation was annotated for convincingness by five different workers. We again applied techniques to pre-qualify workers and remove workers producing low-quality work.

Workers for this stage were also required to read guidelines and examples before passing a qualification test, though with an increased grade requirement of 80%. The test was composed of ten

---

[4]If a worker goes this speed, or faster, they are believed to be clicking answers randomly or *spamming*.

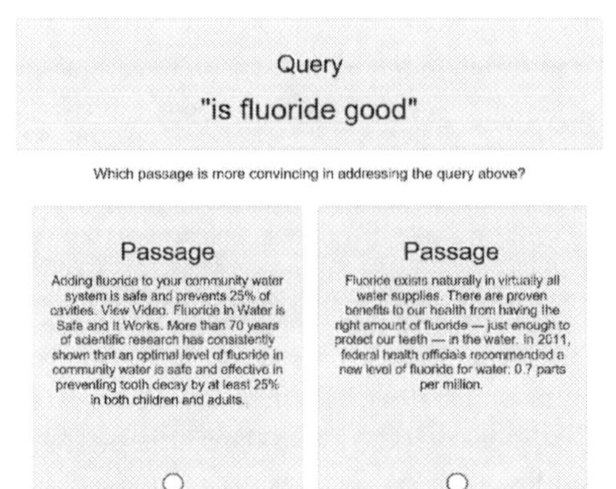

Figure 2: For convincingness annotation, workers are presented with two passages, with the same stance toward a topic (the search query), and are asked to label which passage is more convincing.

judgements, split evenly between easy and hard levels of difficulty, to be made on queries with passage convincingness predetermined. Feedback on the correct option was given after each judgement again and another attempt was provided in the event of failure, however this time without feedback. Workers whose average speed measured less than six seconds per judgement compared to the overall average of 20 seconds or who had low agreement scores with other annotators were blocked with their work being redone by the remaining annotators. The total number of judgements made per worker in this stage was limited to 5% of the total annotations with 12 reaching the limit and an overall average of 907 annotations per worker. A total of 71,840 query-passage pair sets were annotated five times each from a pool of 396 workers.

3.4 Constructing Passage Graphs

One key term for our work is **Passage Graph**, which is the result of using binary annotations of passage pairs to generate a directed graph. Mirroring the process from Habernal and Gurevych (2016), a directed graph is constructed from all the passage pairs that have been annotated with the same topic-stance (query). The nodes of the graph represent the individual passages associated with a topic-stance. For a given passage pair (A,B), if passage A is more convincing than passage B (based on the combined assessments from multiple annotators), a directed edge from node A to node B is created. Assuming that every possible passage pair has been annotated, the initial pas-

sage graph will be complete.

4 Ranking Model for Convincingness

In this section we describe our base model for predicting argument convincingness, as well as the various approaches for using pairwise-labeled data to train a model for ranking passages. We implement all our models in TensorFlow (Abadi et al., 2016) and tokenize text using NLTK (Bird and Loper, 2004).

4.1 Base Convincingness Model

The base model we use for predicting argument convincingness is an extension of the sum-of-word-embedding approach used by Potash et al. (2017). Their model uses pretrained GloVe word embeddings (Pennington et al., 2014), and, instead of continuing to update the word embedding parameters during training, the model learns a fully-connected layer that projects the embeddings into a new embedding space. By doing so, the original 300-dimensional embeddings are transformed into a 100-dimensional space. The model then sums the projected word embeddings to create a single vector representation of the full passage.[5]

We extend the original model by adding further capacity in the form of a Feed Forward Neural Network (FFNN) after summing the word embeddings. Specifically, we add three additional layers (the original model had a single layer after summing embeddings) of sequentially decreasing size, activated by the ReLU function: these layers have dimensions of 32, 16, 8, and 1. Thus, there is a total of four layers after creating the passage representation, where the last layer produces a single score.

Aside from the strong performance of this model, the fact that it only requires pretrained word embeddings as an external resource makes it appealing, as it increases portability and shortens the preprocessing pipeline. In comparison, the linguistic feature proposed by Habernal and Gurevych (2016) require substantial preprocessing, including part-of-speech tagging, named-entity recognition, and sentiment analysis.

Using the publicly available UKP convincingness dataset from Habernal and Gurevych (2016),

---

[5]Simple sum-of-word-embeddings has been shown to be a strong (almost unreasonably so) approach for modeling multi-token sequences (Conneau et al., 2017; Joulin et al., 2017).

Model	Pearson's r	Spearman's ρ	Kendall's τ
GPPL (linguistic+word embedding features)	.44	.67	.50
Sum-of-Word-Embeddings+FFNN (our model)	**.48** ($\pm$.013)	**.69** ($\pm$.003)	**.52** ($\pm$.002)

Table 2: Results on the UKP argument convincingness dataset (Habernal and Gurevych, 2016) from our model (Sum-of-Embeddings+FFNN) and Simpson and Gurevych (2018) (GPPL), which had previously been state-of-the-art. Note that our model uses only pretrained word embeddings as features, whereas the GPPL uses pretrained word embeddings plus a linguistic feature space of 32,010. Our numbers are the average across eight identical runs (standard deviation in parentheses).

we test the effectiveness of our base convincingness model against the the current state-of-the-art (Simpson and Gurevych, 2018): Gaussian Process Preference Learning (GPPL) with word embeddings and linguistic features (of dimensionality 32,010) used to represent passages. The evaluation uses a leave-one-*topic*-out paradigm, measures correlation between our model's predictions and the gold standard scores, and averages the correlation scores across topics. Results of our experiments are presented in Table 2 and show that our model achieves a new state-of-the art on the convincingness ranking subtask across all three correlation measures, which were the metrics used by previous researchers on the dataset.

4.2 Methods for Ranking Model

Although Habernal and Gurevych (2016) used PR over directed graphs induced from the pairwise annotations to create unique convincingness scores for single passages within a set, we posit that such a methodology might be sub-optimal for training a ranking model. We address two primary concerns with this approach, and propose solutions, which we detail below.

Train ranking model directly with pairwise data Regressing to any target induced by pairwise-labeled data introduces a system bias based on how the real-valued scores are calculated. It may be better to use the pairwise annotations directly and train with an objective akin to RankNet (Burges et al., 2005). Thus, our base ranking model produces scores independently for each passage in a pair, with the pair of scores then normalized by the softmax function. The softmax outputs become the input probabilities for optimizing a two-class classification function with cross-entropy, where the one-hot target is the argument annotated as more convincing. At test time, our base model then independently produces

a global convincingness score for each passage.

Optimize regression based on 'Win-Rate', not PR Assuming we keep the regression objective for training, is there a better way to induce real-valued scores for individual passages? Our training data set, despite its wide topical coverage, only averages four passages per query, with many queries only having two passages. When running PR on a graph with two nodes, directed from one to the other, the node scores become roughly $\frac{2}{3}$ and $\frac{1}{3}$. A simpler, intuitive method for scoring passages would be to assign 1 to the more convincing passage, and 0 to the other. Thus, as an alternative to PR we propose the Win-Rate (WR) of a passage as the regression target. We start with our dataset of passage pairs with a *single* label assigned to the passage that is more convincing (produced by the MACE (Hovy et al., 2013) algorithm taking into account the five raw annotations). We calculate the WR for an individual passage by dividing the number of times a passage is labeled more convincing than another passage by the number of passage pairs it appears in. The scores produced by WR are normalized between 0 and 1 but have a higher variance compared to PR because they do not reflect a probability distribution.

Consequently, we propose to evaluate three different methods of leveraging pairwise-labeled data for training a ranking model: 1) Train directly with pairwise data using a classification objective; 2) Optimize a regression model for WR; 3) Optimize a regression model for PR[6].

5 Experimental Design

In this section we describe the details for evaluating the methods we propose in Section 4.2,

---

[6]We use the Python package NetworkX (Hagberg et al., 2008) to create graphs and calculate PR scores.

namely the approaches for filtering the fully annotated dataset, as well as creating a properly curated train/test split.

5.1 Creating Train/Test Split

A goal of the convincingness model is to be agnostic to an argument's topic, i.e. the model should perform well on passages even for topics not seen during training. Thus, we create a train/test split not over individual examples, but over topics (where a topic has an associated set of queries, and each query has an associated set of passages). We assign 80% of topics to the training set and the remaining 20% to the test set.

For evaluation, we require gold-standard rankings for passages in a query set. First, we filter the individual examples in the test set by annotator confidence, using a MACE entropy threshold of .95. Next, to ensure no ambiguity in the resulting ranking, we filter all queries that have cycles in their directed passage graphs induced from the pairwise MACE scores[7] (we also remove graphs that have become disconnected due to MACE filtering removing certain edges). To further ensure that the resulting passage rankings are gold-standard, despite not being set-ordered during annotation, we only keep queries whose passage rankings, determined by both WR and longest walk on the passage graphs, are identical. The resulting gold-standard test set contains 659 queries with an average of 2.23 passages per query.

5.2 Filtering/Weighting Training Data

Although the rigorous filtering process for creating the gold-standard test set maintains that the ranks created by sorting on WR generate an unambiguous ordering, doing so reduces the amount of data available. The question then becomes, is it better to keep data with noisy labeling in order to increase the amount of data available for training? In order to evaluate the effect of filtering data in the training set, we experiment with filtering data based on two methods: (1) removing individual annotated passage pairs with MACE entropy score below 0.95[8], and (2) removing query-passage sets if there are cycles present in the passage-graph. Because MACE assigns entropy to each label given to an annotated pair, we also experiment with weighting the training cost of each training example in the pairwise model using its MACE entropy. Specifically, since the passage rated as more convincing has a MACE entropy between 0.5 and 1, we set the training cost weight to $(2*entropy) - 1$ producing a weight in the interval $(0,1)$.

6 Results

The results of our experiments are shown in Table 3. For each query-passage set in the test set we predict scores for each passage individually, and evaluate the scores against the gold-standard ranking, as described in Section 5.1. We calculate Kendall's tau and the top 1 accuracy (i.e., the proportion of passage sets where the most convincing passage in the set is ranked first)[9,10]. We average the scores on each query across the test set to produce a single number for each metric. We compare the results of our models with the results of a random baseline and the relevancy score assigned by the search engine to the original *passage, query, topic* triple (see Section 3).

An initial result of our experiments is that training a pairwise model leads to better ranking performance compared to regressing to a target score for each passage. Furthermore, the use of weighting in training for the pairwise model makes the model more robust with respect to different filtering scenarios of the training data, though we achieve the best correlation with gold standard without using the weighting. Indeed, without weighting during training, the pairwise model only outperforms regression to WR, in terms of correlation to gold standard, in one out of four scenarios of training data filtering. Alternatively, when training models with the complete dataset,

---

[7] For example, if we have labeled pairs for passages a, b, c, where a is more convincing than b, b is more convincing than c, and c is more convincing than a, then the labeled graph contains a directed cycle.

[8] This process remains the same regardless of whether a model trains on individual passage examples for regression training or passage pairs for pairwise training. However, this procedure affects the amount of data for these types of models differently. For example, given N passages, there are N choose 2 pairs. However, if one pair (edge in the passage graph) is removed due to MACE filtering, there still remains N passages for regression training (assuming the passage graph hasn't become disconnected), but only (N choose 2)-1 passage pairs for pairwise training.

[9] We do not use normalized discounted cumulative gain (nDCG) (Järvelin and Kekäläinen, 2002) because our passage sets are so small. For example, when the set only has two elements, predicting the inverse of the gold-standard still yields an nDCG@2 of 0.63.

[10] Additionally, we do not use Pearson or Spearman correlation, which we used in the UKP experiments, because they are not classical ranking metrics.

Training Objective	Cycles Filtered	MACE Filtered	% Filtered	Kendall's τ	Top1
Pairwise	No	No	0%	.419	.684
Pairwise	No	Yes	43%	.436	.692
Pairwise	Yes	No	61%	**.464***	**.701**
Pairwise	Yes	Yes	48%	.431	.690
Pairwise, Weighted	No	No	0%	.445	.690
Pairwise, Weighted	No	Yes	43%	.451	.701
Pairwise, Weighted	Yes	No	61%	**.458**	**.704***
Pairwise, Weighted	Yes	Yes	48%	.455	.700
Regression to PR	No	No	0%	.408	**.677**
Regression to PR	No	Yes	13%	**.411**	.676
Regression to PR	Yes	No	40%	.392	.657
Regression to PR	Yes	Yes	18%	.399	.669
Regression to WR	No	No	0%	.442	.688
Regression to WR	No	Yes	13%	.445	.692
Regression to WR	Yes	No	40%	**.456**	**.695**
Regression to WR	Yes	Yes	18%	.431	.684
Random	-	-	-	.000	.447
Relevancy Ranking	-	-	-	.204	.585

Table 3: Results of ranking experiments on our newly-annotated dataset. Bold indicates the best performance for a given model on a given evaluation metric, and * indicates the best result across all models.

i.e. not using any filtering, regressing to WR is better than pairwise training *without* weighting.

In terms of regression targets, WR is shown to be a superior objective compared to PR. Furthermore, this holds across all variations of filtering the training data. In fact, PR exhibits its worst performance under the filtering constraints where WR performs the best. These results show that even if one has decided on a regression objective, the way in which one calculates the scores to which the model fits is important.

When examining the effects of data filtering, combining strategies is not always better. Our results show that it is better to filter out whole passage sets that have cycles, as opposed to filtering out individual examples based on MACE score. However, if MACE filtering has already been done, it is generally better to leave cycle-inducing passage sets in the training data. These results indicate that there may be a fine line between removing noise and removing useful information. There is also an interesting relationship between MACE filtering and cycle filtering. We observe that filtering for cycles after initially filtering by MACE results in *more* data being left, when compared with solely filtering by cycles. This implies that MACE entropy scores are able to predict which labels may lead to cycles in a passage graph.

6.1 Convincingness versus Relevancy

Regarding the actual utility of ranking passages by argument convincingness, as opposed to just using topical relevancy, our results show that in fact convincingness and relevancy are separate attributes when it comes to grading a passage. Although the use of relevancy ranking scores results in more convincing passages being selected than random guessing, the relevancy model does not predict argument convincingness as effectively as a model trained specifically to do so. In other words, when constructing a search engine for arguments, the most topically relevant passage may not be the most convincing with regard to its stance on an issue. Future work can evaluate the best practice for combining these different attributes for the best user experience.

7 Conclusion

Our work provides a practical case study in the use of pairwise-annotated data to train a model for ranking passages with respect to their argumentative convincingness. We describe an annotation process that takes the raw output of a search engine and transforms the data into pairs of passages with the same stance toward an issue, annotated for which passage is more convincing. We then construct a base model for predicting argument convincingness that posts state-of-the-art on a publicly available dataset. We conclude with a comprehension evaluation of different ranking models using our newly-annotated dataset. Our results show that a pairwise model trained with cross-entropy objective provides the best performance, though regressing to a simple Win-Rate target can also perform competitively.

Acknowledgments

We would like to thank Frank Guo and Xuan Li for providing the initial seed data for our annotation, Bhaskar Mitra for discussing approaches for ranking methods, and Tong Wang for his help reviewing the manuscript.

References

Martín Abadi, Paul Barham, Jianmin Chen, Zhifeng Chen, Andy Davis, Jeffrey Dean, Matthieu Devin, Sanjay Ghemawat, Geoffrey Irving, Michael Isard, et al. 2016. Tensorflow: a system for large-scale machine learning. In *OSDI*, volume 16, pages 265–283.

Héctor Martínez Alonso, Barbara Plank, Arne Skjærholt, and Anders Søgaard. 2015. Learning to parse with iaa-weighted loss. In *Proceedings of the 2015 Conference of the North American Chapter of the Association for Computational Linguistics: Human Language Technologies*, pages 1357–1361.

Pablo Barberá, John T Jost, Jonathan Nagler, Joshua A Tucker, and Richard Bonneau. 2015. Tweeting from left to right: Is online political communication more than an echo chamber? *Psychological science*, 26(10):1531–1542.

Eyal Beigman and Beata Beigman Klebanov. 2009. Learning with annotation noise. In *Proceedings of the Joint Conference of the 47th Annual Meeting of the ACL and the 4th International Joint Conference on Natural Language Processing of the AFNLP: Volume 1-Volume 1*, pages 280–287. Association for Computational Linguistics.

Steven Bird and Edward Loper. 2004. Nltk: the natural language toolkit. In *Proceedings of the ACL 2004 on Interactive poster and demonstration sessions*, page 31. Association for Computational Linguistics.

Ralph Allan Bradley and Milton E Terry. 1952. Rank analysis of incomplete block designs: I. the method of paired comparisons. *Biometrika*, 39(3/4):324–345.

Chris Burges, Tal Shaked, Erin Renshaw, Ari Lazier, Matt Deeds, Nicole Hamilton, and Greg Hullender. 2005. Learning to rank using gradient descent. In *Proceedings of the 22nd international conference on Machine learning*, pages 89–96. ACM.

Lisa Andreevna Chalaguine and Claudia Schulz. 2017. Assessing convincingness of arguments in online debates with limited number of features. In *Proceedings of the Student Research Workshop at the 15th Conference of the European Chapter of the Association for Computational Linguistics*, pages 75–83.

Xi Chen, Paul N Bennett, Kevyn Collins-Thompson, and Eric Horvitz. 2013. Pairwise ranking aggregation in a crowdsourced setting. In *Proceedings of the sixth ACM international conference on Web search and data mining*, pages 193–202. ACM.

Yuxin Chen and Changho Suh. 2015. Spectral mle: Top-k rank aggregation from pairwise comparisons. In *International Conference on Machine Learning*, pages 371–380.

Wei Chu and Zoubin Ghahramani. 2005. Preference learning with gaussian processes. In *Proceedings of the 22nd international conference on Machine learning*, pages 137–144. ACM.

Alexis Conneau, Douwe Kiela, Holger Schwenk, Loïc Barrault, and Antoine Bordes. 2017. Supervised learning of universal sentence representations from natural language inference data. In *Proceedings of the 2017 Conference on Empirical Methods in Natural Language Processing*, pages 670–680.

Esin Durmus and Claire Cardie. 2018. Exploring the role of prior beliefs for argument persuasion. In *Proceedings of the 2018 Conference of the North American Chapter of the Association for Computational Linguistics: Human Language Technologies, Volume 1 (Long Papers)*, pages 1035–1045.

Yoav Freund and Robert E Schapire. 1999. Large margin classification using the perceptron algorithm. *Machine learning*, 37(3):277–296.

Ivan Habernal and Iryna Gurevych. 2016. Which argument is more convincing? analyzing and predicting convincingness of web arguments using bidirectional lstm. In *Proceedings of the 54th Annual Meeting of the Association for Computational Linguistics (Volume 1: Long Papers)*, volume 1, pages 1589–1599.

Aric Hagberg, Pieter Swart, and Daniel S Chult. 2008. Exploring network structure, dynamics, and function using networkx. Technical report, Los Alamos National Lab.(LANL), Los Alamos, NM (United States).

Sandra Heldsinger and Stephen Humphry. 2010. Using the method of pairwise comparison to obtain reliable teacher assessments. *The Australian Educational Researcher*, 37(2):1–19.

Dirk Hovy, Taylor Berg-Kirkpatrick, Ashish Vaswani, and Eduard Hovy. 2013. Learning whom to trust with mace. In *Proceedings of the 2013 Conference of the North American Chapter of the Association for Computational Linguistics: Human Language Technologies*, pages 1120–1130.

Kathleen Hall Jamieson and Joseph N Cappella. 2008. *Echo chamber: Rush Limbaugh and the conservative media establishment*. Oxford University Press.

Kalervo Järvelin and Jaana Kekäläinen. 2002. Cumulated gain-based evaluation of ir techniques. *ACM Transactions on Information Systems (TOIS)*, 20(4):422–446.

Armand Joulin, Edouard Grave, Piotr Bojanowski, and Tomas Mikolov. 2017. Bag of tricks for efficient text classification. In *Proceedings of the 15th Conference of the European Chapter of the Association for Computational Linguistics: Volume 2, Short Papers*, volume 2, pages 427–431.

Peter John Loewen, Daniel Rubenson, and Arthur Spirling. 2012. Testing the power of arguments in referendums: A bradley–terry approach. *Electoral Studies*, 31(1):212–221.

Sahand Negahban, Sewoong Oh, and Devavrat Shah. 2016. Rank centrality: Ranking from pairwise comparisons. *Operations Research*, 65(1):266–287.

Lawrence Page, Sergey Brin, Rajeev Motwani, and Terry Winograd. 1999. The pagerank citation ranking: Bringing order to the web. Technical report, Stanford InfoLab.

Jeffrey Pennington, Richard Socher, and Christopher Manning. 2014. Glove: Global vectors for word representation. In *Proceedings of the 2014 conference on empirical methods in natural language processing (EMNLP)*, pages 1532–1543.

Barbara Plank, Dirk Hovy, and Anders Søgaard. 2014. Learning part-of-speech taggers with inter-annotator agreement loss. In *Proceedings of the 14th Conference of the European Chapter of the Association for Computational Linguistics*, pages 742–751.

Peter Potash, Robin Bhattacharya, and Anna Rumshisky. 2017. Length, interchangeability, and external knowledge: Observations from predicting argument convincingness. In *Proceedings of the Eighth International Joint Conference on Natural Language Processing (Volume 1: Long Papers)*, volume 1, pages 342–351.

Nihar B Shah, Sivaraman Balakrishnan, Joseph Bradley, Abhay Parekh, Kannan Ramchandran, and Martin Wainwright. 2014. When is it better to compare than to score? *arXiv preprint arXiv:1406.6618*.

Edwin D Simpson and Iryna Gurevych. 2018. Finding convincing arguments using scalable bayesian preference learning. *Transactions of the Association for Computational Linguistics*, 6:357–371.

Christian Stab, Johannes Daxenberger, Chris Stahlhut, Tristan Miller, Benjamin Schiller, Christopher Tauchmann, Steffen Eger, and Iryna Gurevych. 2018. Argumentext: Searching for arguments in heterogeneous sources. In *Proceedings of the 2018 Conference of the North American Chapter of the Association for Computational Linguistics: Demonstrations*, pages 21–25.

Chenhao Tan, Vlad Niculae, Cristian Danescu-Niculescu-Mizil, and Lillian Lee. 2016. Winning arguments: Interaction dynamics and persuasion strategies in good-faith online discussions. In *Proceedings of the 25th international conference on world wide web*, pages 613–624. International World Wide Web Conferences Steering Committee.

Louis L Thurstone. 1927. A law of comparative judgment. *Psychological review*, 34(4):273.

Cristian Vaccari. 2013. From echo chamber to persuasive device? rethinking the role of the internet in campaigns. *New Media & Society*, 15(1):109–127.

Kevin Wallsten. 2005. Political blogs and the bloggers who blog them: Is the political blogosphere and echo chamber. In *American Political Science Associations Annual Meeting. Washington, DC September*, pages 1–4.

Elad Yom-Tov, Susan Dumais, and Qi Guo. 2014. Promoting civil discourse through search engine diversity. *Social Science Computer Review*, 32(2):145–154.

Gradual Argumentation Evaluation for Stance Aggregation in Automated Fake News Detection

Neema Kotonya and **Francesca Toni**
Department of Computing
Imperial College London, United Kingdom
{n.kotonya18,f.toni}@imperial.ac.uk

Abstract

Stance detection plays a pivot role in fake news detection. The task involves determining the point of view or stance – for or against – a text takes towards a claim. One very important stage in employing stance detection for fake news detection is the aggregation of multiple stance labels from different text sources in order to compute a prediction for the veracity of a claim. Typically, aggregation is treated as a credibility-weighted average of stance predictions. In this work, we take the novel approach of applying, for aggregation, a gradual argumentation semantics to bipolar argumentation frameworks mined using stance detection. Our empirical evaluation shows that our method results in more accurate veracity predictions.

1 Introduction

The problem of fake news has existed from time immemorial. But in recent times, both the rise of social media as the go-to platform for receiving news updates and a series of significant politic elections events, the results of which are speculated to have been influenced by misinformation, has culminated in the phrase being pushed to the forefront of our consciousness. It is widely acknowledged (e.g., see (Lazer et al., 2018)) that fake news is an important problem, and that attention should be directed to tackle it.

Fake news is a particularly challenging problem, one that consists of a number of sub-problems, and one for which many approaches have been proposed (e.g., see (Zhou et al., 2019)). Generally fake news detection amounts to collating evidence and counter-evidence from various sources in order to make an assessment regarding the veracity of a given claim, e.g., as in the Fact Extraction and Verification (FEVER) shared task (Thorne et al., 2018).

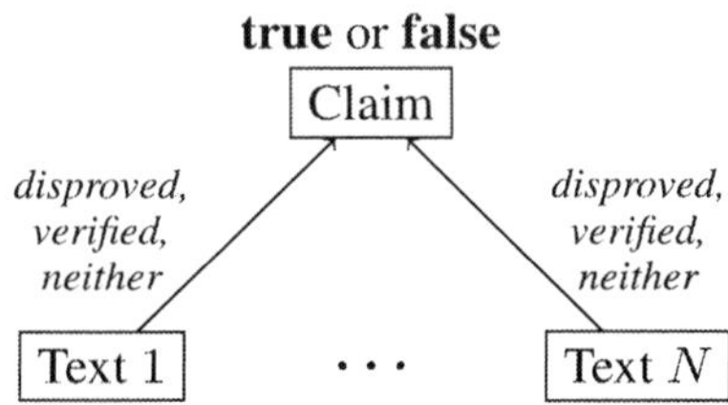

Figure 1: In veracity assessment a true/false label can be acquired by aggregating various texts that *verified* and *disproved* the target claim.

Veracity assessment is typically formulated as a 3-class problem where we aim to arrive at a value for the factuality of a claim, which is based on the stances of Texts $1, \ldots, N$ (see Figure 1). These texts could be headlines, articles, and even other claims. One of the tasks underpinning the prediction of factuality is stance detection. It involves examining agreement expressed by a text in relation to a claim. The text could be a headline (Ferreira and Vlachos, 2016), a topic (Mohammad et al., 2016) or a lengthier text fragment (Pomerleau and Rao, 2017). Stance detection can be thought of as a two-part task: we first aim to determine if the text and claim are sufficiently close with respect to their subject matter, and then, once relatedness of the text and claim is established, we want to know whether the text takes a favourable or unfavourable view of the claim.

The intuition behind the use of stance detection for fake news analysis is that the trustworthiness of a claim is strongly tied to the level of agreement expressed either for or against it in other texts, particularly the agreement or disagreement expressed by sources with high credibility. For that reason, we should be able to aggregate these disjoint stance valuations in order to arrive at a prediction for the veracity of the claim, as described by Conforti et al. (2018).

Proceedings of the 6th Workshop on Argument Mining, pages 156–166
Florence, Italy, August 1, 2019. ©2019 Association for Computational Linguistics

In this paper we draw inspiration from uses of relation-based argument mining (Carstens and Toni, 2015) to generate and evaluate bipolar argumentation frameworks (BAFs) (Cayrol and Lagasquie-Schiex, 2005) in order to perform classification tasks (e.g., in (Cocarascu and Toni, 2018), for deception detection). In the same spirit, we propose and use a stance detection classifier to generate BAFs and evaluate arguments therein with the existing DF-QuAD gradual semantics (Rago et al., 2016) in order to assess veracity of news against evidence. We show empirically, using a stance detection classifier built from the Fake News Challenge dataset (Pomerleau and Rao, 2017) and tested on the RumourEval dataset (Derczynski et al., 2017), that DF-QuAD performs competitively in comparison with a standard stance aggregation method using a credibility-weighted average of stance predictions. The aggregation method resulting from deploying DF-QuAD, unlike the standard aggregation method, considers also the dialectical relationships between different evidence and counterevidence texts in order to gauge the veracity of target claims.

2   Related Work

Stance detection can be framed as a four-way classification problem, as in the Fake News Challenge (Pomerleau and Rao, 2017), where it is aimed at identifying, in pairs consisting of headlines and article bodies, whether the texts are UNRELATED, or if the article body AGREES, DISAGREES, or DISCUSSES the headline. The last label signifies that the two texts are related but no stance (for or against) exists from the body to the headline. The RumourEval rumour verification task in SemEval 2017 (Derczynski et al., 2017) similarly includes a stance detection sub-task and uses data in the format of pairs but labels stances as DENY, SUPPORT, COMMENT and QUERY. In this paper, we see stance detection as a three-way classification problem, as summarized in Figure 2(a), assuming that relatedness has already been ascertained. This is in line with other work, notably in the EMERGENT project[1], using three labels FOR, AGAINST and OBSERVING (Ferreira and Vlachos, 2016).

Given the almost parallel stance labels, when restricted to three, between Fake News Challenge and RumourEval, we choose to develop classifiers

for stance detection using the former and verify them on the latter, for veracity prediction.

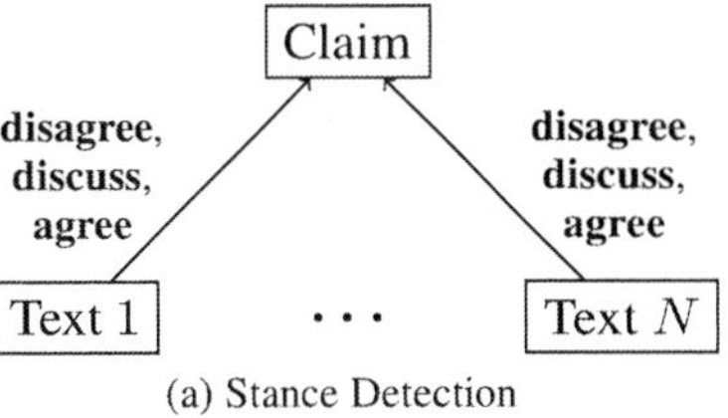

(a) Stance Detection

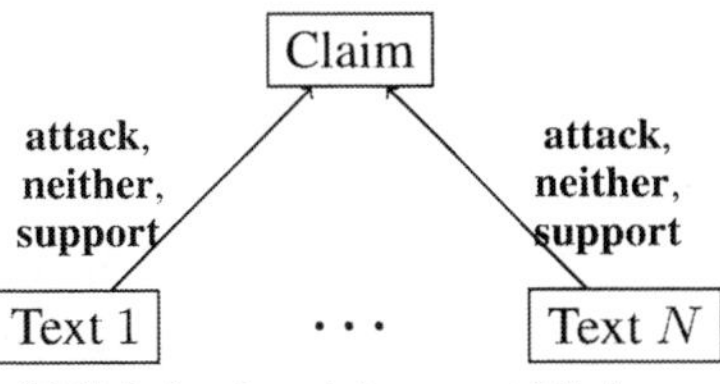

(b) Relation-based Argument Mining

Figure 2: Labels for relation-based argument mining, stance detection and veracity assessment. The labels in bold are those learnt from the task.

A number of techniques have been employed for the purpose of building stance detection systems (Hanselowski et al., 2018), including Long-Short Term Memory networks (LSTMs) (Hanselowski et al., 2018; Shang et al., 2018), term frequency-inverse document frequency (TF-IDF) and bag of word (BOW) features with Multi-Layer Perceptrons (Riedel et al., 2017), end-to-end memory networks enhanced with CNNs and LSTMs (Mohtarami et al., 2018), and non-neural network and neural network classifiers using cue words, Google News word2vec embeddings, and features taken from the Fake News Challenge dataset (Ghanem et al., 2018). We experiment with gradient-boosting, Gated Recurrent Units (GRUs), LSTMs and bidirectional LSTMs (BiLSTMs).

In terms of label aggregation for veracity assessment, Popat et al. (2018) derive credibility assessments for text-based claims aggregating a number of web-sourced articles. Source embeddings for both claims and articles are used to weigh the claims' credibility, and are derived from the names of sources who published the claims e.g., news organisations as well as individuals, typically public figures such as politicians. In this paper we perform aggregation using a gradual semantics for bipolar argumentation (see Section 3), taking into account the stance of responses towards claims and other responses.

Gradual semantics and bipolar argumentation for classification have been used for other tasks, notably in (Cocarascu and Toni, 2018) to contribute features for detecting deceptive reviews. There, bipolar argumentation frameworks were obtained using relation-based argument mining, as understood in (Carstens and Toni, 2015) and summarized in Figure 2(b). In this paper, we perform relation-based argument mining by way of stance detection: when stance detection is modelled as a three-class problem, the labels FOR, AGAINST and OBSERVING bear a strong resemblance to ATTACK, SUPPORT and NEITHER considered in relation-based argument mining (Carstens and Toni, 2015). Thus, we use stance relations as argumentative attack and support relations to evaluate the veracity of claims.

Other forms of argument mining have been studied in conjunction with stance detection. These include argument tagging for insufficiently labelled corpora (Sobhani et al., 2015) and identification of argumentative components in social media conversations (Boltužić and Šnajder, 2014).

3   Background

Our method relies on Bipolar Argumentation Frameworks (Cayrol and Lagasquie-Schiex, 2005) for representing the argumentative relations (disagree and agree) between text pairs, and the Discontinuity-Free Quantitative Argumentation Debates (DF-QuAD) algorithm (Rago et al., 2016) for aggregating the strengths of claims according to these relations. A Bipolar Argumentation Framework (BAF) is the triple $\langle Args, R^-, R^+ \rangle$, in which $Args$ is a set of entities, called arguments, and R^- and R^+ are binary attack and support relations between arguments respectively. The BAF with $Args = \{A_1, A_2, A_3, A_4, A_5\}$, attack relation $R^- = \{(A_1, A_2), (A_2, A_1), (A_2, A_3)\}$ and support relation $R^+ = \{(A_4, A_2), (A_4, A_5)\}$ is shown graphically in Figure 3. Note that the A_i can be instantiated in a number of different ways. For this work, we model claims and counter-claims from the RumourEval dataset as arguments. We identify attack and support relations with the help of stance detection.

Various semantics have been proposed for evaluating the dialectical strength of arguments in BAFs. We use the DF-QuAD algorithm originally defined for QuAD frameworks, which are BAFs

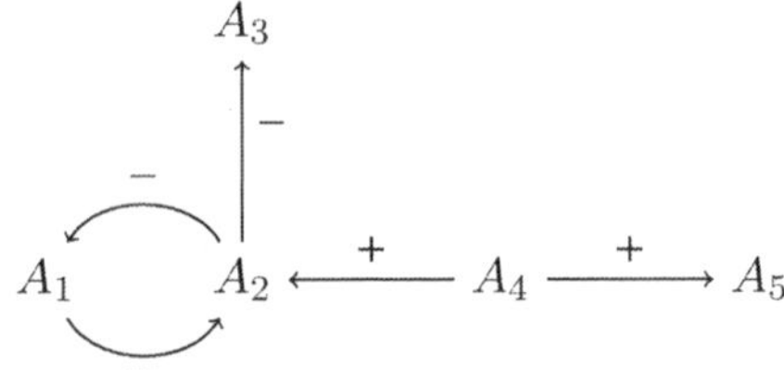

Figure 3: Example BAFs.

$\langle Args, R^-, R^+ \rangle$ forming acyclic graphs with, in addition, each argument $A \in Args$ being attributed a *base score* $\tau(A)$ that denotes its intrinsic strength (prior to considering its attackers $R^-(A) = \{B \in Args | (B, A) \in R^-\}$ and supporters $R^+(A) = \{B \in Args | (B, A) \in R^+\}$).

As required by DF-QuAD, base scores and dialectical strength of arguments are from within $\mathbb{I} = [0, 1]$. In all our experiments, $\tau(A) = 0.5$ for all $A \in Args$. DF-QuAD computes dialectical strength

$$\sigma(A) = \mu(\tau(A), \alpha(\sigma(R^-(A)), \alpha(\sigma(R^+(A)))$$

where $\sigma(R^-(A))$ is the sequence $(\sigma(B_1), \dots, \sigma(B_n)$ for $R^-(A) = \{B_1, \dots, B_n\}$, $n \geq 0$ (similarly for $\sigma(R^+(A))$), $\alpha(()) = 0$, $\alpha((v_1)) = v_1$, $\alpha((v_1, v_2)) = f(v_1, v_2) = v_1 + v_2 - v_1 * v_2$ and, for $n > 2$, $\alpha((v_1, \dots, v_n)) = f(\alpha((v_1, \dots, v_{n-1}), v_n))$, and, finally, the mediating function $\mu : \mathbb{I} \times \mathbb{I} \to \mathbb{I}$ is defined as $\mu(v_0, v_a, v_s) = v_0 - v_0 * |v_s - v_a|$ if $v_a \geq v_s$, and $\mu(v_0, v_a, v_s) = v_0 + (1 - v_0) * |v_s - v_a|$ otherwise. Intuitively, μ represents the idea that attackers of greater combined strength (given by v_a) than the supporters' combined strength (given by v_s) will weaken an argument (with base score v_0) more severely, i.e., these attackers will bring the argument's strength closer to 0. Similarly, supporters of greater combined strength will bring the argument's strength closer to 1. Conversely, the weaker the attackers or supporters, the smaller the effect on the argument's strength.

By employing DF-QuAD for veracity prediction we make the assumption, for example, that false claims will be weakened by the strength and number of their attackers, and thus have a low dialectical strength as computed using the algorithm, because of their lack of supporting arguments and abundance of attackers. However, we are aware that this might not always be the case, given the presence of silos or echo chambers in social media. Indeed, in echo chambers fallacious arguments may be backed up by a number of equally misleading arguments, which would result in a high DF-QuAD strength, despite the evidently false claim.

4 Datasets

Two datasets are employed as part of this study: the Fake News Challenge dataset[2], used to train the stance detection classifiers, and the RumourEval dataset[3], which we adapt for the problem of fake news detection to evaluate our argumentation-based stance aggregation methods.

DATASET	CLASS	SIZE (TRAIN+DEV)	
FNC-1	AGREE	3,678	7.36%
	DISAGREE	840	1.68%
	DISCUSS	8,909	17.8%
	UNRELATED	36,545	73.1%
	ALL	49,972	-
RumourEval Task A	COMMENT	2,907	64.3%
	DENY	344	7.61%
	QUERY	358	7.92%
	SUPPORT	910	20.1%
	ALL	4,519	-
RumourEval Task B	FALSE	62	20.9%
	TRUE	137	46.1%
	UNVERIFIABLE	98	33.0%
	ALL	297	-

Table 1: Summary of FNC-1, RumourEval Task A and RumourEval Task B datasets.

4.1 Fake News Challenge

The Fake News Challenge (FNC-1) is a shared task first presented in 2017 for claim verification in the context of news article headlines using machine learning classifiers. Participating groups in the shared task were granted access to training and development datasets consisting of almost 50K examples of headline and article body pairs.

The stance detection task is composed of two sub-problems. First, a classifier must determine if the input texts are related. If relatedness is established, the classifier must then determine whether the article expresses a positive stance (AGREE), a negative stance (DISAGREE), or no stance (DISCUSS) towards the accompanying headline. The following is a truncated example from FNC-1:

Headline: *Spider burrowed through tourist's stomach and up into his chest.*
Article body: *Fear not arachnophobes, the story of Bunbury's "spiderman" might not be all it seemed. Perth scientists have cast doubt over claims that a spider burrowed into a man's body during his first trip to Bali. The story went global on Thursday, generating hundreds of stories online... a specialist dermatologist was called in and later used tweezers to remove what was believed to be a "tropical spider". But it seems we may have all been caught in a web... of misinformation. Arachnologist Dr Volker Framenau said whatever the creature was, it was "almost impossible" for the culprit to have been a spider...*
Label: DISAGREE.

As shown in Table 1, UNRELATED examples account for a large majority (almost three quarters) of the dataset. We discount the UNRELATED label to focus on the three-way classification task of predicting the stance. Thus, we are left with 13,427 examples.

4.2 RumourEval Task A and Task B

Task 8 of SemEval 2017 focused on verifying rumours pertaining to a number of tweets regarding eight contentious topics from current events, captured in the RumourEval dataset, adapted from the PHEME project[4]. The dataset consists of 297 Twitter conversation threads (the English portion of the PHEME journalism use case data). Rumour verification differs from fake news detection in that rumours are not necessarily presented in the form of traditional news media (e.g., newspapers), but the two tasks are related in that they both require the verification of text-based claims.

We were motivated to use the RumourEval dataset because it is annotated for both stance and veracity. Therefore, even though the original SemEval shared task was not formulated with this problem in mind, this dataset is incredibly well-suited to investigating the relation between stance and veracity. Stance (Task A) and veracity (Task B) labels are provided for each of the 297 Twitter threads in the RumourEval dataset (see Table 1). In total this amounts to 4,161 source tweet and

[2]https://github.com/FakeNewsChallenge/fnc-1
[3]http://alt.qcri.org/semeval2017/task8/
[4]https://www.pheme.eu/

reply tweet pairs, once we disregard the QUERY stance detection label. Furthermore, we adapt the remaining stance detection labels, renaming DENY as DISAGREE, SUPPORT as AGREE, and COMMENT as DISCUSS to match the FNC-1 stance labels. As for the veracity labels, we only consider the TRUE and FALSE source tweets. The following text is an excerpt from a conversation thread in the RumourEval dataset regarding the Sydney siege rumour topic:

> **u1/source tweet**: *Up to 20 held hostage in Sydney Lindt Cafe siege* ⟨URL⟩ ⟨URL⟩ [SUPPORT]
>
> —**u2/reply 1**: *"@u1: Up to 20 held hostage in Sydney Lindt Cafe siege* ⟨URL⟩ ⟨URL⟩*."* [SUPPORT]
>
> —**u3/reply 2**: *Sick. "@u1: Up to 20 held hostage in Sydney Lindt Cafe siege* ⟨URL⟩ ⟨URL⟩*"* [SUPPORT]
>
> —**u4/reply 3**: *@u1 @u10 oh god !!!!* [COMMENT]
>
> —**u5/reply 4**: *@u1 at least they've got good chocolate* [COMMENT]
>
> —**u6/reply 5**: *@u5 you are an insensitive idiot!* [COMMENT]
>
> —**u7/reply 6**: *@u1 all reports say 13* [DENY]
>
> —**u8/reply 7**: *"@u1: Up to 20 held hostage in Sydney Lindt Cafe siege* ⟨URL⟩ ⟨URL⟩*" - wonder if they'll get paid overtime* [COMMENT]
>
> —**u9/reply 8**: *"@u1: Up to 20 held hostage in Sydney Lindt Cafe siege* ⟨URL⟩ ⟨URL⟩*" - Oh. My. God. I am SICK!* [COMMENT]
>
> **Task A label**: See conversation thread.
> **Task B label**: FALSE

In the above example, the level of indentation is used to distinguish between direct and nested replies. Note that user *u10* does not post a response in the conversation thread, but is *tagged* in the conversation by *u4*. Source tweets also have stance labels relating to whether they support the rumour topic which they concern. Each conversation thread in the RumourEval dataset is accompanied by details pertaining to the conversation structure. This provides information about how the tweets relate to each other, including which are direct replies (e.g., reply 1) and which are nested replies (e.g., reply 5) to the source tweet. We use this structure to construct BAFs.

5 Methodology & Experimental Setup

Our methodology is shown in Figure 4. We train a number of stance detection classifiers on the FNC-1 dataset, the best of which we use to predict the labels for the RumourEval Task A dataset. We then perform stance aggregation on the predicted labels, in order to arrive at a veracity prediction. We compare their veracity assessment performance against the gold standard labels from the RumourEval task B dataset. This allowed us to compare and evaluate the usefulness of the stance detection predictions. The reliability of these labels also enabled us to gauge the effectiveness of stance detection as a tool for veracity assessment.

In the remainder of this section, first we describe the methods we employ for stance classification and then our stance aggregation methods. We developed our own stance detection classifiers using gradient boosting as well as (three forms of) neural networks, of which we selected two (LSTM and BiLSTM) as best performing in stance prediction, to generate BAFs. For stance aggregation, a credibility-weighted average, DF-QuAD with only direct replies, and DF-QuAD with both direct and nested replies, applied to appropriately constructed BAFs using the stance detection classifiers.

5.1 Stance Classification

We implemented four stance detection classifiers. Three of these are recurrent neural networks (RNNs) or bidirectional RNNs (GRU, LSTM, BiLSTM), constructed using the Tensorflow[5] and Keras[6] deep learning libraries. A summary of the hyper-parameters selected for our RNN models is shown in Table 2. We also used a non-neural technique, i.e., gradient boosting. We built the gradient boosting classifier using the Scikit-Learn library module for ensemble classifiers[7].

5.1.1 Preprocessing

All four classifiers were trained using headline-article text pairs extracted from the FNC-1 dataset. The effectiveness of the classifiers was tested on the RumourEval Task A dataset. Note that FNC-1 deals with headlines and article bodies, which are more structured than the tweets which make up the RumourEval dataset, so particular care had

---

[5]https://tensorflow.org
[6]https://keras.io/
[7]https://scikit-learn.org

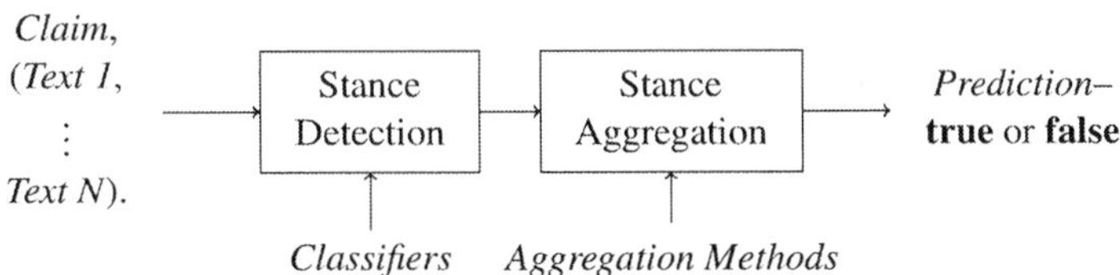

Figure 4: Veracity prediction work flow. As stance classifiers we use LSTMs and BiLSTMs. Methods employed for aggregation are a credibility-weighted average baseline, DF-QuAD (only direct replies), and DF-QuAD (both direct and nested replies).

to be taken in addressing these differences for classifiers trained on the former to perform well when evaluated on the latter.

We used regular expressions to remove links and user handles from tweets. We opted to use 100D pre-trained GloVe embeddings (Pennington et al., 2014) to represent the text inputs. For the deep neural network architectures, we constructed embedding layers. In order to train the non-neural classifier, we computed a mean of each embedding.

We attempted to minimize out-of-vocabulary (OOV) words with lemmatization where possible. Furthermore, we utilized the Stanford Named Entity Recognizer[8] to construct named entity substitutions for locations, organizations, and named people to both minimize OOV words and also prevent over-fitting due to coincidental correlations between named entities and stance labels in the training set, as adopted by Conforti et al. (2018) and Lee et al. (2018). The purpose of employing these techniques was to train more generalized classifiers that would output more accurate predictions when applied to the unseen examples in the RumourEval dataset. This was particularly important given the differences in topics between FNC-1 and RumourEval, but also because FNC-1 contains text pertaining to news articles written in formal English, whereas the RumourEval corpus is composed of short snippets of user-generated text made up of colloquialisms and neologisms which word embeddings is not able to capture semantically.

Furthermore, we made the choice to use stratified cross-validation for training the classifiers. This was because, as can be seen in Table 1, the FNC-1 dataset is highly unbalanced. Although we performed 3-way classification to learn the AGREE, DISAGREE, and DISCUSS labels, only the

AGREE and the DISAGREE labels play a role when it comes to constructing the bipolar argumentation graphs on which the DF-QuAD-based stance aggregation is performed.

HYPER-PARAMETER	VALUE
Batch size	16
Dropout	0.25
Recurrent dropout	0.25
Units (dimensions of output space)	64

Table 2: Hyper-parameters for training RNN models.

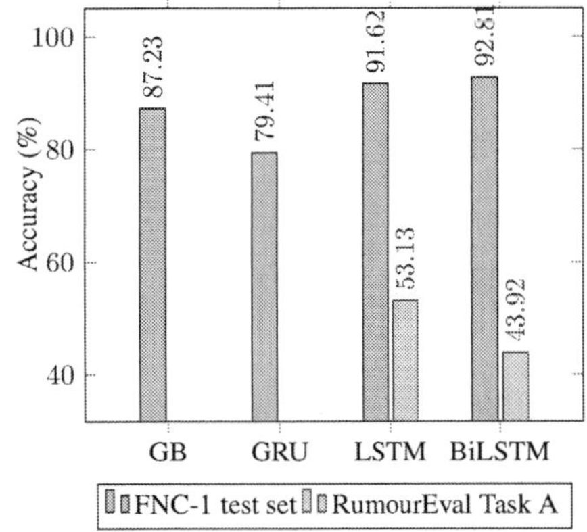

Figure 5: Accuracy of classifiers for 3-way stance problem.

5.2 Stance Aggregation

This section outlines the techniques we employ for aggregating stance labels. Stance aggregation is performed on the RumourEval dataset. We compare the performance of three stance aggregation methods for aggregating both the gold standard stance labels provided for the RumourEval Task B dataset and also the labels generated by the LSTM and BiLSTM models. We choose to only use the predictions generated by the LSTM and BiLSTM models because they display the best test performance on the RumourEval Task A dataset, as we will see in Section 6.

---

[8]https://nlp.stanford.edu/software/CRF-NER.html

Dataset	Model	AGREE			DISAGREE			DISCUSS		
		P	R	F1	P	R	F1	P	R	F1
FNC-1	GB	**.831**	.736	.781	.570	.322	.412	.926	**.972**	.934
	GRU	.645	.685	.665	.402	.244	.304	.876	.887	.882
	LSTM	.817	**.878**	**.846**	.652	**.493**	.562	**.964**	.955	**.960**
	BiLSTM	.829	.840	.835	**.676**	**.493**	**.570**	.949	.965	.957
RUMOUR EVAL	LSTM	.166	**.490**	.248	**.160**	.0119	.0222	.753	.513	.610
	BiLSTM	**.178**	.430	**.252**	.105	**.0448**	**.0628**	.759	.576	**.655**

Table 3: Precision (P), recall (R), and F1-score (F1) of stance detection classifiers on FNC-1 test set and RumourEval dataset (see Section 5).

5.2.1 Aggregation via DF-QuAD Semantics

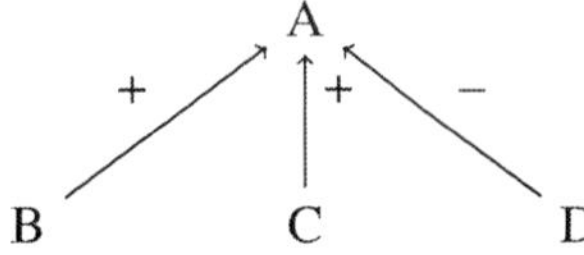

(a) Only direct reply (DR) stance relations for direct and nested replies

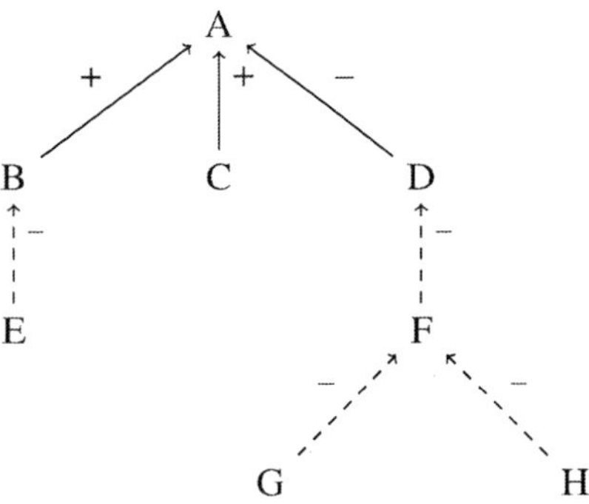

(b) Direct reply (DR) and nested reply (NR) stance relations for direct and nested replies.

Figure 6: Examples of constructed BAFs. A is a source tweet from RumourEval. B, C, D, E, F, and G are all replies. Direct attack and support relations are drawn with solid lines. Nested attack and support relations are shown with dashed lines.

Each conversation thread in RumourEval takes a form similar to the example given in Section 4.2. Argument A in Figure 6 is the claim for which we aim to predict the veracity. A is a source tweet (i.e., start of the conversation thread), so it forms the root node of the graphs shown in Figures 6a and 6b. We construct two BAFs: (1) a BAF in which attack and support relations only exist between source tweet, in this case argument A, and direct replies, as dictated by the stance detection classifier, and (2) a BAF with additional relations between reply tweet nodes, accounting for nested replies as well as direct replies. Figure 6

shows that A has three direct replies in the conversation thread; these are B, C, and D. Only these four arguments (A, B, C, D) are present in the flat BAF described in (1) above. The BAF illustrated in Figure 6b incorporates the responses (arguments and counter-arguments) to A's replies B, C, and D. B is attacked by argument E, and D is attacked by F, which is subject to two counter-arguments G and H. The motivation for the latter graph construction, which incorporates both direct and nested reply tweets, is to learn the credibility of replies through their relation to each other, and incorporate this in the aggregation indirectly, via their dialectical strength. This reflects the acceptability of the claim in the context of the arguments formed with texts that support and refute it, as opposed to the credibility used to compute credibility-weighted averages, which is often based on meta-data pertaining to the source of the claim.

6 Results

Here we discuss the results obtained for both stance detection and stance aggregation for veracity prediction. We evaluate the effectiveness of the four classifiers given earlier for stance detection by cross-validation on the FNC-1 dataset, and the choose the two best performing such classifiers on the RumourEval Task A dataset. We then evaluate the effectiveness of methods for predicting the veracity of the rumour claims presented in the RumourEval dataset: these are, in addition to the two DF-QuAD-based methods presented earlier, a standard credibility-weighted average baseline.

6.1 Stance Classification Performance

As expected the stance detection classifiers performed well on the FNC-1 3-class task, but quite poorly on the RumourEval Task A dataset (see Table 3). This is most likely because of the paucity of DISAGREE examples in the training data. The LSTM and BiLSTM classifiers recorded the best performance on the FNC-1 test set. For this reason, we chose to use these two models for predicting stance labels on RumourEval Task A.

6.2 Aggregation Performance

Table 4 summarizes our stance aggregation results, from which it can be seen that the DF-QuAD-based aggregation methods exhibit comparable or better performance than the non argumentation-based baseline. Figure 7 shows the accuracy achieved by each method for the gold standard labels and the predicted labels. Further error analysis is given in the confusion matrix for each of the aggregation methods provided in Figure 8.

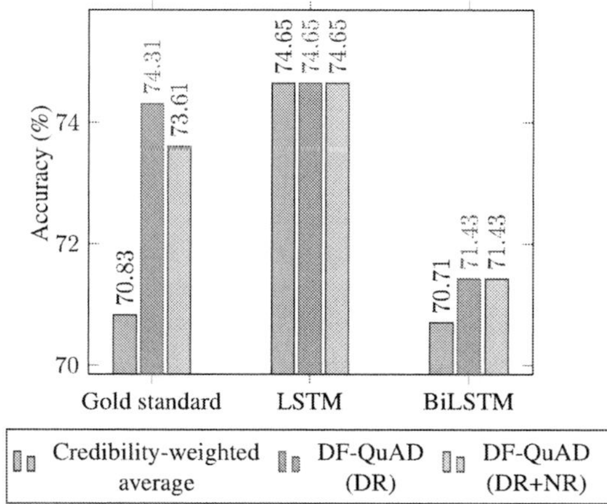

Figure 7: Comparison of stance aggregation accuracy achieved by each method on gold standard labels, and LSTM and BiLSTM stance detection labels.

6.2.1 Baseline

The baseline we devised for our experiments computes a credibility-weighted average of the disagree and agree stance labels relating to a claim.

For the credibility-weighted average we simply defined the credibility to be the number of followers of the account that posts the reply. Since it is often the case that spam accounts will have many followers that are not genuine (i.e., we assigned any account that does not have a profile photo a credibility of zero, assuming that this is not a genuine account. We normalized the Twitter user credibility for each reply in a conversation.

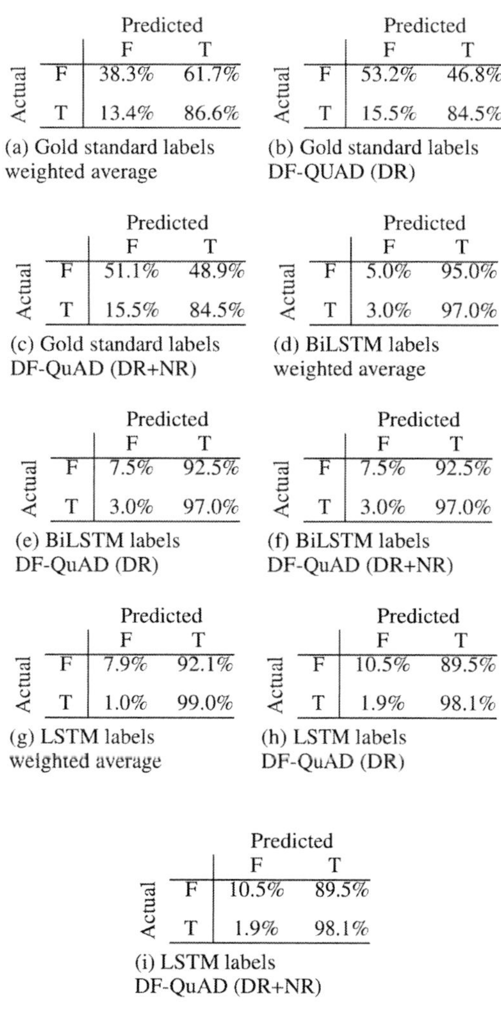

	Predicted	
	F	T
F	38.3%	61.7%
T	13.4%	86.6%

(a) Gold standard labels weighted average

	Predicted	
	F	T
F	53.2%	46.8%
T	15.5%	84.5%

(b) Gold standard labels DF-QUAD (DR)

	Predicted	
	F	T
F	51.1%	48.9%
T	15.5%	84.5%

(c) Gold standard labels DF-QuAD (DR+NR)

	Predicted	
	F	T
F	5.0%	95.0%
T	3.0%	97.0%

(d) BiLSTM labels weighted average

	Predicted	
	F	T
F	7.5%	92.5%
T	3.0%	97.0%

(e) BiLSTM labels DF-QuAD (DR)

	Predicted	
	F	T
F	7.5%	92.5%
T	3.0%	97.0%

(f) BiLSTM labels DF-QuAD (DR+NR)

	Predicted	
	F	T
F	7.9%	92.1%
T	1.0%	99.0%

(g) LSTM labels weighted average

	Predicted	
	F	T
F	10.5%	89.5%
T	1.9%	98.1%

(h) LSTM labels DF-QuAD (DR)

	Predicted	
	F	T
F	10.5%	89.5%
T	1.9%	98.1%

(i) LSTM labels DF-QuAD (DR+NR)

Figure 8: The confusion matrix for each of the aggregation methods performed on the three types of label.

6.2.2 Comparison of Methods

Stance aggregation was performed using four methods, of which two argumentative: one implementation of DF-QuAD on BAFs considering only the argumentation relations on direct reply edges of the BAFs, and another which considers all relations. We performed a DF-QuAD strength evaluation on both the flat and layered BAFs. We interpreted a value of the DF-QuAD strength function (see Section 3) which is > 0.5 to be a true label, otherwise the rumour claim is labelled false.

For all three types of labels, the aggregation-based evaluation either beats the baseline or performs equally as well. Furthermore, the LSTM and BiLSTM predicted labels achieve aggregation accuracy results that are very similar to those achieved using the gold standard labels. The BiL-

	Stance aggregation method	Veracity Assessment (RumourEval Task B)					
		FALSE			TRUE		
		P	R	F1	P	R	F1
Gold standard labels (RumourEval Task A)	CREDIBILITY-WEIGHTED AVERAGE	.581	.383	.462	.743	**.866**	.800
	DF-QUAD (DR)	**.625**	**.532**	**.575**	.789	.845	**.816**
	DF-QUAD (DR + NR)	.615	.511	.558	.781	.845	.811
LSTM stance detection labels	CREDIBILITY-WEIGHTED AVERAGE	**.750**	.079	.143	.746	**.990**	**.851**
	DF-QUAD (DR)	.667	**.105**	**.182**	.750	.981	.850
	DF-QUAD (DR + NR)	.667	**.105**	**.182**	.750	.981	.850
Bidirectional LSTM stance detection labels	CREDIBILITY-WEIGHTED AVERAGE	.400	.050	.089	.719	**.970**	.826
	DF-QuAD (DR)	**.500**	**.075**	**.130**	.724	**.970**	**.829**
	DF-QuAD (DR + NR)	**.500**	**.075**	**.130**	.724	**.970**	**.829**

Table 4: Precision (P), recall (R), and F1-score (F1) of the stance aggregation methods when applied to both gold standard stance labels and the stance labels predicted by the LSTM and bidirectional LSTM trained stance detection classifiers.

STM labels give the worst performance of the three label types. This is likely related to the fact that, although the BiLSTM classifier outperforms the LSTM classifier on the FNC-1 dataset (see Figure 5), it does not accurately predict RumourEval Task A labels as well as the LSTM – particularly DISAGREE labels. As expected, the gold standard tweet labels show the best performance for the two DF-QuAD aggregation methods. They also show comparable results to the LSTM labels, which however are likely to be unreliable because of the classifiers inability to generalize well.

7 Conclusions and Future Work

We have proposed a method for veracity prediction based on a form of argumentative aggregation rather than credibility-weighted average of stance labels. We used stance label predictions for relation-based argument mining to generate bipolar argumentation frameworks (BAFs). We then evaluated the dialectical strength of arguments in these frameworks as a form of aggregation for veracity prediction. Empirical results on a combination of the FNC-1 dataset for stance detection and RumourEval dataset for veracity prediction show that modelling various stance labels within a bipolar argumentation framework may offer a promising new approach to fake news detection via stance detection and dialectical aggregation.

However, there were a number of limitations in our study, in particular the size of the training data and the unbalanced labels of the training data, resulting in stance detection classifiers that performed poorly on the unseen RumourEval dataset.

In order to improve the performance of the classifiers we could incorporate an attention mechanism in our RNN architectures. Furthermore we could train the models on hand-crafted lexical features in addition to word embeddings. In addition, the rumour understanding dataset and the features described in Turenne (2018) could be employed for further experiments into gradual argumentation evaluation of stances.

In order to draw further conclusions about the usefulness of dialectical strength in the task of stance aggregation, studies should be conducted on more robust classifiers. The limitations of the training datasets and classifiers developed from this training data mean that the conclusions we can infer are limited. Also, as we elucidate in Section 3, the nature of the data – conversations taken from social media – also restricts the observations we can draw from our findings. Furthermore, it would be worthwhile to investigate the performance of other gradual semantics for BAFs, as well as non-gradual semantics, to evaluate the strengths of claims in BAFs.

For future work, it would also be worthwhile to explore how BAFs extracted from stance detection classifiers, and the dialectical relations between the arguments in these BAFs, could be used to provide explanations for the veracity prediction of the claim. These explanations would hopefully provide clarification about why a veracity label – true or false – was decided, as well as which evidence or counter-evidence arguments were most pivotal in arriving at that judgement.

References

Filip Boltužić and Jan Šnajder. 2014. Back up your stance: Recognizing arguments in online discussions. In *Proceedings of the First Workshop on Argumentation Mining*, pages 49–58.

Lucas Carstens and Francesca Toni. 2015. Towards relation based argumentation mining. In *Proceedings of the 2nd Workshop on Argumentation Mining*, pages 29–34.

Claudette Cayrol and Marie-Christine Lagasquie-Schiex. 2005. Gradual valuation for bipolar argumentation frameworks. In *European Conference on Symbolic and Quantitative Approaches to Reasoning and Uncertainty*, pages 366–377. Springer.

Oana Cocarascu and Francesca Toni. 2018. Combining deep learning and argumentative reasoning for the analysis of social media textual content using small data sets. *Computational Linguistics*, 44(4):833–858.

Costanza Conforti, Mohammad Taher Pilehvar, and Nigel Collier. 2018. Towards automatic fake news detection: Cross-level stance detection in news articles. In *Proceedings of the First Workshop on Fact Extraction and VERification (FEVER)*, pages 40–49.

Leon Derczynski, Kalina Bontcheva, Maria Liakata, Rob Procter, Geraldine Wong Sak Hoi, and Arkaitz Zubiaga. 2017. SemEval-2017 task 8: RumourEval: Determining rumour veracity and support for rumours. In *Proceedings of the 11th International Workshop on Semantic Evaluation (SemEval-2017)*, pages 69–76, Vancouver, Canada. Association for Computational Linguistics.

William Ferreira and Andreas Vlachos. 2016. Emergent: a novel data-set for stance classification. In *Proceedings of the 2016 conference of the North American chapter of the association for computational linguistics: Human language technologies*, pages 1163–1168.

Bilal Ghanem, Paolo Rosso, and Francisco Rangel. 2018. Stance detection in fake news a combined feature representation. In *Proceedings of the First Workshop on Fact Extraction and VERification (FEVER)*, pages 66–71.

Andreas Hanselowski, Avinesh PVS, Benjamin Schiller, Felix Caspelherr, Debanjan Chaudhuri, Christian M. Meyer, and Iryna Gurevych. 2018. A retrospective analysis of the fake news challenge stance-detection task. In *Proceedings of the 27th International Conference on Computational Linguistics*, pages 1859–1874, Santa Fe, New Mexico, USA. Association for Computational Linguistics.

David MJ Lazer, Matthew A Baum, Yochai Benkler, Adam J Berinsky, Kelly M Greenhill, Filippo Menczer, Miriam J Metzger, Brendan Nyhan, Gordon Pennycook, David Rothschild, et al. 2018. The science of fake news. *Science*, 359(6380):1094–1096.

Nayeon Lee, Chien-Sheng Wu, and Pascale Fung. 2018. Improving large-scale fact-checking using decomposable attention models and lexical tagging. In *Proceedings of the 2018 Conference on Empirical Methods in Natural Language Processing*, pages 1133–1138, Brussels, Belgium. Association for Computational Linguistics.

Saif Mohammad, Svetlana Kiritchenko, Parinaz Sobhani, Xiaodan Zhu, and Colin Cherry. 2016. Semeval-2016 task 6: Detecting stance in tweets. In *Proceedings of the 10th International Workshop on Semantic Evaluation (SemEval-2016)*, pages 31–41.

Mitra Mohtarami, Ramy Baly, James Glass, Preslav Nakov, Lluís Màrquez, and Alessandro Moschitti. 2018. Automatic stance detection using end-to-end memory networks. In *Proceedings of the 2018 Conference of the North American Chapter of the Association for Computational Linguistics: Human Language Technologies, Volume 1 (Long Papers)*, pages 767–776, New Orleans, Louisiana. Association for Computational Linguistics.

Jeffrey Pennington, Richard Socher, and Christopher Manning. 2014. Glove: Global vectors for word representation. In *Proceedings of the 2014 conference on empirical methods in natural language processing (EMNLP)*, pages 1532–1543.

Dean Pomerleau and Delip Rao. 2017. Fake news challenge.

Kashyap Popat, Subhabrata Mukherjee, Andrew Yates, and Gerhard Weikum. 2018. DeClarE: Debunking fake news and false claims using evidence-aware deep learning. In *Proceedings of the 2018 Conference on Empirical Methods in Natural Language Processing*, pages 22–32, Brussels, Belgium. Association for Computational Linguistics.

Antonio Rago, Francesca Toni, Marco Aurisicchio, and Pietro Baroni. 2016. Discontinuity-free decision support with quantitative argumentation debates. In *Principles of Knowledge Representation and Reasoning: Proceedings of the Fifteenth International Conference, KR 2016*, pages 63–73. AAAI Press.

Benjamin Riedel, Isabelle Augenstein, Georgios P. Spithourakis, and Sebastian Riedel. 2017. A simple but tough-to-beat baseline for the fake news challenge stance detection task. *arXiv preprint arXiv:1707.03264*.

Jingbo Shang, Jiaming Shen, Tianhang Sun, Xingbang Liu, Anja Gruenheid, Flip Korn, Ádám D Lelkes, Cong Yu, and Jiawei Han. 2018. Investigating rumor news using agreement-aware search. In *Proceedings of the 27th ACM International Conference on Information and Knowledge Management*, pages 2117–2125. ACM.

Parinaz Sobhani, Diana Inkpen, and Stan Matwin. 2015. From argumentation mining to stance classification. In *Proceedings of the 2nd Workshop on Argumentation Mining*, pages 67–77.

James Thorne, Andreas Vlachos, Oana Cocarascu, Christos Christodoulopoulos, and Arpit Mittal. 2018. Proceedings of the first workshop on fact extraction and verification (fever). In *Proceedings of the First Workshop on Fact Extraction and VERification (FEVER)*.

Nicolas Turenne. 2018. The rumour spectrum. *PloS one*, 13(1):e0189080.

Xinyi Zhou, Reza Zafarani, Kai Shu, and Huan Liu. 2019. Fake news: Fundamental theories, detection strategies and challenges. In *Proceedings of the Twelfth ACM International Conference on Web Search and Data Mining*, pages 836–837. ACM.

Persuasion of the Undecided: Language vs. the Listener

Liane Longpré
Cornell University
lfl42@cornell.edu

Esin Durmus
Cornell University
ed459@cornell.edu

Claire Cardie
Cornell University
cardie@cs.cornell.edu

Abstract

This paper examines the factors that govern persuasion for *a priori* UNDECIDED versus DECIDED audience members in the context of on-line debates. We separately study two types of influences: *linguistic factors* — features of the language of the debate itself; and *audience factors* — features of an audience member encoding demographic information, prior beliefs, and debate platform behavior. In a study of users of a popular debate platform, we find first that different combinations of linguistic features are critical for predicting persuasion outcomes for UNDECIDED versus DECIDED members of the audience. We additionally find that audience factors have more influence on predicting the side (PRO/CON) that persuaded UNDECIDED users than for DECIDED users that flip their stance to the opposing side. Our results emphasize the importance of considering the undecided and decided audiences separately when studying linguistic factors of persuasion.

1 Introduction

Understanding the factors that influence persuasion in the context of argumentation (e.g. debates) has been an important focus in a variety of research areas. Natural language processing (NLP) research on persuasion has focused for the most part on uncovering the *linguistic factors* that determine and define persuasive arguments — features of the language of the argument itself. For example, Tan et al. (2016) and Zhang et al. (2016) have found that the language used in arguments and the patterns of interaction between debaters are important predictors of persuasiveness. Recently, however, studies have emerged that begin to study the effects of *audience characteristics* on persuasion, e.g. features that encode demographic information, the prior beliefs, and debate platform

behavior of individual listeners of a debate or readers of an argument. Lukin et al. (2017), for example, find that different types of people are persuaded by different types of arguments. And Durmus and Cardie (2018) show that the prior beliefs of the audience have a significant impact on predicting whether or not a particular audience member will be persuaded to flip their stance on a debated topic.

Research in psychology and political science moreover suggests that there are key differences in the persuasion of undecided versus decided voters/audience members. For example, Petty and Cacioppo (1996) find that prior experiences and beliefs can lead to the re-framing of a message perceived by a person to maintain consistency between their prior beliefs and their attitudes towards the topic of the message. In particular, studies show that *a priori* decided voters simply ignore certain information in order to maintain this consistency (Sweeney and Gruber, 1984; Vecchione et al., 2013; Kosmidis, 2014). In contrast, an undecided voter is asked to make a decision on an issue for which previously received information was somehow unconvincing; and Kosmidis (2014), Kosmidis and Xezonakis (2010), and Schill and Kirk (2014) show that, as a result, these voters are likely to rely heavily on information conveyed in a new message.

The undecided voter group furthermore holds the highest potential for persuasion (Kosmidis and Xezonakis, 2010; Shehryar et al., 2017). Public support for social and political causes often critically depends on the undecided decision makers. To the best of our knowledge, computational studies of persuasion in NLP have not yet studied this important subset of the audience separately.

This paper studies argumentation in the context of online debate to better understand the factors that govern persuasion for *a priori* UNDECIDED

Proceedings of the 6th Workshop on Argument Mining, pages 167–176
Florence, Italy, August 1, 2019. ©2019 Association for Computational Linguistics

versus DECIDED members of the audience. We study persuasion at the individual (i.e. audience member) level, and find that the linguistic features most important for persuasion differ for the UNDECIDED and DECIDED audience subgroups. Consistent with results of social and political psychology research, the linguistic feature differences correspond to rhetorical styles found to be effective on undecided and decided audiences. Additionally, we find that certain audience features are more important for predicting undecided cases of persuasion than for predicting decided cases of persuasion.

The remainder of this paper is organized as follows. Related work is described in Section 2. We describe the dataset in Section 3 and experiment methodology in Section 4. Results and analysis is in Section 5, and conclusions are in Section 6.

2   Related Work

Language and persuasion. Extensive work has been done in cognitive and social psychology on the linguistic influence on persuasion. Some of the most critical elements of persuasive text include lexical complexity, language intensity, and power of speech style (Dillard and Pfau, 2002). Studies on linguistic factors effecting the persuasion of the listener have shown that language is a key factor in predicting the outcome of debates (Paxton and Dale, 2014; Jorgensen et al., 1998). These studies find the importance of various language features: lexical qualities such as personal pronoun use, word sentiment, and hedging (Paxton and Dale, 2014), and rhetoric qualities such as precision, firmness, energy, and commitment (Jorgensen et al., 1998). These works in psychology highlight the importance of studying linguistic features in arguments and persuasion.

Argument mining. Much recent work in argumentation has focused on the automatic detection of argument structures in text (Lippi and Torroni, 2016; Schulz et al., 2018; Stab et al., 2018; Morio and Fujita, 2018). Research has shown promising results on using extracted argument structures as features on tasks that involve predicting convincingness (Ghosh et al., 2016; Yunfan Gu and Huang, 2018; Cano-Basave and He, 2016).

Specific to debates, work has been done on detecting the stance of the speaker. Walker et al. (2012), for example, find that structuring the debates in terms of agreement relations between

speakers improves prediction. Lexical and syntactic argument features are shown to improve predictive performance in Somasundaran and Wiebe (2010). More relevant to our work, recent studies have examined the role of language in predicting persuasion outcomes in debates. For example, Tan et al. (2016) find that the linguistic interaction between an opinion holder and opposing debater are highly predictive of persuasiveness. And Zhang et al. (2016) find that debaters who target and address their opponent's points are more likely to win the debate.

While these studies motivate the linguistic features examined in our study, they do not take factors corresponding to audience characteristics into consideration. Our work aims to study the linguistic characteristics of persuasive text, while also considering audience characteristics such as prior beliefs and decidedness.

Prior views of the audience. Persuasion of an audience is not solely dependent on the language used by the speaker. Research in psychology emphasizes the significance of people's prior views on their perception of new information. The effectiveness of a message depends significantly on the prior beliefs and the strengths of beliefs of the message recipient (Johnson et al., 1995; Lau et al., 1991).

Recent work has analyzed the influence of audience characteristics on predicting persuasion (Lukin et al., 2017; Durmus and Cardie, 2018). Lukin et al. (2017) examine the effects of audience factors and argumentation types in belief change. They study dialogs from *4forums.com*[1], which contain argument type annotations. Their results show that information on prior beliefs and personality type improves the ability of the model to predict belief change; more conscientious, open, and agreeable people tend to respond more to emotional argument types.

The importance of considering audience-specific prior belief factors is further illustrated in Durmus and Cardie (2018). Using debate and user data from *debate.org*, they study the effects of prior beliefs on various controversial issues along with linguistic factors on predicting the outcome of debates. Importantly, they find that the linguistic features most important for prediction differ when audience features are considered from when

---

[1] http://www.4forums.com/political/forum.php/

they are not. To the best of our knowledge, this work is most relevant to ours because it studies debate text and considers prior beliefs of both the audience and the debaters. Our work differs from this study in that we separately consider persuasion of audience members who were undecided before the debate from audience members who switched sides.

The undecided audience. There has been a substantial amount of research effort in the social and political sciences on undecided and decided voters. A study on the 2005 British general election finds that undecided voters are more susceptible to campaign persuasion (Kosmidis and Xezonakis, 2010). This result, elaborated on in Kosmidis (2014), is because decided voters rely more on their prior beliefs while undecided voters place higher weight on information conveyed in campaigns.

Consistent with this account, studies by Schill and Kirk (2014) on 2008 and 2012 U.S. presidential debate outcomes find that the most critical portions of the debate to undecided voters were the content-rich statements, and that the rhetorical strategies shown to be effective to undecideds are strategies that "transcended the personalities of the candidates". In contrast, studies by Adams et al. (2011) on European election campaigns find that in response to policy statements of political parties during elections, voters adjust their Left-Right positions based on their subjective perceptions of the party's campaign and not on the campaign's actual policy statements. Research on selective exposure (favoring information that aligns with an individual's prior beliefs and attitudes) provides insight into the mechanisms behind this tendency. Voters already decided on an issue tend to avoid information that is inconsistent with their attitudes and are receptive to information consistent with their attitudes (Sweeney and Gruber, 1984; Vecchione et al., 2013).

3 Data Description

The debate dataset from Durmus and Cardie (2018) consists of 67,315 debates and user information on 36,294 users obtained from *debate.org*.

3.1 Debates

Debates span over 23 different categories (e.g. 'Politics', 'Education', 'Movies'). Each debate consists of multiple rounds, where a round con-

ROUND 1	
PRO:	... this reason, you are not free to make threats or defamatory statements against another person in ...
CON:	... laws violate the fundamental freedom of speech which democracy is founded upon ...
ROUND 2	
PRO:	... has ignored my point about hate speech breeding an "us vs them" mentality, and how such ...
CON:	... question is, does our government have the right to tell us what our opinions are, and to define ...
ROUND 3	
PRO:	... evidenced by the rise in violence against Hispanics and Muslims I cited in my second round ...
CON:	... courts to be able to decide which opinions are "moral" and which are not? How fascist do ...

Table 1: An example debate titled 'HATE SPEECH LAWS ARE A GOOD IDEA'.

tains text from the PRO debater and the CON debater. An example debate is shown in Table 1. Other examples of debate titles are: "THE DEATH PENALTY IS A SUITABLE PUNISHMENT" and "ANIMAL TESTING SHOULD BE BANNED".

Users can interact with debates by voting on them. Votes include "AGREE WITH BEFORE THE DEBATE" and "AGREE WITH AFTER THE DEBATE" for each debater/side (users can respond with PRO, CON, or TIE). We focus our analysis on two distinct cases of persuasion based on this vote data.

Case 1: voters persuaded from the middle. This category constitutes voters who indicate TIE between PRO and CON for "AGREE WITH BEFORE THE DEBATE" and indicate one side, PRO or CON, for "AGREE WITH AFTER THE DEBATE". We keep instances of persuasion that correspond to this category and refer to this case as FROM-MIDDLE.

Case 2: voters persuaded from the opposite side. This category constitutes voters who indicate one side for "AGREE WITH BEFORE THE DEBATE" and indicate the opposite side (PRO or CON) for "AGREE WITH AFTER THE DEBATE". We keep instances that correspond to this category, referred

Persuasion Case	#instances	#debates
FROM-MIDDLE	4360	3652
FROM-OPPOSING	2642	2183

Table 2: Dataset statistics.

to as FROM-OPPOSING. In our prediction task, the original side of the voter is not given to the model.

Figure 1 illustrates example user votes for each of the two cases. Distinguishing instances of voters being persuaded into these case groupings allows us to examine what makes an argument persuasive to audience members who are undecided versus decided with respect to a particular debate topic. Table 2 summarizes the dataset statistics relevant to the voter cases.

3.2 User Information

User profiles contain self-identified demographic information, such as GENDER and RELIGIOUS IDEOLOGY. Profiles additionally contain users' opinions on current controversial debate topics (denoted by BIG-ISSUES), such as ABORTION, SOCIAL SECURITY, and MINIMUM WAGE[2]. Users can respond with PRO (in favor), CON (against), UND (undecided), N/O (no opinion), or N/S (not saying).

4 Prediction Task

We aim to study what factors are most important in influencing audience members to be persuaded to one side or the other for each of the cases (*a priori* undecided or decided) of persuasion. Encoding audience-level and linguistic factors as features, we structure the prediction task as follows:

> Given an individual voter, predict which debater/side (PRO or CON) the voter will be convinced by after the debate.

We consider only samples from the data where (1) a voter was undecided before the debate and then adopted a stance, i.e. voted for one of the debaters as the winner; and (2) a voter was (seemingly) decided beforehand and then flipped their stance. We do *not* consider samples where (1) a voter declared a "tie" between the debaters after the debate; and (2) a voter was decided beforehand, and voted for the debater with the stance that they agreed with beforehand.

To study the effect of each of the debaters' linguistic and user-based features on persuasion, in this setting, we specifically look at which side (PRO vs. CON) did the convincing for a particular voter. We believe that restricting the samples in the way described above allows us to best study what influences persuasion when voters are successfully convinced.

4.1 Features

Audience features. User profile data is used to generate a number of features for a voter and the PRO and CON debaters for a given debate.

The *gender* of a voter is one-hot encoded to account for the user's option to not include gender in their profile; the elements of the vector correspond to FEMALE, MALE, and OTHER/DID NOT INDICATE. Additionally, information about the debaters' genders are encoded as whether or not the debater's gender is the same as the voter's.

User profile data is also used to capture the prior opinion similarities of the voter and debaters in two ways, as in Durmus and Cardie (2018). First, the political and religious ideologies are encoded as whether or not each of the debaters' ideologies is the same as each of the voter's. We denote this feature by *matching ideology*. Second, the similarity of the voter and debaters' BIG-ISSUES responses are encoded as follows. Each issue in BIG-ISSUES is represented as a one-hot encoding corresponding to PRO, CON, UND, and N/O. The encoding of an example user can be seen in Figure 2. All issue encodings are concatenated to create a BIG-ISSUES vector for each user. The cosine similarity between the voter's BIG-ISSUES vector and each debaters' BIG-ISSUES vector is used as a feature. We denote this feature by *opinion similarity*.

The number of elements in the voter's BIG-ISSUES vector corresponding to PRO and CON, and the number of elements in the vector corresponding to UND and N/O are used to encode the voter's decidedness or undecidedness, respectively. We denote the feature by *decidedness*. An example of the encoding is shown in Figure 2. This feature captures the degree to which the voter's opinions are established on widely discussed topics.

The frequency of a voter being persuaded is encoded as the percentage of other training debates in which the voter changed their stance, out of all

---

[2]https://www.debate.org/big-issues/

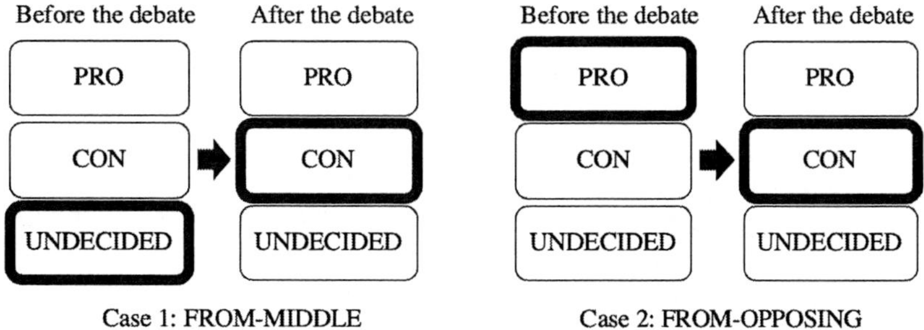

Figure 1: Example votes for a debate showing each case of persuasion.

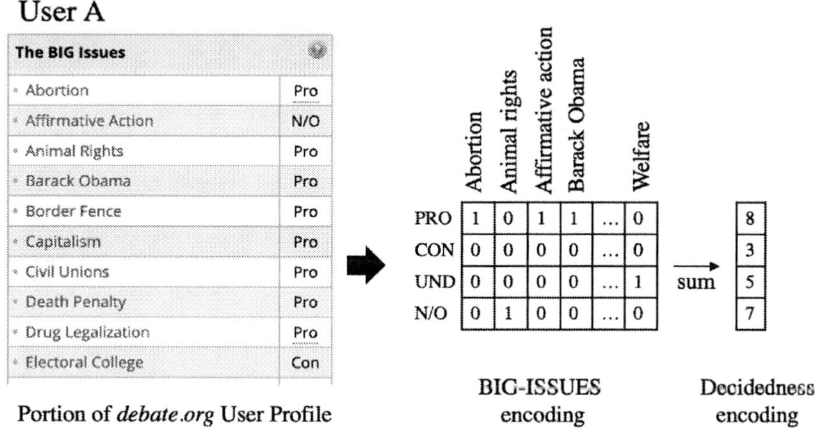

Figure 2: Example user profile and corresponding feature encodings.

training debates on which the voter made a vote. We denote the feature by *persuadability*. This feature is an indication of how persuadable a voter is, in general.

Linguistic features. We process debate text and use linguistic features as is done in Durmus and Cardie (2018). The text from all rounds of PRO are concatenated before feature processing. The same is done for the rounds of CON. We use the same set of linguistic features from Durmus and Cardie (2018), described as follows.

Lexical features include *TF-IDF*, *modal verbs*, *swear words*, *spelling errors*, and *punctuation*. A speaker's word choice (i.e. use of hedging, and particular causal connectors and modal particles) are indicative of the mode of argumentation (Gold et al., 2015; Paxton and Dale, 2014).

Style features include *length, personal pronouns, referring to opponent, use of citations*, and *links*. Using citations and addressing an opponent's points are critical components of justification that affect the reception of an argument. Additionally, the length of a speaker's utterance and the language used when referring to self and the oppo-

nent exhibit characteristics of respect and participation between the debaters, which are important aspects for communication outcomes (Tan et al., 2016; Gold et al., 2015; Paxton and Dale, 2014).

Semantic features include *sentiment, subjectivity* (Wilson et al., 2005), *connotation* (Feng and Hirst, 2011), and *politeness*. The sentiment and subjectivity of an argument impacts the reception of the message, and are predictive of argument stance (Somasundaran and Wiebe, 2010). In addition to these attributes, connotation and politeness cues contribute to the patterns of interaction of debaters, which are critical in predicting persuasiveness (Tan et al., 2016).

Argumentation features, as in (Somasundaran et al., 2007), have been shown to predict the stance and opinion of a speaker. These include the following: *assessment, authority, conditioning, contrasting, emphasizing, generalizing, empathy, inconsistency, necessity, possibility, priority, rhetorical questions, desire*, and *difficulty*.

4.2 Hypotheses

We hypothesize that there are key differences in the linguistic features important for persuasion of an *a priori* undecided audience member and the persuasion of an *a priori* seemingly decided audience member to change their mind. Drawing from social and political science studies, we hypothesize that the persuasion of undecided audience members will critically depend on content-centric language features, while the persuasion of seemingly decided audience members will be more influenced by stylistic language features. Additionally, we hypothesize that audience features will provide important context, improving predictive performance.

4.3 Methodology

We use Logistic Regression to perform the classification task. Prediction accuracy is evaluated using 5-fold cross validation. We use 3-fold cross validation on the training set to select model parameters. We perform ablation analysis first on audience features only and linguistic features only, then on combinations of the best-performing audience and linguistic features. This analysis is done separately for the subsets of data corresponding to undecided and decided cases of persuasion (FROM-MIDDLE and FROM-OPPOSING, respectively). We use majority classifier as a baseline.

5 Results and Analysis

Results for models and feature ablation experiments are show in Table 3. Majority baseline produces 57.43% and 59.42% accuracy for FROM-MIDDLE and FROM-OPPOSING, respectively. This baseline predicts the majority debater/side between PRO and CON in the training set of examples.

Linguistic vs. audience features. As shown in Table 3, the best performance is achieved when both audience and linguistic features are included, obtaining 69.01% and 67.22% accuracy for FROM-MIDDLE and FROM-OPPOSING, respectively. We find that linguistic features are more important for predictive accuracy than audience features. Relying only on audience features obtains accuracies of 61.47% for FROM-MIDDLE and 61.54% for FROM-OPPOSING. Using all linguistic features produces a significant improvement over baseline accuracy, achieving 66.95% and 66.65%

Accuracy of Models

	FROM-MIDDLE	FROM-OPPOSING
Majority Baseline	57.43%	59.42%
All Features	**69.01%**	**67.22%**
Audience Features	**61.47%**	**61.54%**
- persuadability	61.46%	61.51%
- gender	61.44%	61.47%
- matching ideology	61.42%	61.39%
- decidedness	61.33%	61.13%
- opinion similarity	59.04%	59.80%
Linguistic Features	**66.95%**	**66.65%**
- unigram TF-IDF	65.25%	64.54%
- use of citations and referring to opponent	<u>67.20%</u>	66.12%
- subjectivity	66.03%	<u>67.79%</u>

Table 3: **Accuracy results, for majority class baseline, all features, audience features, and linguistic features.** Remaining results are ablation studies, where '- *feature*' denotes the removal of the feature. <u>Underlined</u> results are feature combinations that improve performance over including all features.

for FROM-MIDDLE and FROM-OPPOSING, respectively. This result is surprising and in contrast to results from Durmus and Cardie (2018), who find that audience features improve accuracy more than linguistic features. We suspect that this difference arises because our experiments consider debates from *all* categories, while Durmus and Cardie (2018) restrict analysis to *political* and *religious* debate categories. Political and religious debate topics tend to be more controversial in nature Fichman and Hara (2014), and correspond more closely to the issues encoded in the audience features; the BIG-ISSUES elements consist primarily of political and religious issues [3]. As such, these features will be more informative in *political* and *religious* debate settings.

Audience features. Feature ablation across user-based features shows that all audience features are helpful in predicting vote outcomes for both voter groups. We find that the most important feature is *opinion similarity*[4]; removing this feature decreases prediction accuracy from 61.47% to 59.04% for FROM-MIDDLE, and from 61.54% to 59.80% for FROM-OPPOSING. This result is

[3] https://www.debate.org/big-issues/
[4] For UserA and UserB, the cosine similarity of BIG-ISSUES$_A$ and BIG-ISSUES$_B$.

consistent with research on voter behavior from Arcuri et al. (2008) and Friese et al. (2012), who find that despite reporting uncertainty, undecided voters have implicit attitudes that are predictive of voting behavior.

Linguistic features. The most important linguistic feature for both voter groups is *unigram TF-IDF*[5], whose removal decreases performance to from 66.95% to 65.25% for FROM-MIDDLE, and from 66.65% to 64.54% for FROM-OPPOSING. However, not all linguistic features are helpful in predictive accuracy. For instance, removing *use of citations*[6] and *referring to opponent*[7] features increases accuracy from 66.95% to 67.20% for FROM-MIDDLE. Similarly, removal of the *subjectivity*[8] feature improves accuracy for FROM-OPPOSING from 66.65% to 67.79%.

It should be noted that the linguistic features whose removal improves performance for FROM-MIDDLE and FROM-OPPOSING are different, showing that there are distinctions in the important factors for persuasion between the voter groups. These differences are further explored in the following sections.

5.1 Differences Between Persuasion Groups

5.1.1 Linguistic Feature Differences

We find distinct differences in the important features for predicting the vote outcome for voter groups FROM-MIDDLE and FROM-OPPOSING. Table 4 shows that the best-performing set of linguistic features for FROM-MIDDLE includes all features minus *use of citations*, *referring to opponent*, and *swear words*, while the best-performing set of linguistic features for FROM-OPPOSING includes all features minus *subjectivity*, *modals*[9], and *bi-/tri-gram TF-IDF*[10]. These linguistic feature sets are denoted by MIDDLE* and OPPOSING*, respectively. Using features OPPOSING* increases accuracy for FROM-OPPOSING from 67.22% to 68.39%, while decreasing accuracy for FROM-MIDDLE from 69.01% to 68.51%. Conversely, using features MIDDLE* increases accuracy for FROM-MIDDLE from 69.01% to 69.17%, while decreasing accuracy from 67.22% to 66.92%.

Accuracy of Models

	FROM-MIDDLE	FROM-OPPOSING
All Features	**69.01%**	**67.22%**
- persuadability	68.33%	67.52%
- matching ideology	68.99%	67.30%
User+MIDDLE*	**69.17%**	**66.92%**
- persuadability	69.16%	66.84%
- matching ideology	68.60%	66.92%
User+OPPOSING*	**68.51%**	**68.21%**
- persuadability	68.46%	68.32%
- matching ideology	67.96%	68.39%

Table 4: **Accuracy results, for all features and best-performing linguistic feature sets.** Remaining results are ablation studies, where '- *feature*' denotes the removal of the feature. Underlined results are feature combinations that improve performance over including all features. MIDDLE* denotes the best-performing combination of linguistic features for FROM-MIDDLE, which includes all linguistic features minus *use of citations*, *referring to opponent*, and *swear words*. OPPOSING* denotes the best-performing combination of linguistic features for FROM-OPPOSING, which includes all linguistic features minus *subjectivity*, *modals*, and *bi-/tri-gram TF-IDF*.

The linguistic feature differences of the two groups have subtle differences in nature. A possible analysis that distinguishes the groups is that there is a difference in the rhetorical strategies most effective for undecided versus decided audiences. Use of modals, subjectivity, and general word choice are semantic features of an argument that affect the perception of the content of the argument. Based on our results, these content-based features are more important for undecided voters than they are for decided voters. In comparison, use of swear words, citing sources, and referring to the opponent are stylistic features of an argument that affect the perception of the debater producing the argument. Based on our results, these style-based features are not as important for undecided voters as they are for decided voters. This account is consistent with the findings of Schill and Kirk (2014) that undecided voters respond most to content-rich rhetorical strategies, and the findings of Vecchione et al. (2013); Sweeney and Gruber (1984) that decided voters tend to selectively attend to information in a message based on prior attitudes. The account is also in line with experiments conducted by Adams et al. (2011), which

---

[5]Calculated with a maximum of 50 terms.

[6]The number of explicit source citations.

[7]The usage of phrases like "according to my opponent".

[8]Number of words with negative strong, negative weak, positive strong, and positive weak subjectivity.

[9]The usage of modal verbs, i.e. *can*, *should*, *will*, and *may*.

[10]Calculated with a maximum of 30 terms.

find that affiliated voters do not adjust their positions in response to a party's actual policy statements, but rather do adjust their positions based on their subjective perceptions of the party.

5.1.2 Audience Feature Differences

The inclusion of certain audience features has different effects on prediction accuracy between FROM-MIDDLE and FROM-OPPOSING voter groups. As shown in Table 4, removing the *persuadability* feature improves the accuracy for FROM-OPPOSING from 67.22% to 67.52% when all linguistic features are included, and improves the accuracy from 68.21% to 68.32% when OPPOSING* linguistic features are used. Similarly, removing the *matching ideology* feature improves the accuracy for FROM-OPPOSING from 67.22% to 67.30% when all linguistic features are included, and improves the accuracy from 68.21% to 68.39% when OPPOSING* linguistic features are used. The reverse is true for FROM-MIDDLE. For this voter group, removing the *persuadability* and *matching ideology* features decreases accuracy from 69.01% to 68.33% and 68.99%, respectively, when all linguisitc features are included, and decreases the accuracy from 69.17% to 69.16% and 68.60%, respectively, when MIDDLE* features are included.

It should be noted that the best-performing overall feature set for FROM-OPPOSING includes neither the *persuadability* feature nor the *matching ideology* feature. In contrast, all audience features are present in the best-performing overall feature set for FROM-MIDDLE. This difference suggests that certain audience-level aspects are comparatively more predictive of vote outcomes for undecided voters. The result emphasizes the importance of considering audience factors for people who are undecided with respect to an issue; in order to understand vote behavior of the undecided audience, it is critical to consider audience factors.

5.2 Influence of Audience Features

We perform ablation across linguistic features separately for when audience features are included and for when they are not. Results in Table 5 show that the linguistic features most important for model performance differ when audience features are present. For instance, experiments on voter group FROM-OPPOSING show that including *argument lexicon* features improves performance from 67.22% to 67.52% when audience features are not

Accuracy of Models

	FROM-MIDDLE	FROM-OPPOSING
Linguistic Features	**66.95%**	**66.65%**
- argument lexicon	66.22%	65.90%
- use of citations and referring to opponent	67.20%	66.12%
- swear words	66.65%	66.65%
- subjectivity	66.03%	67.79%
All Features	**69.01%**	**67.22%**
- argument lexicon	68.46%	67.52%
- use of citations and referring to opponent	69.17%	66.99%
- swear words	69.08%	67.20%
- subjectivity	68.76%	67.90%

Table 5: **Accuracy results, for all features and linguistic features.** Remaining results are ablation studies, where '- *feature*' denotes the removal of the feature. Underlined results are feature combinations that improve performance over including all features.

included, while performance is decreased from 66.65% to 65.90% when audience features are included. Comparatively, inclusion of the *swear words* feature improves performance for FROM-MIDDLE from 69.01% to 69.08% when audience features are not included, but negatively impacts performance from 66.95% to 66.65% when audience features are included.

We find that the best-performing sets of linguistic features for FROM-OPPOSING and FROM-MIDDLE differ when audience features are included versus when they are not. The best-performing set of linguistic features for FROM-OPPOSING when audience features are not considered includes *modals* and *bi-/tri-gram TF-IDF*, while these features are not present in the best-performing set of features when all features are considered (denoted by OPPOSING*). Similarly for FROM-MIDDLE, the *swear words* feature is not in MIDDLE*, while it is present in the best-performing set of linguistic features when audience features are not considered.

These results are consistent with findings from Durmus and Cardie (2018) and re-affirm the importance of considering audience features when analyzing linguistic effects of persuasion.

174

6 Conclusion

In this paper, we separately examine what linguistic and audience-level factors are most important for predicting vote outcomes of previously undecided and decided audiences. We show that different linguistic features are critical for predicting the successful side of persuasion of undecided versus decided voters. We find that some audience features that are important for predicting the side of persuasion of undecided voters are not as helpful in predicting persuasion of decided voters.

This paper examines the differences between the undecided and decided audiences in persuasion, which has been under-studied in a computational framework. The results of our work validate the importance of analyzing the undecided versus decided audience separately.

Acknowledgments

This work was supported in part by NSF grants IIS-1815455 and SES-1741441. The views and conclusions contained herein are those of the authors and should not be interpreted as necessarily representing the official policies or endorsements, either expressed or implied, of NSF or the U.S. Government.

References

James Adams, Lawrence Ezrow, and Zeynep Somer-Topcu. 2011. Is anybody listening? Evidence that voters do not respond to European parties' policy statements during elections. *American Journal of Political Science*, 55(2):370–382.

Luciano Arcuri, Luigi Castelli, Silvia Galdi, Cristina Zogmaister, and Alessandro Amadori. 2008. Predicting the vote: Implicit attitudes as predictors of the future behavior of decided and undecided voters. *Political Psychology*, 29(3):369–387.

Amparo Elizabeth Cano-Basave and Yulan He. 2016. A study of the impact of persuasive argumentation in political debates. In *Proceedings of the North American Chapter of the Association for Computational Linguistics: Human Language Technologies 2016*, pages 1405–1413. Association for Computational Linguistics.

James P. Dillard and Michael Pfau. 2002. *The Persuasion Handbook: Developments in Theory and Practice*, pages 371–380. Sage Publications, Inc., Thousand Oaks, CA.

Esin Durmus and Claire Cardie. 2018. Exploring the role of prior beliefs for argument persuasion. In *Proceedings of the North American Chapter of the Association for Computational Linguistics: Human Language Technologies 2018*, pages 1035–1045. Association for Computational Linguistics.

Vanessa Wei Feng and Graeme Hirst. 2011. Classifying arguments by scheme. In *Proceedings of the 49th Annual Meeting of the Association for Computational Linguistics: Human Language Technologies-Volume 1*, pages 987–996. Association for Computational Linguistics.

Pnina Fichman and Noriko Hara. 2014. *Global Wikipedia: International and Cross-Cultural Issues in Online Collaboration*, pages 25–41. Rowman & Littlefield Publishers, Lanham, Maryland.

Malte Friese, Colin Tucker Smith, Thomas Plischke, Matthias Bluemke, and Brian A. Nosek. 2012. Do implicit attitudes predict actual voting behavior particularly for undecided voters? *Public Library of Science One*, 7:1–14.

Debanjan Ghosh, Aquila Khanam, Yubo Han, and Smaranda Muresan. 2016. Coarse-grained argumentation features for scoring persuasive essays. In *Proceedings of the 54th Annual Meeting of the Association for Computational Linguistics*, pages 549–554. Association for Computational Linguistics.

Valentin Gold, Mennatallah El-Assady, Annette Hautli-Janisz, Tina Bgel, Christian Rohrdantz, Miriam Butt, Katharina Holzinger, and Daniel Keim. 2015. Visual linguistic analysis of political discussions: Measuring deliberative quality. *Digital Scholarship in the Humanities*, 32(1):141–158.

Blair T. Johnson, Hung-Yu Lin, Cynthia S. Symons, Laura Ann Campbell, and Geoffrey Ekstein. 1995. Initial beliefs and attitudinal latitudes as factors in persuasion. *Personality and Social Psychology Bulletin*, 21(5):502–511.

Charlotte Jorgensen, Christian Kock, and Lone Rorbech. 1998. Rhetoric that shifts votes: An exploratory study of persuasion in issue-oriented public debates. *Political Communication*, 15(3):283–299.

Spyros Kosmidis. 2014. Heterogeneity and the calculus of turnout: Undecided respondents and the campaign dynamics of civic duty. *Electoral Studies*, 33:123 – 136.

Spyros Kosmidis and Georgios Xezonakis. 2010. The undecided voters and the economy: Campaign heterogeneity in the 2005 British general election. *Electoral Studies*, 29(4):604 – 616.

Richard R. Lau, Richard A. Smith, and Susan T. Fiske. 1991. Political beliefs, policy interpretations, and political persuasion. *The Journal of Politics*, 53(3):644–675.

Marco Lippi and Paolo Torroni. 2016. Argumentation mining: State of the art and emerging trends. *ACM Transactions on Internet Technology*, 16(2):10:1–10:25.

Stephanie Lukin, Pranav Anand, Marilyn Walker, and Steve Whittaker. 2017. Argument strength is in the eye of the beholder: Audience effects in persuasion. In *Proceedings of the 15th Conference of the European Chapter of the Association for Computational Linguistics: Volume 1, Long Papers*, pages 742–753, Valencia, Spain. Association for Computational Linguistics.

Gaku Morio and Katsuhide Fujita. 2018. End-to-end argument mining for discussion threads based on parallel constrained pointer architecture. In *Proceedings of the 5th Workshop on Argument Mining*, pages 11–21, Brussels, Belgium. Association for Computational Linguistics.

Alexandra Paxton and Rick Dale. 2014. Leveraging linguistic content and debater traits to predict debate outcomes. In *Proceedings of the Annual Meeting of the Cognitive Science Society*, pages 592–596. Cognitive Science Society.

Richard E. Petty and John T. Cacioppo. 1996. *Attitudes and Persuasion: Classic and Contemporary Approaches*, pages 95–160. Westview Press, New York, NY.

Dan Schill and Rita Kirk. 2014. Courting the swing voter: "Real time" insights into the 2008 and 2012 U.S. presidential debates. *American Behavioral Scientist*, 58(4):536–555.

Claudia Schulz, Steffen Eger, Johannes Daxenberger, Tobias Kahse, and Iryna Gurevych. 2018. Multitask learning for argumentation mining in low-resource settings. In *Proceedings of the 2018 Conference of the North American Chapter of the Association for Computational Linguistics: Human Language Technologies, Volume 2 (Short Papers)*, pages 35–41, New Orleans, Louisiana. Association for Computational Linguistics.

Omar Shehryar, Kelly Weidner, and Dan Moshavi. 2017. Persuading the undecided: An interdisciplinary approach to increase public support for the arts. *Journal of Public Affairs*, 18(2):e1652.

Swapna Somasundaran, Josef Ruppenhofer, and Janyce Wiebe. 2007. Detecting arguing and sentiment in meetings. In *Proceedings of the SIGdial Workshop on Discourse and Dialogue*, volume 6.

Swapna Somasundaran and Janyce Wiebe. 2010. Recognizing stances in ideological on-line debates. In *Proceedings of the the North American Chapter of the Association for Computational Linguistics: Human Language Technologies 2010 Workshop on Computational Approaches to Analysis and Generation of Emotion in Text*, pages 116–124. Association for Computational Linguistics.

Christian Stab, Tristan Miller, Benjamin Schiller, Pranav Rai, and Iryna Gurevych. 2018. Crosstopic argument mining from heterogeneous sources. In *Proceedings of the 2018 Conference on Empirical Methods in Natural Language Processing*, pages 3664–3674, Brussels, Belgium. Association for Computational Linguistics.

Paul D. Sweeney and Kathy L. Gruber. 1984. Selective exposure: Voter information preferences and the Watergate affair. *Journal of Personality and Social Psychology*, 46(6):1208–1221.

Chenhao Tan, Vlad Niculae, Cristian DanescuNiculescu-Mizil, and Lillian Lee. 2016. Winning arguments: Interaction dynamics and persuasion strategies in good-faith online discussions. In *Proceedings of the 25th International Conference on World Wide Web*, pages 613–624. International Conference on World Wide Web.

Michele Vecchione, Gianvittorio Caprara, Francesco Dentale, and Shalom H. Schwartz. 2013. Voting and values: Reciprocal effects over time. *Political Psychology*, 34(4):465–485.

Marilyn A. Walker, Pranav Anand, Robert Abbott, and Ricky Grant. 2012. Stance classification using dialogic properties of persuasion. In *2012 Conference of the North American Chapter of the Association for Computational Linguistics: Human Language Technologies*, pages 592–596. Association for Computational Linguistics.

Theresa Wilson, Janyce Wiebe, and Paul Hoffmann. 2005. Recognizing contextual polarity in phrase-level sentiment analysis. In *Proceedings of the Conference on Human Language Technology and Empirical Methods in Natural Language Processing*, pages 347–354. Association for Computational Linguistics.

Maoran Xu Hao Fu Yang Liu Yunfan Gu, Zhongyu Wei and Xuanjing Huang. 2018. Incorporating topic aspects for online comment convincingness evaluation. In *Proceedings of the 5th Workshop on Argument Mining*, pages 97–104. Association for Computational Linguistics.

Justine Zhang, Ravi Kumar, Sujith Ravi, and Cristian Danescu-Niculescu-Mizil. 2016. Conversational flow in Oxford-style debates. In *Proceedings of the North American Chapter of the Association for Computational Linguistics: Human Language Technologies 2016*, pages 136–141, San Diego, California. Association for Computational Linguistics.

Towards Assessing Argumentation Annotation – A First Step

Anna Lindahl
Språkbanken Text
University of Gothenburg
Sweden

Lars Borin
Språkbanken Text
University of Gothenburg
Sweden

Jacobo Rouces Gonzalez
Språkbanken Text
University of Gothenburg
Sweden

`(anna.lindahl|lars.borin|jacobo.rouces)@svenska.gu.se`

Abstract

This paper presents a first attempt at using Walton's argumentation schemes for annotating arguments in Swedish political text and assessing the feasibility of using this particular set of schemes with two linguistically trained annotators. The texts are not pre-annotated with argumentation structure beforehand. The results show that the annotators differ both in number of annotated arguments and selection of the conclusion and premises which make up the arguments. They also differ in their labeling of the schemes, but grouping the schemes increases their agreement. The outcome from this will be used to develop guidelines for future annotations.

1 Introduction

Argumentation mining – the automatic recognition and classification of arguments and their components in text – is a useful technology for a number of practical text-processing applications, both commercial and academic, and in the latter case not least as a component of research tools in the digital humanities and social sciences.

Many different annotation schemes for argument analysis have been proposed in the literature (Lippi and Torroni, 2016; Macagno et al., 2017; Visser et al., 2018; Song et al., 2014), and a central concern in the context of argumentation mining is to arrive at a scheme which is both expressive enough for the intended tasks and explicitly defined in a way which makes it amenable to high-accuracy automatic processing.

Automatic linguistic annotation often requires the use of a ground-truth data set – a gold standard – for evaluating – and often training – different kinds of algorithms and software. Since the gold standard annotations will invariably need to be introduced by humans, we require an annotation scheme which human annotators can learn (in a reasonable amount of time) to apply with high accuracy and high inter-annotator agreement.

One of the most elaborate and extensive efforts to devise a comprehensive set of argumentation schemes is that by Walton et al. (2008), which builds on a long line of works in philosophy and law studies. Walton et al. (2008) further explicitly intend their schemes to be usable "in AI". The 60 schemes (with additional sub-schemes in many cases) presented in the book are given detailed, formalized descriptions, and in the present paper we describe and discuss the initial stage in an effort intended to evaluate the suitability and usefulness of this set of schemes for argumentation mining.

As indicated above, a prerequisite for this is that a sufficient amount of suitable text can be manually annotated with high inter-annotator agreement. Consequently, we have initiated an annotation effort (the first of several), where a small set of Swedish political texts (newspaper editorials) have been annotated using the schemes of Walton et al. (2008). To the best of our knowledge, this is the first annotation study which applies Walton's schemes directly to text, without any pre-annotated structure step beforehand. In the present paper, we present and discuss the results of this exercise, and outline what the next steps of this effort should be, based on these results.

Related Work

In Walton et al. (2008) an argumentation scheme is defined by a set of premises and a conclusion, and a label for the scheme. For most schemes, there is also a set of critical questions which are used for identification and evaluation. Walton's schemes, or modified versions of them, have been used to classify argumentation in many cases (Feng and Hirst, 2011; Green, 2015; Song et al., 2014; Lawrence and Reed, 2016). However, when annotating argumentation schemes, in these cases the annotation has been done on already pre-

Proceedings of the 6th Workshop on Argument Mining, pages 177–186
Florence, Italy, August 1, 2019. ©2019 Association for Computational Linguistics

segmented text, identified as containing argumentation.

Visser et al. (2018) use Walton's original schemes for annotating nodes in an argumentation structure. They reach an inter-annotator agreement of $\kappa = 0.723$ (Cohen's Kappa), but note that there are some schemes that are difficult for the annotators to distinguish, despite the use of a decision tree based on Walton et al. (2008). The issue of distinguishing schemes and the need for a taxonomy or classification of the schemes have been also been discussed in Walton (2012), and there have been many suggestions for this (Walton et al., 2008; Walton and Macagno, 2015; Macagno et al., 2017). Because of this, in addition to using the original schemes, we also use groups suggested in the classification system mentioned in Walton et al. (2008).

2 Data Set Creation and Annotation

The Data Set

The data for this study were originally compiled by Hedquist (1978), who investigated emotive language[1] in Swedish newspaper editorials. He selected a total of 30 editorials from 6 newspapers, all published in the period May–September 1973, shortly before the Swedish national parliament elections at the end of September 1973. The newspapers were selected so as to reflect the five political parties then represented in the Swedish parliament, and the editorials were selected on the basis of topic, with two general and three specific topics per newspaper. The total number of words in this data set is about 19,000, for an average word count per editorial of about 640.

For his investigation Hedquist annotated all texts manually for emotive language, using a scheme which he developed specifically for this work. Together with the existing and planned argumentation annotation described in this paper, this data set comprises a small but rich foundation for future work on argumentation mining in Swedish in particular, but also in more general terms on the relationship between argument structures and sentiment.

Annotation Procedure

The editorials were annotated by two annotators with solid training in linguistic analysis, master students of linguistics at Uppsala University.

The instructions given to the annotators were minimal. In preparation for the annotation task, they were initially given three editorials, asked to identify and classify all arguments in them manually according to Walton et al. (2008). After this they met with the project leader, for a discussion of differences and difficulties. Other than that, they were expected to be able to understand the description of the argumentation schemes as given by Walton et al. (2008), as it was believed that somebody with their extensive training in linguistics should be well equipped to understand and apply these descriptions, which are couched in terms quite familiar to somebody who has been exposed to linguistic semantics and pragmatics.

The annotation was done with the Araucaria tool for argument analysis (Reed and Rowe, 2004) which has support for Walton's argument schemes. For the annotation, the 30 most common schemes were used, as originally presented in Walton (2013). In Araucaria, for a given text, the annotator selects any consecutive passage of text, labels it and possibly connects it to any other labeled passage of text. From here on, these passages are referred to as *units*. The available labels are 'premise' and 'conclusion'. A premise can only have one conclusion, but a unit can be annotated multiple times. This is suitable for chained argumentation. After labeling, an argument scheme is connected to a conclusion and one or more premises, and these parts together make up the argument. Araucaria also allows adding so-called 'missing' units if an annotator feels a conclusion or premises are left unstated/implied.

3 Results

The results from the two annotators differ significantly, both regarding what is annotated and how it has been annotated. More specifically, they differ both in numbers of arguments annotated and the distributions of units, and they even differ in how they use the annotation tool, which results in different structure of the file containing the argument

---

[1]The phenomena investigated and described by Hedquist largely come under the heading of what is now generally referred to as *sentiment analysis*.

	Annotator 1	Annotator 2
No. of arguments	345	195
Avg. no. of premises per arg.	1.26	2.03
Premises, in text	395	380
Premises, missing	42	16
Conclusions, in text	292	194
Conclusions, missing	53	1
Total no. of units	782	591

Table 1: Annotation statistics

information, although the retrieved information is the same.

The number of annotated argument instances and units is shown in Table 1. Annotator 1 (A1) has annotated about 150 more argument instances than annotator 2 (A2), although the latter has annotated more premises on average. By inspection it was observed that A1 often pairs a conclusion with each of its premises into individual arguments with one conclusion and one premise each, but assigns all of these arguments the same scheme. A2 usually includes all premises attached to a conclusion as a single argument. This could be either a difference in interpretation or usage of the tool, but this may be the reason for the difference in the average number of premises.

The annotators have used the option of adding missing units differently, with A1 having added about 100 missing units and A2 17 as shown in Table 1. The identification of implied conclusions or premises is a well-known problem, and might be the reason for this discrepancy. In Table 2 the statistics of multiple occurrences are shown. A1 has both more units repeating as conclusions, and occurring as both premise and conclusion. On the other hand, A2 has 26 repeating premises while A1 has none. Most of A2's occurrences are only repeating once, but A1 has many conclusions which occur many times. This is related to the difference in how the annotators divide the premises between arguments. If a conclusion has 6 premises and A1 turns each conclusion-premise pair into a separate argument, then the conclusion will occur 6 times.

Of the 30 schemes described by Walton (2013), A1 uses 12 and A2 uses 21. Together they use 22 different schemes.[2] Both annotators use 4–5 schemes for the majority of identified arguments,

with the rest of the schemes having only a few occurrences each. Even though A1 annotates more argument instances, fewer schemes are used. Table 3 shows the the used schemes and their occurrences for A1 and A2. The schemes ARGUMENT FROM CONSEQUENCES and ARGUMENT FROM SIGN are both heavily used by both annotators. The description of these schemes are seen below.

ARGUMENT FROM SIGN:
Premise: A is true in this situation.
Premise: Event B is generally indicated as true when its sign, A, is true in this kind of situation.
Conclusion: B is true in this situation.

ARGUMENT FROM CONSEQUENCES:
Premise: If A is brought about, then good (bad) consequences will (may plausibly) occur
Conclusion: A should (not) be brought about.

From these descriptions it is seems that these schemes could be applied to a wide range of argumentation, and this is probably why the annotators have used them the most. Compared to some of the descriptions of the other schemes, they are also possibly easier to understand and therefore easier to apply. But they are also very general, and this raises the question in which cases an annotator chooses the more specific scheme in favor of a more general one. Interestingly, the scheme A1 annotated the most (ARGUMENT FROM EVIDENCE TO A HYPOTHESIS) is only used 6 times by A2. Likewise, A2's most annotated scheme (ARGUMENT FROM CORRELATION TO CAUSE) is only used 5 times by A1. The descriptions of these two schemes are seen below. These schemes both describe correlation between events, and one could possibly see the first as a subset of the second. The similarities of the schemes are further explored in the next section.

___

[2]23 of the annotated units of A1 are not marked with an argument scheme and are thus not included.

Annotator 1		Annotator 2	
Units as both conclusion and premise	72	Units as both conclusion and premise	12
Units as repeating conclusion	80	Units as repeating conclusion	7
Units as repeating premises	0	Units as repeating premises	26

Table 2: Occurrences of units

Scheme	A1	A2
Argument from Evidence to a Hypothesis	105	6
Argument from Consequences	90	20
Argument From Sign	47	22
Argument from Cause to Effect	30	18
Argument from Falsification of a Hypothesis	30	4
Argument from Commitment	11	3
Argument from Verbal Classification	9	15
Argument from Expert Opinion	8	7
Argument from Popular Opinion	7	12
Argument from Correlation to Cause	5	42
Argument from Analogy	2	1
Ethotic Argument	1	–
Argument from Popular Practice	–	17
Argument from Position to Know	–	8
Argument from Bias	–	5
Causal Slippery Slope Argument	–	4
Argument from Precedent	–	3
Argument from an Established Rule	–	2
Argument from Arbitrariness of a Verbal Classification	–	2
Circumstantial Argument Against the Person	–	2
Argument from Vagueness of a Verbal Classification	–	1
Argument from an Exceptional Case	–	1
Total	195	345

Table 3: Usage of schemes for Annotator 1 and 2

ARGUMENT FROM EVIDENCE TO A HYPOTHESIS:

Premise: If hypothesis A is true, then a proposition B, reporting an event, will be observed to be true.

Premise: B has been observed to be true in a given instance .

Conclusion: A is true.

ARGUMENT FROM CORRELATION TO CAUSE:

Premise: There is a positive correlation between A and B.

Conclusion: A causes B.

4   Evaluation

In order to measure inter-annotator agreement (IA) we use the measure in Equation 1 based on the Sørensen–Dice coefficient, where a_1 and a_2 are the sets of annotations from each annotator, and m is the set of pairs of annotations from a_1 and a_2 that are matching (i.e. they are considered equiv-

alent). Annotations can be either units (spans of text representing premises or conclusions) or arguments (a conclusion with one or more spans).

$$c = 2 * |m| / (|a_1| + |a_2|) \tag{1}$$

We don't use measures such as Fleiss' kappa or Krippendorff's alpha because these measures calculate agreement over annotation tasks that consist of assigning a discrete label or score to each element in a set, which is different to annotating spans over continuous text. Previous work on argumentation annotation such as as in Stab and Gurevych (2017) uses them because their annotation task is defined as marking whether predefined spans of texts do or do not contain annotations or units, but in our annotation task the annotators themselves create the spans.

To determine if two units are matching, the amount of overlap between the strings representing the units is compared to a given threshold α. The strings are defined as ranges of character indices within the text. The amount of overlap is measured as the ratio between the length of the longest common continuous substring to both strings and the length of the longest of both strings. For example, the units below have an overlap of 0.68.

Unit 1. *7:48 Utgången kan leda till regeringsbyte, men den kommer inte att leda till någon förändring av trygghetspolitiken i det svenska välfärdssamhälllet.*[3]
'The result might lead to a change of government, but it will not lead to any change in the Swedish welfare state.'
Unit 2. *den kommer inte att leda till någon förändring av trygghetspolitiken i det svenska välfärdssamhälllet.*
'it won't lead to any change in the Swedish welfare state.'

Two values of α are used in the experiments. A strict one of 0.9, which can still account for small differences in whitespace, and a more lenient threshold of 0.5. In order to compare how well the annotators agree, the arguments are compared unit by unit. First, the conclusions of the arguments are compared, and if the conclusion matches, the premises are compared. Given both a matching conclusion and premise, the schemes of the two matching arguments are compared. If a unit occurs more than once, it will belong to different arguments. Each occurrence is thus treated as a unique occurrence.

Conclusions

In Table 4 the number of matching conclusions is shown. The IA is calculated as per Equation 1, and is 0.26 for an α of 0.9. The average number of matching conclusions per editorial is 2.37, with two editorials having no matches and one having seven matches.

	α	
Conclusions	0.9	0.5
m	71	92
IA	0.26	0.34

Table 4: IA and m for conclusions.

---

[3]The number at the beginning of the sentence is sentence numbering present in the source of the texts.

Premises

Given a matching conclusion between two arguments, the premises of the same arguments are compared. Since the number of premises in an argument can vary between the annotators, both matches with all premises matching and at least one is displayed in Table 5. With the full overlap α, used for both premises and conclusions, the IA is 0.56 for at least one matching premise. With the same α, only 6 of the matching conclusions have all premises matching. Using the 0.5 α, the IA is 0.71 for at least one matching premise, and 0.20 all premises matching. The IA within all arguments is low for both α.

	α	
At least one matching premise	0.9	0.5
m	20	33
IA, within matching conclusions	0.56	0.71
IA, within all arguments	0.07	0.12
All premises match		
m	6	9
IA, within matching conclusions	0.17	0.20
IA, within all arguments	0.02	0.03

Table 5: IA and m for premises, given a matching conclusion.

It is important to note that even if two arguments have a matching conclusion this does not necessarily mean that they should have the same premises, a conclusion can be reached through different premises and argumentation. This could explain why there are 71 matching conclusions, but only 20 of them share at least one premise. An example of this can be seen below:

Premise A1: *den visar sig redan i form av kraftiga höjningar av olje- och bensinpriserna.* 'It is already showing in the form of increasing oil and gas prices.'
Premise A2: *Vi är i det här landet inte särskilt vana att spara på något.* 'We are not especially used to saving anything in this country.'
Conclusion: *Men nu är energikrisen inte långt borta* 'But now the energy crisis is not far away'
Scheme A1: ARGUMENT FROM SIGN
Scheme A2: ARGUMENT FROM CAUSE TO EFFECT

In the same way, a premise can be used for different conclusions. Table 6 shows the matching premises, regardless of whether they have a matching conclusion or not. There are 14 arguments

At least one premise match	α	
	0.9	0.5
m	74	99
IA, within all arguments	0.27	0.37
All premises match		
m	14	20
IA, within all arguments	0.05	0.07

Table 6: IA and m for only premises.

where all premises match. Of these 14 matches, three have also a matching argumentation scheme. This means that even if the premises match, there is disagreement about which scheme they participate in. The two following examples show this. The first example is a match in both conclusion and premises, but the schemes differ. The next example has the same premise but different conclusion and scheme. This indicates that a premise can be used for different schemes, and result in different conclusions.

Premise: *Den är inte obegränsad*
'It is not unlimited.'
Conclusion: *Allmänt sett är det nödvändigt att hushålla med energin*
'It is widely considered necessary to economize energy.'
Scheme A1: ARGUMENT FROM CONSEQUENCES
Scheme A2: ARGUMENT FROM SIGN

Premise: *En växling vid makten medför att vi inte riskerar några socialistiska experiment under valperioden utan kan bygga vidare på välfärdssamhällets grund.*
'A shift of power will result in us not risking any socialistic experiment during the elected term and instead we can further build on the foundations of the welfare society.'
Conclusion A1: *Väljare bör rösta på oppositionen*
'Voters should vote for the opposition'
Conclusion A2: *Rösta inte bort samverkan!*
'Do not vote away collaboration!'
Scheme A1: ARGUMENT FROM CONSEQUENCES
Scheme A2: CAUSAL SLIPPERY SLOPE ARGUMENT

Argument schemes

After finding which arguments match in conclusion and premise, the argumentation schemes are compared. Using 0.9 as the α, only 2 arguments have a match in scheme, conclusion and premises. The schemes in these two arguments are ARGUMENT FROM SIGN and ARGUMENT FROM CAUSE TO EFFECT. Using 0.5 as α instead, there

are 4 matches. Three of them have only 1 premise and they all overlap fully. The last one has half of the premises matching.

Based on the low numbers of matching schemes in the case where both conclusion and premise match, conclusions and premises were compared separately. Of all the matching conclusions, 9 have the same scheme, see Table 7. Figure 1 shows how the schemes co-occur when the conclusion is the same. The schemes that match are the schemes which are most commonly used by both annotators.

Scheme matches	α	
	0.9	0.5
m	9	10
IA, within matching conclusion	0.25	0.22
IA, within all arguments	0.02	0.02

Table 7: IA and m for schemes, given a matching conclusion.

In Figure 1 we can see that ARGUMENT FROM CONSEQUENCES and ARGUMENT FROM POPULAR PRACTICE have a high co-occurrence, compared to the others. This could be because the annotators have have chosen different premises, for the same conclusion and thus chosen different schemes. The descriptions of these schemes are shown below.

ARGUMENT FROM CONSEQUENCES:

Premise: If A is brought about, then good (bad) consequences will (may plausibly) occur.
Conclusion: A should (not) be brought about.

ARGUMENT FROM POPULAR PRACTICE:
Premise: If a large majority (everyone, nearly everyone, etc.) does A, or acts as though A is the right (or an acceptable) thing to do, then A is a prudent course of action.
Premise: A large majority acts as though A is the right thing to do.
Conclusion: A is a prudent course of action.

It seems that the difference between these schemes is dependent on the reason for a proposed action. Should it be done because there is a desired outcome (Consequences) or is the right thing to do because it is a popular practice? An example of this disagreement is seen below. Possibly this example could be argued to be both schemes.

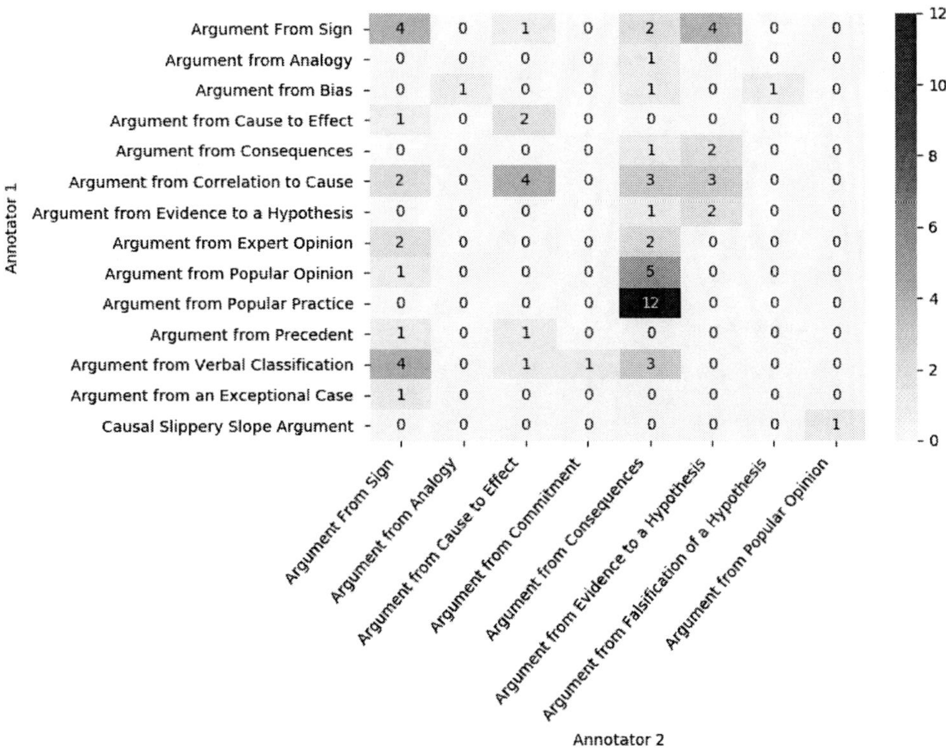

Figure 1: Co-occurrence matrix for the schemes with the same conclusion (α 0.9)

Premise: *Den höga arbetslösheten i Sverige är inte acceptabel ur några synpunkter, detta måste slås fast med skärpa.* 'The high unemployment rate in Sweden is not acceptable from any angle, this must be firmly established.'
Conclusion: *Att skaffa fram nya jobb, måste vara den viktigaste uppgiften för närvarande.* 'To create new jobs must be the most important task for now.'
Scheme A1: ARGUMENT FROM CONSEQUENCES
Scheme A2: ARGUMENT FROM POPULAR PRACTICE

As mentioned above, matching premises were also compared, regardless of conclusions. One could expect this to generate more scheme matches, as similar premises would possibly be used in similar kinds of argumentation. However, as noted in the previous section, of all the 540 arguments, only 14 have all premises matching. Out of these, only 3 have the same scheme, as compared to 9 scheme matches for the conclusions.

Because of the noted difficulty of distinguishing the schemes, both here and in previous research, and the low number of matches, the schemes were divided into groups and these groups were compared instead. This division is suggested by Walton et al. (2008) as a classification system for the schemes.

Matching schemes	α	
	0.9	0.5
m	3	7
IA, within matching	0.08	0.15
IA, within all arguments	0.01	0.03
Abductive reasoning	2	5
Casual reasoning	1	1
Practical reasoning	0	1

Table 8: Matching schemes with the new groups of schemes, given a matching conclusion and at least one premise.

Using the new groups results in more matching schemes, but still the numbers are low for a match of both conclusion and premise, see Table 8. Table 9 shows the same numbers but for only conclusions. The co-occurrence matrix is again showed for an α of 0.9 and only conclusions, see Figure 2. Most noteworthy are the 10 matches in the ABDUCTIVE REASONING group and the 17 co-occurrences between the groups ARGUMENTS FROM POPULAR PRACTICE and PRAC-

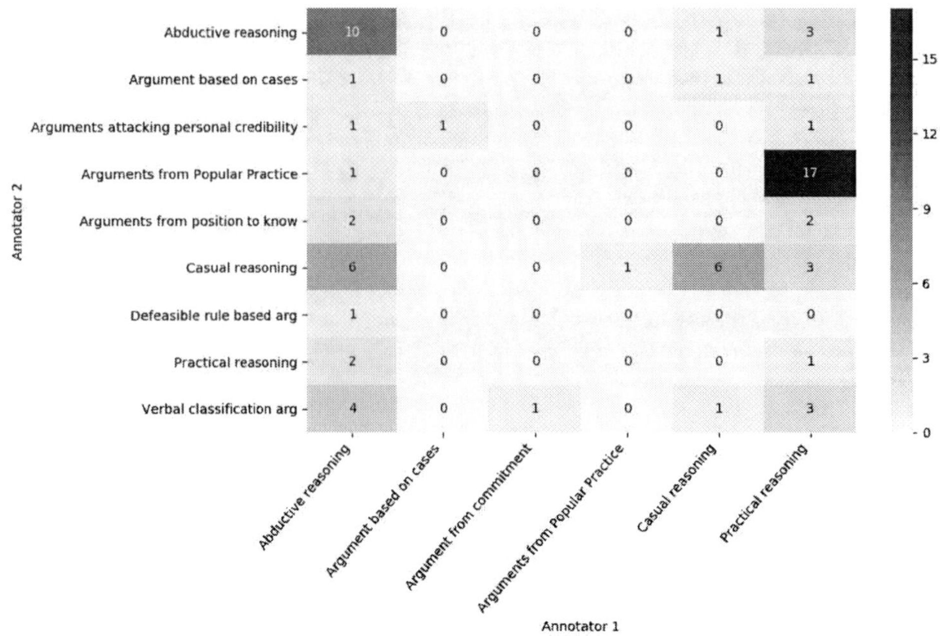

Figure 2: Co-occurrence matrix for the schemes in new groups, with the same conclusion (α 0.9)

	α	
Matching schemes	0.9	0.5
m	17	20
IA, within matching conclusions	0.48	0.43
IA, within all arguments	0.06	0.07
Abductive reasoning	10	12
Casual reasoning	6	6
Practical reasoning	1	2

Table 9: Matching schemes with the new groups of schemes, only conclusions.

TICAL REASONING. This mismatch in groups is due to the previously discussed co-occurrence of the schemes ARGUMENT FROM CONSEQUENCES and ARGUMENT FROM POPULAR PRACTICE. The former scheme is in the group PRACTICAL REASONING and the latter scheme is in the ARGUMENTS FROM POPULAR PRACTICE group, thus transferring the co-occurrences to the new groups.

Again, a comparison of the schemes in the new groups but for only matching premises was done. This however only led to 4 scheme matches and no pattern in the co-occurrences.

5 Conclusions and Future Work

In this first annotation exercise, we wanted to investigate whether annotators with a strong background in linguistics but who were given little explicit instruction for this specific annotation task would be able to recover the argumentation schemes described by Walton et al. (2008). This turned out not to be the case, with the annotators agreeing neither on whole arguments nor on the units and schemes which make them up.[4] This could be for at least three reasons: (1) that the annotators would have needed more detailed and precise instructions; (2) that the argumentation schemes themselves are too difficult to recover from free natural text (despite their seeming formal characterization); or (3) that the annotation task should be structured differently, in a first step where spans representing argument instances are identified followed by a second step where the instances and their components are labeled.[5]

Some of the differences between the annotators would have been avoided if they had more spe-

---

[4]The use of only two annotators possibly influenced the result, making it difficult to conclude when we are dealing with 'normal' disagreement or not.

[5]It was suggested by the anonymous reviewers that this would make for more effective annotation and higher inter-annotator agreement. We are not aware of any strong arguments in the literature unequivocally supporting this view, nor of any empirical studies comparing the end-to-end efficiency and efficacy of these two annotation workflows while controlling for other potentially relevant variables. We note this as an interesting topic for future research.

cific instructions for the tool. More strict and detailed instructions for the annotation itself could probably improve the inter-annotator agreement, but might come with a loss of information. For example, a rule such as marking sentences instead of spans would result in some loss of information, since an argument might not be restricted to sentences. However, most of the disagreements come from differences in the interpretation of argument components and schemes, as shown in the examples in the previous section. For example, the same premises and conclusions are used in different schemes, and a single premise is used more than one scheme. In order to minimize information loss but achieve high inter-annotator agreement a necessary next step in annotating argumentation needs to be a discussion of what should be marked as premises and conclusions and why the annotators have made the choices they did.

Interpretation seems also to be the reason for the difference in the annotation of the argumentation schemes, although the low inter-annotator agreement in the argument components evaluated before the schemes might influence this. If the annotators were given already annotated units they would possibly agree more. The results of Visser et al. (2018) indicate this, where they use already predefined nodes and reach a high inter-annotator agreement.

As previously shown, and also observed by others (Walton and Macagno, 2015; Macagno et al., 2017), the original schemes can be difficult to distinguish from each other. If they are to be used by annotators, then they need better instructions on when to use which scheme. As the post-annotation grouping of schemes improved agreement, perhaps it would be effective to collapse them already in advance, instructing annotators to use coarser groupings in cases of doubt.

For the immediate future we plan to design two annotation exercises to follow up on the experiment described in this paper and to address some of the questions raised above. Further, the exercises will be carried out using two different annotation workflows. In the first exercise, the annotators will be instructed to use the schemes of Walton et al. (2008), but this time according to an explicit annotation manual. In the second exercise the annotators will be asked to annotate the same texts according to some other proposed scheme, possibly a less fine-grained version of the original

schemes as this was shown to have a positive effect on the inter-annotator agreement, but the exact scheme to be used remains to be determined. We will also organize two versions of each exercise, one corresponding to the previous annotation round, where annotatoras are asked to identify argumentation spans and classify them in one operation, and another where argumentation span identification is separated from labeling of schemes and components.

In all cases we plan to employ more than two annotators and there will be a different set of annotators for each of the four annotation setups. The texts to be annotated will include the editorials used for the work described in this paper, but we may also decide to extend the data set. Hopefully, the planned experiments will allow us to gain a better understanding of the advantages and disadvantages of different schemes for argumentation annotation, as well as for alternative organizations of the annotation workflow.

Acknowledgments

The work presented here has been partly supported by an infrastructure grant to Språkbanken Text, University of Gothenburg, for contributing to building and operating a national e-infrastructure funded jointly by the Swedish Research Council (under contract no. 2017-00626) and the participating institutions.

We would also like to thank the anonymous reviewers for their detailed and constructive comments.

References

Vanessa Wei Feng and Graeme Hirst. 2011. Classifying arguments by scheme. In *Proceedings of the 49th annual meeting of the association for computational linguistics: Human language technologies*, pages 987–996.

Nancy Green. 2015. Identifying argumentation schemes in genetics research articles. In *Proceedings of the 2nd Workshop on Argumentation Mining*, pages 12–21. Association for Computational Linguistics.

Rolf Hedquist. 1978. *Emotivt språk: En studie i dagstidningars ledare [Emotive language: A study in newspaper editorials]*. Umeå University, Dept. of Nordic Languages, Umeå.

John Lawrence and Chris Reed. 2016. Argument mining using argumentation scheme structures. In *COMMA*, pages 379–390.

Marco Lippi and Paolo Torroni. 2016. Argumentation mining: State of the art and emerging trends. *ACM Transactions on Internet Technology (TOIT)*, 16(2):10.1–10.25.

Fabrizio Macagno, Douglas Walton, and Chris Reed. 2017. Argumentation schemes. history, classifications, and computational applications. *History, Classifications, and Computational Applications (December 23, 2017). Macagno, F., Walton, D. & Reed, C*, pages 2493–2556.

Chris Reed and Glenn Rowe. 2004. Araucaria: Software for argument analysis, diagramming and representation. *International Journal on Artificial Intelligence Tools*, 13(04):961–979.

Yi Song, Michael Heilman, Beata Beigman Klebanov, and Paul Deane. 2014. Applying argumentation schemes for essay scoring. In *Proceedings of the First Workshop on Argumentation Mining*, pages 69–78.

Christian Stab and Iryna Gurevych. 2017. Parsing argumentation structures in persuasive essays. *Computational Linguistics*, 43(3):619–659.

Jacky Visser, Lawrence John, Wagemans Jean, and Reed Chris. 2018. Revisiting computational models of argument schemes: Classification, annotation, comparison. In *Proceedings of the 7th International Conference on Computational Models of Argument (COMMA 2018)*.

Douglas Walton. 2012. Using argumentation schemes for argument extraction: A bottom-up method. *IJCINI*, 6:33–61.

Douglas Walton. 2013. *Argumentation schemes for presumptive reasoning*. Routledge.

Douglas Walton and Fabrizio Macagno. 2015. A classification system for argumentation schemes. *Argument & Computation*, 6(3):219–245.

Douglas Walton, Christopher Reed, and Fabrizio Macagno. 2008. *Argumentation Schemes*. Cambridge University Press, Cambridge.

Author Index

Association for Computational Linguistics
209 N. Eighth Street
Stroudsburg, Pennsylvania 18360

ISBN 978-1-5108-9115-9